D0680352

THE LONG SURRENDER

OTHER WORKS BY BURKE DAVIS

Biography:

They Called Him Stonewall
Gray Fox: R. E. Lee & the Civil War
Jeb Stuart, the Last Cavalier
Marine! The Life of Lt. Gen. Lewis B. (Chesty) Puller, U.S.M.C. (Ret.)
The Billy Mitchell Affair
Old Hickory: A Life of Andrew Jackson

History:

To Appomattox
Our Incredible Civil War
The Cowpens-Guilford Courthouse Campaign
A Williamsburg Galaxy
The World of Currier & Ives (with Roy King)
The Campaign That Won America: The Story of Yorktown
Get Yamamoto
George Washington and the American Revolution
Sherman's March

Novels:

Yorktown
The Ragged Ones
Whisper My Name
The Summer Land

For Children:

America's First Army
Heroes of the American Revolution
Black Heroes of the American Revolution
Biography of a Leaf
Biography of a Kingsnake
Mr. Lincoln's Whiskers
Roberta E. Lee

THE LONG SURRENDER

Burke Davis

VINTAGE BOOKS
A Division of Random House, Inc.
NEW YORK

FIRST VINTAGE BOOKS EDITION, November 1989

 Published in the United States by Vintage Books, a division of Random House, Inc., New York, and simultaneously in Canada by Random House of Canada Limited, Toronto. Originally published, in hardcover, by Random House, Inc., New York, in 1985.

Grateful acknowledgment is made to:

Bertram Hayes-Davis of Richardson, Texas, president of the Davis Family Association, for permission to quote from the correspondence of Jefferson and Varina Davis.

Southern Historical collection, Wilson Library, University of North Carolina at Chapel Hill, for permission to quote from the John Taylor Wood Diary.

Manuscript Department, Perkins Library, Duke University, Durham , N.C., and to Mrs. Mary Elizabeth Stowe, for permission to quote from the Clement Claiborne Clay Papers.

Mrs. Frances Stern Lowenstein of Greensboro, N.C., for permission to quote from the correspondence relating to Abram Weill.

Library of Congress Cataloging-in-Publishing Data
Davis, Burke, 1913–
The long surrender / Burke Davis.—1st Vintage Books ed.
p. cm.
Reprint. Originally published: New York : Random House, c1985.
Bibliography: p.
Includes Index.
ISBN 0-679-72409-5: $8.95
1. Confederate States of America—History. 2. Davis, Jefferson, 1808–1889. 3. United States History—History—Civil War, 1861-1865.
I. Title.
[E487.D25 1989]
973. 7'13—dc20 89-40077
CIP

Manufactured in the United States of America

10 9 8 7 6 5 4 3 2 1

To Juliet

The Confederates have gone out of this war, with the proud, secret, deathless, dangerous *consciousness that they are THE BETTER MEN, and that there was nothing wanting but a change in a set of circumstances and a firmer resolve to make them the victors.*

—*Edward A. Pollard,* The Lost Cause, *1866*

Acknowledgments

For aid in the preparation of this narrative I am indebted to numerous descendants of chief actors in the drama, including:

Bertram Hayes-Davis of Richardson, Texas, great-grandson of Jefferson Davis; former Congressman Robert Grier Stephens of Athens, Ga., collateral descendant of Confederate Vice-President Alexander H. Stephens; George Rountree III of Wilmington, N.C., great-grandson of Confederate Attorney General George Davis; Mary Elizabeth Stokes of Gurley, Ala., great-granddaughter of Virginia Clay's adopted daughter, Betty Lumsden; Mary Lewis Rucker Edmunds of Greensboro, N.C., great-great-granddaughter of N.C. Governor John M. Morehead; Frances Stern Loewenstein of Greensboro, N.C., great-granddaughter of Abram Weill; Anne Springs Close of Fort Mill, S.C., and Jane Carlton Anderson of Charlotte, N.C., great-great-granddaughters of Colonels A. B. Springs and Wm. Elliott White; Will Molineux of Williamsburg, Va., great-grandson of Gen. Edward L. Molineux, USA.

Also:

Ms. Mary Willey, Special Collections Librarian, Seymour Library, Knox College, Galesburg, Ill.; Dr. Martha Russell, director, and Ms. Ellen G. Gartrell, Manuscript Dept., Perkins Library, Duke University, Durham, N.C.; Ms. Carolyn Wallace, Director, and Richard A. Strader, Reference Archivist, Southern Historical Collection, Wilson Library, University of North Carolina, Chapel Hill, N.C.; Ms. Linda L. Crist, Editor, The Papers of Jefferson Davis, Rice University, Houston, Texas; Newton W. Carr, Jr., Superintendent, Beauvoir, Biloxi, Miss.; R. C. Peniston, Director, and John Hughes, former Curator, Lee Chapel, Washington & Lee University, Lexington, Va.; Chester D. Bradley, M.D., former Director, Jefferson Davis Casemate, Hampton, Va.; William J. Moore, Director, Greensboro Historical Museum, Greensboro, N.C.; Jack Claiborne, Associate Editor, Charlotte *Observer,* Charlotte, N.C.; Patricia Rosenthal, History and Genealogy Librarian, Rowan Public Library, Salisbury, N.C.; Ms. Pattie J. Scott, Richmond, Va. Public Library; Ms. Charlene S. Marinka Alling, Curator of Manuscripts and Archives, The Museum of the Confederacy, Richmond; Ms. Edie Jeter, Librarian, Valentine Museum, Richmond; Helmi Raaska, Research Assistant, Michigan Historical Collections, Bentley Historical Library, University of Michigan, Ann Arbor; Ms. Trudy Mignery, Archivist, duPont Library, University of the South, Sewanee, Tenn.

Dr. Lenox Baker, Durham, N.C.; J. Victor Brandt III, Charleston,

S.C.; former Justice Francis O. Clarkson, Charlotte, N.C.; Mr. & Mrs. Archie K. Davis, Winston-Salem, N.C.; Mrs. William B. Guerrant, Williamsburg, Va.; Jack Huguley, Charleston, S.C.; Elizabeth Lawrence, Annapolis, Md.; Mrs. Thomas F. Motley, Chatham, Va.; D. J. Nickell, Lewisburg, W. Va.; Lowell Reidenbaugh, St. Louis, Mo.; Dr. Frances Roberts, Huntsville, Ala; Stephen Rowe, Raleigh, N.C.; Peter Browne Ruffin, Wilmington, N.C.; Mr. & Mrs. Leroy Simms, Huntsville, Ala.; Dr. Fred Hobson, Jr., Tuscaloosa, Ala.; Mrs. Benjamin Withers, Charlotte, N.C.

And I am particularly grateful to my wife and close collaborator, Juliet Halliburton Davis, and to my editor of more than thirty years, Robert D. Loomis.

Tsuga —Burke Davis
Patrick County, Va.
Feb. 6, 1985

Contents

PART 1

Flight

1. *"Now . . . they will repent"* 5
2. *"We should abandon our position to-night"* 19
3. *"Blow her to hell"* 33
4. *"A fire bell in the night"* 44
5. *"We could rally our forces"* 63
6. *"I* cannot *feel myself a beaten man!"* 82

PART 2

The Pursuit

7. *"Why are you still in the field?"* 101
8. *"You're Southern gentlemen, not highway robbers"* 121

PART 3

The Capture

9. *"God's will be done"* 135
10. *"He must be executed"* 149
11. *"This is not like being Secretary of State"* 159

PART 4

The Prisoner

12. *"Oh, the shame! The shame"* 173
13. *"Ankle deep in gold and silver"* 183
14. *"Watch and wait for the morning"* 190
15. *"We cannot convict him of treason"* 200
16. *"The President is bailed!"* 211

PART 5

The Phoenix

17. *"Preserve the traditions of our fathers"* 227
18. *"Alas for frail humanity!"* 243
19. *"My ambition lies buried"* 256
20. *"No infidelity to the Union"* 265

EPILOGUE 273

A NOTE ON SOURCES 287

BIBLIOGRAPHICAL NOTES 289

INDEX 307

PART 1

FLIGHT

"We have to save the people, spare the blood of the Army and save the High Civil functionaries. Your plan, I think, can only do the last . . . Commanders believe the troops will not fight again. We think your plan impracticable. [You should flee] without loss of a moment."

—GENERAL JOSEPH E. JOHNSTON TO JEFFERSON DAVIS

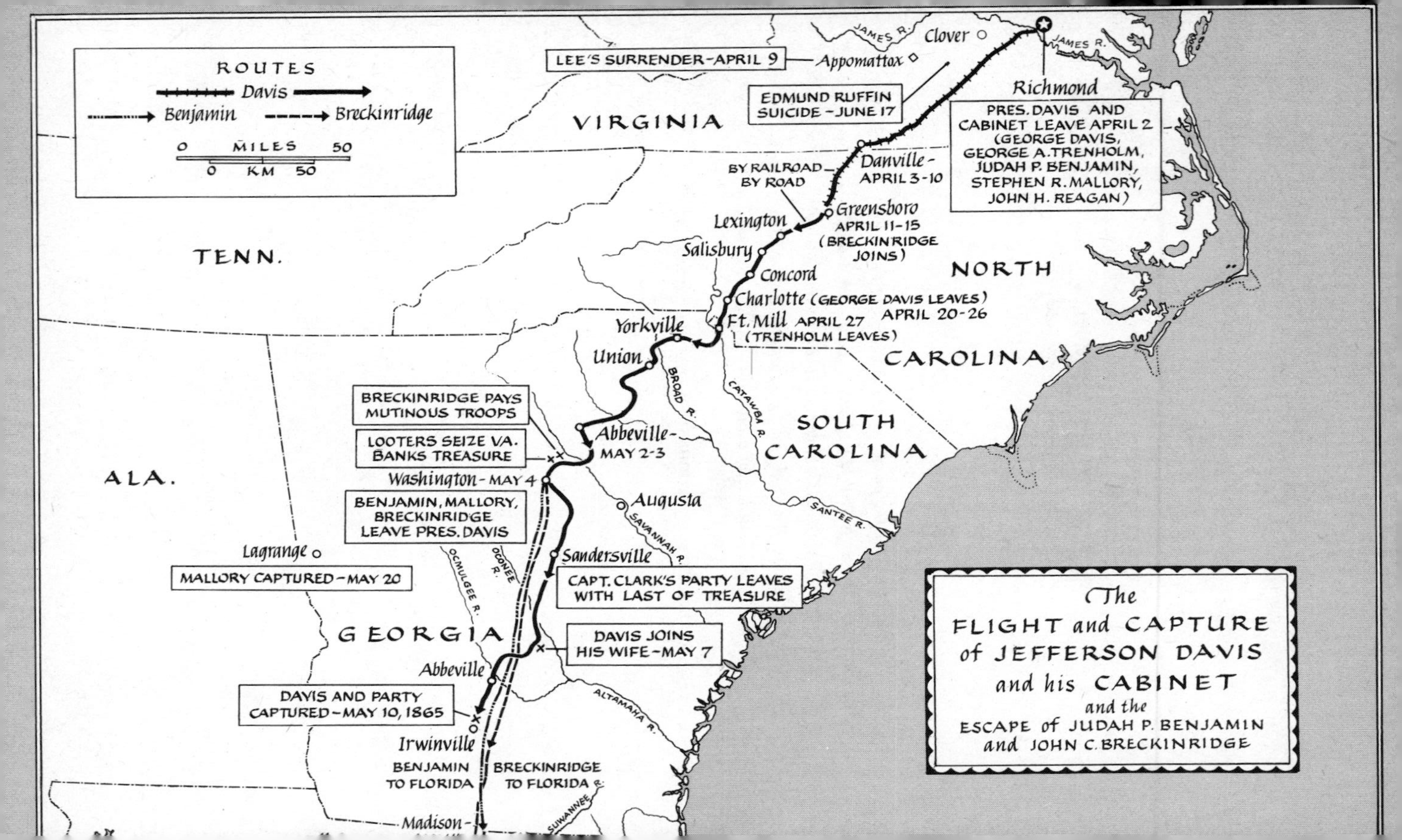

The FLIGHT and CAPTURE of JEFFERSON DAVIS and his CABINET and the ESCAPE of JUDAH P. BENJAMIN and JOHN C. BRECKINRIDGE
ROUTES
Davis
Benjamin
Breckinridge
0 MILES 50
0 KM 50
VIRGINIA
TENN.
NORTH CAROLINA
SOUTH CAROLINA
GEORGIA
ALA.
JAMES R.
Clover
Appomattox
LEE'S SURRENDER-APRIL 9
EDMUND RUFFIN SUICIDE-JUNE 17
Richmond
PRES. DAVIS AND CABINET LEAVE APRIL 2 (GEORGE DAVIS, GEORGE A. TRENHOLM, JUDAH P. BENJAMIN, STEPHEN R. MALLORY, JOHN H. REAGAN)
Danville-APRIL 3-10
BY RAILROAD
BY ROAD
Greensboro APRIL 11-15 (BRECKINRIDGE JOINS)
Lexington
Salisbury
Concord
Charlotte (GEORGE DAVIS LEAVES) APRIL 20-26
Ft. Mill APRIL 27 (TRENHOLM LEAVES)
Yorkville
Union
BROAD R.
CATAWBA R.
BRECKINRIDGE PAYS MUTINOUS TROOPS
LOOTERS SEIZE VA. BANKS TREASURE
Abbeville-MAY 2-3
Washington-MAY 4
BENJAMIN, MALLORY, BRECKINRIDGE LEAVE PRES. DAVIS
Augusta
SAVANNAH R.
SANTEE R.
Lagrange
MALLORY CAPTURED-MAY 20
OCMULGEE R.
OCONEE R.
Sandersville
CAPT. CLARK'S PARTY LEAVES WITH LAST OF TREASURE
DAVIS JOINS HIS WIFE-MAY 7
Abbeville
DAVIS AND PARTY CAPTURED-MAY 10, 1865
ALTAMAHA R.
Irwinville
BENJAMIN TO FLORIDA
BRECKINRIDGE TO FLORIDA
SUWANNEE
Madison-

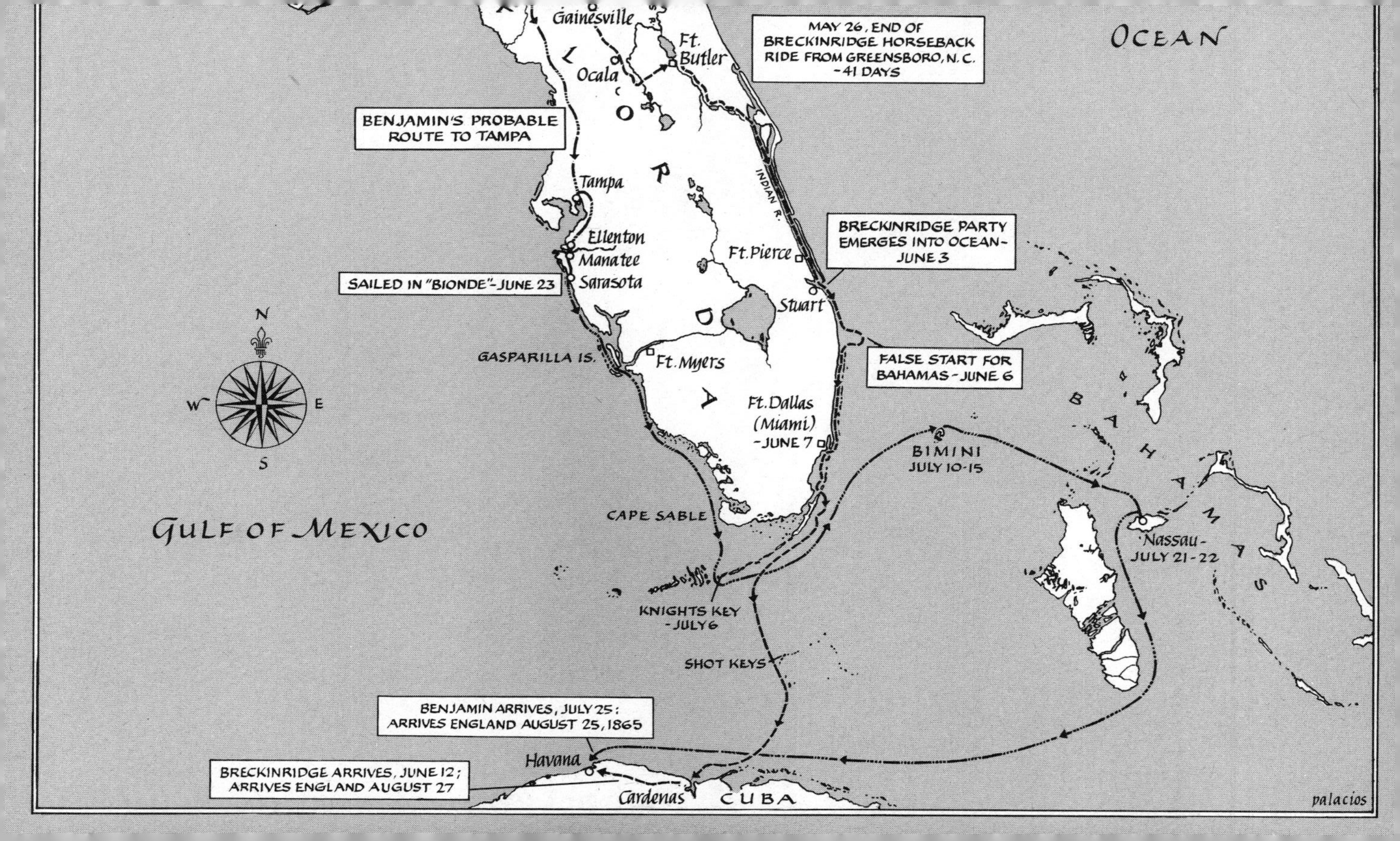
OCEAN
Gainesville
Ft. Butler
Ocala
MAY 26, END OF BRECKINRIDGE HORSEBACK RIDE FROM GREENSBORO, N.C. -41 DAYS
BENJAMIN'S PROBABLE ROUTE TO TAMPA
INDIAN R.
Tampa
Ellenton
Manatee
Sarasota
SAILED IN "BIONDE"-JUNE 23
Ft. Pierce
BRECKINRIDGE PARTY EMERGES INTO OCEAN-JUNE 3
Stuart
N
GASPARILLA IS.
Ft. Myers
FALSE START FOR BAHAMAS-JUNE 6
W
E
S
Ft. Dallas (Miami) -JUNE 7
BIMINI
JULY 10-15
B A H A M A S
CAPE SABLE
GULF OF MEXICO
Nassau-
JULY 21-22
KNIGHTS KEY -JULY 6
SHOT KEYS
BENJAMIN ARRIVES, JULY 25: ARRIVES ENGLAND AUGUST 25, 1865
Havana
BRECKINRIDGE ARRIVES, JUNE 12; ARRIVES ENGLAND AUGUST 27
Cardenas
CUBA
palacios

1

"Now . . . they will repent"

SPRING came to central Virginia in late March 1865, in a season of cold rains. Fruit trees bloomed in the city of Richmond and in the scarred, desolate landscape beyond, where a ragged crescent of entrenchments sheltered a Federal army of some 100,000 men. The siege of Richmond and nearby Petersburg was in its ninth month. Within a few days the American Civil War would be four years old.

It seemed unlikely that the Confederate capital would survive to celebrate the anniversary. A perceptive diarist saw symptoms of approaching crisis in the disintegration of the army defending the capital:

"Desertions from the army were assuming fearful proportions that no legislative or executive rigor could diminish. Every day saw brigades double-quicking back and forth through the suburbs . . . inadequate to man the vast extent of the lines."

Inflation ravaged the city and threatened the unfortunate with starvation. Flour sold for $1,500 per barrel, live hens for $50 each, butter for $20 per pound and beef for $15. The plight of Richmonders was a grim joke to a woman from Georgia, who had come to be near her husband at his post in the trenches: "Close times in this beleaguered city. You can carry your money in your market basket and bring home your provisions in your purse."

But there were those who suffered more keenly. Young A. R. Tomlinson, a wounded soldier serving as a hospital guard, though so weak that he could barely stand watch, could not bring himself to eat as his companions did: "The surgeons and matrons ate rats and said they were as good as squirrels, but having seen the rats running over the bodies of dead soldiers, I had no relish for them."

The past few days in the capital had been quiet despite growing pressure from General Ulysses S. Grant's Federal besiegers, so near at hand. Though it was clear that the city must soon fall, a stranger might have assumed that all was well. Overcrowded Richmond's 200,000 people went about their affairs almost as usual. The gadfly editor Edward Pollard of the Richmond *Examiner* wrote: "For months past the government had been reticent of all military news whatever; the newspapers had been warned not to publish any military matters, but what should be dictated to them from the War Department; and the public was left to imagine pretty much what it pleased. . . . Indeed, the idea current in the streets . . . was rather pleasant and assuring." Pollard repeated rumors of possible reinforcements for General Robert E. Lee's dwindling ranks from the army of General Joseph E. Johnston, now in North Carolina as the last barrier in the path of the invading horde led by General William T. Sherman. The grim Sherman had already driven through the Carolinas after sweeping from Atlanta to the sea. Even in face of such news of disaster in the air, Pollard wrote, Richmonders "had not the slightest inkling of the situation" as the Confederate capital neared its hour of doom.

But the partisan Pollard, who had heaped vituperation upon President Jefferson Davis and his administration during the war, was not always to be taken literally. By now, at least, Richmond's civilians were less naïve than the fault-finding editor assumed. A French businessman who came to the city noted that "everyone wore a haggard, scared look." And Captain Micajah Clark, a clerk in the President's office, said that the Treasury had been issuing coin for more than a month, changing currency into silver "for the relief of the people"—coins rarely seen in the wartime Confederacy. Clark and most other Richmonders realized that this exchange had but one purpose: coin might be spent after the fall of the city, when Confederate bills would be worthless. The ratio of paper to silver dollars was 60 to 1, and rising.

As Pollard charged, government propaganda had indeed misled many people, but more observant residents saw that the end was at hand. The fall of the city was so obviously imminent that only one Cabinet member's wife remained. An early exodus of government clerks and archives had begun March 1, and supplies of machinery, arms and food had been shipped southward with them to the relative safety of the interior. Congress had disbanded soon afterward with no plans to reconvene, departing amidst bitter exchanges with Davis that left the President "worn and exhausted," so his wife said. Another observer, noting that Congress had turned "madly against him," saw Davis as a sick lion attacked by jackals: "It is a very struggle for life with him . . . He is in a sea of trouble, and has no time or thought for anything but the safety of the country."

More recently, within the past few days, President Davis was known to have sent most of the food in his mansion to the city's hospitals, as if preparing for his own flight. The enigmatic Confederate President, whose public manner was that of a stern, unyielding ascetic, became the focus of attention in the final days of the capital's life. The leader of the failing rebellion, though by no means a chameleon in dealing with people, did seem to inspire the most impassioned —and extreme—reactions from his frustrated subjects, reactions ranging from hatred to adoration. Those who knew him best still regarded him as the salvation of the Southern cause—but his early role as hero and founder of the Confederacy had altered greatly in recent months.

Thousands of Southerners, inconsolable in face of defeat and with passions inflamed by a press hostile to Davis, had made him a scapegoat, a symbol of their blasted hopes.

Physically Jefferson Davis had been stricken by pressures of war. No longer did he look "every inch the President," as he had during his 1861 inaugural. As now seen on Richmond's streets he was pale, feeble and distraught. He had become an incurable insomniac, and his condition could not have been improved by the regimen imposed upon him by his wife, Varina, and his doctors. She forced Davis to sniff chloroform and rubbed the anesthetic on his temples. The President also inhaled the vapors of burning rosemary leaves, and for a time had been dosed daily with two grains of opium, five grains of quinine, a teaspoonful of "calchocum wine"* and a portion of castor oil. Despite ailments, Davis kept to his usual rapid stride, his gaze fixed forward as if about some all-consuming business. Though he was, at fifty-six, a year younger than General Lee, Davis looked much older. One eye, now useless, was a stone-gray orb; he

*Actually a potion made from the autumn crocus, of the genus colchicum.

had been almost blinded by an ulcerated cornea and attacks of neuralgia. Varina, his second wife and eighteen years his junior, had also begun to age. She had lost the sensuous, doe-eyed beauty of her girlhood and was no longer "The Mississippi Rose"—she was now spoken of as "that Western squaw." An officer's wife had lately described the couple, "He looks badly—old, grey and wrinkled . . . But she is enormously fat, and very cross and ill-tempered."

In the defensive trenches outside Richmond, where men lived like conies in their miserable burrows, firewood sold for $5 per stick. Under sporadic bombardment from enemy cannon and deadly rifle fire from sharpshooters, the gray line, always sparsely manned, had stretched so thinly that Robert E. Lee's troops could not hope to withstand an attack from the bluecoat hordes at their front. Hundreds of men stole away each night, drawn homeward by letters from their desperate families, many of whom lived in the path of General Sherman's pillagers. The rate of Confederate desertions had become ruinous.

General Lee had served barely a month as commander-in-chief after a belated promotion forced upon President Davis, who was incensed by such an infringement upon his powers. Though he admired Lee and had supported him stoutly through most of the war, Davis was zealous in defense of his presidential role.

This surprised no one who knew Davis, whose watchwords in life were pride, honor, duty and courage—and he had always been steadfast in purpose. Critics saw him as fanatical, so zealous in pursuit of his goals as to inspire Sam Houston of Texas to exclaim, "One drop of Jeff Davis' blood would freeze a frog."

There were similar estimates of Davis by his adversaries, particularly those who did not know him well and were repelled by the haughty exterior the President displayed to the world. Even the President's admirers found him somewhat distant, for he rejected intimacies. His manner seemed to sharpen criticism by political opponents, who became more vociferous in the last months of the war. There was a clamor by some to remove him from office—an ironic twist in the career of a man acknowledged as one of the most capable leaders of his era. A Kentuckian by birth, he had grown up in Mississippi, where his brother Joseph was a planter. Young Jefferson attended West Point and, fascinated by war, served in the Black Hawk War, fought Indians on the frontier and commanded his state's troops in the war with Mexico.

As senator from Mississippi, Davis had become the successor to South Carolina's John C. Calhoun, an eloquent spokesman for southern planters in the increasingly ominous debates over states' rights—and, more vitally, in the quarrels over the dilemma of controlling slavery as the nation expanded westward.

As Secretary of War under Franklin Pierce, the forceful and energetic Davis had dominated the Cabinet and became known as the most capable and creative secretary to fill the post. It was Davis who had engineered the Gadsden Purchase, under which the U.S. acquired 30,000 square miles of Mexican territory. He had increased the standing army of the United States from 11,000 to 16,000 men, begun development of rail connections between the Mississippi Valley and the West Coast and experimented with camels as cavalry mounts in the Southwestern deserts. In an attempt to improve military education he lavished attention on West Point, where Robert E. Lee was then superintendent (and under fire for his kindly refusal to enforce the iron discipline customary in that era).

His years in the U.S. Senate had won Davis a reputation as a strict constitutionalist who repeatedly asserted the rights of the states. As one of the best-educated men in the Senate and its leading intellectual, well versed in history and the classics, he had attracted crowded galleries on the January day in 1861 when he made his farewell speech—his voice, as his wife said, "a silver trumpet." He had waited until Mississippi had left the Union, when he had no other recourse, and his brief address moved men on both sides of the aisle and in the throng above. "Unshed tears were in it," Varina Davis recalled, "and a plea for peace permeated every tone."

The South, Davis said, was merely following the lead of the founding fathers when they made their revolution, and though they bore no hostility toward others, Southerners would resist all enemies and "vindicate the right as best we may." When he had finished, to roars of applause, Davis had slumped to his desk, hiding his face, his shoulders shaking—with sobs, it was assumed. He was sleepless that night, blinded by neuralgia. In the next days he wrote or telegraphed leaders of each southern state, advising caution and reason. To ex-President Pierce, the New Englander, he said, "Civil war has only horror for me, but whatever circumstances demand shall be met as a duty and I trust be so discharged that you will not be ashamed of our former connection or cease to be my friend."

Davis had gone home at once, hoping to command troops in

defense of the South, but he had been summoned, instead, to lead the Confederacy. He had accepted promptly enough but, as Varina said, he spoke of the call "as a man might speak of a sentence of death."

In the early years of the war, when Southern independence had seemed a certain prospect, Davis had been a hero to his people. Though unable to convince his friends of the grim outlook, he foresaw a long, desperate war. When the governor of Mississippi had told him that he overrated the risk Davis had replied, "I only wish I did." But once he had accepted this risk, Davis would be loath to abandon the cause until death. Supremely confident of his own powers, he would be psychologically unable to accept defeat.

This stern, almost painfully upright man seemed to have changed but little since youth. Varina had written perceptively of him after their first meeting: "I do not know whether [he] is young or old. He looks both at times; but I believe he is old . . . a remarkable kind of man, but of uncertain temper, and has a way of taking for granted that everyone agrees with him . . . which offends me; yet he is most agreeable and has a peculiarly sweet voice and a winning manner." The young, inexperienced Mississippi country girl had accurately plumbed the personality that was to baffle so many of Jefferson Davis's Confederate cohorts and historians of later years.

The war had brought dramatic changes in the reputations as well as the physical appearances of the Confederate chief and his commanding general. As the end of the struggle neared, it was Lee who had become the hero. Davis, whose earlier popularity had faded with the ebb of the South's military fortunes, had now become an object of scorn. The public, press and politicians had increasingly assailed the President for his role in the failure of the rebellion. Oddly, little of the blame for Confederate collapse seemed to attach to Lee.

War had taken its toll of the celebrated general, but as his soldiers saw him he was in apparently robust health. His jet-black hair and mustache of 1861 had grown gray, and there was a thick gray beard as well. By now Lee's face had become a popular image, a tintype or engraving of which was hung, almost reverentially, in thousands of homes. This was a form of hero worship that was to become embedded in a romantic legend of Southern folklore—a gently born warrior knight who had led devoted Anglo-Saxon legions against foemen unworthy of his steel, though superior in numbers and resources. It was a concept that was to shape regional attitudes toward other sections of the country for generations.

A staff officer who observed Lee during the last days of war was reassured by the presence of this beau ideal of Southern aristocracy: "He had aged somewhat in appearance . . . but had rather gained than lost in physical vigor, from the severe life he had led. His hair had grown gray, but his face had the ruddy hue of health, and his eyes were as clear and bright as ever . . . he seemed to be able to bear any amount of fatigue."

In January, at the insistence of Lee and Davis, Congress overcame fears of a slave rebellion and approved black troops for the army, but rejected Lee's proposal that they be freed for their service. The experiment was a failure, and a bitter disappointment, since Confederate losses from desertions were severe (more than one-ninth —100,000 men—were away without leave). Northern desertions, even more severe, were largely made up by 200,000 blacks in uniform.

Lee had also warned that the army must be disbanded unless food supplies were improved. He urged the dismissal of Commissary General Lucius B. Northrop, an ineffectual officer whose chief qualification for the post seemed to be his long friendship with President Davis, dating from their days as West Point cadets. An eccentric who had been on permanent sick leave from the prewar United States Army for twenty-two years, Northrop wore newspapers inside his shirt rather than underclothing, and rustled remarkably at every move, a bizarre display of penury. But though Davis had finally replaced Northrop, supply had not improved. By now few trains were left to serve Richmond—and in addition some Southern states refused to share with the Confederacy in its time of need, though their warehouses were filled with food, uniforms and arms.

The desperate Lee rode into Richmond in early March to beg aid for his army from Virginia's congressional delegation, but despite his alarming reports, the politicians were not moved to action. After a disappointing session with them, Lee dined with his invalid wife and some of their family, and later, in talking with his son Custis, the general seemed "deeply troubled." He paced the floor, oblivious to all but the plight of his army, and then he turned abruptly to face his son.

"Well, Mr. Custis, I have been up to see the Congress and they don't seem to be able to do anything except eat peanuts and chew tobacco, while my army is starving. I told them the condition we're in . . . but I can't get them to do anything."

Lee paused to add sharply, "Mr. Custis, when this war began I was opposed to it, and I told these people that unless every man should do his whole duty, they would repent it; and now . . . they will repent."

Lee visited Jefferson Davis in the presidential mansion, "The Gray House," with little hope. The general was loyal to Davis but made no secret of his belief that the war was lost and that peace should be sought on the best terms possible, though he knew the President would not hear of this. Lee had not criticized Davis's views, though he had approached doing so in a mild comment to a trusted officer, "You know that the President is very pertinacious in opinion and purpose." This opinion was not disrespectful, for Lee had praised Davis's "remarkable faith in the possibility of still winning our independence, and his unconquerable will power."

Varina Davis noted that the general wore a "dispirited and wretched" look during the last days of the Confederacy. Mrs. Davis, a shrewd if sometimes contentious woman, had a lively appreciation of Lee's importance to the Southern cause. As confidante and adviser to her husband, she was uniquely qualified to judge the great Virginian and his relationship with the President, for she had witnessed the growth of their friendship and their wartime collaboration, and realized how vital their complex association had been to the Confederacy's struggle for survival. Though prone to view Lee through her husband's eyes, she must have regarded the Virginian as a fellow aristocrat—she came from a distinguished lineage that included her grandfather, Richard Howell, who had been a governor of New Jersey. Robert Lee's background as well as his sacrifice on behalf of the Confederacy disposed Varina Davis to respect and admiration—but not awe—of Lee.

The general, who was the son of a Revolutionary hero, had been a lifelong soldier, first-ranking graduate in his West Point class, a leading figure in the campaigns of the war with Mexico, a distinguished army engineer in peacetime, and commander of United States troops on the western frontier. Rejecting an offer to command the United States Army at the outbreak of the Civil War, Lee had come south instead, to serve Virginia and the Confederacy in a subordinate position. It was only after a year of war, upon the wounding of the senior general Joseph E. Johnston, that Lee had assumed command of the Army of Northern Virginia, which he was to make his own. Lee had become world famous in this role, though he had exhibited an unexpected aggressiveness which had caused a ruinous casualty rate. Some later historians were to conclude that the Southern dogma of incessant attacks had actually cost the Confederacy its slim chance of victory, since the rolls of dead and wounded were virtually as large as those of survivors in the field. Still, Lee's reputation was intact, and he was to be known as one of the great commanders of history.

Though Jefferson Davis thought of himself as a gifted military strategist, his challenges of Lee's judgment had been rare. The President's astuteness and the modesty and devotion of the talented Lee combined to assure their effective cooperation as they strained against great odds to keep Confederate hopes alive into the fourth year of the war.

As they met in the President's study on this March day of 1865, Davis abandoned the grim reserve with which he faced most of the world. In his conversation with Lee there was no hint of his celebrated quick temper, often displayed in spectacular outbursts that further irritated his enemies within the Confederacy and spurred some to intemperate criticism. General Henry A. Wise, a quixotic former governor of Virginia, had said of Davis, "There is a screw loose in him . . . He is a small, weak . . . jaundiced bigot and vain pretender."

This assessment by a political adversary was unduly harsh but Davis was known for his occasional tantrums, some of which may have damaged the Confederate cause through the creation of new enemies, many of whom were men of political influence. The mercurial Davis had engaged in numerous quarrels in his youth, and had narrowly averted involvement in several duels. He had once confessed, "I have an infirmity of which I am horribly ashamed: when I am aroused in a matter, I lose control of my feelings and become personal." Now, closeted with his trusted field commander as they faced the final ruin of the four-year-old empire whose leadership he had assumed with reluctance, Davis was outwardly the picture of self-assurance. Lee, in fact, found him to be overconfident of Confederate prospects.

But, to his surprise, Lee found Davis willing to give up Richmond at once, weeks before the general felt the retreat might be necessary. But it was clear that Davis felt that, since the army was still full of fight, and manpower was still available, the Confederacy should fight on. After the failure of several of his peace initiatives, which found the Federal government unyielding and unwilling to offer terms, Davis was resolved to resist to the end.

The war must go on. Lee certainly perceived long before this meeting that the President was virtually incapable of surrendering the cause to which he had given so much of himself, even in the face of catastrophe. But Lee could also understand this unyielding defiance of the enemy, for he, too, clung tenaciously to a dream that the Confederacy might endure. He had recently told Davis, "With my army in the mountains of Virginia I could carry on this war for twenty years." But today, returning to the front, Lee was apparently without hope.

It was obvious that President Davis foresaw the fall of Richmond. He had lately sent his family southward by train, reluctant refugees to Charlotte, N.C., where Davis had sought to rent a house for them by sending a quartermaster officer ahead. With Varina were her children, her sister, Maggie Howell, three servants, and the daughters of George Trenholm, the Secretary of the Treasury. Their escort was Burton Harrison, Davis's secretary, a dignified, Yale-trained Virginia aristocrat.

Varina carried the visible remains of the family fortune, a handful of U.S. gold coins and a bundle of almost worthless Confederate currency. She would not forget those moments when a somber Davis, his manner "gentle but decided," had told her he must soon flee, and that the presence of his family would only "grieve and embarrass" him. She protested that she could not leave him; she did not trust their housekeeper, Mrs. Omelia, to pack their belongings. Davis was firm. "If I live, you can come to me when it is over. But I don't expect to survive the destruction of constitutional liberty." He expected her to await him in North Carolina with the children, who ranged in age from nine-year-old Maggie to Varina Anne, a teething infant of nine months called "Piecake"—later to be known as Winnie.

Davis had also shown his wife a pistol, twirling its chambers to show her how to load and fire the menacing weapon. "If you fall into . . . the wrong hands," he said, "you can at least force them to kill you." He urged her to follow his directions: "When you hear the enemy approaching . . . you must go . . . Make for the Florida coast and take a ship."

Davis had put his wife and children on a train of three cars, one of which held the family's carriage horses. The party entered a ruined coach whose worn interior of weathered paint and peeling varnish was revealed by smoky oil lamps. They settled upon soiled brown plush seats which were infested with fleas. Rain began to fall. Davis led Harrison outside and gave him final instructions: Federal cavalry was moving to cut the railroad and the train might be halted en route to Danville, some 140 miles to the southwest. He asked Harrison to see the family to safety if possible, and to return to him when he could.

At the last moment Davis almost relented and took Varina and the children off the train. The older children seemed to sense their father's fear that they would not meet again. Seven-year-old Little Jeff begged to be left behind, and Maggie clung to her father "convulsively." Davis soon recovered his aplomb, said his goodbyes and moved to the trackside, where he smiled fixedly upward at the blurred images of Varina and the children behind the dirty windows which now streamed with rain. The train lurched into motion and swayed away down the track.

The cars rolled into the rainswept darkness with the women and children huddling miserably as they tried to avoid drips from the leaky roof. The engine broke down just outside the city and the train sat all night in a downpour. There was no food aboard, but Harrison somehow found crackers and milk to quiet the hungry children, at a cost of $100 in Confederate bills. It was long after dawn when the train creaked off on its journey.

The departure of the First Lady of the Confederacy came as no surprise to Richmond's sharp-eyed housewives. Varina's old gowns, silks, feathers and gloves had appeared in store windows for weeks past. Friends of the family also noted that paintings, silver and furniture from the presidential mansion were offered for sale. Many of Varina's belongings had been sent to an auction house, where they were snapped up by eager shoppers. The auctioneers had sent Davis a check for $28,400—but that value was reckoned in depreciating Confederate currency, and was now worth only $500 in coin, the only easily negotiable money of the day.

March 28 brought a crisis to Richmond. General Lee saw by the morning's light what he had long feared: massive blue columns crawling to the southwest to assail his flank, moving steadily despite flooded roads and fields. Ulysses S. Grant was making the inevitable move to pry the defenders from their trenches and take the Confederate capital. Lee hurried to meet this threat with the inadequate forces he could muster, most of them under command of General George Pickett, a hard-drinking Virginian who had been in eclipse since his fateful charge at Gettysburg almost two years earlier.

Lee sent the first of a series of warnings that Richmond must be abandoned, spread his forces even more thinly along the Petersburg front and called to him the troops of General James Longstreet from the north bank of the James. Longstreet was slow, as some of his rivals were to charge later that he had been in a fateful hour at Gettysburg. By late Saturday, April 1, the fatal blow had fallen—General Philip Sheridan, with a large force of combined cavalry and infantry, smashed Pickett's band at a rural settlement called Five Forks, inflicted heavy casualties and turned the Confederate flank. Grant then opened a furious barrage against Lee's main line and followed that with an infantry advance. By Sunday, April 2, Lee's situation before Petersburg was hopeless. The Confederate general spent a wakeful night, suffering so intensely from rheumatism that he complained of it to staff officers, who seldom heard him mention his infirmities.

Longstreet arrived at Lee's headquarters before dawn and found him still abed, in a house called Edge Hill, the home of the William Turnbull family. Lee spoke rather calmly of the disaster, placing no blame upon Pickett. He began giving instructions for the deployment of Longstreet's troops, but was interrupted by an officer. "General, the lines have broken in front. You'll have to go."

Longstreet admired the coolness with which Lee pulled his robe about him and went to the door. The commander saw, as Longstreet reported, "as far as the eye could cover the field, a line of skirmishers in quiet march toward us." Within a few moments Lee was dressed and riding from the place, mounted on gray Traveler and accompanied by a few officers. A telegrapher who had been in the house had been halted in the midst of sending a message to Richmond:

> It is absolutely necessary that we should abandon our position tonight, or run the risk of being cut off in the morning. I have given all the orders . . . It will be a difficult operation. Please give all orders that you find necessary in and about Richmond . . .

The telegrapher, galloping away with the headquarters band, was sent sprawling as a shell burst beneath his horse and left him to flee afoot. Colonel Walter Taylor of Lee's staff said, "He quickly gathered his instrument together and the last I saw of him he was making very good time for the city." By now enemy shells had set afire the Turnbull house, to which Lee looked back ruefully. "I'm afraid it was burned because they knew I had been there. I should not occupy a private house."

To another staff officer, Colonel Armistead Long, Lee said, "This is a bad business, Colonel. Well, it has happened as I told them at Richmond it would. The line has been stretched and it has broken." As he rode toward Petersburg, to prepare for holding a defensive position until nightfall, Lee had a message from Jefferson Davis complaining that such an early departure from Richmond would cause "the loss of many valuables." But Lee's orders had already gone to his commands, giving routes of retreat along both sides of the James River—a general movement which was to lead westward up the valley of the Appomattox River, in the direction of Lynchburg or Danville, small cities in the foothills. Field officers were ordered to pull their troops from the Petersburg front, cross the James and Appomattox, and burn bridges behind them. The movement was to begin at 8 P.M.

Furious fighting raged most of the day, since many Federal assaults were necessary to overcome strong points in Lee's defensive line, such as the redoubtable Fort Gregg, where windrows of blueclad bodies were piled up before the defenders were swept away. Once the Confederate bastions were gone, retreat became a rout. Lee's officers described the first moments of flight. Lieutenant J. F. J. Caldwell, a South Carolinian, wrote: "Now was the most disorderly movement I ever saw among Confederate troops. We had to pass from 200 to 300 yards through a clear field under the fire of infantry from flank and rear, and under artillery. The whole air shrieked with missiles, the whole earth trembled. We fled for the cover of woods and distance." Another saw this as "a perfect bedlam. Officers and men, mixed together in the wildest confusion, fled before the withering fire until the point of danger was passed, when they came together, were assorted out and formed into some kind of organization and continued the retreat."

Soon afterward Caldwell rode amid the retreating men, who were calmer now: "A weary, mortified, angry stream of men poured through the field and roads, some pushing toward Amelia Courthouse, some making direct for the river."

There was still savage resistance to the Federal advance during the day. General John B. Gordon's front held out so stubbornly that General Grant was obliged to call off pursuit of the retreating rebels and send a warning to Sheridan that Lee might turn upon him in full force. Still, Grant planned to push forward his entire army the next day, and in midafternoon he sent a telegram to Abraham Lincoln, who had come down from Washington hoping to see the end of the fighting. Lincoln eagerly accepted an invitation to come up to the front:

> Allow me to tender you and all with you the nation's grateful thanks for the additional and magnificent successes . . . I think I will meet you tomorrow.

It was only a few days earlier that Lincoln had come here on his first visit, to meet with Grant and William T. Sherman, then planning the final moves of the war. Lincoln's mind, as it was now, had been on peace rather than vengeance.

When asked about the fate of Jeff Davis and his Cabinet, Lincoln had said quickly, "That door will be left open; let them go! We don't want to be bothered with them . . . "

This theme, repeated so frequently near the end of his life, seemed to indicate that Lincoln's chief concern at the war's end was to extend humane treatment to the Southern people and to welcome the erring states back into the Union.

2

"We should abandon our position to-night"

POSTMASTER General John Reagan, a bluff Texan, had spent most of the night at the War Department in Richmond, following news from the Petersburg front, some twenty-five miles distant. Others had joined him, including Francis R. Lubbock, a former governor of Texas who was now an aide to President Davis. Since Lee's messages had become increasingly urgent, Reagan returned to the office early on Sunday morning, April 2. At 10:40 A.M. a telegram arrived from Lee addressed to Secretary of War John Breckinridge, who had recently taken office:

> I see no prospect of doing more than holding my position here till night. I am not certain that I can do that . . . I advise that all preparations be made for leaving Richmond to-night . . .
>
> R. E. Lee

Reagan was hurrying this news to the presidential mansion when he met Jefferson Davis and Frank Lubbock, who were strolling toward church at a leisurely pace. Reagan reported Lee's dispatch to the President and was taken aback by his reaction. Davis seemed "oddly distracted," as if he did not comprehend the reality of the moment. Nor did Lubbock seem to share Reagan's sense of alarm, despite all he had learned during the night's vigil. Davis walked on toward St. Paul's with his aide, having taken little note of Reagan's message or even his presence, so far as the Texan could observe.

Reagan was not one of his close friends, so Davis may have

given his report less credence than it deserved; he thought Reagan "uncouth . . . unpolished." The President's true state of mind on this day of the Confederacy's downfall could have been fathomed only by his intimates. One who would have seen beneath the unsmiling mask was Varina, who knew him to be "a nervous dyspeptic," so extremely sensitive to criticism that "even a child's disapproval discomposed him." Davis had been so hurt by attacks of adversaries that he had frequently withdrawn for several days, refusing all but the most vital appointments. He had sought refuge in work at such times, sitting at his desk from 10 A.M. until 7 or 8 P.M. without food. Though Varina often sent lunches to him, he usually left them forgotten and could be persuaded to eat only when she went there to insist that he pause.

The sensitive Davis had been severely tested during the war by a hostile press, particularly by Pollard of the Richmond *Examiner,* whose barbs had literally affected Davis's health. "I wish I could learn to let people alone who snap at me," the President told his wife, but few could have remained calm under the vicious assaults of Pollard, whom Davis called "that vile scavenger." One Rebel congressman had assailed the newspaper as a "low, pitiful, dirty, scurrilous sheet . . . a common sewer of falsehood and infamy" and urged Davis to close it. This advice, said the congressman, James Leach of North Carolina, was not to send editors into the army "in a position more congenial to their disposition—giving aid and comfort to the enemy . . . I mean hang them up with a cord of porcupine quills and lash them with a thong of scorpions, until they are dead, dead, dead —and then turn them over to their rightful owner, the father of lies."

The *Examiner,* an inspiration to a claque of the President's most vindictive critics, had drawn bitter response from the Confederate administration, and such exchanges became more frequent as Southern hopes faded, public squabbles that did not improve the President's reputation.

Criticism of Davis was neither new nor unusual, for his Confederacy was by no means a monolithic state. Secession had been imposed upon many loyal Unionists in the South, devoted patriots who, though subdued, remained hostile to the Rebel government; Union conventions had been held in the Confederacy during the war, and thousands of Southerners served in Union armies out of conviction that slavery and secession were twin evils. Many more thousands deserted the Confederate army to spend most of the war at home or in hiding. The more numerous poor whites and small farmers, who owned no slaves and worked their own lands, usually despised the few wealthy planters who controlled the slave system and the political apparatus as well. North Carolina's Governor Zebulon Vance, in his forthright fashion, had put this issue to Jefferson Davis himself in terms that had become a rallying cry: "It's a rich man's war and a poor man's fight."

Conflicts among fervent Secessionists were equally strident. Some, like Vice-President Alexander Stephens, deplored the centralization of power in Richmond and complained that Davis had trampled the rights of the Confederate states. In the collapse of the rebellion the complex social, political and economic currents in the South seemed to swirl about Davis, the capable, experienced, humane and honest but remarkably unbending, man who had led the Confederacy through its brief, apocalyptic life.

Today, on the sunlit morning of April 2, Davis and Frank Lubbock went into St. Paul's Episcopal Church at about 11 A.M. and entered the presidential pew, Number 63. Davis wore his familiar "Confederate gray" trousers and vest and a Prince Albert coat. His wide-brimmed felt hat lay on the pew at his side. It was Communion Sunday. Most of those in the large congregation were women, many of whom wore mourning. Correspondent Francis Lawley of the London *Times* admired their elegance of dress as an "unfailing wonder," after four years of war and blockade. The Reverend Charles Minnigerode, a German immigrant who had become a beloved figure in Richmond, opened the service in his quaint, thick accent, raising his voice to be heard over the rumble of distant guns from the front.

Worshipers who sat near the President in church on this first Sunday in April studied him covertly for signs of the city's fate, but, as Secretary of the Navy Stephen Mallory observed, Davis wore that "cold, stern" expression that had become so familiar during Richmond's four years of war. The stiffly upright Davis was a presence not easily forgotten: ". . . a slight, light figure, little exceeding middle height . . . his manner plain, and rather reserved and drastic . . . a fine, full forehead covered with innumerable fine lines and wrinkles . . . the cheek bones too high, and the jaws too hollow to be handsome; the lips thin . . . the eyes deep set, large and full—one seems nearly blind, and is partly covered with a film . . . Wonderful to relate, he does not chew, and is neat and clean-looking, with hair trimmed and boots polished . . . he has a very haggard, careworn and pain-drawn look."

The service was under way when a young man entered the church and whispered to William Irving, the elderly sexton. The messenger insisted upon seeing the President, but Irving refused to interrupt the prayer. As worshipers turned toward the sound of this commotion, the courier passed the latest dispatch from General Lee to the sexton, this one more insistent: "I think it is absolutely necessary that we should abandon our position to-night . . . "

Irving moved down the aisle with the telegram, "pompous and swaggering," a plump figure in a faded old-fashioned blue suit with brass buttons, foaming with ruffles at neck and wrists. Davis glanced at the message and rose at once, as if convinced at last that Richmond could not be held. His face was impassive, but Constance Cary, the pretty fiancée of Burton Harrison, saw a gray pallor on the President's face. Some of those in the church watched anxiously as Davis left, and became restive when Irving returned to summon others: General Josiah Gorgas and Colonel William Broun of the Ordnance Department and General Joseph Anderson, director of the Tredegar Iron Works, which turned out Confederate cannon.

Minnigerode was called into the vestry room, where the city's provost marshal, Major Isaac Carrington, told him that the city must be evacuated. The little German returned to the chancel to find his congregation streaming out.

He called, in his heavily accented voice, "Stop! Stop! There is no neccessity for leaving the church."

Most of the people returned to take Communion despite their fears, but Minnigerode recalled later that they "felt as if they were kneeling there with the halter around their necks."

Even so, as Francis Lawley observed, Minnigerode "did not omit to make the usual collection."

In the street outside, Connie Cary saw that there was little discussion among agitated churchgoers. "People . . . would exchange silent hand grasps and pass on." But though many had pale faces, she saw no signs of panic.

Dallas Tucker, a boy soldier who had come to church, saw piles of new Confederate bills burning in the street—the first intimation that the end was actually at hand, he thought. Neither Tucker nor the city's civilians realized that other fires were planned—army officers were under orders from General Lee to burn valuable supplies after Confederate troops left Richmond.

The Richmond *Whig* noted that news of the city's crisis had spread with incredible rapidity. "Suddenly, as if by magic, the streets became filled with men, walking as though for a wager, and behind them excited Negroes with trunks, bundles and baggage of every description. All over the city it was the same—wagons, trunks, bandboxes and their owners, a mass of hurrying fugitives . . . "

The fear which swept the city arose partially from war-long propaganda depicting the enemy as "Yankee mudsills" and "degraded foreigners," beneath the contempt of true Southerners—who were idealized as aristocratic gentlefolk, the hope of American civilization and rightful heirs to the fruits of the Revolution. Already, as if to confirm this mythology, Sherman's "bummers," advancing from the South under a 1000-mile pillar of fire, had frightened Richmond civilians and kindled their imaginations. Tales of looting and rapine were commonplace. Sherman understood the phenomenon. He said of his own troops: "No Goths or Vandals ever had less respect for lives and property of friends and foes." And he realized that he and his troops would be reviled by the Southern people for generations to come: "I doubt if history affords a parallel to the deep and bitter enmity of the women of the South. No one who sees them and hears them but must feel the intensity of their hate . . . women and children bred in luxury, beautiful and accomplished, begging with one breath for the soldiers' rations and in another praying that the Almighty or Joe Johnston will come and kill us, the despoilers of their homes and all that is sacred." Though it was Grant's army, and not Sherman's, that battered at Richmond's gates, Sherman had added to the fears of the capital's civilians through the brutal terrorism which the general justified as tending to shorten the war, and thus, "mercy in the end."

The throngs in Richmond streets, in any case, felt bitterness as well as fear—and beneath the fear and bitterness a feeling of superiority to the enemy and all his works, his industrial cities with their swarms of immigrant laborers, his speech, his fast-paced way of life, his patterns of social behavior which were cavalierly dismissed by Southerners as "lack of manners." Thousands of people in the desolated region had imbibed these attitudes and were to impart them to their progeny as part of a unique heritage—the only American heritage based upon memories of charred cities, ruined farms, pillage and rape. The final days of the war did much to ensure the survival of such a conviction.

At the call of the President, Cabinet members and other officials went to the War Department through the growing pandemonium in Richmond's streets. The most composed of these figures was the "keg-like" Secretary of State Judah P. Benjamin, who walked jauntily through Capitol Square, twirling a gold-headed cane and smiling around his cigar at passersby. His olive features betrayed no hint of agitation.

The Cabinet met at noon in the President's office in the old U.S. Customs House, with Governor "Extra Billy" Smith, former Governor John Letcher and Richmond's aging mayor, Joseph Mayo, present. Davis read the latest message from Lee in a calm voice and ordered government papers packed, and destruction of those that could not be moved readily. Though the President usually insisted upon full discussion of important matters, there was no debate today. Reagan reported that files were already moving toward the railroad station. Cabinet members left the meeting to prepare for flight. They were to meet at the station at 7 P.M., ready for the 140-mile train ride to Danville, a small town in the Piedmont region, near the North Carolina border.

Davis was in his office most of the afternoon. He called in Lewis Harvie, president of the Richmond & Danville line, to confer on the problems of supplying trains for the retreat from the city toward the west and south. He also telegraphed Lee to ask whether he could hold the Petersburg lines one day longer to avoid loss of valuable government property in a hasty evacuation. Lee responded only at 3 P.M. and then in a lengthy message concerning enlistment of Negro troops in the army. The general ended with an insistence that Richmond be evacuated by 8 P.M. The need for haste had been anticipated by the Treasury Department, whose steady conversion of banknotes into coin had become an emergency program of financial relief for the public.

Some Treasury clerks had fled the city the previous night, leaving behind Mann S. Quarles, the youngest of the staff. When he saw that no one had recorded the value of money containers, Quarles improvised an account book of rough paper to note values on each of them. He closed the containers with a seal. Most of the money, in Mexican dollars, was packed in wooden kegs. The U.S. gold coins, in sacks of $5,000 each, were packed in coin boxes, five sacks to each box. Quarles also burned a vast stock of currency: "We kept the furnace . . . red hot with Confederate notes, bonds, papers, etc. until it was all destroyed."

At the railroad station the next afternoon, under heavy guard, uniformed men unloaded eight wagonloads of money in chests, bags and barrels, all with the fresh official Confederate seal affixed by Quarles. Walter Philbrook, the senior teller of the Treasury Department, watched the money stowed on a car. The shipment was rather casually estimated at about half a million dollars. (Philbrook later said its value was "less than $600,000"). In addition to the Mexican silver dollars and American golden double eagles, there were also ingots, nuggets and silver bricks. And though not reported in the totals, there were also millions in Confederate banknotes and bonds, some 16,000–18,000 pounds sterling in "Liverpool Acceptances," negotiable in England, and a chest of jewels donated by Southern women to buy a warship. The deposits of the Richmond banks were loaded into the same car as the official treasure.

These private funds, which were to be kept distinctly separate from the official treasure, were grossly underestimated at a value of about $200,000. Judge W. W. Crump of Richmond, Assistant Secretary of the Treasury, was to accompany the bank funds on their journey, assisted by several bank tellers.

The treasure car was guarded by midshipmen, one of whom was the President's brother-in-law, Jefferson D. Howell. Some of these guards were only twelve years old. Their commander was William H. Parker, an old salt of thirty-five who had served in the prewar U.S. Navy. Parker, assisted by John F. Wheless, a navy paymaster, saw the treasure packed on a train which was to carry Treasury Department clerks and officials; it was to follow the presidential train.

In the absence of Burton Harrison, Davis worked with his aides, Governor Lubbock and Colonel William Preston Johnston, as they packed his executive papers and saw them off for the depot. Several of his associates noted an unusual air of detachment in the President's manner.

He had made methodical preparations for his flight, but because of the chaotic military situation, his future movements could not be predicted. Plans for regrouping Confederate forces remained vague. Davis hoped to make a stand in western Virginia, or if that were impossible, in the Deep South or southwest. In addition to Johnston's army in North Carolina facing Sherman, there were substantial forces elsewhere. These were being rapidly reduced by desertions, and thus were not actually available, but Davis was to be haunted for years by visions of the wasted troop strength still theoretically at his command, if it could be concentrated: 52,000 in Georgia and Florida under various commanders; 42,000 under General Richard Taylor in Alabama and Mississippi; some 18,000 under General Edmund Kirby Smith west of the Mississippi. Adding some 90,000 deserters from the ranks of Lee and Johnston, as Davis did in his distraught condition, the South still should have been able to muster more than 200,000 troops. It was enough to confirm the iron-willed Davis in his belief that the war was not lost but was merely entering a new phase.

In the late afternoon the President locked his office and went home to oversee the packing of his household effects. He found that he was needed. Several of his slaves had fled and four who remained were drunk. Mrs. Omelia, the housekeeper, was in a pet. When Davis ordered groceries and bedding sent to the farm of a friend outside the city, Mrs. Omelia bridled. "The Missus told me to have the Sisters at the Convent to take things," she said. Davis asked her to follow his orders and added, "I want Miss Maggie's saddle taken with the rest of the tack."

The President entrusted a servant, John Davis, with a crated marble bust which was Varina's favorite likeness of her husband. John also carried off the prized war painting, "Heroes of the Valley," which depicted Stonewall Jackson and his officers.

Davis was interrupted by a courier bearing a message from the War Department, and sat to read it amid the bustling of Mrs. Omelia, who harried the Negroes as they dismantled the stately rooms.

During these moments Davis was surprised by the arrival of his old friend Clement Clay, who was only now returning from an abortive peace mission to Canada. A frail, asthmatic figure, Clay had served Alabama as both U.S. and Confederate senator, and a few months earlier had been sent by Davis as a commissioner on an ill-starred attempt to end the war through the offices of Horace Greeley of the New York *Tribune,* who had shown sympathy for Secessionists. The mission had collapsed after an inconclusive meeting with Greeley in Niagara Falls, N.Y. The peacemakers were forced to make their way home through the Federal blockade.

. . .

Davis and Clay—and their wives—had been frequent companions during the prewar years of Senate service. Davis and Mrs. Clay seemed to have much in common, but Clay found Davis distant and inscrutable. As he wrote a friend, the President "would not ask or receive counsel—he was predisposed to go exactly the way that his friends advised him not to go." Though he had sought to form closer ties, Clay found in Davis some indefinable perversity which led him to isolate himself: "He *will* be in a minority." Today, as their world was crashing around them, there was time for no more than a greeting between the old friends whose friendship had been so enduring, yet so lacking in intimacy. It was agreed that Clay would join Davis and the Cabinet in their flight, and travel with them until he left to overtake his wife, the vivacious, coquettish Virginia Clay, who was now a refugee in rural Georgia. Mrs. Clay was to play an intriguing role in the later life of Jefferson Davis.

Davis turned to speak with government officers who came, seeking orders. To John Hendera, the Confederate treasurer, he gave the check for $28,400 he had received from the auction of his wife's furniture and silver plate and asked him to have it cashed into U.S. coins, the only money then negotiable at par in the city. (Banks were open, in haste to close their books before Federal troops burst into Richmond.)

From the porch of the mansion the President spied the family cow in the backyard but forgot her as he read fresh dispatches from the front. Lee had already evacuated the river lines south and east of the capital and Richmond was exposed. Petersburg was also doomed. James Grant crossed the street from his house to help carry valuables from the mansion to his farm but declined to take Varina's carriage. "I don't believe I'd risk that, sir," he said. Davis realized that Grant was afraid of retaliation by Federal troops, should they discover the carriage on his place.

"Well, then," Davis told Grant, "take it to the depot. I'll carry it along with me."

As the carriage and the President's light baggage left for the station, Davis remembered the cow and sent a servant after Grant with a message, asking him to send for her. Davis saw several articles in the mansion that his wife had urged him to take to safety but with time short he could delay no longer. He asked Mrs. Omelia to save an inkstand decorated with figures of the Davis children, but left behind many family possessions. For himself the President took only bedding, a comb and brush, toothbrushes, some freshly ironed shirts and some socks. A few grocery staples also went into his luggage. He felt an urge to take his sword, but remembered that it was in the Arsenal for repairs.

His mind turned to the women and children who must remain behind in the city, and as an afterthought he sent his most comfortable chair to Mrs. Robert E. Lee, an arthritic invalid who was to remain to face the invading troops. His own wife was much on his mind. Today, though he was not aware of it, Varina and her children had arrived in Charlotte, N.C., to the surprise and alarm of local citizens, who saw in their coming the fall of Richmond and catastrophe for the Confederacy.

Varina's party arrived in Charlotte to find that the house rented for them by the President was unfurnished, its rooms completely bare. Though Burton Harrison noted that the people of the city "did not rush forward" to greet Mrs. Davis, there was an immediate and generous response from a few local families, which sent furniture and linens to the house to help make the party comfortable.

Varina was forced to wait for an hour or so before she went to her house, and during this time a mob, "stragglers, deserters and conscripts, the very scum of the army," gathered about the railroad car to shout at Varina. James M. Morgan, a young sailor who accompanied Mrs. Davis, wrote, "The wretches reviled her in the most shocking language"—an ironic display of the furies loosed in the dying Confederacy and the range of passions inspired by the public image of Jefferson Davis, the defeated and discredited leader.

Morgan and Harrison, alarmed by the menace of the "blackguards" around the train, closed the car windows and rushed to the doorways, just as "several of the most daring of the brutes climbed up the steps." Though Morgan was armed with a sword and revolver, it was the firm, calm voice of the unarmed Harrison that dispersed the rowdies, and, in the words of James Morgan, "the cowards slunk away" before the scolding of the soft-voiced Virginia aristocrat.

Harrison found one man in Charlotte brave enough to give further aid to Mrs. Davis. He was Abram Weill, a Jewish railroad official whose "courage and chivalric hospitality" prompted him to provide food and other comforts for Varina's party, despite the threat of later retaliation. Some of the Davis party, too numerous to be sheltered in the house, were given quarters in an adjoining warehouse by Weill, where food was carried to them under cover of darkness, evidently to conceal them from the desperadoes roaming the streets.

In distant Richmond, the President left his mansion only when a messenger came with word that the Cabinet awaited him at the depot. It was dark when Davis rode his horse, Kentucky, through the city's streets, accompanied by John Taylor Wood, the grandson of the late President Zachary Taylor. Young Wood was one of Davis's secretaries, as well as his nephew by his first marriage. Other riders included Clement Clay and the aides, Colonel William P. Johnston and Governor Lubbock. The streets were quiet at first, but as they neared the depot there was a rising roar from unruly crowds. Davis and his companions forced their way through a press of men, women and vehicles near the station. Many of these desperate people, hoping to escape the enemy, evaded guards and clambered atop the overcrowded trains.

Davis was besieged by government officials as well as by his household servants. About this time John Hendera came with the check, to say that the banker had refused to cash it, though it was drawn on one of the city's most respected firms.

"Take it along," Davis said. "Perhaps we can cash it in Danville." The lack of ready money was a serious problem, since Davis had given his wife all their cash except for a five-dollar gold piece and a roll of Confederate bills which were now depreciating so rapidly that many Richmonders refused to accept them at any value.

Robert Brown, a house servant, appeared. "Miz Omelia won't leave me pack the stuff," he said. "She taken out the groceries and Miss Maggie's saddle ain't nowhere."

Davis then attempted to deal with the carriage, which trainmen refused to put aboard for lack of room. He ordered it put on the next train and was assured that it would be done.

"All aboard!" a soldier bellowed. " 'Board!"

Still Davis lingered. His slave Tippy had been left at home in the confusion, but another, Spencer, had defied an order from Davis and come to the train. A third slave cried out to him over the din, "They done an' lef' the spoons and forks, sir!" Davis sent still another of his black men, David Bradford, to find the silver at the mansion and ordered him to leave the city with General Breckinridge, who was delaying his departure in order to supervise the withdrawal of troops from the city. Breckinridge was to join the Presidential party somewhere along its line of flight, as events dictated.

The Cabinet was a striking group in the thronged station: The swarthy Benjamin, who had become such a familiar figure in his service in three Cabinet posts, still smiled and smoked one of his perpetual Havana cigars, calling debonair pleasantries in his resonant voice. Some critics who found Benjamin unctuous said his chief talent was a knowledge of how to please Davis, who admired the secretary's air of perpetual cheerfulness—real or assumed. An observant War Department clerk said of Benjamin, "Upon his lip there seemed to bask an eternal smile, but if it be studied it is not a smile." Tonight, at any rate, the Yale-trained intellectual of the Cabinet managed to look as if he were off on a pleasant outing.

The handsome, courtly Attorney General, George Davis of North Carolina (who was not related to the President) was a well-known orator and lawyer himself. He had joined the Cabinet only the year before, and though he had been an adversary, was now the President's friend and adviser. The Attorney General, like Benjamin, was considered a Cabinet "intellectual" and was personally attractive. Varina Davis found him "one of the most beautifully proportioned of men."

Postmaster General John Reagan, "The Grand Old Roman" of Texas politics, was a fat bear of a man whose frock coat strained across his enormous chest. Though noted for his gregariousness, he seemed to be subdued tonight.

Secretary of the Navy Stephen R. Mallory, a genial, witty, round-faced Floridian known as the Beau Brummell of the Davis circle, had a deceptively breezy manner that served to conceal a superior intelligence and rare executive ability. A favorite of Richmond society during the war, his public reputation was that of a lively conversationalist and raconteur—and an especially accomplished flatterer. It was said that he and his highly born Spanish wife served the most delicious mint juleps in the Confederacy.

There was also Secretary of the Treasury George A. Trenholm, who was so ill that he had gone to the train in an ambulance. His wife, the only woman in the official party, had come along to nurse him. Numerous others had joined the party—at least twenty more officials, military and civilian.

Secretary of War John Breckinridge, who had come to see them off, was a large, handsome Kentuckian who had been Vice-President, the youngest man who had served in that office. His drooping mustache gave him a forlorn look, as if—so detractors said—he had been long deprived of his favorite potion—Kentucky bourbon. As a presidential candidate in the crowded field of 1860, Breckinridge had finished second to Lincoln in electoral votes. In only two months as Confederate Secretary of War he had made a favorable impression in Richmond. The War Department clerk John Beauchamp Jones wrote, "Gen. Breckinridge seems to have his heart in the cause, not his soul in his pocket, like most of his predecessors."

Despite short notice and the pandemonium in the station, the departure of the presidential train had been ably organized; it was said to be so well stocked that the refugee government could resume operations in the field at once—in tents, wagons or log cabins. This train was to lead the way westward, closely followed by the treasure train.

Secretary of the Treasury George Trenholm went aboard the Davis car, and others of the Cabinet stood outside, mustering such dignity as they could amidst the bustle. The Navy's Captain Parker, whose middies had taken over security of the entire station, was not impressed by most of the departing leaders. He wrote later, "Mr. Davis was calm, dignified as usual, and Gen. Breckinridge . . . was as cool and gallant as ever—but the others, I thought, had the air, as the French say, of wishing to be off."

Parker and his boys kept watch as the Presidential train ahead sat, inexplicably waiting. "Both trains were packed," Parker said, "not only inside, but on top . . . on the engines—everywhere, in fact, where standing-room could be found; and those who could not get that 'hung on by their eyelids.' " Parker's young men, posted at the depot's gates, were "cool and decided . . . prompt and brave" in keeping the rapidly growing mob at bay, Parker felt, but Secretary Mallory noted that a few "terrified" women and "artful dodgers" managed to board the Presidential train despite the guards.

All others were aboard for an hour or more when Davis entered the car about 11 P.M. The Cabinet had been uneasy at this delay. They did not realize that he and Breckinridge had been closeted in President Harvie's railroad office hoping for "better news" from Lee, messages that never came. Davis entered the railroad car, and the decrepit engine started and the train lumbered across the bridge to the south bank of the James and was off toward Danville—where Davis hoped to establish a new capital and await news from Lee. Looking northward across the dark waters of the river, the fugitives had their last glimpse of Richmond. Tonight the doomed capital had a peaceful, even slumberous, appearance. Constellations of gas lights were flung across the Seven Hills of the city where Thomas Jefferson, inspired by ancient Greece and Rome, had made a new seat for the government of Virginia during the throes of an earlier revolution. The Confederacy's eminent refugees, though they faced an uncertain future, were to be spared the sights and sounds of the city's destruction at the hands of its own people.

3

"Blow her to hell"

WITH the departure of Davis and the Cabinet, Captain Parker's young sailors formed closely about the treasure train, their muskets and bayonets gleaming in the dim light.

Parker became more anxious as time passed. Near the station were "large numbers of ruffians . . . breaking into stores searching for liquor . . . We heard the explosions of vessels and magazines, screams and yells of drunken demons in the streets. Fires were now breaking out in every direction, and made it seem as though hell itself had broken loose."

About this time a slave dealer, known to history only as "Lumpkin," approached the station with a gang of about fifty black men and women who shuffled along with chained ankles. One of the midshipmen thrust a bayonet at Lumpkin.

"There's no room here for you or your gang," he said. The infuriated Lumpkin turned back, unlocked his Negroes in the street and watched them scatter, perhaps the last group of salable slaves in the nation. They were valued at $50,000. It was almost two-and-a-half centuries since the first shipload of African captives had landed at Jamestown, only a few miles distant to the east.

By now fires had sprung up in the heart of the city, nearer the railroad station. Joseph Haw, an Ordnance Department clerk, watched a mob plunder government supplies: "The storehouses were wide open and filled with men, women and children, white and black. For light they were burning bits of paper and dropping them on the floor still burning."

General Richard S. Ewell, the city's last Confederate commander, had urged the raising of a volunteer corps to prevent such looting—but only one man had offered to serve. A Richmond *Times* reporter, drawn to a warehouse where soldiers were smashing whiskey barrels under Ewell's orders, saw civilians flock to the spot: "They contrived to catch most of the liquor in pitchers, bottles and basins . . . the crowd became a mob and began to howl . . . So frenzied had the mob become that officers in charge had to flee for their lives . . . men, women and children traversed the streets, rushing from one storehouse to another, loading themselves with all kinds of supplies . . . [S]traggling soldiers . . . set about robbing the principal stores on Main Street, followed by a reckless crowd, drunk as they."

Some of this mob approached the midshipmen on guard and began jeering them—already rumors had spread that the combined treasure of the Confederacy and the city's banks amounted to many millions.

As one observer wrote, "after filling themselves with the fiery liquor out of the ditches they [the mob] became very brave and determined to divide the assets of the Confederacy among themselves." The crowd rushed the train, "But something happened!—and before those ruffians realized it, they were all on the outside. Those midshipmen were regulars, and the mob instantly appreciated the fact that the guns and the bayonets in the hands of these youngsters were going to be used at the word of command, and the scoundrels . . . fled."

Near midnight Captain Parker heard the rumble of artillery caissons on a nearby bridge and sent a sailor to investigate. He brought a report that it was the rear guard of the Confederate army. To Parker's relief, the treasure train shuddered into motion about this time, the young sailors leapt aboard and the treasure crossed the river bridge to the south bank of the James, from where the sailors watched the burning city across the water. Parker and his men steamed off with their precious burden, moving westward at about ten miles an hour, just in time to avoid witnessing the final agonies of the capital.

Among those who were to follow them was a more colorful band of seamen led by the celebrated Admiral Raphael Semmes, home from his wartime career of burning Yankee shipping halfway around the world. The hero had returned only a few weeks earlier, having lost his raider *Alabama* in a fiery battle with the U.S.S. *Kearsarge* in the English Channel. Semmes had escaped to England and returned home after a triumphal tour of Europe.

The red-haired admiral had been given command of a landlocked little fleet—four ironclads and five wooden ships which were anchored helplessly in the James River, blocked by Federal ships which lay downstream. The day brought him belated warning of the city's fall; it was only at 4 P.M. that he had a sealed dispatch from Secretary Mallory with word that Lee advised evacuation of the city during the night. The grizzled veteran twitched his fierce mustaches as he read Lee's urgent suggestion that he destroy his ships and join the retreating army with his remaining seamen.

Semmes had had no previous orders from Lee—nor even a hint of the evacuation—and Mallory's note took him by surprise. "This was rather short notice," he said ". . . here were my 'forces,' but where the devil was General Lee, and how was I to join him?" Still, he ordered his flagship, the *Virginia,* packed with explosives, ready to be blown up with the rest of the small fleet after nightfall.

Elsewhere in the city army officers prepared the last stages of evacuation. Lieutenant General Richard S. Ewell, still vigorously active despite the gray fringe of hair about the pointed dome of his bald skull and a wooden leg as a result of a battle wound, directed an arson squad. As he had been ordered, Ewell prepared to burn tobacco and ordnance warehouses to deny their contents to the enemy. City officials had protested such arson as a threat to the entire city, but John Breckinridge, though he also opposed the plan, had not countermanded the order and Ewell made ready for action. The lieutenant general, known as "The Woodcock" because of his long, pointed nose and reedy voice, was conferring with the Secretary of War in front of the War Department building when they were glimpsed by Captain Charles Dwight, who had come to get orders for his regiment: "Breckinridge as he sat on his fine horse was simply magnificent, bright and cheerful, giving no sign of anguish." Ewell presented a striking contrast: "He looked the wreck that he was, his thin narrow face, wizened and worn, twitched nervously, as did his hands and arms."

Nearby some troops were pouring out liquor from kegs in streams "quite as large as would be caused by a summer shower," from which Dwight saw "hundreds of men, women and boys . . .

dipping the liquor in all kinds of vessels, even with their hands . . . some even lying flat and swilling it."

Dwight returned to his regiment through roaring fires. He rode flattened on the back of his galloping horse between walls of flame that gushed from burning houses on 14th Street, but went through safely, though "singed and almost suffocated." Looking back, Dwight could see Richmond's flour mills, Haxall and Gallego, beginning to burn. These mills were among the largest in the world: "They were nine or ten stories high. Out of . . . the several hundred windows rushed great tongues of flame mixed with boiling black smoke; and finally, as the roofs were burned through or fell in, huge pyramids of fire and smoke shot up high above the towering walls . . . [T]he view of the burning city was at once sublime and terrible."

Explosions soon rocked the city and houses for miles about—the arsenal had gone up. To the eyes of a South Carolina cavalryman across the river, "It was marked by a peculiar blackness of smoke; from the middle of it would come the roar of bursting shells and boxes of fixed ammunition, with flashes that gave it the appearance of a thunder cloud of huge proportions with lightning playing through it . . . The old war-scarred city seemed to prefer annihilation to conquest."

Late in the night Mayo's Bridge began to burn, after thousands of retreating soldiers and civilians had crossed to the south bank of the river. In the confusion of the shouting mob and the rumored approach of the enemy, no one could be sure which troops were the last across the bridge. But General Ewell crossed, past the flames of freshly set fires, just as South Carolina soldiers of General Joseph Kershaw's brigade hurried over to safety. Kershaw called to Captain Clement Sulivane of his command: "All over. Good-bye. Blow her to hell."

Sulivane's men joined the retreat, tossing lighted pine knots on the planks until the bridge was a roaring inferno, dropping its flaming brands into the swift current below. The escape route from the city to the south bank of the James was closed. Only a handful, such as those who retreated with Admiral Semmes, could now evade the enemy by way of the southern bank, along which lay the route of the western railroad to Danville.

Shortly before the arsenal exploded, Semmes had left his flagship with fires burning in her hold and watched from a distance as the *Virginia* was destroyed: "The spectacle was grand beyond description . . . The explosion of the magazine threw all the shells, with their fuses lighted, into the air . . . as the shells exploded by twos and threes, and by the dozen, the pyrotechnic effect was very fine. The explosion shook the houses in Richmond."

Semmes mustered a band of sailors and naval cadets aboard a wooden gunboat and moved upstream at a snail's pace. They passed the burning school ship, *Patrick Henry,* and saw several blocks of the city in flames. As they went by, the Tredegar Foundry caught fire, and the remarkable plant which had produced Confederate cannon and other arms was soon a roaring furnace. As Semmes knew so well, the Tredegar was one of the few heavy industrial plants in the South, a bulwark of Confederate arms production. But though the Rebels had striking success in turning out some types of arms and ammunition, most of their weapons had been imported from England.

In fact, the Confederacy had lacked an industrial base, and the fragile Southern agricultural economy, founded on cotton and manned by slaves, had been in ruins for many years.

Both Admiral Semmes and Jefferson Davis realized that any plans for postwar revival of the South must, in the absence of basic industrial capacity, a large commercial class and effective local governments, be laid from the ground up. Though Confederate leaders were to play major political roles in the Southern renaissance that was to come, the impetus for industrial development was to come from outsiders, chiefly Northerners.

No such reflections concerned Admiral Semmes as he went ashore on the south of the James with his absurd little command: "I was about the most helpless man in the whole crowd. I had just tumbled on shore, with their bags and baggage, 500 sailors, incapable of marching a dozen miles without becoming footsore."

A passing cavalryman taunted them, "How you like navigating afoot, boys?" and the sailors marched forward, "blinded by the dust kicked up by those vagabonds" on horseback. Semmes saw his men as some of the most hapless in the retreat, "Loaded down with pots and pans and mess kettles, bags of bread, chunks of salted pork, sugar, tea, tobacco, pipes. It was as much as they could do to stagger under the load."

When they reached the station Semmes asked for a train and was told that the last one had left hours earlier, bearing officials of the government. Semmes persisted until he found three old cars on a siding crammed with men, women and children. He ordered his sailors to clear them out with bayonets. While the unfortunates wailed, the admiral investigated a decrepit old engine that stood nearby, without a fire in its furnace and without fuel. Under his orders the sailors shoved cars together and coupled them by hand; Marines chopped down a picket fence and soon had steam hissing from the locomotive's boiler. Semmes then opened the cars to all the civilians he could carry. The train moved off, almost imperceptibly, but stalled on the first slight slope, within view of Richmond, and though the engine was stoked until the boiler glowed white-hot, the train refused to budge.

Across the river, Semmes saw the blue columns of enemy infantry approaching the city, and heard, above the tumult, the rumbling of Federal cannon. To Semmes this was the fulfillment of the prophecies of Patrick Henry in his opposition to the Constitution—warning Virginia of her ruin if she surrendered her sovereignty as a state and joined the Union.

A sailor then found a second locomotive that had been hidden by fleeing workmen. Semmes had it hitched to the useless engine, and the train puffed off under a cloud of black wood smoke shot with sparks, moving at no more than six miles an hour. The sailors soon reached a railroad woodpile, where they took on better fuel; the train thundered ahead, beyond reach of oncoming Federal troops. Semmes halted to pick up stragglers in uniform, most of them, the admiral said, "unattached generals and colonels" fleeing the army. When the train was well on its way to Danville, safe from General Sheridan's cavalry, three men made their way through the crowd, announced to Semmes that they were conductors and engineers and demanded to be given charge of the train. Semmes merely roared with laughter at the belatedly courageous volunteers. The fleeing sailors escaped, but barely. An hour and a half after they rolled through the village of Burkeville Junction, Sheridan's cavalrymen ripped up the rails.

The Confederate capital, abandoned now by Rebel officialdom and its armed defenders, also lost civilians by the thousand—most of whom fled along the northern bank of the James, vying with retreating troops for places in the miserable roadway. Colonel William Blackford, an army engineer who had fought with Jeb Stuart during the days of Confederate glory, rode amidst this "pitiable spectacle" of people streaming westward. Blackford passed some navy veterans less imposing than those of Admiral Semmes:

"The sailors did well enough on the march, but there were the fat old captains and commodores, who had never marched anywhere but on a quarter-deck . . . limping along puffing and blowing, and cursing everything black and blue." Following the sailors was a "perfect army of bureau clerks, quartermasters, commissaries, and ordnance officers . . . in fine uniforms, with white faces, scared half to death, fellows who had for the most part been in . . . bombproof offices ever since the war began . . . [T]here were citizens in broadcloth, politicians, members of Congress, almost all on foot . . . some ladies too might be seen occasionally and generally they were calmer than the men."

During this hectic retreat, Blackford silently cursed the President, expressing the view of many soldiers who did not know him personally, but accepted the popular opinion that the army's valor and sacrifice had been set at naught through the vanity of the inflexible Davis. Blackford fumed, "Why Jeff Davis should have preferred to be kicked out of Richmond to evacuating it in a dignified manner I suppose he himself does not know. It was the egotistical, bullheaded obstinacy of the man no doubt."

In the defenseless city, families of rebel leaders had been left to face the invaders. General Josiah Gorgas, the ordnance chief, fled soon after Davis, apparently without a qualm at leaving his wife, Amelia, "still standing like a brave woman over the remnants of her household goods." Her ten-year-old son, Willie, who remained with her, was to become a hero by beating out fires on the roofs of houses —and in manhood was an international hero, Dr. William C. Gorgas, conqueror of yellow fever and "the man who made possible the Panama Canal."

But the enduring symbol of Richmond's defiance was Mary Custis Lee, the crippled wife of the commander-in-chief. Only the week before, General Lee had written to ask what she would do in case of a retreat: "Will you remain, or leave the city? You must consider the question and make up your mind." Though immobilized by arthritis and left alone with her daughter Agnes and a few black servants, Mrs. Lee never considered flight. In the last hours of their stay, two Confederate officers had called on her in her tall brick house on Franklin Street and found her gay and lighthearted. She would remain in the city, she said, come what may.

The fires that swept the heart of the city during the night of April 2 roared down Franklin Street. A blaze sprang up on the roof of a house next to the Lee home, crackling briefly until it was extinguished. Just across the street, a church burned to the ground. A woman friend who called on her a few hours later found Mrs. Lee calmly knitting, as usual. She had sat up in her invalid's chair most of the night. She seemed to be unshaken by the fall of the capital. "The end is not yet," she said. "Richmond is not the Confederacy."

The first Federal soldier came into sight about 7 A.M., April 3, just as the city's elderly mayor, Joseph Mayo, rode out in a rickety carriage with two other men, eager to surrender to the enemy and prevent pillage. The first invader was glimpsed by the indomitable Phoebe Yates Pember, matron of Chimborazo army hospital, said to be the world's largest. A lone enemy appeared on her grounds high above the still-burning city: "A single Federal bluejacket rose over the hill, standing transfixed with astonishment at what he saw." Mrs. Pember heard the clatter of horses and saw U.S. cavalry winding into the city in long columns, followed by infantry, "Company after company, regiment after regiment, they poured into the doomed city, an endless stream."

A United States flag rose, a band played the "Star-Spangled Banner," and in one house near the residence of Mrs. Lee, women wept at sight of the now-strange banner atop the Capitol dome: "We covered our faces and cried aloud. All through the house was the sound of sobbing. It was as the house of mourning." Blue-clad soldiers now filled the streets, marching between dying fires. Negroes besieged them, dropping to their knees and clutching the legs of horses, overcome by joy at their liberation. For the first time Richmond's slaves saw the prospect of freedom of which they had dreamed for so long. The Federal soldiers who had become deliverers by chance were often indifferent to the reactions of the deliriously happy blacks, but nothing dampened the ardor of the newly freed men and women. It was a scene to be repeated frequently throughout the South as invading armies penetrated to the heart of the Confederacy.

Among the hundreds of women who begged Federal officers for guards to be posted over their homes was Agnes Lee, sent by her mother. Agnes explained that her mother was an invalid. "She can't leave her home. Will you help us if the fire comes that far? She's Mrs.

Robert E. Lee." A corporal and two privates of the 9th Vermont Cavalry were soon posted at the house, and an army ambulance was kept waiting, ready to rescue Mrs. Lee if the flames should come closer.

The invalid was not content. She peered through the blinds and saw that one of the guards was a black man, and wrote a note of protest to the provost marshal, charging that the Negro had been posted there as an insult. The marshal then sent a white soldier instead, but though Mrs. Lee subsided, the officer commented that there was "not much hope of her recovery" from racial bias.

The invaders sought to reassure all Richmond's whites. Soldiers halted Negroes at their looting and a bluecoat officer told a crowd, "We'll picket the city with a white brigade. I assure you there won't be a bit of molestation, ladies. Not a particle." There was also an order posted: "No one will be on the streets after 9 P.M. Soldiers and civilians found out after that hour will be arrested."

Capitol Square, in the midst of the burning section of the city, was quickly filled by Federal troops, most of them black. To the cheers of Negroes outside the fences the newcomers stood guard over furniture and parcels dragged into the Square by those whose homes had been burned.

One Richmonder fled to the Square as to an oasis in the stricken city. "Fathers and mothers, and weeping frightened children sought this open space for a breath of fresh air. But here, even, it was almost as hot as a furnace. Intermingled with these miserable beings were the Federal troops . . . All along the north side of the Square were tethered their horses, while dotted about were seen the white tents of the sutlers, in which were temptingly displayed canned fruits and meats, crackers, cheese and so forth."

George Bruce, a Federal soldier, found in Capitol Square ironic symbols of the death of the Confederacy and the city—and of the American past: "Inhabitants fleeing burning houses, men, women and children, black and white . . . bureaus, sofas, carpets, beds, bedding, baby toys, costly mirrors scattered on the green. All the sick who could move retreated there to lie . . . Wind like a hurricane from the fire . . . Rising among the trees in the center of the square, amid this carnival of ruin, stood the great statue of Washington, against which firebrands thumped and rattled."

Richmond had rejoined the Union.

. . .

A few miles west of the city, seventy-one-year-old Edmund Ruffin, a refugee on a plantation where he was hiding from Federal armies, reflected bitterly on the catastrophe in Richmond. With his zealot's eyes burning in his pallid face, and lank gray curls across his shoulders, the old evangelist of Secession wrote in his diary: "Richmond was evacuated last night. All Virginia . . . will be occupied by the vindictive and atrocious enemy . . . Every . . . resident must now choose between flight and remaining to suffer every insult and indignity added to impoverishment if not destitution . . . My utter ruin is now completed . . . I am without any resources either of property or escape . . . I cannot consent to live a pauper on the charity of strangers abroad or of impoverished children and friends . . ."

In prewar years, as one of the most famous of living Americans, Ruffin had devoted himself to the twin passions of his life: the salvation of Southern agriculture by applying lime to wornout fields, and his grim gospel of Armageddon, warning that Northern Abolitionists were plotting to free the slaves, who would rise in bloody vengeance to annihilate Southern whites. With the Northern victory now at hand, Ruffin was lost in despair.

Ruffin spoke for thousands of desperate men throughout the South who found themselves unable to face the subjugation of their region—but none could feel the sting of defeat more keenly than he. It was almost precisely four years since Edmund Ruffin, an elderly recruit among men young enough to have been his grandsons, had fired the "first shot" against Fort Sumter in Charleston harbor, plunging into the stone fortress a huge and symbolic shell that had opened the war, a climax to his career as a self-styled "itinerant missionary of disunion of the south & north."

It was a feat that brought him a bizarre and instant fame. Babies and Confederate military units were named for him, and a Georgia legislator cast a ballot for Ruffin as President of the Confederacy. The aging hero, one of the first men to prowl through the ruins of fallen Fort Sumter, collected shell fragments as souvenirs, one of which he sent to Jefferson Davis. General Beauregard said Ruffin had done as much to take the fort as any younger man. Davis sent "grateful acknowledgment of your heroic devotion to the South, of truth and Constitutional Government," as well as thanks for the historic shell fragment. But though Southern newspapers acclaimed him, the New York *Post* declared that "a piece of the first hemp that is stretched in South Carolina should be kept for the neck of this venerable and bloodthirsty *Ruffian.*"

Now that Richmond had fallen, Ruffin's thoughts turned, as they had turned before, to suicide. Once more he told himself "I have lived too long . . . It is my earnest wish that I may not live another day."

Though he was but one of many Southerners to declare that they had no desire to survive the Confederacy, Ruffin was to become one of the few to carry out his threat of self-destruction. But there were others who could not bear to face life under "the nutmeg-eyed, muslin-faced Yankee." Among them was John Milton, the war governor of Florida, who had committed suicide only a few days earlier.

4

"A fire bell in the night"

JEFFERSON DAVIS and his official party jolted along on their westward journey through the night of April 2–3, halted frequently as workmen repaired war-worn tracks. Through the barren country on each side of them Lee's shrunken army plodded in the same direction, on a route roughly parallel to that of the railroad. The Davis party, badly shaken by the loss of Richmond, spent a sleepless night on the first leg of the flight.

But the Confederate cabinet could not justly be charged with the collapse of their experimental nation. They were among the ablest men in the public life of the region, experienced in government, well educated and devoted to their cause. They were representative of the Southern ruling class, though some had reached high position through their own efforts and abilities rather than birth. They had worked effectively with Jefferson Davis, who had chosen them with care. These survivors of Cabinet duty, who had replaced less productive predecessors, were probably the most capable the South could offer.

Yet the high officials of the disintegrating Confederacy were not an inspiring sight as they endured the overnight passage in their "frightfully overcrowded" train. John Reagan felt that the refugees were "oppressed with sorrow for those we left behind us," but Stephen Mallory observed that they were "very depressed," not merely because they had been forced to flee their capital—but also because every member of the party was fearful that the rail line would be cut by Federal cavalry at any moment. Almost to a man these leaders expected to be hanged if captured, probably without trial. Most of them were acutely aware of the violent ends that had come to unsuccessful leaders of revolutions and civil wars of the past.

Secretary of the Navy Mallory, who left a record of this journey in a brief diary, had served as chairman of the Naval Affairs Committee in the prewar U.S. Senate and had been familiar with the navy's facilities and personnel in the South. He had launched a vigorous and imaginative program which was to make the Confederate Navy a formidable fighting force in the face of overwhelming odds.

Despite the lack of naval yards, machinery, iron and rolling mills, Mallory had created an amazingly large fleet of ironclads and wooden ships. To accomplish this he assembled about 300 former U.S. naval officers, among whom were such men of genius as Matthew Fontaine Maury, "The Pathfinder of the Seas"; John M. Brooke, a noted designer of ordnance; and the formidable sea captains Admiral Raphael Semmes and Franklin Buchanan. Not only had these men assembled a navy of 199 vessels, they had also made history by developing submarines, mines, torpedoes and floating gun batteries. The Navy's growth had stemmed largely from the initiative and industry of the competent Mallory.

Tonight the gregarious, smiling Floridian studied his fellow passengers with an appreciation for the unique historical aspects of the flight that was to bear the Confederate leaders to such varied fates.

Anna Trenholm nursed her husband as he lay across a seat, apparently unruffled in her role as the only woman in the car filled by thirty men and their servants and a swarm of visitors from other parts of the train. The Secretary of the Treasury had been sedated by a doctor before departure, treatment for neuralgia and a stomach ailment, and he was now "quite sick from the effects of the morphine as well as the pain in his head." Trenholm had grown wealthy from steamship lines, wharves, railroads, South Carolina cotton plantations and the labor of hundreds of slaves. The ships of Frazer, Trenholm & Co. had carried contraband through the blockade and its Liverpool offices had become a vital Confederate outpost.

The second man to hold office as Confederate Treasurer, Trenholm was not a politician but a banker and international trader who had been one of the wealthiest Americans in 1861. After serving as adviser to Treasurer Christopher Memminger from the opening of the war, he had succumbed to the pleas of Davis and taken over the office in the summer of 1864, when it was too late to save the South from financial ruin. When Congress refused to raise taxes or to put the new nation on a cash basis, Trenholm turned to the public, begging gifts of cash, jewelry, even food for the government. Though he himself contributed $200,000 in cash and bonds to aid the cause, it was all in vain. Inflation raged out of control. As early as mid-1864 many soldiers deserted, disgusted because they were seldom paid.

The Treasurer's distinguished appearance and charming manner were of little moment in this crisis. The new nation's currency neared a state of collapse that presaged doom for the Confederacy. Since he had campaigned so insistently for a sound fiscal policy, Trenholm seemed to suffer no loss of public confidence, but affluent Southerners refused to buy most of his bonds and the Confederacy drifted into bankruptcy. Trenholm had failed because the people had lost faith in victory.

Mallory felt that the most anxious of the group was John Reagan, who sat "whittling a stick down to nothing, his eyes bright and glistening as beads," as if they were unseeing. Reagan, too, had taken his office reluctantly, but since he had served on the House Postal Committee of the U.S. Congress, and was also familiar with the Southern territory, Davis was able to persuade him to become his Postmaster General. The resourceful Reagan had quickly made the Confederate system profitable by the simple expedient of confiscating the U.S. postal network in the South and hiring some postal officials to come down from the North to join him. Reagan created early surpluses at the cost of efficient operations, and despite innovations —such as the establishment of a school for clerks—complaints of poor service had been incessant.

A loyal, energetic official, Reagan was a self-made man, a Tennessee farm boy who went to the Texas frontier to become an Indian fighter, surveyor, lawyer, judge and congressman. The habits of his youth remained with him; a Richmonder had seen him at a party, "ill at ease and looking as if he might have left his carry-log and yoke of oxen at the door." Though regarded as a rough countryman who was out of his element in the society of the capital, Reagan had been one of the most dependable members of the Cabinet.

But, like most other Confederate officials, the Texan had seen his labors come to naught in recent months, his scattering of post offices across the South falling into disrepair, manned by a handful of clerks and postmasters who were isolated by the destruction of the railroads.

Judah Benjamin, "the brain of the Confederacy," was the center of attention in the refugees' car. Mallory suspected that his air of unconcern was a pose, since Benjamin's face was "a shade or two darker than usual" as he munched a late sandwich by the light of the swinging oil lamps, but Benjamin was well known for his aplomb. An observer said that he had "moved through the most elegant or simplest assemblages on rubber-tired and well-oiled bearings." Benjamin's companion tonight was the Reverend Moses Hoge, a Presbyterian minister from Richmond said to be "the only man Benjamin trusted." Nearby was the tiny Jules St. Martin of New Orleans, Benjamin's brother-in-law, who was a clerk in the Department of Justice.

Davis, who admired "the lucidity of his intellect," had defended Benjamin against all critics during the war, even after his brief, stormy, term as Secretary of War, when one of his orders had so offended General "Stonewall" Jackson that he threatened to resign. Jackson never knew that, in this case, Benjamin was merely carrying out an order from Davis. A hostile press assailed Benjamin as "the chief thief in a Cabinet of liars," and Davis removed him, but only to make him Secretary of State. Though it was little known even in Richmond, Benjamin's capacity for work was so phenomenal that he had not only performed his own duties with dispatch, but near the end of each day entered the President's office to labor with Davis until late evening, lending his considerable skill and experience to help cope with the recurrent crises of the Confederacy.

Benjamin had joined the government early, in a lowly position, had supported it with all his energy, and had become a major influence in its affairs. Born in St. Croix to British parents who were Sephardic Jews, Benjamin was brought up in Wilmington and Fayetteville, N. C., and Charleston, S. C. In three years at Yale—he had failed to graduate—he gained a superior education and was fluent in several languages. He had arrived in New Orleans with only five dollars in his pocket, and by prodigious effort became a prosperous lawyer and then a United States senator. Benjamin had been known as the wealthiest lawyer in Washington, with a thriving international practice—though much of his income was spent at gambling tables. He was a founder of the railroad that became the Illinois Central, had served nine years as U.S. senator from Louisiana and had once declined a seat on the United States Supreme Court. He had become popular as a host in Washington's Decatur House, where

Martin Van Buren and Henry Clay had been tenants before him; Benjamin had lived there alone after his lovely French-born Catholic wife Natalie, whom he adored, left him to live in Paris. He had visited her annually, but rumors of her several love affairs had so shaken him that he sold the fine furniture and objets d'art he had collected for her—though there had been no divorce, probably out of consideration for their daughter, Ninette. Tonight, as usual, Benjamin was smiling, urbane and loquacious, as if determined to make the best of approaching catastrophe.

Attorney General George Davis was also a prominent figure in the car. The North Carolinian, though not regarded as brilliant, had become one of the President's chief advisers because of his practical approach to Confederate problems. He was a capable lawyer and a noted orator and had been an honor graduate of the University of North Carolina. Of medium height, poised and unaffected, Davis had gained a reputation as an honorable man of cosmopolitan tastes, a personable gentleman of the old Southern school.

George Davis had turned to politics belatedly, and after serving as a conservative Whig leader in his home state he had abruptly changed his position to become a Democrat and an ardent Secessionist—and a Confederate senator. He had served as Attorney General for little more than a year.

Among others on the train were the presidential secretaries, Frank Lubbock and William Preston Johnston. Lubbock, a wartime governor of Texas, was born in Beaufort, S. C. into a wealthy family of shipowners and cotton planters, and was brought up in Charleston. At seventeen he had joined the States' Rights movement during the South Carolina nullification crisis of 1832, and was thus a seasoned Secessionist. After a brief career as cotton merchant and buyer, Lubbock had moved to New Orleans, where he married a wealthy Creole woman, but after a financial panic in 1836 had moved to Texas, to the small tent city called Houston. Lubbock won the friendship of Sam Houston, became clerk of the House of Representatives and then Comptroller of Texas at the age of twenty-two. Lubbock was now almost fifty years old.

Johnston, the son of the ill-fated western commander who was killed at Shiloh, was a thirty-four-year-old lawyer, an honor graduate of Yale, and a former field officer who had been forced to give up his command by illness. For three years he had served as a presidential aide, chiefly as liaison between Davis and his generals. Johnston was a gentle, courtly, introspective man, a poet whose major interests were literature and history.

Also in the car were Samuel Cooper, the aged Adjutant General; Captain Micajah Clark of the Davis staff; Dr. A. Y. P. Garnett, the President's personal physician; Robert G. Kean, chief of the War Bureau; and the Davises' old friend Clement Clay.

To John Reagan it appeared that the most composed of the fugitives was Davis himself. Everyone in the car, the Postmaster General thought, was "impressed with his calm and manly dignity, his devotion to the public interest and his courage." In fact, Reagan felt that Davis was beyond question the greatest man he had known. The other two Cabinet secretaries who had served throughout the war and had come to know Davis well also admired the President extravagantly. Benjamin said he had never known a more dedicated or patriotic man, and that he had never heard Davis express an "ungenerous or unworthy thought" about others. Secretary Mallory praised Davis as patient, energetic and industrious, with a shrewd understanding of human nature, the prompt, businesslike methods of a merchant and a keen, analytical mind.

But even among those aboard the car, estimates of the President's gifts as a leader were in such striking contrast that it seemed impossible that friends and foes were speaking of the same man. Robert Kean of the War Department reflected bitterly that Davis himself had been the cause of Confederate catastrophe: ". . . peevish, fickle, hair-splitting . . . a man with a passion for detail and a grandiose reluctance to delegate authority."

As the little train rattled on its slow way toward Danville, Kean, with a bemused eye on the President, thought of a friend who had spoken of Davis as a "mule," but withal "a good mule." Now, Kean thought, his friend would be forced to agree that the President had turned out to be "a jackass."

A theme common to much criticism of Davis was that he had been overbearingly dictatorial, a charge most often heard from bureaucrats in the War Department, who had experienced presidential intrusion more than most government officials. One critic, in fact, had charged: "He was not only President and Secretary of five Departments—which naturally caused some errors—but that spice of the dictator in him made him quite willing to shoulder the responsibilities of all the positions."

Davis had indeed found it difficult to delegate authority, particularly in military affairs, a field in which he felt himself most competent. At times he had interfered in the operations of the War Department, even to dealing personally with officers in the field, or signing purchase orders and expense vouchers himself. His friends maintained that he felt obliged to take such steps in light of staff incompetence, and pointed out that the President's failure to impose his strategic concepts on some field commanders had cost the Confederacy dearly. Davis had also failed to exert authority over certain governors who put the welfare of their states above that of the Confederacy. In truth, though its armies and navy had fought with a valor and ferocity seldom equaled and though many of its leaders were able and resourceful, the government of the Confederate States had been something of a paper tiger, basically ineffectual because of its inability to enforce its will upon the States (and Congress itself). From the start the Davis administration was forced to deal with a bureaucracy torn by faction and dissension.

In many respects, Jefferson Davis was to remain an enigma to his contemporaries and to scholars of later generations. But despite the salvos of criticism he inspired in the twilight of the Confederacy's life, there were few who questioned his single-minded devotion to the Southern cause. His obvious sincerity of purpose did not prevent a striking diversity of opinion about this complex, sternly repressed leader. Later scholars have been forced to the conclusion that there was truth even in the most extreme expressions about Jefferson Davis, by both supporters and adversaries.

Tonight, in any case, a president in retreat but not yet a fugitive, Davis radiated confidence, giving most of his associates the impression that neither his will nor his faith had flagged. Against all logic this doggedly resolute Rebel chief held out to these experienced men of mature judgment the hope, even the expectation, that the Confederacy would survive. Not until the very end, in the face of utter catastrophe, would he concede defeat.

It was now for the first time that Davis had leisure to hear of the adventures of Clement Clay on his foray into Canada, where he had gone under the leadership of Jacob Thompson, a talented North Carolinian who had made his fortune in Mississippi before the war. A flamboyant spymaster, Thompson had been sent northward to foment rebellion in the hope of creating a northwestern confederacy to force peace upon the North. His propaganda persuaded many midwesterners to oppose Lincoln's re-election, and he was involved in a plot to burn New York City—an attempt that had failed after Barnum's Museum and a dozen hotels had been set ablaze (but only because of faulty "Greek fire" incendiaries and the prompt work of city firemen).

Clay and Thompson had spent some $300,000 of a secret fund on their Canadian foray and other ventures, including a raid by armed men on St. Albans, Vt., and plots to rescue prisoners from Federal pens. In the end the two had created little more than a nuisance and their efforts to promote a peace treaty with the aid of Horace Greeley had failed.

In returning home, Clay had barely escaped with his life as the blockade runner *Rattlesnake* ran aground in Charleston harbor on a bitter February day. When the ship was set afire by enemy guns, Clay got into a lifeboat, which also grounded, forcing him to wade ashore in chin-deep waves. Miraculously, he managed to salvage not only a trunk of valuables meant for Judah Benjamin but also saved a large Newfoundland dog which had been stolen from Robert E. Lee by a Union soldier who sold him into Canada, where Clay found him. After a month-long illness caused by exposure, Clay had made his way to Richmond just as the Confederacy began to collapse.

Long after midnight the President's train slowed to a stop at Clover Station, a village some eighty miles southwest of Richmond, where an eighteen-year-old army lieutenant, John Wise, saw the fleeing Cabinet. The boy officer was the son of ex-Governor Henry A. Wise of Virginia, the President's adversary. For the past two days young Wise had learned of accumulating Confederate disasters through the chattering key of the railroad telegrapher. Trains from the capital had begun passing early Sunday night, and by midnight young Wise thought that most of Richmond must have been moving westward on the cars that swayed above the fragile rails.

When these trains halted for wood or water Wise heard the bland assurances of Confederate officials as they greeted the small crowd at the country depot. "The army's not beaten or demoralized," one of these men said. "It's retreating in good order, and Lee is now out from under the burden of holding those long lines. Why, he'll whip the Yanks yet. Wait and see!"

Wise took heart, but his despair returned at 3 A.M. when he saw the train bearing the President and his Cabinet come to a halt in the torchlit darkness.

Davis smiled wanly at the few people along the track and waved a thin hand. Wise saw "physical and mental exhaustion" in his bony face and languid gesture.

The train was soon on its way, laboring westward with a dwindling of its lanterns and a subdued soughing of its ancient engine. Other trains were in its wake, and Wise watched them all: the Treasury Department train with its burden of silver and gold, both official and private, guarded by Captain Parker and his midshipmen and the bank tellers led by Judge W. W. Crump; later trains bore archives and employees of the Post Office and the Bureau of War.

The boy lieutenant realized that he was witnessing the death of the Confederacy: "I saw a government on wheels . . . the marvelous and incongruous debris of the wreck of the Confederate capital . . . indiscriminate cargoes of men and things. In one car was a cage with an African parrot, and a box of tame squirrels, and a hunchback." All, including the parrot, were intensely excited at the sight of the people clustered about the Clover station.

As the last train that crept through the village passed on, a man standing at the rear shouted to them: "Richmond's burning. Gone. All gone."

Soon afterward Lieutenant Wise was sent on a perilous mission through enemy lines to reach General Lee and carry news of the army's progress to President Davis in Danville. Wise and a young trainman roared off into the night aboard a decrepit engine, running without lights toward Burkeville Junction, which the enemy was thought to have occupied by then.

It was 4 P.M. of April 3 before the presidential train reached Danville, after an eighteen-hour journey that covered only 140 miles. A local delegation met the party and carried the passengers to their homes; offices and living quarters had been made ready for the establishment of a new Confederate capital. Davis and his staff were housed in the large home of Major W. T. Sutherlin on Main Street, where he found a warm welcome that was in vivid contrast to Varina's experience in Charlotte. "Nothing," Davis said, "could have exceeded the kindness and hospitality of the patriotic citizens. They cordially gave us an 'Old Virginia welcome' . . ." This did not include the cashing of his check, which he found non-negotiable.

The anxious President asked for news of Lee, but learned that there was none. He wrote his wife in Charlotte, N. C., of his arrival in Danville and of the fall of Richmond, warning her that "military necessity" might force him to further flight. Varina responded loyally in a letter brought back to Danville a few days later by Burton Harrison: "I . . . know that your strength when stirred up is great, and that you can do with a few what others have failed to do with many." She was confident that he would "deliver" the South, but confessed that news of Richmond's fall "came upon me like the 'abomination of desolation.' "

Davis turned vigorously to the improvement of Danville's inadequate defenses; both soldiers and slaves dug new trenches and gathered supplies for the expected arrival of Lee's troops. The refugees then settled for an indefinite stay in the town.

The traveling Treasury Department, which had arrived in Danville a few hours later than the presidential train, now opened for business. Captain Clark and Chief Teller Philbrook paid out from the official treasure an unspecified amount under "informal requisitions" and also redeemed more Confederate bills, exchanging silver for them in a ratio of $1 to $70. After three days of brisk activity the Treasury moved south by rail through Greensboro to Charlotte, N. C., where the money was to be stored in the old U.S. Mint, still under guard of Parker's young sailors.

The Confederate treasure was assigned its first precise value by Captain Clark as his train left Danville: $327,022.90. No one was to explain further the substantial reduction of the treasure from its supposed value estimated on departing Richmond at between $500,000 and $600,000. Since there was no estimate of the "informal requisitions" or of the amounts of coin paid out in currency redemption, future efforts to account for all the official funds were to be in vain. Whatever the facts of the Danville transactions, this casual reporting of payments inspired suspicions. Wild and absurdly misleading rumors were already circulating that Davis carried millions in gold and silver specie—rumors that were to plague the guardians of the treasure to the end.

The Virginia bank funds, which left Danville at the same time, remained intact and separate from the official Confederate treasure. Judge Crump's coin containers had not been opened.

On April 5, after a Cabinet session, Davis issued a proclamation exhorting the people of the South to further exertions. Judah P.

Benjamin wrote the document, using a sheet of dingy foolscap, and took it to the Danville *Register* for publication. Davis's call to his people, as a biographer of Benjamin wrote, was a cry of "desperation rather than reasoned hope":

"We have now entered upon a new phase of the struggle. Relieved from the necessity of guarding particular points, our army will be free to move from point to point to strike the enemy . . . Let us but will it, and we are free . . .

"I will never consent to abandon to the enemy one foot of the soil of any of the states of the Confederacy . . .

"Let us not despond then, my countrymen; but, relying on God, meet the foe with fresh defiance and . . . unconquerable hearts."

Also on April 5 there was finally a report from Lee, this one "favorable"—though the army was still retreating. Thus encouraged, the President, Captain Wood, Dr. Garnett and the staff opened a mess and prepared for an extended stay—though Wood left the city the following day to visit his family, for whom he had rented quarters in Greensboro. Troops arriving in Danville, among them the sailors of Admiral Semmes, were posted for defense of the town. Davis immediately commissioned Semmes as a brigadier general so that he could assume command of all forces there. Semmes pointed out that this was lower than his naval rank, but that he would not protest. "I will waive my rights pending further discussion," the grinning admiral said.

Davis gave him one of his rare smiles. "That's the right spirit," he said, and entrusted Danville's safety to the admiral-general.

Semmes found that desertions had reduced his strength to 400 men. He formed these into skeleton regiments and, after some drilling, moved them into the Danville trenches on April 7. One of his command was his youngest son, Cadet Raphael Semmes, aged thirteen.

The refugees, whose pause in flight was unknown to most of the country, were the object of intense speculation by now. A jubilant Northern public hailed the fall of Richmond as the end of the long, bloody war, but *Harper's Weekly* cautioned that the Confederate leaders were "not men who will relinquish the struggle until the defeat . . . of their soldiers assure them that there is no alternative. These soldiers comprise the most desperate men of the insurrection . . ." The Northern press also debated the fate of the Confederate

President and his Cabinet. The New York *Times* said that Davis was already fleeing for Mexico, and that it was doubtful he would ever be captured, "But if he is caught he should be hung . . . He was the prime mover of the conspiracy . . . To forgive his followers, will be noble and wise. To forgive Jeff Davis himself will be a miserable and most mischievous weakness."

Horace Greeley's *Tribune* challenged the vengeful *Times,* pointing out that Davis had left the Union later and more reluctantly than most Southern leaders and could not be charged with the instigation of the rebellion. Severe punishment for Confederate leaders, the *Tribune* said, would merely single out each victim as "conspicuous hero and martyr" to the Southern people—particularly if the government hanged Jefferson Davis.

In occupied Richmond, now that order had been restored, Abraham Lincoln appeared on the streets, where he was greeted by vast crowds of Negroes, many of whom fell to their knees. The President seemed to be embarrassed. "Don't kneel to me," he said, "that's not right. You must kneel to God only, and thank Him for liberty . . . But you may rest assured that as long as I live no one shall put a shackle upon your limbs." When the blacks refused to disperse even after a few Marines pushed forward with bayonets, Lincoln quieted them with an impromptu speech:

"My poor friends, you are free—free as air . . . Liberty is your birthright. God gave it to you as he gave it to others, and it is a sin that you have been deprived of it for so many years. But you must try to deserve this priceless boon. Let the world see that you merit it . . . Learn the laws and obey them; obey God's commandments and thank Him for giving you liberty . . ."

When the crowd fell quiet, Lincoln said, "There, now. Let me pass on. I have but little time to spare. I want to see the capital."

An officer saw Lincoln toiling up a hill with a crowd at his heels, "walking along with his usual long, careless stride and looking about him with an interested air and taking in everything."

Lincoln sat for a few moments at the desk of Jefferson Davis, who had left it so recently. The President was moved by the poignancy of his presence there, a moment that marked a turning point in American history, the end of a fratricidal war that had claimed more than half a million lives. "This must have been President Davis's chair," Lincoln mused, staring out a window with "a dreamy expression," as if he felt a new awareness of the dreadful dilemmas his wartime adversary had dealt with in this place. But if he experienced a tug of sympathy for the departed Rebel chief, Lincoln kept it to himself.

The President was soon gone, after brief inspection of the city's grim prisons and the legislative halls, where he saw "dreadful disorder, with Confederate scrip and . . . documents lying on the floor." In Capitol Square Lincoln paused before the bronze equestrian statue of Washington, whose eyes seemed to fix upon each passerby, and whose right hand was raised. Lincoln said, "Washington is looking at me and pointing to Jeff Davis."

When the city's new commanding officer asked what should be done with Richmond's people, Lincoln said, "I don't want to give any orders on that, General, but if I were in your place, I'd let 'em up easy. Let 'em up easy."

Meanwhile, Secretary of War John Breckinridge, who had tarried in Richmond to oversee final details of the evacuation, was making his way westward with a small party on horseback. They moved amidst Lee's retreating troops. Hoping to overtake Davis, Breckinridge led his band toward Danville: Quartermaster General A. R. Lawton, Commissary General Isaac St. John, Colonel James Wilson, and Breckinridge's oldest son, Cabell. The Secretary of War and his party rode with General Lee for several miles, but left him on April 5 or April 6 with the feeling that the cause was hopeless.

Breckinridge had one adventure during this brief period. When Federal cavalrymen attacked a wagon train a couple of miles away, a panic-stricken quartermaster fled along the column shouting, "The Yankees! The Yankees are coming!" Teamsters and others fled across a bridge, leaving Breckinridge and a handful of men in an isolated position. The general collected about twenty horsemen and a hundred men on foot, and marched toward the enemy, his command including nearly as many generals and colonels as it did privates. This advance opened with a wild charge led by a drunken captain, against an unoccupied woodland. But soon afterward, when a Federal party cut off a few rear wagons, Breckinridge led his motley force to the site and drove off the enemy—thereby distinguishing himself as the only American Cabinet officer to lead troops in battle.

Breckinridge telegraphed Davis to say that he had left Lee at the small town of Farmville, Va., adding: "There was very little firing yesterday and I hear none today . . . The straggling has been great and the situation is not favorable . . . Will join you as soon as possible." By now the enemy had cornered a wing of Lee's army at Sayler's Creek, capturing 7,000 men, including half-a-dozen generals, among them Richard Ewell, who was soon on his way to prison.

In Danville on the night of April 8, as the Cabinet met in the Sutherlin dining room, a disheveled Lieutenant Wise appeared with a verbal message from Lee—the general had feared to send a written dispatch. Wise told of the disintegration of the army as Federal forces gathered in its path. When Davis asked if Lee might escape, Wise replied, "I regret to say, no. From what I saw and heard I am satisfied that General Lee must surrender. It may be that he has done so today."

The men about the table, shocked by this devastating news on the heels of a favorable report from the army, said nothing. Wise noted that they shifted uneasily when he added glumly, "It is a question of only a few days at most." For the first time Davis and his Cabinet began to consider the actuality of a surrender of Lee's army, but since there was as yet no definitive report, they clung to their hopes.

The exhausted Lieutenant Wise was given supper and then reported more fully to Davis, a recitation taken down by the secretary, Burton Harrison. Wise quoted from memory Lee's plan to retreat along two rail lines, the Richmond and Danville and the Southside: "The enemy's cavalry is already flanking us from the south and east. You may say to Mr. Davis that as he knows, my original purpose was to adhere to the line of the Danville road. I have been unable to do so, and am now endeavoring to hold the Southside Road as I retire in the direction of Lynchburg." Wise said he had asked Lee if he planned to make a last stand along the route, but the general had shaken his head and said slowly, "No. I shall have to be governed by each day's development . . . A few more Sayler's Creeks and it will be all over—ended—just as I have expected it would end from the first." Davis, as Burton Harrison noted, sat quietly for a moment, "peering into the gloom outside," perhaps recalling Lee's air of optimism after his victories in the summer of 1862, when Confederate hopes had been high. Davis entrusted Wise with orders to Lee, urging that the army be kept together.

It was in Danville that Senator Clement Clay left the party. He spent a few days there with his cousin, Dr. Robert Withers, but was so anxious to hurry southward to join his wife, Virginia, that the President urged him to precede the caravan on its journey. Davis himself was fond of Virginia Clay, with whom he corresponded occasionally on a rather intimate basis; he, too, appeared to be drawn to this attractive—though far from beautiful—woman who had been so alluring to men throughout her life.

On Palm Sunday, April 9, Davis sent Lee a telegram: "You will realize my reluctance to leave the soil of Virginia and appreciate my anxiety to win success north of the Roanoke . . . I hope soon to hear from you at this point . . . May God sustain and guide you."

But the army was in the final stages of disintegration. The British correspondent Francis Lawley, who had followed Lee, wrote of the march: "Every mud-hole and every rise in the road choked with blazing wagons—the air filled with the deafening reports of ammunition exploding and shells bursting . . . dense columns of smoke ascending . . . exhausted men, worn-out mules and horses lying down side by side—gaunt Famine glaring hopelessly from sunken, lacklustre eyes—dead mules, dead horses, dead men everywhere."

It was thus that, on Sunday, Robert E. Lee, wearing a new uniform, a yellow sash, gold spurs and new boots embroidered in red silk, rode out from his army to meet General Grant in the McLean House at Appomattox Courthouse; an exchange of messages over the past few days had prepared the way for a peace conference. Brief, sharp fighting had begun about dawn, but ceased when Lee saw that he was surrounded, his lines of retreat and supply severed.

Though he said, "I would rather die a thousand deaths," Lee endured the surrender ceremony with calm dignity. Grant's terms were generous, even magnanimous, and were to influence American military and foreign policy for many years—but Confederate troops received the news as the end of their world.

The engineer, Colonel William Blackford, watched Lee as he returned to his troops: "Tears filled his eyes and trickled down his cheeks. . . . The men's cheers changed to choking sobs as with streaming eyes and many cries of affection they waved their hats. . . . Grim-hearted men threw themselves on the ground, covered their faces with their hands and wept like children. . . . One man held his arms wide over the crowd and shouted, 'I love you just as well as ever, General Lee.' " Men passed their hands affectionately over Traveler's flanks as the general rode by.

A few moments later, Lee halted and spoke to a small group of soldiers. "Men, we have fought the war together, I have done my best for you. My heart is too full to say more."

On this day in Danville, Davis and some of the Cabinet went to church, a combined service of all the city's congregations. Though the day was otherwise uneventful, forlorn soldiers straggled in from Lee's army, deserters who had fled to avoid surrender. The sight of them caused consternation among the townspeople, who had been told little of events in the field. A number of young officers had also escaped through enemy lines, vowing to fight to the last; one of these was the commander's son, Robert E. Lee, Jr.

On the late afternoon of this day—April 9—nearing the end of a homeward voyage up the Potomac, Abraham Lincoln entertained his wife and a few guests by reading somberly from *Macbeth,* lingering over the lines so obviously familiar to him:

Duncan is in his grave;
After life's fitful fever he sleeps well;
Treason has done his worst; nor steel, nor poison,
Malice domestic, foreign levy, nothing,
Can touch him further.

Soon afterward, when the *River Queen* docked in Washington, Mary Lincoln swept the capital lying before them with an agonized glance. "That city is full of enemies!" she said.

Lincoln turned to her with an impatient gesture, "Enemies! Never again must we repeat that word."

The party entered the city in a carriage, past bonfires blazing in the streets and crowds of shouting, laughing people. Lincoln's bodyguard called out, "What has happened?"

A man stared at them in amazement. "Why, where have you been? Lee has surrendered."

On the afternoon of April 10, Davis and others were in conference in Danville when Captain W. P. Graves arrived from the army with "positive" news of surrender. This, as Mallory said, "fell upon the ears of all like a fire bell in the night." The men passed the message around the table and became silent, "a silence more eloquent of great disaster than words could have been."

The President seemed to recover from this blow by sheer power of will, but was then told that enemy cavalry was approaching from the west—some 6,000 veteran riders led by General George Stoneman, driving in from East Tennessee, looting, burning and cutting communications. The party must flee at once, before the enemy cut rail lines leading southward into North Carolina.

Under Burton Harrison's direction, government documents were repacked and hauled to the railroad station. Davis telegraphed General Joseph E. Johnston about the emergency, and asked him to meet the Cabinet in Greensboro. The official party was told to prepare to leave for the fifty-mile journey by 8 P.M. so that they could meet Johnston, who was falling back before Sherman. Davis contemplated nothing but continued defiance toward the enemy, and he was not alone in his delusion. Mary Lee, who heard news of Appomattox in her invalid's chair in Richmond, told a friend that all would yet be well. "The end is not yet," the resolute cripple said firmly. "General Lee is not the Confederacy. There is life in the old land yet."

But the reported surrender struck dread to the heart of Judah Benjamin in Danville. He was reading poetry—Tennyson—to a young woman when he was interrupted by word of the army's disaster at Appomattox. Benjamin at once sought his friend the Reverend Hoge, whom he found in the parlor of the Johnston house talking with several women. The secretary of state, who seemed as cheerful as ever, joined the conversation and said nothing of the grim news, but signaled Hoge and led him to their room. "I didn't have the heart to tell those good ladies what I have just learned," he said. "General Lee has surrendered and I fear the Confederate cause is lost."

Hoge was silent for a moment. "What will you do?"

"I will go with Davis and the Cabinet to Greensboro. Beyond that, I don't know."

"How can you escape? Federal troops will be scouring the country for you, and you'll be with the President and the whole Cabinet."

Hoge long remembered Benjamin's "pitiless smile" and firm words: "I will never be taken alive."

. . .

Davis returned to the Sutherlin mansion through a rainstorm, and told his hostess "almost in a whisper" that he must flee, since Lee had surrendered. Though he was evidently overwhelmed by this "astounding misfortune," the vigorous Davis continued to pack bags for further flight. As he said farewell, Mrs. Sutherlin offered Davis a bag of gold. His eyes brimmed with tears, "I cannot take your money," he said. "You and your husband are young and will need it . . . I doubt if I shall need anything much very long." He gave her a small gold pencil as a keepsake.

Eight o'clock found the Danville station roaring with the confusion of flight—there was an air of panic after news of Lee's surrender, and a desperate scramble for places on the train. Heavy rains had left bogs in the city streets, and men floundered toward the depot knee-deep in mud. Mule teams struggled, teamsters and soldiers bellowed curses, horses whinnied in terror when driven up makeshift ramps into cars, and a growing crush of men threatened to overpower the guards and fight their way aboard the train. The crowd was excited by a rumor that the enemy had already cut the line to Greensboro, and that to make the railroad journey would be as perilous as to remain in Danville.

It was 10 o'clock when members of the Cabinet and a few other officials appeared near the train, where they sat on their luggage, waiting silently in darkness "lighted only by Mr. Benjamin's inextinguishable segar." It was even later when Davis arrived and entered the train, followed by his aides. The car was locked against the press of soldiers and civilians, but a few unexpected passengers went aboard despite the efforts of guards.

Robert S. Rankin, a Confederate officer based in the area, had been ordered to board the train with eight men, and when he found the Davis coach locked, simply led his troops to the roof. The train rattled off in a cold drizzle just before midnight, moving slowly over the dangerously worn rails. Rankin and his men "doubled up around a stove pipe" atop the Davis car and piled blankets over the flue in an attempt to keep themselves warm; this forced smoke downward through the wood stove and filled the car with stifling clouds. There was a roar of "expostulative remarks" from the presidential car, but Rankin's men continued to cover the flue, until the coughing, choking officials were obliged to open windows and endure blasts of cold night air in order to breathe.

The train made halting progress, with frequent short stops, until dawn enabled the engineer to see that the rails ahead of him had not yet been broken by enemy cavalrymen. The small engine resumed its labored chuffing and the train careered along at top speed.

The train reached Greensboro about noon of April 11, having averaged four miles per hour on its journey. It was in the nick of time. A few moments after the President's party had passed over, Federal troopers burned a tall trestle just north of the town. When Davis was told of his narrow escape he said only, "A miss is as good as a mile."

5

"We could rally our forces"

GREENSBORO, a pleasant small town whose tree-shaded streets were lined with comfortable homes, was now in an uproar, thronged by straggling soldiers from the armies of Lee and Johnston. Few civilians were to be seen when the presidential party arrived, and those gave scant attention to the fugitive officials. Davis and his friends were shocked by the cold reception they found here.

Captain John Taylor Wood noted the mood of the townspeople in his diary. "Houses all closed. The people are afraid to take anyone in."* Avenging enemy troops were expected on the heels of the presidential party. After a vain search to find quarters for him, Davis took a tiny upper room of the modest house on South Elm Street in which Wood had rented rooms for his wife and children. The President's room was furnished only with a bed, table and a couple of chairs. Even this arrangement was protested by Wood's landlord, who rushed in shouting that he might as well burn the house himself, since the enemy would surely do so when they appeared. Wood resisted, however, and Davis remained there during most of his five-day visit in the town.

Stephen Mallory was incensed by the lack of hospitality in the city: ". . . at Greensboro it was the old story, of which political history presents too many chapters. The ship was sinking, and in their haste to desert her, the expeditious rats would not even see

*Some Greensboro citizens, then and later, indignantly rejected these charges of inhospitality toward the party, but this narrative accepts the versions of Mallory, Wood and Burton Harrison. (See Notes, Chapter 5.)

those who still stood by her colors." The town's doors were closed, and "their latch strings pulled in against the members of the retreating government"; the party was fortunate to find shelter in "a dilapidated, leaky passenger car" on a railroad siding. The naval secretary added (erroneously) that "this pitiable state of human nature" was to be the only instance of rejection encountered by the party on its long flight through the South.

It was not surprising that some of Greensboro's people feared to harbor Davis and the Cabinet. They were shaken by the avalanche of Southern disasters—the ominous approach of Sherman, the collapse of the Confederate government and the threat of anarchy posed by rioting, pillaging Confederate troops in the town's streets. North Carolina had been the last state to secede, and Union sentiment there was still strong, especially in and around Greensboro, where Quaker pacifism was a restraining influence upon the wartime community. Guilford County had voted heavily against Secession in 1861; only a few months before Davis arrived, a mass meeting in Greensboro had declared the war lost and urged that the South sue for peace. Delegates to that meeting had complained bitterly of "the state of things in Richmond." Still, the county had supported the Confederacy. The Guilford Grays, a local militia unit, were among the first Confederate troops in action and had suffered heavy casualties during the war.

And in some ways Greensboro was hospitable. Local men saw to it that the presidential party was supplied with liquor. And Mrs. Alphonso Whittington, the wife of a trainman who had helped bring Davis from Danville, sent the President a pie and inspired other women to send delicacies to the fugitive dignitaries. But Davis and the Cabinet were largely confined to their old railroad coach, which was so crowded that Colonels Lubbock and Johnston slept on the floor. The party usually ate simple meals of bread and bacon from navy stores, supplemented by eggs, coffee and flour foraged by cooks and aides. Their utensils were one tin cup and spoon and a few pocket knives.

Meals were cooked in the open by a young Negro, who built his fire alongside the tracks. Mallory described a dinner during which Attorney General Davis stuffed himself with "a piece of half-broiled middling in one hand and a hoecake in the other," grimacing at the taste of the elderly bacon; Benjamin divided his attention between a bucket of stewed dried apples and a haversack of hard-boiled eggs; Reagan whacked away at a ham with his Bowie knife; and Mallory himself gulped scalding coffee in order to give Adjutant General Cooper his chance at "the coveted tin cup."

Only George Trenholm, the stricken Secretary of the Treasury, found comfortable lodgings in Greensboro. He was met at the station by ex-Governor John M. Morehead, the town's wealthiest and best-known citizen. As Burton Harrison reported it, Morehead came "effusively to the train" and carried Trenholm off to Blandwood, his large mansion, which stood a few blocks distant. Morehead, who had invested heavily in Confederate bonds and currency, was alarmed by the prospect of their total depreciation, and Harrison felt that his show of hospitality toward Trenholm was prompted by the ex-governor's hope that he could induce the secretary to redeem his securities in silver or gold. Harrison reported that Trenholm's illness continued during his stay at Blandwood, and added that "his symptoms were said to be greatly aggravated by importunities with regard to that gold."

However accurate Harrison's charge, the bulk of the official Confederate treasure was not available to Trenholm. Some days earlier, before the arrival of Davis in Greensboro, Captain Parker and his men had left this town and gone to Charlotte with their burden. It was only now that a part of the much-discussed official Confederate hoard accompanied the Davis party in its flight, for Captain Parker left behind in Greensboro two boxes of gold sovereigns valued at $35,000, for the use of Davis and the Cabinet. In addition, Parker left $39,000 to pay the troops of General Johnston.*

In Greensboro Davis was greeted by the mercurial Creole, General P. G. T. Beauregard, whose relationship with Davis had been strained. When Beauregard had reported boastfully of his victory at the battle of Manassas/Bull Run, Davis had rebuked him for this "attempt to exalt yourself at my expense." Today's meeting, however, was cordial enough. Beauregard reviewed the army's status and said General Johnston would arrive the next day.

The President invited Beauregard and Johnston to a meeting of the Cabinet in the old railroad car the next morning.

It was an occasion marked by irony as the fugitive Davis faced his two most difficult generals, seeking at this moment to inspire them to fight in a cause which they felt was lost. The complex

*In Greensboro the official treasure was reduced to about $253,000 in coin and bullion. This excluded currency, "Liverpool Acceptances" and jewels. The Virginia bank funds, of course, remained separate and intact.

emotions at work as these old adversaries met were evident in the set faces of Davis and Johnston. The vain, fussy, pompous general had been a persistent critic of the President. As a shrewd woman diarist of Richmond society had noted, Johnston's "hatred of Jeff Davis amounts to a religion. With him it colors all things."

In commissioning five full Confederate generals early in the war, Congress and Davis had placed Robert E. Lee and two others ahead of Johnston, who had been the senior U.S. officer to join the Southern army. Such a breach of Confederate law angered Johnston, who blamed Davis personally. "This is a blow aimed at me entirely," he wrote. Davis rejected the complaint, but his reputation suffered in his clash with the popular commander, and the resulting war-long hostility between the two damaged the Confederate cause. It was not their first quarrel, for they had become enemies as West Point cadets when they staged a fistfight over the affections of a tavern-keeper's daughter. Johnston, the heavier of the two, had won the fight, and their relationship had been strained ever since.

Near the end of the war, when Congress had urged that Johnston be restored to command in hope of halting Sherman, Davis had refused. He had relieved Johnston earlier, after Sherman had forced him into Atlanta's trenches, and now told Congress that he considered the general unfit for further command. Despite the attitude of the President, R. E. Lee, in one of his first acts as Commander-in-Chief, had chosen Johnston to face Sherman in North Carolina, a show of confidence that was lost on the restored general, who said sourly, "They're only calling me back so that I'll be the one to surrender." He berated Jeff Davis once more. "He would sacrifice wife, children, country and God to satisfy his hate for Joe Johnston." Mrs. Mary Chesnut, a Confederate general's wife, deplored Johnston's plight, but was unsure of his basic loyalty to the Confederacy: "He always gives me the feeling that all his sympathies are on the other side."

Though Johnston, with a makeshift army, had failed to check Sherman's march through the Carolinas, he had fought the invaders with ferocity at Averasboro and Bentonville, N. C., then retreated so adroitly that his army had every chance to escape, even now. His survivors were concentrated near Raleigh, some 80 miles to the east of Greensboro.

Beauregard and Johnston were surprised when the President opened their meeting with talk of raising a new army. Reagan found the conference "most solemnly funereal," but Davis still refused to face the reality of defeat, insisting that, though recent disasters were crushing, they need not be fatal. Lee's veterans were ready and willing to fight again, the President said, and he could round up deserters and draft others to continue the resistance. Johnston heard him out, stiffly erect, tight-lipped and disdainful. "It would be the greatest of human crimes," the general said, to attempt to carry on the war—the South had neither money nor credit, and its only weapons were those in the hands of his soldiers. "The effect of our keeping the field would be, not to harm the enemy, but to complete the devastation of our country and the ruin of its people."

Johnston proposed that he open peace negotiations with General Sherman. Davis protested that the Federal government would insist upon unconditional surrender, which would be unacceptable —and that failure of the conference would further demoralize the Southern people. "Neither soldiers nor civilians have shown a disposition to surrender," Davis said, and he intended to have the government protect them to the last.

Only Judah Benjamin agreed with Davis, whom he supported in a brief, eloquent speech—which prompted Johnston to remark later that he was "baffled by the occult Jew's intransigence."

When he saw that the austere Johnston remained unmoved, Davis recessed the meeting until the next day, April 13.

About this time, Captain Robert E. Lee, Jr., arrived in Greensboro, one of several officers who had escaped the net at Appomattox.

The junior Lee had been at some distance from army headquarters when he heard that his father had surrendered, a report he could not accept until several officers assured him of its truth. "I had never heard the word 'surrender' mentioned or even suggested," he said—but Bob Lee had made his way southward, still confident that the war was to continue despite the surrender of the Army of Northern Virginia. He was aware that his father had scorned suggestions that the army "scatter like rabbits and partridges in the bushes" to carry on guerrilla warfare. General Lee had said, "You young fellows might go bushwhacking, but the only dignified course for me would be to go to General Grant and surrender myself and take the consequences."

Young Robert, still full of the hope his father had lost, reached the President's quarters in Greensboro just as Davis was declaring that he could "rally our forces west of the Mississippi."

But while young Lee was there, Davis got official confirmation from General Lee of the Appomattox ceremony. As Captain Bob watched, Davis read the message and passed it around.* The President's face was stricken, as if the certainty of Appomattox had only now overcome him, despite the receipt of earlier reports. The others watched Davis "silently weep bitter tears." Bob Lee remembered later. "He seemed quite broken at the moment by this tangible evidence of the loss of his army and the misfortunes of its General. All of us, respecting his great grief, withdrew, leaving him with Captain Wood."

Wood himself was stunned to read Lee's dispatch. "I can hardly realize this overwhelming disaster," he wrote that night. "It crushes the hopes of nearly all."

John Taylor Wood was a welcome ally to his Uncle Jeff in adversity. One of the most capable men in the President's party, Wood had fought at the age of sixteen in the Mexican War, the conflict which had brought his grandfather to the presidency. He was a graduate of the U.S. Naval Academy and had later taught seamanship and gunnery there. As a U.S. Navy captain with ten years of service, he had joined the Confederate Navy in 1861 and helped to fight the old *Merrimac,* rechristened *Virginia,* in her duel with the *Monitor.* Wood, as skipper of the raider *Tallahassee,* had made daring raids on U.S. supply centers and captured numerous enemy ships. Only Raphael Semmes had caused greater havoc among U.S. fleets.

Wood's aunt, the beautiful Sarah Knox Taylor, had been Davis's first wife, whose death after three months of marriage had changed Davis from a carefree boy to a stern, reserved stoic.

The party had hardly reached Greensboro before Wood began planning later stages of the flight, even before Davis had come to a decision as to his destination. Colonel Charles E. Thorburn, a blockade runner and naval purchasing agent who appeared in Greensboro on April 12, had already hidden a boat on the Indian River on Florida's east coast. Thorburn agreed to have the boat ready if and when Davis reached Florida. This plan may not have been known to Davis at the time, but Wood and others of the party had foreseen

*It was probably at this time that Davis learned that he and members of his Cabinet were excluded from the protection offered parolees at Appomattox. Only officers and men paroled there were to be allowed to return home and be left in peace. Even Lee, as a ranking officer, was to be denied American citizenship for life.

that land routes through Georgia, Alabama and Mississippi were likely to be cut off by Federal forces penetrating the region and that Davis could reach the Trans-Mississippi area commanded by General Edmund Kirby Smith only by sailing from Florida through the Gulf of Mexico.

Even now, in the vast "second Confederacy" west of the Mississippi, General Smith was wooing Mexico's Emperor Maximilian in hope of providing a sanctuary for Davis. Smith expected to raise a force of 15,000 men at Marshall, Texas, ready for the President to lead into Mexico. Such half-formed plans, little more than improvisations, were seized upon by the President during these uncertain days when he fled before a Federal pursuit which was only now being organized. Since ruined railroads, telegraph lines and bridges had virtually destroyed communications in the South, Davis would be forced to grope his way, in hope of joining distant Confederate armies before it was too late.

John Breckinridge arrived in Greensboro late on April 12, bringing more details of Lee's surrender. He conferred with Johnston and Beauregard during the night, and agreed with them that further resistance would be useless. There was still the matter of convincing Jefferson Davis.

The experienced and judicious Breckinridge, from whom Davis expected support in contending against Johnston and Beauregard, joined the April 13 conference. Davis admired his fellow Kentuckian, "a man of a high order of talents, of most fascinating manners." As Vice-President, Breckinridge had remained in Washington in 1861 longer than Davis, hoping to prevent war. He denounced Lincoln's forceful acts on the eve of the war as illegal: raising troops without congressional consent, blockading the South, suspending habeas corpus, ordering unlawful searches and seizures. Breckinridge charged Republicans with changing the character of the U.S. government, in a speech the Associated Press was forbidden to wire across the country.

The Vice-President presided firmly over the session in which the presidential electoral votes of 1860 were counted, a day when army guards surrounded the Capitol and many senators were armed. Refusing to recognize a Southerner who wished to expel the guards, Breckinridge announced Lincoln's majority, and his own second-place finish. He administered the oath of office to Vice-President

Hannibal Hamlin and remained after Lincoln's inauguration, hoping for peace even after the battle of Bull Run opened the bloodshed. Breckinridge denounced the "unnatural, fratricidal, horrible war," visited Confederate prisoners at Old Capitol Prison, joked with his cousin Mary Lincoln about the new Confederacy—and at last, after many threats against his life, went home to Kentucky. Even here he was forced to flee arrest by the pro-Union legislature of his divided state and was driven into the Confederate army, one of the most reluctant of rebels.

Breckinridge had been a capable general officer during the war. In the final months of the struggle, President Davis had named him Secretary of War, the sixth man to hold the post, in the hope that he might help turn the tide. General Lee had found him to be a stout ally. "He is a great man," the commander said, "a lofty, pure strong man. . . . If I had an army I would at once put it under his command."

Now, in mid-April, as he joined the flight of the leaders of the rebellion, Breckinridge felt that the President's last-ditch resistance was foolhardy.

The conference of April 13 was a somber repetition of the session of the previous day. Davis protested once more that Lee's surrender was not the end; the remaining Confederate armies could carry on the war until the people of the North wearied of it, and acceptable peace terms might be won. He reasoned that Lincoln would be forced to grant Southern demands if Rebel armies remained in the field, but surrender of the Confederacy, the President insisted, would bring ruin to the South. If Southerners believed that their cause was just, they would "do and dare to the last extremity." Though he did not speak of it to his associates, Davis likened his role to that of George Washington during the dark days of the Revolution—clinging to a vision of eventual victory when almost all others had despaired.

To his unresponsive generals Davis said, "I think that we can whip the enemy yet, if our people will turn out. We must look at matters calmly, however, and see what is left to do. We haven't a day to lose."

In the silence that greeted his plea Davis turned to the expressionless Johnston. "We should like to hear your views, General Johnston."

The officious little general did not hesitate. His manner was without respect toward Davis, "almost spiteful," as John Reagan recalled. "My views are, sir, that our people are tired of the war, feel themselves whipped, and will not fight," Johnston said. "Our country is overrun, its military resources greatly diminished . . . My small force is melting away like snow before the sun and I am hopeless of recruiting it. We may, perhaps, obtain terms which we ought to accept." Johnston was a general who would fight no longer.

Davis heard him out with downcast eyes, nervously folding and unfolding a small piece of paper as Johnston's rapid, precise words filled the room. When silence fell, the President did not look up, but murmured, "What do you say, General Beauregard?"

"I concur in all General Johnston has said."

Then, still folding and refolding the paper, Davis said to Johnston, "You speak of obtaining terms." He reminded the group that he had made several attempts to open negotiations with the enemy but had been offered nothing more than "surrender at discretion"—meaning unconditional surrender.

"I think Sherman will offer terms," Johnston said. "I recommend that you exercise at once the only function of government still in your hands, and open negotiations." He offered to ask Sherman for an interview. Four members of the Cabinet agreed with the generals—Reagan, Mallory, George Davis and Breckinridge. (The invalid Trenholm was not present.) Only Secretary of State Judah Benjamin agreed with the President that the war should continue.

"Well, sir," Davis said at last, "you can adopt this course . . . " but he said firmly that he had no faith in the outcome. The group agreed that Johnston should hold a conference with Sherman and obtain the best terms possible. Stephen Mallory offered to transcribe Johnston's thoughts, but the little general was determined that Davis should assume full responsibility, and insisted that he dictate terms he would be willing to accept at the hands of Sherman. Davis did so: Johnston could offer to disband Confederate troops, and Federal authority would be recognized—but *only* on condition that existing state governments were preserved, that all political and property rights be respected and that there would be no penalties for having engaged in rebellion. In brief, Davis wished to restore the prewar South, just as if the war had not been fought and lost.

An odd omission, in the eyes of later generations of Americans, was the lack of emphasis, or even comment, on the future status of the Negro slave. Though this issue was to become the flash point in

Washington's formulation of Reconstruction policies, neither Federal nor Confederate field commanders raised the question in surrender negotiations. But it was an issue which was to cause agony in the new South, and incidentally to threaten ruin to the career and reputation of General Sherman, whose "insensitivity" to the plight of freed slaves angered Abolitionists and others in the North.

As the Davis-Johnston conference ended, the President asked Johnston for his plan of retreat. The general said he would fall back into South Carolina on a line to the east of Charlotte, but Davis urged him to make a stand in Charlotte and, if defeated, to retreat to Texas "as a final goal." This was another indication that the Davis party could actually make no specific plans, since little was known of the fates of distant Confederate armies—nor of the anticipated Federal pursuit of the President and his Cabinet.

When Cabinet members urged Davis to think of his own safety, Johnston reported Sherman's remark that Abraham Lincoln was willing to send Davis out of the country on a Navy ship and allow him to "take with him whoever and whatever he pleased." Davis straightened and said sharply, "I will do nothing to place myself under obligation to the Federal government"—and was then off once more on his plans to go to Texas and carry on the fight, perhaps for years to come. "I have no idea whatever of leaving Confederate soil so long as there are men in uniform ready to fight."

But soon after the session ended Davis wrote Varina, in quite another mood:

> I will come to you if I can— Everything is dark—you should prepare for the worst by dividing your baggage so as to move in wagons . . . I have lingered on the road and labored to little purpose . . .

He entrusted the letter to an officer who was riding horseback to Charlotte, some 90 miles to the southwest—the only possible method of delivery, since the enemy had cut the rail line somewhere south of Greensboro.

The letter was late in reaching Varina, since she and her party had left Charlotte on the day the President reached Greensboro. For safety, Mrs. Davis accompanied Captain Parker's treasure train, with its guard of middies now increased to a strength of about 150, including a few Confederate Marines. Mrs. Davis left the hospitable home of Abram Weill to ride into South Carolina by rail—tracks were intact as far as Chester, S. C., but beyond that point the fugitives would be forced to travel by road.

In Chester, Varina climbed into a rickety wagon to begin a memorable phase of her journey. A sailor recalled the "distressing spectacle" of the few wagons drawn by "broken-down and leg-weary mules," and never forgot "that stately and serene woman, the wife of the President of a nation of Anglo-Saxons, as she sat, surrounded by her helpless children, on one of those primitive vehicles while the half-starved animals slowly dragged her over the weary miles.

"And not far away, on either flank and in their rear, hovered deserters waiting either for an opportunity or the necessary courage to pounce upon the, to them, untold wealth which those wagons contained." There were rumors that Varina, as well as her husband, carried vast riches in her wagons—rumors intensified by Chief Teller Philbrook, who left a scattering of gold and silver coins in his wake to aid hungry soldiers who were homeward bound: "Various stops were made on the Journey and payments were made to commissary and other officers in sums varying from $200 to $40,000, informal vouchers being given of necessity . . . These payments were made for the subsistence and pay of soldiers and for forage."*

Varina found old friends among the refugees in Chester—Generals John B. Hood, John S. Preston and James Chesnut. Clement Clay was also there, and Mrs. Chesnut noted that Clay was as attentive to Varina now "as if they had never quarreled in her prosperity"—a hint of persistent but unexplained tensions between the Davis and Clay families.

While Parker and his men transferred the treasure into wagons for the next stage of the flight, Mrs. Davis dined with General Chesnut and his wife, Mary, a perceptive diarist who had been one of Varina's intimates in wartime Richmond.

The diners talked of the fall of Richmond and exchanged news and rumors that had come to them. Though Varina was "calm and smiling" throughout the evening, Mary Chesnut noted a striking change in the status of the First Lady since Lee's surrender. Once

*Captain Micajah Clark, who made the only accounting of the Treasury's funds on the flight, did not mention these expenditures, nor the "further payments" reportedly made in Charlotte.

defeat became a reality, new attitudes had begun to affect even the highest Confederate officials.

One former member of the President's staff did not trouble to rise when Varina entered the room: "[T]here were people here so base as to be afraid to befriend Mrs. Davis," Mrs. Chesnut wrote. She realized that once-proud Confederates, now ruled by fear, had abandoned the leaders they had so recently acknowledged.

During her last moments in Chester, Varina penciled a hurried note to her husband on a scrap of rough paper. Though she felt "wordless, helpless," she told him she felt more secure in traveling with Parker and his treasure wagons. She was uncertain as to whether she should go to Abbeville, S. C., or Washington, Ga. She added, "Would to God I could know the truth of the horrible rumors I hear of you. One is that you have started for General Lee, but have never been heard of. . . ."

Near nightfall Varina and the children and two servants resumed their journey, huddled in a wagon which rumbled along in the tracks of the treasure. Her own overloaded vehicle came to a halt in a quagmire. Varina's nurse was too ill to walk, and her maid refused to clamber down into the mud. Varina climbed out, carrying Piecake. She walked five miles through darkness with mud over her shoetops, "with my cheerful little baby in my arms." Her children seemed to enjoy the excitement of the slow march, but Varina, making her way by following the sounds of the wagons and drivers, only now began to realize the desperate plight of the Confederacy and of her husband. During the night, she said, it became clear to her that he was an outcast without friends, a fugitive deprived of his power to give orders.

The caravan was unmolested, despite several alarming reports that Yankee troops or marauders were nearby. At 1 A.M. the wagon reached a country church—Woodward Baptist—where the wagon guards had halted. Captain Parker slept in the pulpit, with his men lying on the floor. The communion table had been saved for Varina, but she declined to commit the sacrilege of sleeping there. She settled on the floor beside her sleeping children, where she lay awake through the night, her mind ranging restlessly over the prospects of the family's ruined life and the plight of the Southern people.

Fearful that Federal riders were close behind, Captain Parker led the little train rapidly southward, halting at farmhouses for meals and overnight rests. The Davis children were hungry. A glass of milk or a biscuit sold for fifty cents to one dollar, and Varina was happy to have them at any price.

On April 16, when they reached the small town of Newberry, S. C., Parker and his men transferred the treasure from the wagons to a train once more. Here the fugitives read a local newspaper which rejected reports of Lee's surrender and declared that the rumor "must be an unmitigated falsehood of the enemy." The caravan reached Abbeville, S. C., where John C. Calhoun had practiced law and politics and perfected his theories of the rights of states to secede from the Union. The peaceful town was abloom with roses and flowering vines, which clung to fences and chimneys. The fragrance of gardens filled the place. Varina arrived "more dead than alive," but found a warm welcome that was in striking contrast to the reception of the Davises in North Carolina. She was now among the original Secessionists, most of them of unwavering loyalty to the Confederacy.* She met Colonel Armistead Burt, an old friend from prewar Washington days, when Jefferson Davis entered the U.S. Senate; Mrs. Burt was a niece of John C. Calhoun.

When Varina told Burt his house might be burned if he sheltered her, Burt replied, "Madam, I know of no better use my house could be put to than to be burned for such a cause."

While Varina remained in the town, Captain Parker and the treasure train moved southward, seeking greater safety in Georgia.

Varina wrote her husband that news of Lee's surrender, "fills me with horror . . . I do not believe all, yet enough is thrust upon my unwilling credence to *weigh* me to the earth. Where are you? How are you? What ought I to do with these helpless little unconscious charges of mine are questions which I am asking myself always. Write to me of your troubles freely for mercy's sake. Do not attempt to put a good face upon them to the friend of your heart."

Back in North Carolina the Confederacy faced a fresh crisis. Joe Johnston had left Greensboro to open talks with Sherman, whom he was soon to meet in a farmhouse near Durham, N. C., in negotiations that would lead to eventual surrender—just in time to prevent the

*An exception was the native dissenter James L. Pettigru, S. C. Attorney General and a staunch Unionist. On the eve of war, when the Secession Convention sat in Columbia, a stranger asked Pettigru to direct him to the insane asylum, and was directed to the church where the Secessionists were meeting. "It might look like a church," Pettigru said, "but it's really an asylum, filled with 164 maniacs."

dissolution of Johnston's army from wholesale desertions.

Admiral Semmes, whose sailors had been attached to Johnston's army upon arrival in Greensboro, was already in despair. He had lost 250 of his small band of men in ten days, and his most reliable sailors were no longer trustworthy: "Commissioned officers slunk away from me one by one and became deserters! I was ashamed of my countrymen." But after he saw the effects of news of Lee's surrender upon Johnston's army, he knew that his problems had been minor ones. Soldiers were leaving Johnston by the thousands: "There was a stampede away from his army. It melted away . . . whole companies deserted at a time."

David Conyngham, a Northern journalist who had been following Sherman and had made his way into Rebel lines, saw that Johnston's men were now pillaging and becoming bolder by the day: "They even stole most of the headquarters horses, leaving the General and his staff to shift for themselves."

The reporter saw a band of Confederate soldiers rob their officers of horses: "You damned sons of bitches have rode long enough," a Rebel soldier cried. "Hit's our turn now—git off before I let some light through ye!" The triumphant infantrymen disappeared, now mounted for the first time during the war.

Captain Wood took note of the general state of anarchy almost as soon as the Cabinet meeting of April 13 had ended: "The depression is universal & disorganization is setting in." Wood was making plans for departure; he arranged to leave his wife and children with friends in Greensboro while he fled with the President. Already Wood noted disorder in Greensboro's streets that presaged the end of the rebellion. The inner discipline that lay at the heart of the Southern war effort had snapped. Pillaging soldiers were no longer under control and were undeterred by the presence of Davis and his Cabinet and many ranking Confederate generals. Wood wrote: "Troops greatly demoralized, breaking into and destroying the public stores."

Unlike the scenes in Richmond during its last hours as the Confederate capital, the rioting in Greensboro was led by soldiers. These men felt themselves released by Lee's surrender. They knew their cause was lost; freed from the rigid controls they had known for four years, they threw off inhibitions and stole whatever they wished.

Warehouses were stormed and rifled, and rioting bands fought up and down the streets with struggling guards. Cavalry galloped to and fro, campfires were built on sidewalks and guards were posted at every corner, to little avail. One reckless band broke into the quartermaster warehouses and virtually emptied a large building before Major S. R. Chisman arrived. He "rushed into their midst with a flaming torch, crying out that he would set fire to a barrel of powder and blow the whole concern up." The men fled and a reinforced guard was posted.

The hungry, ragged, unpaid men had only begun. A unit of Wheeler's cavalry charged a North Carolina quartermaster warehouse, overwhelmed the guard and stole or destroyed everything in the building. Amidst this bedlam men of the 45th North Carolina appeared. When their captain shouted to the pillagers someone fired at him, and the officer shot the leader of the looters from his horse. The troops opened fire: "For a few minutes the crack of musketry was rapid and deadly . . . but soon the desperate mob fled over fences, through yards and back streets, and as far as one could see a huge sea of heads appeared running. . . . Four men were shot and slain in the melee—all belonging to the mob."

A day later a local officer, Major James R. Cole, was assigned to post 300 guards over the stores. A large mob appeared, roaring and swearing, but dispersed after a look at the soldiers with bayonets at the ready. There was soon another threat, for civilians also lost their heads and joined in the looting: "Then came the old women from far and near, who had been charging over the guards, relying upon their sex to protect them from bullets. . . . They were urged on by men who desired to follow after they broke the line. But once in his life [Major Cole] was not to be influenced by the 'smiles of the fair' nor their frowns, but very ungallantly told the guards to shoot anyone attempting to enter."

Women screamed at Cole, "We want some of them goods!"

"You can't have them."

"Why ain't you distributing them?"

"We're distributing them to the soldiers."

After more shouts and taunts the women turned away, and the goods were saved for troops, who were issued most of them before Federal units reached Greensboro.

But the scene in Greensboro was not entirely one of violence. One spectator who enjoyed the influx of armies was three-year-old William Sydney Porter, the nephew of a local druggist, who watched the soldiers as they pillaged, or romped after them as they marched in the streets. He was especially taken by the sound of fifes and drums. Young Porter was to become famous as O. Henry, the short-story writer who chronicled life in New York City, his "Bagdad on the Subway."

Anticipating failure of Johnston's negotiations with Sherman, President Davis on April 14 began packing for his further flight, in face of new difficulties. Since General Stoneman's Federal cavalry had swept through the area, cutting rail lines, the band could not ride on trains in the next leg of their journey. Since the Cabinet must henceforth move southward more slowly, over the primitive roads of the region, their chances of eventual escape were now sharply reduced.

As a result, horses and wagons suddenly became scarce and much more expensive. The price of sound horses trebled overnight. Captain Micajah Clark, who was in charge of transport, found that looters had stolen so many horses and supplies from government stocks in Greensboro that he could provide only the weakest of horses and mules and the most rickety wagons. He assembled these through streets echoing with gunfire.

There was a welcome addition to the caravan: an escort of a few squadrons of Tennessee cavalry commanded by General George Dibrell, a sensible country merchant who was beloved by his troops. These men were reinforced by a dozen or so Kentucky cavalrymen led by Captain Given Campbell, riders who were to serve as scouts and couriers.

In Washington, D. C., on April 14, as Davis and his band prepared to leave Greensboro, Abraham Lincoln held a Cabinet meeting to discuss means of taking the southern states back into the Union. Except for Secretary of State Seward, who had been injured in a carriage accident, the full Cabinet was present.

General Grant, who had joined the group, reported that he expected to hear from Sherman at any moment—and that Joseph Johnston was sure to surrender.

Lincoln talked of the future of the South, and spoke kindly of Lee and other officers, and of enlisted men who had fought so bravely for their cause. Secretary of War Edwin Stanton presented a plan that would erase old state boundaries and redraw the map of the

South, but Lincoln rejected it. He said he was glad Congress was not in session, so that he might establish friendly relations with the rebellious states before it returned. "There are men in Congress who possess feelings of hate and vindictiveness in which I do not sympathize and can not participate." He hoped there would be no persecutions, "no bloody work." Postmaster General William Dennison spoke of the rebel leaders, "I suppose, Mr. President, you would not be sorry to have them escape out of the country."

"Well," Lincoln drawled, "I shouldn't be sorry to have them out of the country; but I should be for following them up pretty close, to make sure of their going." He waved his huge hands as if shooing animals from a barn lot. Lincoln seemed to be anxious to establish as a basic political policy the swift return of the Southern states to the Union. He intended to deal directly with Davis—a hope in which he was to be foiled by Stanton and Andrew Johnson and the Radicals in Washington.

Grant remained after the session to decline the President's invitation to attend the theater that evening; the general and his wife planned a visit to their son.

It was the last of Lincoln's Cabinet meetings—in fact, the last day of his life.

Confusion marked the departure of the Davis party from Greensboro, for the overloaded wagons sank into quagmires left in the road by spring rains. Some Cabinet officials, as soldiers complained, carried absurdly large loads of baggage, and the worn-out horses and mules were taxed to the limits of endurance.* In the procession moving southwestwardly toward Charlotte were several boxes of presidential documents and two exceptionally heavy containers of coin—the $35,000 left by Captain Parker for the use of the President and his companions.

As the party left town, Breckinridge, Mallory, Reagan and a few others rode horseback with the escort, but many of the fugitives jostled along in carriages, ambulances and common wagons. Among those in wagons trailing the President was the rotund, short-legged Benjamin, who had vowed that he would not mount a horse, whatever the peril. During this departure the President's reserve failed

*The precise size of the caravan is unknown, but it is reasonable to assume that the party traveled with at least half-a-dozen wagons.

him for the first time and he gave his friends an intimation that his spirits were flagging and that he had begun to despair. Mallory noted the striking change: "Mr. Davis was very moody and unhappy, and this was the first day on which I had noticed in him a thorough surrender & abandonment of the cause of Southern independence."

There was a newcomer in the party, a huge red-bearded English artist who moved along the column, sketching portraits and landscapes. He was Frank Vizetelly of the London *Illustrated News,* who had spent four years covering the war's campaigns with both Federal and Confederate armies and had become a Southern sympathizer. He had been made an "honorary captain" in the Confederate army for his bravery under fire, a volunteer courier at the battle of Chickamauga. The thirty-four-year-old Vizetelly had enlivened Richmond's wartime social life, directing and playing in amateur theatricals, for which he also designed sets, painted scenery and fashioned wigs.

The young artist, already celebrated for his coverage of other wars around the globe, was a hearty, laughing man who was to shorten the hours with his ribald tales and songs and lively impromptu dances. A friend of Charles Dickens and other luminaries of the London Press Club, the visiting Englishman was to become a fascinating companion to the refugees. As the only newsman in the President's caravan, he left the sole pictorial record of the epic flight.

Slowed by the wagons, the caravan made only ten miles the first day. Burton Harrison, one of the last to leave, overtook the wagon which bore the invalid Trenholm, Benjamin, Jules St. Martin, the elderly Adjutant General Cooper and George Davis. The battered vehicle was forced to make frequent halts: "Heavy rains had recently fallen, the earth was saturated with water, the soil was sticky red clay, the mud was awful." Harrison, who was charged with keeping the train in motion, found this wagon to be a constant laggard, but he had occasional help from some passengers. When wheels sank into the mud and ground to a halt, St. Martin and George Davis pried the wheels loose with fence rails, enabling the straining horses to move the wagon forward.

Just after nightfall Harrison rode back to find this rear vehicle stalled in the darkness. Harrison spied the covered wagon by the bright occasional glow of Benjamin's cigar. All others in the ambulance sat in glum silence, but as Harrison drew near he heard the "silvery voice" of Benjamin as he recited to his comrades the almost endless verses of Tennyson's "Ode on the Death of the Duke of Wellington":

> *. . . Let the long, long procession go, . . .*
> *All is over and done.*
> *Let the bell be tolled,*
> *And a deeper knell in the heart be knolled;*
> *. . . We are a people yet.*
> *Though all men else their nobler dreams forget, . . .*

Even now, Benjamin's cheerful nature and considerable learning made him "a most agreeable companion," Harrison said.

The day ended in comfort at last, in the home of a hospitable farmer named John Hiatt, four miles north of the village of Jamestown. Here Davis and his friends had their "first good meal since leaving Danville" and a good night's sleep. As they departed the next morning, Hiatt gave the President a handsome filly to help carry him on his flight.

6

"*I* cannot *feel myself a beaten man!*"

THE caravan toiled over a poor road following the route of the railroad south and west, an ancient track worn by buffalo herds, nomadic Indian tribes and Colonial cattle drovers. The Davis party passed through the village of High Point and after failing to find a farm family willing to take them in, camped near Lexington. The first night in the open seemed to bring Davis both new vigor and relaxation. To Mallory's surprise the President became pleasantly talkative beside the campfire, where he lay on blankets with his head on a saddle, smoking a cigar and telling tales of old times. "He decidedly preferred the bivouac to the bedroom," Mallory said. The Cabinet now saw a Davis they had not seen before, his conversation bright and humorous, his manner "singularly equable and cheerful."

Governor Zebulon Vance, who had escaped from Raleigh as Sherman's horde neared the capital, overtook Davis in Lexington. The governor had sought to save Raleigh from burning by sending two elderly North Carolina leaders to negotiate with Sherman, to the outrage of Davis, who had ordered the emissaries arrested.

Governor Vance was one of the most colorful politicians in North Carolina annals, "a coarsely handsome, barrel-chested, six-foot mountaineer with a leonine head, flowing locks and intense blue eyes." He had opposed Secession until the moment Lincoln called for troops, and had, in fact, opposed the Davis administration throughout the war, his policy being to "fight the Yankees and fuss with the Confederacy."

Still, Vance's leadership inspired impoverished North Carolina to a remarkable war effort. The state had only 115,000 voters, but sent 125,000 troops to war and lost some 41,000 of these.

When desertions among North Carolina troops reached epidemic proportions, Vance declared, "It shows what I have always believed, that the great *popular heart* is not now & never has been in this war. It was a revolution of the politicians not the people." Despite his reservations, Vance had followed the President to Lexington, anxious to discuss the military situation with him. Davis called the Cabinet to meet with the governor.

"Mr. President, I have come to see what you wish me to do," Vance said.

Davis launched upon a "long and solemn" review of the South's plight, insisting that an army could be rallied to fight in the West, and intimating that Vance should raise North Carolina troops to join General Kirby Smith. Vance was impressed by the President's determination but was relieved when Breckinridge broke "the sad silence" that followed Davis's statement.

"Mr. President," Breckinridge said, "I don't think you have answered the governor's question."

"Well, what would you tell him to do?"

"I don't think we are dealing candidly with him. Our hopes of accomplishing what you set forth are so remote and uncertain that I, for my part, could not advise him to follow our fortunes further . . . "

The Kentuckian turned to Vance. "My advice would be that you return to your responsibilities and do the best you can for your people and share their fate, whatever it might be."

Davis sighed. "Well, perhaps, General, you are right." He rose and shook the governor's hand. "God bless you, sir," he said. "God bless you and the noble old state of North Carolina."

The Davis caravan reached the Yadkin River on Easter Sunday, and crossed on a ferry and a railroad bridge that had been saved a few days earlier when a local garrison beat off some of General George Stoneman's raiders.

Frank Vizetelly sketched the scene of the crossing for his British readers, and explained that each wagon, with its mule team, was ferried across in turn, delaying the caravan so that the rumored approach of Federal cavalry made the crossing "a very anxious affair." Alarms were sounded often, and "the excitement among the rear guard and teamsters was excessive." Riders stripped off their clothing, removed saddles and forced cavalry horses to swim across the swift current. Frightened horses turned back, threw their riders, struggled to the bank and charged wildly through the crowd. "Notwithstanding this," Vizetelly said, "the entire train passed safely over this and many other streams."

In Salisbury, where ruins of a Confederate prison and the rail depot were still smoldering after Stoneman's raid, Davis and others were invited to the home of the Reverend Thomas A. Haughton, rector of St. Luke's Church. Davis sat on the veranda with friends until late in the night, talking cheerfully, as if he had put aside his troubles. Even when he told of Lee's surrender, speaking rapidly while holding an unlighted cigar in his mouth, the President's tone was not doleful or despairing. Several soldiers spent the night on the veranda as guards, and Burton Harrison slept there with them as an added precaution, in case Federal cavalry should return.

At breakfast the next morning Haughton's young daughter burst into tears, "Oh, Papa. Old Lincoln's coming and going to kill us all."

Davis turned her woeful face up to his own. "Oh, no, little lady. Mr. Lincoln isn't such a bad man, he doesn't want to kill anybody, and certainly not a little girl like you."

The child was soon reassured, and began chatting away gaily of other things.

About this time a courier tracked down the fleeing Davis with a telegraphed appeal from Joseph Johnston—Breckinridge was needed in negotiations with Sherman; the eloquent former Vice-President might win more favorable terms from the enemy. Breckinridge and John Reagan turned back toward Greensboro at once, riding horseback from 10 o'clock one night to midnight the next, to join the negotiations. Reagan did not attend the sessions in a farmhouse near Durham, N. C., but wrote a proposed truce agreement which Johnston presented, only to have Sherman reject it as "too verbose"—whereupon the Federal victor wrote a version of his own, also verbose and almost as favorable to the South as Reagan's.

The Davis party rode steadily southward. They stopped overnight in the village of Concord, where the President and nine others slept in the home of Judge Victor C. Barringer before moving on to Charlotte, the largest town in the Carolinas border region. Harrison found that rooms had been located for them here—though in the President's case it had not been an easy task. Members of the Cabinet were welcomed by leading citizens of the town, including Abram Weill, who had taken in Varina Davis and her children during their visit a few days earlier. Weill now took in Benjamin, St. Martin and Burton Harrison. George and Anna Trenholm went to the William F. Phifer house, and George Davis stayed in the home of William Myers.

But fear of retaliation by Stoneman's raiders against anyone who sheltered Davis was so strong that officers could find only one householder daring enough to welcome the President. Harrison accepted the offer, though the house, he felt, was "not at all a seemly place." The host was Lewis F. Bates, a Northerner who represented an express company, "a bachelor of convivial habits" who lived alone except for Negro servants and kept "a sort of open house" and a generous supply of liquor. Bates was said by local gossips to be a Yankee spy—or at least "a graceless scamp."

Davis had just arrived at Bates's home, in the absence of his host, when a body of Kentucky cavalry rode up in a cloud of dust, waving flags and cheering at the sight of the President. At that moment Davis was handed a telegram from Breckinridge:

> President Lincoln was assassinated in the theatre in Washington on the night of the 11th inst.
>
> Seward's house was entered on the same night and he was repeatedly stabbed and is probably mortally wounded.

Davis read the telegram twice, apparently without comment, then passed it to William Johnston, a Charlotte lawyer and railroad executive who was said to be "the richest man in North Carolina." Davis said, "Here is a very extraordinary communication. It is sad news."

Whatever the precise words of the exchange, the incident grew into a controversy. A few weeks later Lewis Bates would tell the Congressional Committee on the Conduct of the War that General Breckinridge was with the President when the telegram was opened, and expressed regret over Lincoln's death—and that Davis had replied, "Well, General, I don't know; if it were done at all it were better it were well done; and if the same were done to Andy Johnson, the beast, and the Secretary, Stanton, the job would be complete."

Of this allegation Davis said, "The man who invented the story of my having received the news in exultation had free scope for his imagination as he was not present."

In any case Bates was in error about the presence of Breckinridge, who had sent the telegram himself, from a point more than a hundred miles distant.

As Davis recalled the incident, he read the telegram, passed it to Johnston with a brief comment, then turned to the Kentucky cavalrymen, who were shouting for a speech. He thanked them, urged them to resist to the last and, pleading fatigue, had turned to enter the house. Johnston read Breckinridge's telegram to the crowd, and when someone cheered, Davis turned back and raised a hand. The people in the street fell silent.

Davis expressed distress over Lincoln's murder to Burton Harrison later in the day, "I am sorry. We have lost our best friend in the court of the enemy."

Davis, Harrison and the Cabinet had often discussed the possibility of Andrew Johnson's becoming President, and agreed that this Southern Democrat, who had been named to the national Union ticket in 1864 to win wider support for Lincoln's re-election campaign, would deal harshly with defeated Secessionists. A North Carolinian by birth, Johnson, a tailor's apprentice, had run away to Tennessee as a ten-year-old. There he had become a popular politician, serving as a senator and governor. Though he had held slaves, Johnson opposed secession and remained with the Union, and Lincoln had named him military governor of Tennessee during the war. He made no secret of his distaste for the planter aristocracy which he felt divided the country. Partly because he knew Johnson so well, Davis maintained that Lincoln's death was "a great misfortune for the South"—though he conceded that the Rail-Splitter had been so relentless an enemy of the Confederacy that "we could not have been expected to mourn" his passing.

Far behind Davis, on the farm west of Richmond where he remained safe from Federal patrols, the embittered Edmund Ruffin followed the President's progress. Ruffin hoped that Davis and his Cabinet would reach the Southwest in safety and raise fresh armies to liberate the prostrate Confederacy. If he were younger, the old Secessionist leader declared, he would shoulder his musket and go west to fight the Yankees. As it was, he could not attempt escape—it would be "undignified & humiliating." He still contemplated suicide, but would "try to time my action so as [to] cause the least damage to my children."

Ruffin's reaction to the news of Lincoln's death was that of a diehard Southern extremist. The President's murder on Good Friday struck him as peculiarly ironic. He said that Lincoln was "lucky" that an assassin had rescued him from obscurity, and noted in his diary every scurrilous remark he had heard about the martyred President. He conceded, however, that Lincoln's conciliatory policy of Reconstruction had surprised him. Ruffin did not expect such mercy from the new President, Andrew Johnson, "the low & vulgar & shameless drunken demagogue" who had made no secret of his hatred for "stuck-up aristocrats" who "are not half as good as the man who earns his bread by the sweat of his brow." Johnson, "The Tailor King," as Ruffin styled him, was "despicable" in the eyes of the Virginia fire-eater. Ruffin, like many others, feared that Johnson would carry out his threats to eradicate the Southern ruling class and supplant it with "poor white trash." Not even Ruffin, for all his venomous hatred of the North and his conviction that black slaves were little more than animals, could imagine that the South was to be ruled by illiterate ex-slaves.

It was not until the following day that Davis learned that Lincoln had been shot by the radical John Wilkes Booth, and that a massive manhunt was underway for Booth and his fellow conspirators. There was yet no hint that Davis was suspected of complicity.

On April 23, the first Sunday after Easter, Davis went to church in Charlotte with some of the Cabinet, a few congressmen, General Cooper, Burton Harrison and other aides, making "a congregation the like of which Charlotte had never seen before, and will, doubtless, never see again." The Reverend George M. Everhart, Rector of St. Peter's Episcopal Church, was not inhibited by his distinguished visitors. He delivered an angry, impassioned sermon on the murder of Lincoln, "a blot on American civilization, which in this 19th century of the Christian era is doubly deep in infamy. It is the tapping of a fountain of blood, which, unchecked, will burst forth and flow onward through the South as well as the North, and bear on its gory bosom a reign of terror like unto which that in the days of Robespierre would fade into insignificance." Anarchy, Everhart said, was threatening all of America, "with its outbreaks of passion and madness, crime and outrage. This event, unjustifiable at any time, but occurring just now, renders it obligatory upon every Christian to set his face against it—to express his abhorrence of a deed fraught with consequences to society everywhere, and more especially to Southern society."

Davis sensed that the sermon was meant for him. As he left the church with Colonel Johnston and Harrison he said, smiling, "I think the preacher directed his remarks at me; and he really seems to fancy I had something to do with the assassination." Oddly enough, it did not seem to occur to Davis that the ideas expressed by Everhart were also being heard in Washington.

Distressing news came to Davis in Charlotte. There was word of the fall of Mobile, one of the last Confederate ports, on April 12, and two days later news that Federal Major Robert Anderson had raised the American flag over Fort Sumter in Charleston harbor, just four years after he had surrendered the post to the Rebels.

It was also in Charlotte that Davis received from Lee his explanation for his surrender, a report written just three days after Appomattox. Davis read with surprise:

"Upon arriving at Amelia Court-House on the morning of the 4th with the advance of the army on the retreat . . . and not finding the supplies ordered to be placed there, nearly twenty-four hours were lost. . . . The delay was fatal . . ."

Lee's weary troops, then near starvation, had been forced to scour the countryside for provisions, losing so much time that pursuing Federal armies had cut them off before they could reach Lynchburg. Had the Confederacy died because of a commissary order gone astray? This controversy was to drag on for more than a century. Davis did not recall a request for the rations from Lee and resolved to investigate. He felt that Lee was mistaken, and had been the victim of his tendency to issue imprecise orders. Historians were to concur in this conclusion.

By this time, though Davis did not know of it, General Lee had returned to his family in Richmond. So far as the greatest soldier of the Confederacy was concerned, the war was over. "The questions at issue," he said, had been decided, and henceforth he was to devote his life to building a New South. He was soon to declare that he felt no resentment toward the North: "I believe I may say, looking into my own heart, and speaking as in the presence of God, that I have never known one moment of bitterness or resentment."

The contrast between Lee's calm resignation and the fierce defiance of the fleeing President was symbolic of attitudes important to the Southern future, as public opinion polarized about the heroes of the defeated nation. Only years later were the views of Lee and Davis toward the enemy to be reconciled.

Burton Harrison needed no reminder that the inflexible Davis was unlikely to abandon his position, but during their stay in Charlotte even he was impressed anew by the depths of the President's feelings. Davis clung to hope of eventual victory with the fervor of a zealot, all the while torn by frustrations as his closest advisers urged his acceptance of the inevitable. The emotional roots of his inability to surrender had not been revealed, even to his most trusted aide, Harrison. But there was a day when Davis, his face wreathed with a cheerful smile, said impulsively to his secretary, "I *cannot* feel myself a beaten man!" It was as if the fate of the South were no longer a sectional or national issue, but had become for him a highly charged personal one, linked to attitudes formed during a lifetime. Davis might yet be forced to concede defeat for the South, but he could not conceive of his own. Harrison was to remember the remark for years.

Soon after learning of Lincoln's death, Davis sent Burton Harrison to Abbeville to guide his wife and family farther to the south, and to carry to her messages about the rapid movement of events. Varina was deep in South Carolina when she read of the murder of Lincoln, and said, "I burst into tears, the first I had shed, which flow from the mingling of sorrow for the family of Mr. Lincoln, and a thorough realization of the inevitable results to the Confederates," who, she felt, were now at the mercy of Northern radicals.

Varina begged Davis to make no attempt to join her, "unless I happen to cross your shortest path to your bourne, be that what it may." She repeated this in later letters, "Do not try to meet me. I dread the Yankees getting news of you so much, you are the country's only hope . . ."

Much more quickly than her husband, Varina seemed to sense that Lincoln's murder placed Davis's life in danger. She feared that radical Northerners saw Lincoln's death as "a divine rebuke" to those who favored leniency toward the Confederates. A fanatic spirit of revenge was already sweeping the North.

Varina asked her husband's approval of her plans for continued flight, though they were confused and shifting: She might go to Washington, Ga., then perhaps to Atlanta, or to Florida for passage to Nassau or Bermuda and thence to England unless she happened to find a good school for the children elsewhere. She might join him in Texas, "and that is the prospect that bears me up, to be once more with you." She added domestic news: Her sister Maggie Howell sent "a thousand loves," Piecake had become "too playful to suck," and the boys were well. She also mentioned that their black playmate, Jim Limber, was especially so, "thriving but bad." The Davises had rescued Jim Limber from his cruel father in Richmond, and through kind treatment had healed his sores and wounded spirits and restored him to happiness. Varina ended with a note of finality in farewell: "God bless you, keep you. I have wrestled with God for you. I believe He will restore us to happiness."

Though Harrison and the Burts sought to persuade her to remain longer in Abbeville, where she would be safe among friends, Varina left the next morning, feeling that her presence in the town would endanger her husband when he arrived. Harrison agreed to ride with her for several days—though he had planned to precede her to Florida, where he might arrange transportation to the coast for her party. Varina and Harrison left Abbeville by wagon with an escort of young Kentucky cavalrymen who were on sick leave.

In Charlotte, Davis was temporarily cheered by the support of the South Carolina firebrand, General Wade Hampton of the cavalry, who had accompanied Johnston to his conference with Sherman. Hampton agreed with Davis that the military situation called for stout resistance, rather than despair; he claimed that at least 40,000 Confederate troops east of the Mississippi were still in a fighting mood, and that he would like to lead them: "Give me a good force of cavalry and I will take them safely across the Mississippi—and if you desire to go in that direction it will give me great pleasure to escort you."

Hampton vowed that he himself would never surrender to the base Yankees: "A return to the Union will bring all the horrors of war coupled with all the degradation that can be inflicted on a conquered people."

Both Hampton and Davis feared that war-weary Southerners, desperately anxious for peace, failed to realize what grim conditions they faced as a conquered people. The huge South Carolinian's impassioned message may have helped to stiffen the President's resolve after the lapse noted by Stephen Mallory as the caravan left Greensboro. Davis soon reiterated his faith in the Confederacy.

John Breckinridge, after appearing briefly at the Sherman-Johnston surrender conference near the small town of Durham's Station, returned to Greensboro with Reagan and then rode horseback southward to the point where the railroad had been cut. Davis sent a train from Charlotte to hurry them to headquarters, but stragglers from Johnston's army seized the train and ousted the officials.

Breckinridge and Reagan arrived belatedly in Charlotte with a surrender document signed by Sherman and Johnston. Unlike General Lee, Johnston had insisted that Davis approve and sign his surrender terms, evidently to forestall criticism of his action. Under terms of armistice brought to Davis, Confederates would disarm, and existing state governments would remain and be welcomed back into the Union. The U.S. would protect Southern people and property, and guarantee complete freedom from molestation by Federal authorities. Even in this formal document there was no mention of slavery. Sherman believed he was following the wishes of Abraham Lincoln.

Ironically, Sherman, the man most feared and reviled by Southerners, offered more liberal terms than any other Federal conqueror —and Davis agreed that they were liberal indeed.

In fact, Davis was certain that these overgenerous terms would have been rejected even by the humane Lincoln, and predicted that Andrew Johnson and Edwin Stanton would scorn them.

Davis called a Cabinet session and asked members to write their assessment of choices facing the government. John Reagan's report was typical: "The country is worn down by a brilliant and heroic, but exhausting and bloody, struggle of four years. Our ports are closed. . . . The supplies . . . are limited . . . and our railroads are . . . broken and destroyed. . . . Our currency has lost its purchasing power."

Reagan concluded that Southerners could not "reasonably hope for the achievement of our independence" and that it would be both "unwise and criminal" to continue the struggle. He urged Davis to sign the agreement.

But Reagan and his colleagues were unwilling to surrender on less favorable terms. If Washington rejected this agreement then "it will be our duty to continue the struggle as best we can, however unequal it may be; as it would be . . . more honorable to waste our lives and substance . . . than to yield both to the mercy of a remorseless conqueror."

All of his advisers urged Davis to sign. Attorney General George Davis pointed out that the Southern states would re-enter the Union with the same status they had enjoyed in 1861. Even Judah Benjamin joined the majority and said he felt that no better terms could be had. The President then signed the document.

The President's own emotions at this moment had been poured out in a long, impassioned letter to Varina, written while his Cabinet members were composing their reports:

> The dispersion of Lee's army and the surrender . . . destroyed the hopes I had when we parted . . . Even after that disaster, if the men who "straggled," say thirty or forty thousand in number, had come back . . . we might have repaired the damage; but panic has seized the country . . .

He wrote of the Sherman-Johnston agreement and its terms and added:

> The issue is one which it is very painful for me to meet. On one hand is the long night of repression which will follow the return of our people to the "Union"; on the other, the suffering of the women and children, and the carnage among the few brave patriots who . . . would struggle but to die in vain.

Of himself and their family he wrote:

> . . . I have sacrificed so much for the cause of the Confederacy that I can measure my ability to make any further sacrifice required, and am assured there is but one to which I am not equal—My Wife and my Children—How are they to be saved from degradation or want is now my care.

He repeated his plea that Varina sail abroad, or to Texas. His own plan was still rather vague: ". . . it may be that a devoted band of cavalry will cling to me, and that I can force my way across the

Mississippi, and if nothing can be done there . . . I can go to Mexico and have the world from which to choose a location."

He closed melodramatically:

> Dear Wife, this is not the fate to which I invited you when the future was rose-colored to us both; but I know you will bear it even better than myself . . . Farewell, my dear, there may be better things in store for us than are now in view, but my love is all I have to offer, and that has the value of a thing long possessed, and sure not to be lost. . . .

All the agonizing over the truce agreement was in vain, for it was hardly an hour after Johnston received the copy signed by Davis that news of the Federal rejection came. U. S. Grant was sent south to impose a much sterner peace—and was ordered to remove Sherman from command if he did not comply. Edwin Stanton publicly accused Sherman of disloyalty and intimated that he had been "bribed by Jeff Davis gold." The new terms to be offered were those that Grant had extended to Lee at Appomattox, which were purely military.

Stanton's charges stirred a nationwide reaction; people throughout the North refused to believe that their hero, Sherman, had been in collusion with the enemy to thwart the government's war aims.

From Charlotte, Davis sought to prevent Johnston's surrender under the new terms proffered. Over the signature of Breckinridge the President urged Johnston to march his troops to some rendezvous beyond the reach of the enemy: "Such a force could march away from Sherman and be strong enough to encounter anything between us and the Southwest. If this course be possible carry it out and telegraph your intended route."

The more realistic Johnston, with his distaste for Jeff Davis still evident, responded that the presidential plan for continued resistance was "impracticable," that its only beneficiaries would be Confederate high officials—and that its victims would be the men in ranks and the civilians at home. Johnston urged Davis to abandon all escorts and wagons and flee at once.

Johnston said he would accept the best terms he could get but, to the dismay of Davis, he surrendered not only his own army but most Confederate troops still in uniform throughout the eastern theater, including remnants of the Army of Tennessee under his command in North Carolina and scattered forces in South Carolina, Georgia and Florida. Only the army of General Richard Taylor in Alabama, Mississippi and Louisiana was excluded. Captain John Taylor Wood, perhaps reflecting the President's view, noted that this wholesale surrender by Johnston was "something unparallelled without good reason or authority."

Davis was bitterly critical of Johnston's surrender in defiance of orders. He accepted the fact that Lee had given up the fight when surrounded and helpless, but he felt that Johnston had dishonored the Confederacy by surrendering his army before it could be brought to bay, rather than retreating southward as Davis had urged: "Had General Johnston obeyed the order sent to him from Charlotte, and moved on the route selected by himself . . . he could not have been successfully pursued by General Sherman." Johnston's army, he said insistently, could have been reinforced in Charlotte and could then have marched unchallenged to the Mississippi.

On April 24, in the Phifer house on Charlotte's North Tryon Street, Davis presided over the last full session of the Confederate Cabinet, and sought to make plans for flight. It was not an easy task. As Wood noted, the cavalry escort had become unreliable: "They are committing many depredations." Wood heard that some members of the party planned to leave the President. "So we are falling to pieces," he wrote.

Attorney General George Davis became the first Cabinet member to leave the caravan. He asked the President's advice about resigning. "I want to stand by the Confederacy," he said, "but my children are here in Charlotte and my only property is in Wilmington. I don't know where my duty is."

"By the side of your family," the President said.

George Davis agreed. His wife had died during the war, and though he felt that his children could safely remain in Charlotte, he expected to be jailed if caught in "Union-infested" North Carolina. The President was sorry to see him go, for he had come to value the opinions of the Tarheel lawyer whose advice had often guided him in important decisions. With an eye upon recorded history, the President responded to the Attorney General's resignation in writing, and the courtly fugitive was soon off on an escape route of his own.

As the party prepared to leave Charlotte, Secretary Trenholm was so ill as to be bedridden, but gamely insisted to Davis that he could bear the jolting of the wagon on the way southward. It was decided that old General Samuel Cooper, the Adjutant General, should remain behind in the city and await the arrival of Federal troops. Officials, soldiers and local civilians spent the day of April 25 preparing the President's party for continued flight.

A few more troops appeared in Charlotte, and General Braxton Bragg, who had retreated into central North Carolina, was ordered to march his little command to the city, and to follow the Cabinet.

In New York City on this day the funeral procession of Abraham Lincoln wound through the streets, one of the several ceremonies planned for the slain President's long journey homeward to Springfield, Ill. As the procession passed the corner of Broadway and 14th Street, two small boys watched from an upper floor—Theodore Roosevelt, the future President, aged six and a half, and his young brother Elliott, the future father of Eleanor Roosevelt. The boys were nephews of James D. Bulloch, the Confederate chief of staff in Europe, spymaster, paymaster and procurer of those remarkable British-built ships which became Rebel raiders on the seas of the world.

Back in Greensboro the wily Admiral Semmes, who had been trained as a lawyer before the war, realized that his exploits as a sea raider might bring charges of piracy against him, and sought to protect himself in a unique surrender ceremony. He went before General William Hartsuff, the Federal commissioner in the town, and presented the muster roll of his command. When he was told that his officers and men need only sign printed forms, Semmes said, "I prefer, if you have no objection, to fill and complete my own here in your presence."

"Oh, that makes no difference," Hartsuff said, but when Semmes insisted, the general had an aide complete the form as dictated by Semmes, who pointedly signed himself "Rear Admiral in the Confederate States Navy, and a Brigadier General in the Confederate States Army, commanding a brigade." He now had recognition from the enemy of his legitimate rank as a general as well as an admiral, and was not merely a "pirate"—a factor that was to help foil later efforts to prosecute him. The parole pledged Semmes to fight no more, and in return he was permitted to return home, "not to be disturbed by the U. S. authorities, so long as he observes this obligation . . . "

John Breckinridge's chief contribution to Confederate history was made while he was in Charlotte—the salvage of the official archives of the government. The general put the collection under the care of Robert G. Kean, the chief of the War Bureau. Breckinridge told Kean that the U. S. had rejected the Sherman-Johnston truce and that the enemy might overrun the state. Kean accepted orders to store the documents in Charlotte and to surrender them to the Federal commander when the enemy occupied the city, "preserving them from being destroyed, if I could."

Breckinridge also asked General Samuel Cooper to help protect the voluminous archives, since they were "essential to the history of the Confederacy." As the general's biographer wrote, "This was Breckinridge at his best. His family had always had a keen sense of their own history, and diligently preserved over a span of two centuries every scrap of correspondence, receipts and records."

There was a new, if temporary, air of cheerful confidence as the party left the city. Emergency calls for troops had brought in three new skeleton brigades, so that the escort had been reinforced to a strength of more than 2,000, all under command of Breckinridge, but led by new field officers: General S. W. Ferguson, an energetic West Pointer from South Carolina who was a Davis favorite; Colonel J. C. Vaughan, a "brave and earnest" Tennessean; and General Basil Duke, an exceptionally able Kentucky cavalryman. Like most of the others, Duke's men were veterans, but of uncertain discipline in these last days of the Confederacy.

Discipline was breaking down elsewhere. Captain Fred Emory, chief of the baggage guard, had been "drunk continually" in Charlotte and was supplanted by Captain Watson Van Benthuysen, a nephew of the President. The new baggage guard included young soldiers who were thought to be among the most trustworthy men in uniform. Two were brothers of Watson Van Benthuysen—Alfred and Jefferson D.—and five others were scions of prominent families of Maryland's Eastern Shore. One of the Marylanders was Tench Tilghman, whose great-grandfather, an aide to Washington during the Revolution, had carried to Congress news of victory at Yorktown. Also in the baggage guard were two scouts from Captain

Given Campbell's Kentucky company. In addition there were five Negro servants, including Watson, the President's cook. Though the flight was to become desperate, the President intended to enjoy the comforts to which he was accustomed.

The caravan entered South Carolina on April 26, a long procession of soldiers, officials and wagons—perhaps fifty men in the President's immediate party, the 2,000 troops of the expanded escort, and five wagons. Their passing trailed clouds of orange dust across newly green fields.

PART 2

THE PURSUIT

"... let them go! We don't want to be bothered with them. ... Frighten them out of the country. Open the gates, let down the bars. Scare them off."

—ABRAHAM LINCOLN ON JEFFERSON DAVIS AND HIS CABINET, APRIL 14, 1865.

"... Follow them to the ends of the earth if necessary."

—BRIGADIER GENERAL GEORGE STONEMAN, U. S. CAVALRY, TO TROOPS IN PURSUIT OF DAVIS PARTY, APRIL 27, 1865.

7

"Why are you still in the field?"

SOUTH CAROLINA, the mother of Secession, greeted the band of refugees as if they were heroes and saviors rather than hunted fugitives who had led a lost cause. Each day became a triumphal progress, for this state gave them a welcome in striking contrast to their reception in North Carolina.

Civilians and discharged soldiers lined the roads as the caravan entered villages and towns of a region untouched by raiding armies. Schoolchildren were sent out to greet Davis and his officers. Scores of women who had lost sons or husbands hailed him tearfully, still looking to him to save the Confederacy. Davis smiled and responded courteously, but William Preston Johnston recorded his inner distress.

"It must be gratifying to find people with so much confidence in you, even now," Johnston said.

Davis sighed. "That makes me the most miserable of all," he said.

In fact, Davis had political enemies even within this state. One of these, Confederate Senator James L. Orr, had said bitterly, "We have failed through the egotism, the obstinacy and the imbecility of Jeff Davis." Such opinions were heard from others as the people of the South awaited the end.

After the Davis party entered South Carolina, all of its wagons were guarded day and night by soldiers paired off for the duty, two men to each wagon. The elongated train now contained the nucleus from which Davis hoped to re-establish the Confederacy in the west:

loads of official documents and supplies in addition to the gold and silver and personal baggage of the President and the five remaining Cabinet secretaries. Even here sudden alarms were frequent, and the unwieldy vehicles of the procession sometimes plunged into frantic flight. Frank Vizetelly saw these moments with the eye of an artist, and sketched one of them. He had a long memory of one stampede: ". . . everything went helter-skelter along the road—President, Ministers, cavalrymen, four-muled wagons, and terrified Negro servants, all jumbled up together."

During brief halts, Davis conducted business at the side of the road and called Cabinet members to informal discussions of their problems. Vizetelly sketched one such meeting, which he entitled "Government by the Roadside," a homely scene depicting Benjamin as he handed papers to the seated Davis for his signature. There were also frequent halts combining social visits with meals or overnight stops.

THE LIBRARY OF CONGRESS

Soon after the party crossed the South Carolina border—no more than seventeen miles below Charlotte, in fact—"a bevy of ladies" emerged from a handsome mansion to strew flowers in the path of the President and insisted that his party stop there for the night. "They would not listen to us going further that day," Frank Lubbock said.

This stop was made in the small town of Fort Mill, where Davis spent the night in the home of Colonel A. B. Springs, a leading planter of the region. Secretary Trenholm and others went to the nearby home of Colonel William Elliott White, who was later to join descendants of Colonel Springs to found a major textile empire. The President put aside his cares during the overnight visit and, with Reagan, Benjamin and Breckinridge, got down on his knees to play a game of marbles with the two Springs boys, thirteen-year-old Eli and eleven-year-old Johnny. Stephen Mallory watched in surprise as Davis and his officers laughed and played with the boys "an animated and well contested game of marbles" for almost an hour. The boys were delighted to find that Davis was familiar with the complex rules of the game.

The Cabinet lost another member at Fort Mill when Secretary of the Treasury George Trenholm told Davis that the pain of riding in the lurching ambulance had become unbearable, and that he must go home. Davis named Postmaster General Reagan as his successor. Benjamin laughed and drew the President into a rare exchange of jocularity. "I believe you will find it unconstitutional for him to hold both places at once," Benjamin said.

And when Reagan resisted the added burden, the President made a joke, "You can look after that without much trouble . . . there's not much for the Secretary of Treasury to do. There's but little money left for him to steal."

Davis and the Cabinet met on the Springs lawn the next morning, April 27, to discuss the route of retreat, and later went to the White home, where another of the "last" meetings of the Cabinet was held.

Here the Cabinet was caught up in a more urgent discussion. Fresh enemy troops were reported approaching, and the informal council agreed to continue its efforts to join the army of the President's brother-in-law, Lieutenant General Richard Taylor, who commanded in Alabama, Mississippi and Louisiana. With communications cut, Davis did not realize that Taylor's position was hopeless and that he would soon surrender the three key states. Davis was, however, painfully aware that Taylor did not share his determination to resist to the last man. General Taylor dismissed the President's plans to escape westward with the hope of joining the Emperor Maximilian as "much wild nonsense"—and had warned Davis against heeding the advice of men "more disposed to tell him what was agreeable than what was true."

The Davis party understood the need for haste to avoid capture, but, since they knew nothing of the specific charges against them, were unaware of the extraordinary vigor with which the Federal pursuit was being pressed. The manhunt was directed by Secretary of War Edwin M. Stanton who, ignoring Sherman, commanded field officers to "pay no attention to any orders but your own or from Gen Grant & spare no exertions to stop Davis and his plunder." He repeated gossip that Davis was carrying from $6 million to $13 million in coin, a rumor relayed from Richmond by General Henry Halleck. General Sherman scoffed at this tale. He conceded that it "might find willing ears," but was absurd on its face. Such a vast treasure, Sherman calculated, would require a train of from fifteen to thirty-two money wagons, each drawn by a six-mule team. (The fugitives had used no more than three or four wagons for the purpose, even when all the treasure had been concentrated in a single caravan.)

This quarrel between the conquerors was rich in irony. Sherman, the bête noire of the Southern people, was urging a realistic view upon his civilian masters—who not only failed to give it credence, but suspected that he was collaborating in the escape of Davis in return for a share of the loot. Yet already (though Edwin Stanton was evidently ignorant of it) Sherman had spread even wider the net designed to capture Davis. The accused traitor had foreseen the possibility of the President's flight through Florida, and had sent an aide on the long voyage to Key West to close that avenue of escape. As a result, U.S. Admiral Cornelius Stribling was patrolling Florida waters on both coasts, and had alerted all his officers to join the search for Davis. By the end of the first week of May three Federal expeditions were on the alert in Florida.

The Confederates knew nothing of the squabble between Sherman and Stanton, but the Northern people were aghast at the controversy. The popular general, who had virtually ended the war with his famous march, had now been completely stripped of his authority by Secretary Stanton.

General George Stoneman's cavalrymen, already on their way

home, were ordered by Stanton to turn about and pursue Davis. Irritated by this assignment and outraged by news of Lincoln's murder, the troopers set forth in a vengeful mood. The Federal column was led by the aggressive General W. J. Palmer, who pushed his brigades to the limit of their endurance through upland South Carolina toward Augusta, Ga.—under orders passed to him by Stoneman to follow Davis "to the ends of the earth" if necessary.

The image of Davis in flight with vast sums of money appealed to such newspapers as the Boston *Transcript,* which called him "a haughty, insolent and malignant traitor . . . a swindling bankrupt and fugitive thief, running away from justice and his creditors, with the assets of the Confederacy he has sunk in boundless debts, accompanying him in wagons."

Reflecting the public mood in the North in the wake of Lincoln's death, the *Transcript* called for the blood of Davis and his Cabinet: ". . . The whole mass of individual murderers since Cain has not produced in forty centuries so much misery and ruin as these malignant traitors have wrought in four terrible years."

A few days later the New York *Times* repeated its call for the head of Davis, since he had perpetrated the "greatest crime of the ages—a crime costing the lives of half a million men, and aimed at the overthrow of the best government the world ever saw." The editor lumped Davis and his cohorts with Catiline and Benedict Arnold, and declared that they should die "the most disgraceful death known to our civilization—death on the gallows."

President Johnson joined the chorus. He urged the "halter and gallows" for Davis and all other "conscious, intelligent, leading traitors."*

The Davis caravan crossed the nearby Catawba River on a ferry at Nation's Ford, since the railroad bridge had been burned. Tench Tilghman, who watched the passage with his fellow Marylander, Captain William Dickinson, was moved by a sense of tragic history: "What a sight to see Jeff Davis and Breckinridge and the Cabinet standing on the pontoon. Dickinson and I thought of The Bruce and his retreat in the mountains surrounded by a few of his

*General Grant firmly opposed this policy. When Johnson and Stanton proposed to arrest all Confederate colonels and generals, including those surrendered at Appomattox, Grant declared, "You will have to whip me and my army before one hair of one head of the men whom we captured, and to whom we promised protection, shall perish."

faithful followers." Tilghman added a note of dejection: "This cause has gone up. God only knows what will be the end of all this."

In an effort to bolster morale, Davis and Breckinridge and others of the Cabinet mingled freely with the soldiers of the escort during these marches. Breckinridge, a superb horseman, rode one of the few good mounts left to the party, but most of the others rode in wagons. The common soldiers concluded that Davis, Breckinridge and Mallory were vigorous and alert and would escape pursuit if they wished. But they felt that the corpulent Benjamin, so obviously unaccustomed to outdoor life, had no chance to escape. The Jewish lawyer-diplomat fascinated the troopers, who had heard him described as the evil genius of the Davis administration; they were quickly won over by his lighthearted humor and ingratiating manner. Some of them were anxious over Benjamin's fate.

Other members of the party were less popular with the escort. In General Duke's opinion, only Breckinridge "knew what was going on, what was going to be done, or ought to be done." As the flight continued and conditions worsened, soldiers no longer regarded the officials with awe. There were rising complaints about the excessively heavy baggage carried by the Cabinet, which had created cruel burdens for the wagon horses and mules and at times for the men themselves.

The caravan halted in the village of Yorkville, where troopers scouted the area for Federal riders reported to be nearby. Davis and a few others spent a night in the home of Dr. James Bratton, the President in such straits that he was forced to borrow a nightshirt from one of the doctor's neighbors. The party moved on, crossing the Broad River at Pinchersville Ferry, thence following the stream's west bank to Love's Ford, where it made camp. There was a stop at Unionville in the home of General William H. Wallace, who had not yet returned from the war. In the southern part of Union County, the party spent the night in the home of Lafayette (Fate) Young, and on May 1 crossed the narrow, muddy Saluda River at Puckett's Ferry, some nine miles northeast of Greenwood. That night was spent in the town of Cokesbury, the home of General Martin W. Gary of the Confederate army.

During this halt the Davis party was joined by General Braxton Bragg, who was leading a few troops retreating out of Sherman's path. Davis greeted his favorite with obvious pleasure, but there was little warmth in the greeting of others.

When Bragg appeared at Cokesbury he immediately removed his hat and stood obsequiously before Davis. Breckinridge remained impassive as Bragg turned to him with equal deference. Earlier in the war, after the battle of Murfreesboro, the insecure Bragg had blamed Breckinridge for his failure, complained of him bitterly in reports to Davis—and had falsely accused the Kentuckian of drunkenness at the battle of Missionary Ridge. Though Davis seemed to be oblivious to the air of tension, other officers watched with amusement as Bragg went through a charade. Captain Given Campbell, the young Kentuckian, reflected on the contrast between Bragg's present fawning manner toward Breckinridge and his "treatment of the same man at and after the battle of Murphysborough." Davis had clung to Bragg throughout the war in face of widespread criticism of the inept general, leading the acidulous Senator James Orr to comment, "The President's attachment for General Bragg could be likened to nothing else than the blind & gloating love of a mother for a deformed and misshapen offspring." Yet even now Davis found comfort in Bragg's presence.

The President's affection for Bragg was rooted in their friendship, which was formed during the Mexican War. Though he was an excellent organizer, the stern General Bragg had failed in several major commands, chiefly because of an inability to work in harmony with other officers. He had remained a Davis favorite despite his lack of attractiveness and a certain psychological instability. Before the fall of Richmond the President had told General Josiah Gorgas that with Bragg absent "he could get no information or help from anybody else."

Gorgas was unimpressed by this comment, for he found Davis incapable of choosing the most competent advisers: "The President seems to respect the opinions of no one; and has, I fear, little appreciation of services rendered, unless the party enjoys his good opinion. He seems to be an indifferent judge of men, and is guided more by prejudice than by sound, discriminating judgment."

It was obvious that Bragg retained the confidence of Davis even now as the Confederacy neared its end, for he rode southward with the fleeing caravan, a source of comfort and a respected counselor to the President. The general did not inspire universal admiration from observers along the route. One discerning young woman who saw the Davis entourage on its flight conceded that John Breckinridge might well be, as she had heard, the handsomest man in the South, but she added, "Bragg might well be the ugliest . . . he looks like an old porcupine. I never was a special admirer of his."

Tench Tilghman and his companions were sorry to leave this region of South Carolina, where two of the guard were given an elegant breakfast in a farmhouse: "They also enjoyed a dish of strawberries, the first of the season of which I got none." There were compensations: "Young ladies were out in the porches to bow and wave their handkerchiefs. Bouquets were given us and we marched gaily on." But scouts had brought Davis word that Federal riders might be only ten miles behind, and the caravan hurried out of Cokesbury on the morning of May 2, prepared for battle.

In fact, U.S. General Palmer did not follow the route of Davis, who had a lead of two days. Fearing that the Confederates would slow pursuit by burning bridges and ferry boats, Palmer led his troopers southward on a parallel course, and was soon far in advance of the fugitives. The bluecoats reached the headwaters of the Savannah River in upper South Carolina and turned eastward along the Georgia border, hoping to intercept Davis at a river crossing. Palmer now deduced, erroneously, that the fugitives were bound for Athens, Ga., and resolved to block their path.

By this time, though it was unknown to Davis, overland passage to Texas was being blocked by U.S. occupation of Alabama, whose governor, Thomas H. Watts, was in prison. General Richard Taylor had not yet surrendered, but he could no longer give the President safe conduct through the area.

During the same week, Andrew Johnson approved the offer of rewards for Davis, Clay, Jacob Thompson and their alleged co-conspirators in the murder of Lincoln. The President had been told that Stanton had evidence linking them with the plot—Clay and Thompson apparently because of their mysterious foray into Canada in the last days of the war. Posters were prepared for distribution:

> WHEREAS, it appears, from evidence in the Bureau of Military Justice, that the atrocious murder of the late President Abraham Lincoln and the attempted assassination of the Honorable William H. Seward, Secretary of State, were incited, concerted, and procured by

> and between Jefferson Davis, late of Richmond, Va., and Jacob Thompson, Clement C. Clay . . . and other rebels and traitors . . .
>
> NOW, THEREFORE . . . I, Andrew Johnson, President of the United States, do offer and promise . . . the following rewards: $100,000 for the arrest of Jefferson Davis; $25,000 for the arrest of Clement C. Clay. . . .
>
> ANDREW JOHNSON

Johnson ordered the proclamation telegraphed to hundreds of cities and towns—and went so far as to send photographs of the hunted men to police departments in Europe, on the theory that they had already left the country. But broken communications delayed news of the offer for many days in rural Georgia, and even General Wilson's Macon headquarters was late in learning of it. The Davis party knew nothing of the proclamation.

About this time Varina Davis responded to the eloquent outburst her husband had sent from Charlotte: "Your very sweet letter reached me safely and was a great relief—I leave here in the morning at 6 o'clock for the wagon train going to Georgia—Washington will be the first point I shall 'unload' at—and wait a little until we hear something of you— . . . Let me beseech you not to calculate upon seeing me . . . "

She reassured him that she treasured their lives together, whatever might come to them now: "It is surely not the fate to which you invited me in brighter days, but you must remember that you did not invite me to a great Hero's home, but to that of a plain farmer. I have shared all your triumphs, been the *only* beneficiary of them, now I am but claiming the privilege for the first time of being all to you now that these pleasures have passed for me." She told him of the exceptional hospitality of the people of Abbeville, "here they are all your friends . . . I shall never forget all their devotion to you." But she added a warning that he should not expect to find support in that region: "I have seen a great many men who have gone through—not one has talked fight. A stand cannot be made in this country; do not be induced to try it— As to the Trans-Mississippi, I doubt if at first things will be straight, but the spirit will be there. . . ."

Offering her own view of General Braxton Bragg's shortcomings—and unconsciously revealing the difficulties of influencing her husband's course—she begged him not to give Bragg a role in this crisis: "Though I know you do not like my interference, let me entreat you not to send B.B. to command here . . . the country will be ruined by its intestine feuds if you do so. . . . If I am intrusive forgive me for the sake of the love which impels me."

Davis made no comment on Bragg, but agreed with his wife that further organized resistance in the east was impossible. Still he cherished the dream of limited warfare on the Texas plains he knew so well. There, in the Trans-Mississippi of Edmund Kirby Smith, "where they would not be flanked by rivers and railroads," the President felt that Confederate troops could hold out for months or years, until he could win from the North "immunity from plunder of the people's private property." Though some Radical Republicans did advocate seizure of estates and their distribution to freed Negroes, neither they nor Davis could envision the coming "long night" of a subjugated South ruled by carpetbaggers and illiterate ex-slaves.

The vast Trans-Mississippi region to the west which held the key to Confederate hopes stretched from the Mexican border to New Orleans and northward to Missouri, thence westward to Arizona Indian territory. The states and territories of Texas, Louisiana, Arkansas, Missouri, Oklahoma, New Mexico and Arizona made up a virtual empire scarcely penetrated by Federal troops. It was a country sparsely populated, much of it wilderness where guerrilla forces might hold out for years.

Edmund Kirby Smith, the thirty-nine-year-old general in command of this region, had greeted news of Lee's surrender with a show of defiance that would have delighted Jefferson Davis. Forecasting victory, Smith appealed to his men "in the name of your bleeding country, whose future is in your hands. You possess the means of long-resisting the invasion . . . protract the struggle and you will surely receive the aid of nations who already deeply sympathize with you. . . .

"The great resources of this department, its vast extent, the numbers, the discipline, and the efficiency of the army, will secure to our country terms that a proud people can accept."

For almost two years, since the fall of Vicksburg, Miss., had isolated the western theater, Kirby Smith had ruled the sprawling territory with absolute authority. The distant general had seized the responsibility granted from Richmond by Davis with a resourcefulness that made his command singularly efficient. He had been forced to finance his own operations: "I bought cotton through my Cotton Bureau at three or four cents a pound, and sold it at fifty cents in gold. It passed in constant streams by several crossings on the Rio Grande, as well as through Galveston to the agents abroad." Mass production of meat and grain enabled Smith to feed troops of this second Confederacy, and his factories and foundries provided textiles, tools, weapons and many essential supplies. Smith's fleet of blockade runners had carried on a thriving trade with Caribbean and European ports, importing arms and ammunition, hardware, medical supplies, shoes and salt—all of which were paid for in cotton.

The economic heart of this territory was the state of Texas—larger than France and Belgium combined—which had flourished during the war, drawing immigrants from throughout the South, almost doubling its population.

Kirby Smith, the son of Judge Joseph L. Smith of Litchfield, Conn., had been reared in Florida, where the judge served as an appointee of Andrew Jackson. The West Point-trained Kirby was a veteran of the Mexican and Indian wars and was one of seven full generals of the Confederacy, a resolute professional officer in whom Davis had complete confidence.

In Washington, Ga., only a few day's ride south of the Davis party, Clement Clay had rejoined his wife, the vivacious Virginia, in whose safety the President also had a keen interest—an interest that was later to inspire sensational gossip.

The North Carolina-born Mrs. Clay had been reared by wealthy relatives in Alabama, where, at the age of seventeen, she had married Clement Claiborne Clay, one of the most eligible bachelors of the region. Clay was a law graduate of the University of Virginia and the son of Clement Comer Clay, who had served as congressman, governor of Alabama and a justice of the State Supreme Court.

From the time of their marriage Virginia had assumed a role of dominance over her husband, who was eight years her elder and was already asthmatic and in delicate health. Within four years of the wedding Clay had begun to express fears of losing her. During one of their early separations Clay wrote Virginia, "You are so pretty and fascinating that I fear some fine-looking fellow will forget you are a married woman and make love to you."

In prewar Washington, when both Clay and Jefferson Davis were U.S. senators, the couples had become close friends. Though she lacked beauty, Virginia still attracted men strongly and was a belle of capital society, devoted to the endless rounds of social life, spending extravagantly on fashionable clothes.

The vain, rather snobbish Virginia continued her role as professional Southern belle during the war years in Richmond, where she was celebrated for her keen mind, lively sense of humor and animated conversation. She was evidently more handsome than she had been in youth, though her weight had soared to 155 pounds.

Virginia was vulnerable to flattery. When John Breckinridge had complimented her on her beautiful hair, she gave him a dimpled smile of pleasure. "And all my own," she said—something of an exaggeration. Her fashionably tall coiffure had been achieved by folding a pair of soft boots atop her head and carefully concealing them with her long hair.

A Richmond newspaper of 1862 praised Virginia's "grace and *savoir faire* and brilliant conversation. . . ." She was lauded as "an inimitable raconteur" who "sparkles and glows with fun and vivacity and absorbs the attention."

Since the Clays did not know the whereabouts of President Davis and his party during their flight in the spring of 1865, they eagerly sought news of them from other fugitives who had encountered the caravan during their own journeys southward from Richmond. As prominent members of the Confederate hierarchy, the Clays realized that their own futures were closely linked with that of the President.

At this time Davis and his companions were nearing the village of Abbeville, S. C. Entering the town, riding with Reagan in advance of their column, the President stopped at a roadside cabin and asked a woman for a drink of water. As he drank, a baby crawled across the porch and down the crude steps. The woman, who had been staring at Davis, asked, "Ain't you President Davis?"

"Yes, I am."

She nodded to the child. "He's named for you."

Davis took a gold piece from his pocket and gave it to her.

"Please keep this for him, and tell him about it when he's old enough to understand."

The woman gazed after them until they had disappeared.

"That's the last coin I have to my name," Davis told Reagan. "I wouldn't have had that but for the fact that I've never seen one like it, and kept it for luck."

He turned to Reagan with a rueful smile. "My home is a wreck, Benjamin's and Breckinridge's are in Federal hands. Mallory's at Pensacola has been burned by the enemy, your house in Texas has been wrecked . . ."

Davis drew a sheaf of Confederate bills from his pocketbook. "That is my entire estate at this moment."

The President's arrival in Abbeville caused consternation among the guards of the Confederate treasure. The resourceful Captain Parker had just returned to the town after making a frustrating hegira with his burden of gold. The Captain had planned to carry the treasure to Macon, Ga., but after a brief stop in Washington, Ga., had turned instead to Augusta, where Confederate officials refused to share the responsibility for the funds. These men feared lawless Confederate troops more than they did the enemy, now that there were no constraints on the disbanded rebel veterans, who were stung and shamed by defeat and hungry and penniless as well.

Parker was further perplexed by a telegraphed order from Secretary Mallory, directing him to disband the corps of midshipmen. Loath to obey this order and abandon the treasure, Parker and his young men returned northward with their "onerous burden," hoping to turn it over to President Davis himself, who until now had carried with him only the two boxes of gold coin, valued at $35,000.

Already there were widespread rumors even among Confederates that Davis was fleeing with the official treasure and that he planned to retire in luxury in some foreign country. Such rumors were so persistent that Walter Philbrook, the Chief Teller of the Treasury, felt compelled to write years later, "Mr. Davis never saw this treasure from the time it left Richmond until we reached Abbeville. . . . His wife and children . . . were with our train, but he was not."

Just before Davis arrived in Abbeville, Captain Parker came in to store his coin in a warehouse. Early one morning, aroused by the cry, "The Yankees are coming!", the sailors hurriedly repacked the treasure once more, this time on a train bound for Newberry. At dawn, just as the task was finished and the train was ready to depart, armed riders approached Abbeville—but, to the relief of the sailors, they were recognized as men of the President's party.

As he and his escort entered Abbeville, Davis went to the home of the Armistead Burts, where he was given a rousing welcome and shown to his room, the room which had been used such a brief time before by Varina. His wife was now only a few days ahead. If he did not tarry along the route, Davis could soon overtake her for a final reunion before disappearing on his flight to Texas or beyond—wherever the movements of the enemy permitted. Though his information was scanty, Davis realized that invading armies were pushing into the heart of the South from several directions, and that his plans must await developments.

Varina and Harrison and their charges, meanwhile, entered an isolated, swampy region of south Georgia, where they heard reports of a raging smallpox epidemic. Since Piecake had not been vaccinated, Varina stopped at a roadside house and, as Harrison said, "heroically" had the planter who lived there infect the baby with "a fresh scab from the arm of a little Negro."

Varina's party approached the small town of Washington, Ga., through a countryside in its full spring glory. Smilax and jessamine flowered at the roadsides amidst tangles of myrtles, magnolia, live oaks and palmettos. White garlands of Cherokee roses hung from trees. The small but now-bustling town of Washington, which had been founded in the colonial era, had become the trading center of a prosperous plantation district. The remote village was untouched by war. Ordinarily a sleepy town of 2,200, Washington had become the stronghold of the Confederacy and was thronged with refugees. Remnants of the naval and medical departments had been sent here, paroled veterans were passing through, and several Confederate generals had gathered in the town.

Young Eliza Andrews was moved by the sight of Mrs. Davis arriving in Washington: "The poor woman is in a deplorable condition—no home, no money, and her husband a fugitive . . . I am very sorry for her, and wish I could do something to help her, but we are all reduced to poverty, and the most we can do is . . . to open our doors . . ."

Once more Varina was warmly welcomed, even by General Robert Toombs, the President's archenemy. Ignoring their embittered relationships of the war years, Toombs called on Varina to offer his help. A number of women also befriended Varina, and, Eliza Andrews noted, "to the honor of our town it can be truly said that she has received more attention than would have been shown her even in the palmiest days of her prosperity."

There were further signs of the Confederacy's dissolution in the town. Varina complained of "unruly" soldiers who boldly seized horses and mules from her camp.

News of Johnston's surrender reached her here, and like her husband, Varina was stunned. She felt that the President's old enemy had betrayed the South through his "treacherous surrender of this dept." In any case, the surrender of most Confederate forces east of the Mississippi imperiled the President's attempt to reach Texas by the overland route. Varina could not conceal her fears of pursuing Federal troops. She wrote her husband: "I so dread their stealing a march and surprising you." She urged him to drop other plans and flee to safety abroad.

Harrison had already changed the route of her own flight—they would now move between Macon and Augusta, hoping to reach Pensacola and find passage to Europe. She had lost all hope of seeing Davis soon: "Oh, my dearest, Precious Husband, the one absorbing love of my whole life, may God keep you from harm."

Harrison also wrote to Davis to say that, though anxious to see him, Varina was resolved that she would not hamper his efforts to escape. With seven fresh horses, good wagons, forage and dependable drivers, her party was ready for the journey to "safety in or beyond Florida." This had been the President's first plan for his wife, but Captain Wood thought it "a most quixotic enterprise."

Varina's final glimpse of the village of Washington convinced her that the Confederacy was collapsing. Amid Lee's ragged veterans passing through town begging for food, water or shelter, she again saw the tall figure of Robert Toombs, who was now so poorly dressed that she hardly recognized him in his "ill-cut Websterian coat the worse for wear, his face concealed under a broad-brimmed black hat." Toombs stood beside an old buggy and its spavined horse, making the air "murky with blasphemies and denunciations of Yankees."

General Humphrey Marshall, an immensely fat Kentuckian, bade them a laconic farewell: "Well, Harrison, in all my days I never knew a government to go to pieces in this way." Marshall stared after the departing wagons of Varina's caravan with his mournful, heavily seamed face.

As Mrs. Davis and her band moved on southward, they met another caravan, a few wagons accompanied by men who were remarkably well dressed for travel on this remote roadway—city men who wore business suits. These men and their drivers looked anxiously at the oncoming strangers—for this was a portion of the treasure train which bore the deposits of Richmond's banks, on the way northward in search of safety.* This small party with its burden of private funds was to be confused in later accounts with the larger train of official Confederate funds, but the distinction meant nothing to lawless soldiers and civilians prowling the area in search of rumored treasure. Public or private, the rich hoards were tempting targets for the brigands. The Virginia bankers were soon to come to grief.

Far behind in Abbeville, the President and his party also saw ominous signs that disintegrating Confederate forces were beyond control. When he had a false report that a bandit band from the mountains calling themselves guerrillas planned to fall upon the treasure train and its boy guards, Davis made an appeal for help to Confederate soldiers in camp nearby. He rode out to face these men, now on their way home from the armies of Lee or Johnston, and told them that the approaching bandits had been ravaging the western Carolinas, committing such atrocities that both Federal and Confederate forces had attacked them.

"They are robbers and murderers," Davis said. "I want you men to go out with me and attack them and drive them away." He paused.

A Confederate private pushed his horse forward and called boldly, "Our lives are just as precious to us as yours is to you. The war is over and we're going home!"

The troops then dispersed, leaving Davis with his still-loyal personal escort. It was clear that even the President could no longer depend upon Confederate troops at large—disillusioned men who had lost respect for their leaders and whose only thoughts were now of home.

*The private bank funds had accompanied the official Confederate treasure on its round trip to Augusta, Ga., under guard of Captain Parker and his midshipmen, and were now returning to Washington for temporary deposit in a local bank vault.

Soon afterward the President's staff, alarmed by reports of a Federal advance in their direction, burned several boxes of papers and entrusted some of the most valuable ones to Mrs. Henry Leovy of New Orleans, who was living in the town as a refugee. Her husband, Colonel Henry Leovy, decided to accompany the Davis caravan southward.

Even in this emergency Davis called a council of war on May 2 in the parlor of the Burt house, "a historic scene" one participant said. The brigadiers entered to find Davis seated between Generals Breckinridge and Braxton Bragg. Young General Basil Duke commented, "I have never seen Mr. Davis look better or show to better advantage. He seemed in excellent spirits and humor; and the union of dignity, graceful affability, and decision, which made his manner usually so striking, was very marked in his reception of us."

It was obvious that Davis had girded himself for a supreme effort to save the Confederacy. "It is time that we adopt some definite plan," he said. He hoped to continue the war, but, "I feel that I ought to do nothing now without the advice of my military chiefs." Duke detected irony in the President's smile, and thought, "such a term addressed to a handful of brigadiers, commanding altogether barely three thousand men, by one who so recently had been the master of legions, was a pleasantry, yet he said it in a way that made it a compliment."

After each brigadier had reported on the condition of his command, Davis repeated his now-familiar plea—the cause was not hopeless. If loyal soldiers would band together, they might still win freedom for the South. "Even if troops now with us be all that I can rely on . . . 3,000 brave men are enough for a nucleus around which the whole people will rally when their panic has passed away."

But when he called for specific plans for future operations there was an embarrassing silence, and his officers exchanged glances of dismay. After a moment Duke confessed that they had given up hope of victory—admissions that were all the more impressive because of their obvious sympathy for the President. "Our respect for Mr. Davis approached veneration," Basil Duke said, "and not withstanding the total dissent we felt . . . that respect was rather increased than diminished by what he had said."

The generals agreed that Southern resources were exhausted and that the people were "broken down and worn out." Any attempt to fight another campaign would merely bring more miseries to the region.

Davis stiffened. "Then why are you still in the field?"

"We are here to help you escape," Duke said. "Our men will risk battle for that, but they won't fire another shot to continue the war."

The President was silent for a moment, staring at the officers with a pained and accusatory expression, as if he had been betrayed by the last of the faithful. He spoke sharply. "I will entertain no proposal that looks merely to my personal safety." He then launched an eloquent plea that appealed to "every sentiment and reminiscence that might move a Southern soldier," begging his generals to have faith and follow him. But at the end his officers again looked at him "in sorrowful silence."

Davis paled, as if he realized only now that the Confederacy was doomed. He put his head in his hands. "All is lost indeed," he said. "I see that the friends of the South are prepared to consent to her degradation." He went unsteadily from the room, supported by Breckinridge.

The officers sat in glum silence when Breckinridge returned. "I will urge Mr. Davis to get out of the country without further delay," Breckinridge said. He suggested that all of them get some sleep, but soon afterward, about 10 P.M., Basil Duke was aroused by Breckinridge, who asked him to provide guards for the treasure. The Kentuckians moved the hoard from open box cars, money packed in shot bags, money belts, boxes of many sizes (some "of the frailest description"). Duke and his men transferred the money back into wagons for the return trip to Washington, Ga., where Davis was bound.

Captain Parker and his young sailors thus ended more than a month of arduous duty as guards, and Parker prepared to send the youngsters to their homes—but first demanded pay for them. He was so insistent upon this that he sent General John F. Wheless after the caravan, and waited in Abbeville for several days until he returned with $1,500 for the sailors and $300 for the tiny detachment of Confederate Marines. (This reduced the value of the official treasure to about $251,000.)

Elsewhere in the country there was intense interest in the flight of Davis and the Cabinet. The Richmond *Whig,* now published under Federal censorship, said, "Great curiosity is naturally felt North and

South to learn what has become of Jefferson Davis, the head and front of the greatest rebellion the world has yet seen . . . His one object is now to escape to the Trans-Mississippi and he cannot regard himself as out of extreme danger until he has run the gauntlet of the United States Armies now operating in Alabama . . . [H]is escort of two thousand horsemen form today a gloomy cavalcade as they toil along the sandy southern roads under a southern sun. . . . Davis, Breckinridge, Trenholm, Benjamin, St. John and Reagan all ride in the centre of that forlorn band. . . . They bear with them no affection of the people of Richmond, though they have left us a lasting memento in the charred and blackened ruins of the fairest portion of our beautiful city."

Southern newspapers beyond Federal control also expressed interest. The Augusta (Ga.) *Constitutionalist* published a rumor that Davis and his Cabinet had returned to Richmond to open negotiations with the enemy. The Edgefield, S. C., *Advertiser* said, "We would like to inform our readers where these gentlemen are and what they are doing, but we cannot. Their whereabouts and doings are shrouded in mystery unfathomable to mortal ken. We would not insinuate for a moment that President Davis is not in the right place and doing the right thing; we believe he is. We honor him and trust him still, and hold the opinion that he will yet prove himself to be what we thought him when we placed him in the presidential chair."

The New York *Times* urged on the hunters of the Rebel leaders, "We trust that the government will spare no efforts to catch Jeff. Davis, and all his lieutenants in treason. . . . Most of them are undoubtedly in flight for Texas, thence into Mexico. . . .

"Yet it is a ride of a thousand miles to the Mississippi . . . on horseback, as all the great lines of railroad are either destroyed or in our possession. . . . With prompt activity on the part of the government, it is not unlikely that capture can yet be made."

The *Times* favored large enticements for pursuers: "Even should these rewards fail to produce the captures, they would do much to attach disgrace. The very fact that these men fled their country with a price on their heads, would put them more distinctly into the category of criminals."

Though Northern editors were unaware of it, U. S. military leaders were deeply concerned lest Davis escape into Mexico to organize an invasion of the United States with the aid of Emperor

Maximilian's French troops. This threat seemed ominous, since Mexico was already a base for smuggled Confederate supplies. U. S. Grant was particularly "oppressed" by the thought of Davis's Rebel troops joining Maximilian to assure foreign domination of Mexico—and he planned to prevent that alliance at all costs.

8

"You're Southern gentlemen, not highway robbers"

DAVIS rode out of Abbeville at midnight of May 3 in a chilly rain. Benjamin, General Bragg, Breckinridge, Mallory and Reagan rode with the President, accompanied by a reduced troop of bodyguards. Since Breckinridge had authorized brigade commanders to discharge men who wished to return home, a thousand or more had departed. Of the escort of 2,000 which had left Charlotte with Davis, only half remained after the stop in Abbeville.

Davis and his Cabinet were still followed by Captain Micajah Clark, as well as the President's kinsman, Quartermaster Watson Van Benthuysen, commander of the elite guard which was keeping watch over the Davis baggage. In one of the President's two wagons rode the two heavy boxes containing the $35,000 in gold sovereigns. The residue of the official Confederate treasure, which had passed from the protection of Captain Parker and his sailors to General Duke, rode in wagons with the rear guard of the column. The value of this gold and silver was still $251,000 (little changed since departing from Greensboro, N. C., according to Captain Clark).

The pace of the caravan was swift. Even Judah Benjamin forsook his vow and submitted to the discomfort of riding horseback, his plump cheeks aquiver with each step of his mount.

Breckinridge, though weakened by illness, rode for several miles at the side of the President, seeking to placate the frustrated leader who was still fuming over the refusal of his brigadiers to carry on the fight. Breckinridge tried to explain that these officers had by no means lost their courage—they merely sought to avoid further loss of life in a forlorn cause. He also tried to persuade Davis that he must flee in earnest and give up hope of reorganizing their forces. Breckinridge then fell back along the column to join Ferguson's rear guard. He had seen Davis for the last time.

The caravan reached the Savannah River before daybreak, crossed on a pontoon bridge near Vienna, S. C., and entered the state of Georgia. Stephen R. Mallory resigned his post as Secretary of the Navy during this ride, and even in the haste of flight exchanged letters with Davis before leaving the column. Mallory said he wished to protect his family, now refugees in Georgia, but offered to remain with Davis and guide him along the Florida coast he knew so well. The President urged him to think of his own welfare and the Secretary departed. Davis praised his "zeal, ability and integrity." Though the two separated as friends, Mallory felt that the Confederate cause was lost: "I regarded all designs . . . for continuing the war as wrong," he said later. Mallory found his way to one of the few rail lines in Georgia which had been restored in the wake of Sherman's destructive march, and rode via Atlanta to the village of La Grange, Ga., where his wife and children awaited him.

Breckinridge, who had so confidently assured the President of the loyalty of his brigadiers, now discovered a breakdown of discipline among the troops. While Davis rode steadily at the head of the column, Breckinridge faced a threat of mutiny among Ferguson's rear guard. The column was still near the river, not far from the home of the Reverend Dionysius (Nish) Chenault, a 300-pound Methodist minister who was also a planter.

Many Rebel riders, surly and grumbling, had discarded their arms and threatened to seek out the enemy and surrender. Now a number of them vowed to seize the money from the wagons, rather than wait for the enemy to capture it. As unpaid troops, they declared, they had first claim upon the Confederacy's last resources, and they would be paid now, rather than waiting until they reached Washington. Most of the men gathered around the heavy wagons at each halt. The wagon guards grew nervous. It was obvious that the angry troops could easily overpower the handful of sentries—and that the cavalrymen assigned to the wagon guard duty could not be depended upon to fire at their companions.

Breckinridge, who bore ultimate responsibility for the safety of the treasure as overall commander of the escort troops, rode up from the rear during the night to find the wagons halted, surrounded by cavalrymen. "We'll never get these wagons to Washington," one man said. "Why not take the money now?"

Breckinridge moved to the center of the mob and tried to face down the men; he had been a favorite of his troops throughout the war, but felt their implacable hostility tonight. Clad in his familiar hunting jacket, he sat his horse so calmly that his presence forced the troops to listen.

"You're still Confederate soldiers," he said. "It's your responsibility to act the part."

The general's face was a fierce white mask in the glare of pine torches.

"You're Southern gentlemen, not highway robbers. On a hundred battlefields you have shown that you know how to face death like brave men. Now, in these dark times, you must show that you can also live honorably."

He paused and swept the crowd with a glance from his pale eyes. "As soon as we reach Washington, you will be paid from the treasure train—just as I told you yesterday."

The troops were not persuaded. They would have their pay now, while it could be had, they said. No one could be sure they would reach Washington safely, with the enemy so near at hand.

Breckinridge succumbed to them. "If you want me to make good my promise immediately, I'll do it," he said. He ordered the wagons drawn up across the road, not far from the crossing of the Savannah River. Boxes were broken open as a circle of watchful men pressed about the treasure wagons in the half-light of dawn. By Captain Clark's official account, at least, each man received about $26 from paymasters—but this must have been in error, since Clark also reported that $108,322.90 was paid to troops at the riverside (leaving only $143,000 in the official treasure). This accounting indicated that more than 4,000 troops had been paid, rather than the 1,000-odd who were reported there.*

*There was a tantalizing hint that Breckinridge and Clark may have glossed over a much more serious breach of discipline. One C. E. L. Stuart, identified only as a Davis staff officer, left a vivid account of the behavior of the troops: "They were impatient, and helped themselves as soon as they discovered where to get it. The result was an inequitable distribution—many got too much, many got nothing; and 'dust hunters' picked up a good deal the following day —a good deal that was trampled under foot during the contemptible scramble."

Breckinridge, who had so recently sought to allay the President's anxieties about the loyalties of his brigadiers, was now responsible for the treasure, and may indeed have endured the wild scene depicted by Stuart—and found himself unable to admit to Davis that he could no longer depend upon his troops. The author located no corroborative evidence of Stuart's

Breckinridge had become too ill to ride forward and overtake Davis, but he kept watch over the mutinous men, and wrote Davis, "Nothing can be done with the bulk of this command. It has been with difficulty that anything has been kept in shape." He reported that though he had paid out the silver, only a few of the treasure's containers had been opened, and he would bring the rest of them forward to Washington the next day. None of the gold coins or bullion had been touched, he said. Anxious to be rid of this burden, Breckinridge added, "I hope Judge Reagan will take it."

The general conceded to the President only that some troops had thrown away their arms and refused to leave the site where the money was divided, saying that they would surrender to the enemy when they could. Breckinridge ruefully reported that no more than "a few hundred" of his men were still reliable, and that he was fearful of what remaining troops might do. As he wrote to the President, "Threats have just reached me to seize the whole amount of treasure but I hope the guard at hand will be sufficient."

This report was followed by a baffling silence from Breckinridge. Neither he nor Captain Clark, whose official accounting of the treasure's fate was to include the payout at the riverside, reported further action by the mutinous troops.

Whatever the extent of the mutiny, Breckinridge was evidently fearful that he would lose all control of the men, and he sought a safe hiding place for the jewelry that was part of the treasure—the chest of jewels and silver which had been contributed by Southern women toward the building of a Confederate warship. The general left the chest in the care of Mrs. J. D. Moss, who lived near the Chenault house, between the Savannah River and the small village of Danburg.

By the time Jefferson Davis responded to Breckinridge's dispatch from the riverside the money was already in the hands of the mutinous troops. Captain Clark's official report said, in a phrase seldom used by accountants, that the President "ratified" the distribution, suggesting irregularities as well as belated approval. At the urging of Davis, Breckinridge marched toward Washington with the remaining loyal troops.

. . .

---

version of the incident, but the language of Clark's report argues strongly that the troops might have taken their pay by force.

The President continued to resist suggestions that he try to escape on his own, and seemed to resent the implication that he was in flight rather than retreat. He had rejected earlier pleas of Breckinridge and Reagan that he disguise himself as a soldier and slip into Florida, then travel westward to join Kirby Smith's force to establish a new Confederacy. Davis had replied firmly, "I will not leave the country while a single Confederate regiment is on our soil."

Davis and his advisers still did not realize that they were engaged in making futile plans, since most routes of escape to the south and southwest were already blocked, with enemy soldiers flocking into the area in growing strength. By now it would be difficult for Davis to lose himself even among the wild fastnesses of the Florida coastal regions, and it was virtually certain that he could not make the overland ride to the Mississippi without detection.

Judah Benjamin left the President at this time, determined to make good his own escape and to rejoin Davis later, if he managed to elude the enemy. The two hastily arranged a rendezvous in Texas, where they still hoped to organize a final stand. During a brief private conversation, Davis entrusted Benjamin with "certain public duties," the nature of which was not to be revealed. Captain Clark gave the Secretary some gold for travel expenses and he turned to depart. Benjamin's last words were to Reagan. "I am going to the farthest place from the United States if it takes me to the middle of China."

It was with regret that the party saw Benjamin go; his inexhaustible stock of anecdotes and his beaming optimism had lifted the spirits of the refugees and shortened the miles of their flight.

Henceforth Benjamin was literally a new man. Aware that as the third-ranking Confederate official he would be a prize catch for Federal troopers now only a few miles distant, and realizing that he would be recognized at once, Benjamin bought a farmer's buggy and disguised himself as a Frenchman, one Monsieur Bonfals. Accompanied only by Colonel Henry J. Leovy, Benjamin set out over back roads for the Florida interior.

Captain John Taylor Wood, who saw him near the beginning of his journey, was surprised by the effectiveness of Benjamin's disguise. "With goggles on, his beard grown, a hat well over his face, and a large cloak hiding his figure, no one would have recognized him as the late Secretary of State of the Confederacy." Benjamin pretended that he spoke no English beyond a few broken phrases, and planned to depend upon Leovy to deal with people he met on his way.

At the end of his forty-mile ride through stormy weather, Davis entered Washington on the sunny morning of May 3 still erect and smiling, but gray-faced and near exhaustion. He had missed Varina by four hours, and was bitterly disappointed not to have seen her and their children.

A few men seated on the porch of the town bank recognized the spare, upright figure in gray and rose at once, baring their heads. Dr. J. J. Robertson, the cashier of the local branch of The Bank of Georgia, offered rooms in his apartment above the bank. Davis accepted. Someone passed him a note from Varina, urging that he escape alone, and not attempt to join her: ". . . Why not cut loose from your escort? Go swiftly and alone with the exception of two or three . . . May God keep you, my old and only love."

Washington greeted Davis as a hero. As Micajah Clark said, the people of this small town, though they knew the Confederacy had come to "the bitter end," gave Davis a welcome which, "though fearful, was full of love, warmth and tenderness." The village was more receptive than others on the route had been, perhaps because of Varina's recent visit, the establishment of supply depots there and the presence of Confederate generals and other officials. Washington was a temporary sanctuary for Mr. Davis.

The President went to bed and slept until evening, when a crowd gathered in the public square to see him. Several old Confederates, including General Arnold Elzey and his wife, burst into tears at sight of Davis, the symbol of their lost hopes whose presence even then was so reassuring to them. Judge Garnett Andrews, though a strong Union man, told his daughter Eliza after talking with Davis that the President was so calm and dignified that he "could not help admiring the man."

The next morning Davis presided over a final "Cabinet meeting," which was attended by John Reagan, in his dual capacity as Postmaster General & Secretary of the Treasury, and by General Bragg, Colonels Johnston, Lubbock and Thorburn, Captain Wood and a few others. Here too Davis spoke "with surprising calmness" of his hopes of re-establishing the Confederacy in the west. He also performed what was to become known as his last official duty by appointing Captain Micajah Clark Acting Treasurer of the Confederacy.

To the last Davis took seriously his responsibilities as head of his government, which he felt he lacked the authority to dissolve. In an effort to cope with this problem as a lawyer might have done, he resolved to surrender only when overpowered—since he was still technically commander of all Confederate armed forces.

To establish official sanction for disbanding the government, the President asked several army officers and Reagan, the lone remaining Cabinet member, for their written opinions. Their letters declared that the government could no longer function and that its officials should scatter. Davis then asked Captain Given Campbell, the commander of his escort of Kentuckians, if he could find ten volunteers to accompany him on his way southward—the escort was now too small to resist the enemy if attacked but too large to slip unnoticed through the countryside.

Campbell left the room, but soon reappeared to report that every man of the unit had volunteered. Davis smiled, and asked Campbell to select ten men for the duty. These men, like most of the presidential escort throughout the flight, were troops paroled after surrender, and had merely volunteered to help guide and protect Davis on his way.

The President also asked Captain Clark to assume responsibility for his personal baggage, which included the $35,000 in gold. Davis was to ride ahead with his little escort, and Clark and Reagan were to follow after they had paid out to responsible agents the remainder of the official Confederate treasure—which was being brought into Washington by Breckinridge. Clark secretly sewed the President's "Letter Books"—a veritable log of his daily orders throughout the war—and a few other documents into a quilt and concealed them in Washington.

Like others of the shrunken escort, Clark was moved to admiration by the President's manner: "I saw an organized government . . . fall to pieces little by little, until there was left only a single member of his Cabinet, his private secretary, a few members of his staff, a few guides and servants, to represent what had been a powerful government . . . Under these unfortunate circumstances, Mr. Davis' great resources of mind and heart shone out most brilliantly. He was calm, self-poised; giving way to no petulance of temper at discomfort; advising, consoling, laying aside all thought of self for our unhappy and despairing people, and uttering words of consolation."

On the morning of May 4 Davis emerged from the Robertson apartment to discover a crowd waiting to bid him farewell; several women had brought flowers. While his mounted aides waited impatiently, Davis spoke gravely with each woman and accepted wishes for a safe journey. The President turned to the homeward-bound escort party to thank them for their services, and then, for the first time, the black servant Robert saw tears in the eyes of his master. Tench Tilghman, the Marylander, confessed in his diary that he lacked the words to describe his emotions at "witnessing the head and representative of a great and mighty people fleeing for his life," but the young soldier saw that though the gray eyes of Davis had lost "some of their lustrous power," he was still a confident figure, and left with the Washington crowd the impression of "being yet hopeful."

The aides of the President now left town, followed by a reduced caravan of three wagons. Still Davis lingered. Frank Vizetelly made his last sketch of him there in the square, hat in hand, saying goodbye to men of his guard. The English artist, who had become an admirer of Davis, covertly gave someone a fifty-pound note to help the party on its way. He left an impression of the moment: "It was there that President Davis determined to continue his flight almost alone. With tears in his eyes he begged the men to seek their own safety and leave him to his fate."

Before departure Davis gave Mrs. Robertson some books, an inkstand and dressing case, which she was to treasure for years. He also left with her for safekeeping some of his personal papers.

It was 10 A.M. when Davis turned his horse out of town at last. Eliza Andrews noted that he left "with a single companion, his . . . escort having gone on before." She then repeated what someone had told her of security measures taken by Davis on the march with his caravan, a habit of ranging up and down his column of escorts, never remaining in one position for long: "He travels sometimes with them [the escort], sometimes before, sometimes behind, never permitting his precise position to be known." If her report was accurate, it was one of Davis's few precautions. In fact, Basil Duke noted that the President was recklessly heedless of his personal safety. As Davis left town Duke felt that though he and his aides were superbly mounted, and should outdistance all pursuit, Davis had other ideas: "I can only believe that he had resolved not to escape."

With the President's departure, Eliza Andrews was overcome by sensations of loss and desolation: "The most terrible part of the war is now to come, the 'bloody assizes' . . . Yankee troopers are closing in . . . our own disbanded armies, ragged, starving, hopeless . . . are roaming about without order or leaders . . . The props that held up society are broken . . . We have no currency, no law save the primitive code that might makes right. We are in a transition state from war to subjugation . . . far worse than was the transition from peace to war. The suspense and anxiety in which we live are terrible."

The President had hardly disappeared when John Breckinridge and his band of troops, including the mutinous cavalrymen, arrived near Washington. It was here, within a mile of the town, that Captain Clark joined the camp, and beneath a large elm tree, conducted his first official duty as Acting Treasurer of the Confederacy.

Of about $143,000 remaining after the payments (or looting) at the riverside, Clark entrusted $126,000 to two men who were to carry heavy burdens of coin and bullion to safety for the benefit of other Confederates.

Clark's payments included:

Gold coin and bullion amounting to $86,000 to James A. Semple, identified as "a trusted naval officer" who was nonetheless placed under bond. Semple was ordered to conceal his gold in the false bottom of a carriage and take it to Charleston or Savannah, whence it was to be shipped to Nassau, Bermuda or Liverpool for safekeeping. President Davis and John Reagan were to draw upon this gold to finance further resistance in case they reached the Trans-Mississippi.

Clark also paid $40,000, all in silver bullion, to Major Raphael J. Moses, who was to use it in feeding impoverished Confederate soldiers returning to their homes.

With the payment of these sums the treasure was reduced, by Clark's accounting, to about $17,000. Of this, John Breckinridge was paid $10,000 (from this sum, he was to transfer $1,000 to the Trans-Mississippi Department if he could reach there; he drew $5,000 for the Quartermaster Department in Washington, Ga.; and $4,000 to pay troops still under his command).

General Braxton Bragg was also given $2,000 to be taken to the Trans-Mississippi.

Of the some $5,000 remaining of the treasure, accounting was rather imprecise. Breckinridge is said to have taken $5,000 to Senator Robert Toombs in a meal sack, and to have placed small amounts in other "trustworthy" hands. In any event, the gold and silver treasure had now been dissipated, except for the $35,000 in gold which was still in the President's baggage.

The "Liverpool Acceptances," valued at £16,000 to £18,000 were entrusted to John Reagan—who spent his last hour or so in Washington burning "millions" in Confederate money and bonds. The funds of the Virginia banks were placed temporarily in a local bank, but Judge Crump and his tellers from Richmond were eager to move them to a safer place to avoid confiscation or robbery.

Breckinridge spent a busy day near Washington. His own horses and wagons had been used to transfer money from the caravan to Washington, evidently for delivery to Semple and Moses. The general also disbanded the War Department, ordering Quartermaster General A. R. Lawton and Commissary General Isaac St. John to dispose of remaining government property as they saw fit. He then authorized the final resignation from the Department, that of James B. Clay, Jr., grandson of Henry Clay, who had foreseen the coming of the war, and had given so much of himself in a futile effort to prevent it.

After Reagan and Clark had left to follow the President, Breckinridge set his volunteers on another road in an effort to confuse Federal pursuit. He was soon to move off on his own, in the hope of rejoining Davis farther south.

Varina Davis and her party, after leaving Washington, had rattled off down a back road toward the Florida border, hoping to be lost in anonymity. Teamsters were warned to speak to no one on the route and to refer to Varina only as Mrs. Jones. Burton Harrison was amused by the responses of soldiers and teamsters when irrepressibly curious countrymen called to them, "Who's that lady?"

"Mrs. Jones."

"Where'd you come from?"

"Up the road."

"Where you going?"

"Down the road a bit."

Varina's caravan traveled ten miles the first day and halted at the roadside for the night. Mrs. Davis and her sister, Maggie Howell, were there with the children and servants, making tea "in the awkward manner of townspeople camping out," when Richard Nugent, a nephew of the President, arrived with a note from Davis offering advice and expressing regret at his having missed her in Washington. The exceptionally dark night in the remote camp depressed Varina, who began to fear that she might not see her husband again, and was tormented by anxieties: "The ground felt very hard that night as I lay looking into the gloom and unable to pierce it even by conjecture."

Each day, as it made its way southward, Varina's party passed more soldiers from the defeated army, "plodding along depressed and sorrowful, in the direction of their homes." On the third night out from Washington the women and children were frightened by a raid on the camp, when a band of Confederate stragglers overran the site in the belief that the wagons were filled with gold. The raid was halted when its leader, an ex-captain, recognized Varina as the woman who had once dressed a battle wound for him in Richmond: he apologized and ordered his men out of the camp.

This was not the last of the party's trials. One evening when they camped near Milledgeville, the Georgia capital, Varina sent her coachman, Jim Jones, into town to find milk for the children. Some ruffians seized his mule, and Jim overheard someone say that a band of Alabama cavalrymen planned a raid on the camp that night.

Burton Harrison organized the campsite for battle. The wagons were placed in a circle to protect the horses and mules, and guards were posted outside the camp. Varina produced the Colt revolver that her husband had given her and another pistol that she had brought along from his collection and lay down, weapons in hand, to await the setting of the moon and the anticipated attack.

PART

3

THE CAPTURE

"I drew a net around Mr. Davis that would have reflected credit upon a detective policeman."

—MAJOR GENERAL JAMES H. WILSON, U.S. ARMY

9

"God's will be done"

THE President's party, now moving rapidly in the wake of Varina's caravan, was joined by some unwelcome—but unrecognized—escorts: twenty troopers of the U.S. First Ohio Cavalry, disguised in Confederate uniforms. These spies rode southward in the crowded roadway, unchallenged as they mingled with bands of Rebel troops who were returning homeward.

Davis evidently did not see these intruders, who were led by Lieutenant Joseph E. Yeoman of the First Ohio; they had been sent into central Georgia in hope of striking the President's trail so that pursuing columns could be guided in to capture him.

Yeoman did not catch a glimpse of Davis, either, but he satisfied himself that he was riding with his caravan and then led his band of spies away, carrying a report to the Federal command in Macon. Despite his ignorance of this intrusion by the enemy, Davis realized that pursuers were closing on him and that his chances of escape were dwindling: "They will make every effort in their power to capture me and it behooves us to face these dangers as men." He still hoped to move west to find General Forrest, or, failing that, "we will cross the Mississippi and join Kirby Smith, where we can carry on the war forever." After more than a month in flight he still knew nothing of his distant armies.

By now General Richard Taylor was ready to surrender his troops, which included Forrest's cavalry, with the feeling that further resistance would be foolish. He had told his troops: "We owed it to our manhood, to the memory of the dead, and to the honor of our arms, to remain steadfast to the last." Honor satisfied, Taylor surrendered on May 8 to General E. R. S. Canby near Mobile, Ala. Taylor and his staff were dining with Canby, their bands alternately playing "Hail, Columbia" and "Dixie," while Davis made camp in the barren Georgia woods near Sandersville.

It was here that Captain Clark and his wagons overtook Davis, at "a miserable out of the way place, the President wishing to be as secluded as possible." It was also here that Davis took the desperate step of abandoning "everything on wheels," even the wagon bearing the $35,000 in gold he had brought from North Carolina. He had evidently chosen between the remaining money and the hope of freedom, and turned southward toward the Florida border. Clark and his party were to follow a more westerly route to Madison, Fla.

THE LIBRARY OF CONGRESS

Before leaving Sandersville, Clark distributed some of the President's store of gold—$1,500 each to Colonels Lubbock, Johnston and Thorburn and Captain Wood, plus $10 each as pocket money. Though Clark said he expected most of this money to be spent for supplies and boats in Florida, he issued official receipts specifying that it was to be taken abroad as Confederate States property, subject to later accounting. He then persuaded a reluctant John Reagan to accept $3,500 in gold coin. Reagan hesitated to do this, since he already carried $2,000 in gold coins in a money belt—a ten-pound burden—and it was only after some discussion that Reagan agreed to carry the additional money in his saddlebags. Davis himself had only paper money, including the 50-pound note contributed by Vizetelly, and he could not be persuaded to take coins. Clark and his men left with the wagons, including the treasure, now reduced to about $25,000 in gold coins.

As they rode toward the Florida border, Davis made another concession to his aides. He agreed to pose as a Confederate congressman from Texas, while Reagan played the role of "a Texan judge" —but this was merely an added subterfuge, since neither man attempted an actual disguise. The small band turned to the southeast through a sparsely settled region of pines, swamps and semitropical growth.

But during the evening, while camp was being prepared on the bank of the Oconee River, Colonel Johnston overheard some local gossip: a large wagon train had passed that way a few hours earlier, followed by a party of soldiers who planned to rob it during the night. Davis became alarmed when Johnston told him the story, for the wagon train, as it was described, was almost certainly Varina's. Impulsively, without further thought for his own safety or the efforts of his companions to protect him throughout the long flight, Davis resolved to go to the aid of his wife, all previous precautions forgotten in a moment.

Though the President, who was just short of his fifty-seventh birthday, had dismounted from a tiring ride, he climbed back into the saddle. "I'll probably be captured or killed for this," he told his aides. "I don't feel that you're bound to go with me, but I must protect my family."

In a spontaneous display of loyalty to the President, the entire party immediately prepared to follow him—his four aides, John Reagan, Captain Given Campbell and ten of the Kentucky cavalrymen.

After several hours of hard riding in the darkness, Captain Campbell reported that the horses of his escort were too worn to continue without rest. The ten young Kentuckians halted, but the distraught Davis pushed on, accompanied now only by Reagan, the four aides and his servant Robert Brown. To the astonishment of his companions the President rode on at top speed through the night, trying first one road and then another in the confusing network of back-country trails, hoping to locate Varina's camp. Except for John Reagan, who was ten years his junior, most of the men in the party were young enough to have been the President's sons, yet he pushed on at an exhausting pace until, by one account, he had ridden an estimated sixty miles "without drawing rein." It was an almost incredible feat. It was also an impulsive act which placed him in peril of immediate capture.

It was nearly dawn when Varina heard horses approaching. Dim figures of riders on horseback loomed at the edge of the grove. Varina sat up with her pistols at the ready, expecting the worst. But Burton Harrison, who recognized a familiar form, called out from the shadows. Jefferson Davis responded, identifying himself as he dismounted. Varina embraced her husband and the children flung themselves upon him. The exhausted President, animated by the presence of his family, talked with Varina for an hour or more, recounting the events of his journey from Richmond. He told her of his continuing hope of reaching Forrest, crossing the Mississippi and carrying on the war to a victorious conclusion.

The expected attack did not come. Through the next day the President and his men rode with Varina's party and camped with it that night. Davis and his escort departed after breakfast, however, in response to Varina's plea that he hurry on his way, leaving to her the "wagons and encumbrances."

The President, Reagan, the four aides and Robert rode off at a brisk pace, still with the prospect of outdistancing the Federal pursuit. Davis moved vigorously all day until, by nightfall, he halted at the village of Abbeville, Ga., where he took shelter in an unfinished house near the town. Before he slept, the President sent a warning to Varina by courier: Federal cavalrymen were on their trail, and were reported to be at Hawkinsville, only twenty-five miles away. The exhausted Davis then fell asleep, oblivious to a severe thunderstorm that raged over the countryside during the night of May 8–9.

Varina and her children had suffered as their wagons lumbered southward after the President. Her teamsters had forced the wagons through mucky bottomlands of the Ocmulgee River to make a crossing of the stream on a ferry. The party was camped miserably in sodden beds when the President's courier arrived with the warning.

Harrison responded by breaking camp after midnight and driving the caravan onward through the storm. Teamsters lashed the weary animals and the white-faced women and children clung to their seats, staring about in terror during the frequent flashes of lightning and peals of thunder. Harrison, who had suffered from dysentery and fever for the last four days, was near the end of his endurance, but he rode doggedly at the head of the caravan until they approached Abbeville.

Harrison found the President wrapped in a blanket on the floor of the abandoned house, but Davis was so worn that he did not rise to greet Varina, who waited in the ambulance outside.

"Go ahead immediately," Davis told Harrison. "We'll catch up as soon as the horses have rested."

Once more, in the face of growing danger, the bizarre pattern of separating and rejoining was followed haphazardly by the Davis family in its two caravans. Despite all the President's planning and Varina's continual pleas that he go on without her, the two seemed to be unable to remain apart. The opportunity for the escape of Davis, once so favorable, was now fading.

Harrison led Varina's party into the darkness through the downpour, along a narrow, winding road blocked by fallen trees. The drenched teamsters were often forced to await lightning flashes to see their way. Davis and his party overtook Varina several hours later and the two groups then rode southward together for about twenty miles before pausing to eat breakfast and bathe. Captain Wood noted that the Davises had adapted themselves to the primitive conditions —he saw them bathing "al fresco" in a stream that morning, their chalk-white bodies gleaming through the thickets.

Burton Harrison turned out of the road at about 5 P.M. on May 9 and chose a campsite beside a stream just north of the village of Irwinville, Ga., a site partially screened from the road by thickets. An extensive swamp lay beyond the creek. The Florida border was still some 65 miles distant. While servants and soldiers pitched the tents and built fires, Colonel Preston Johnston rode into Irwinville to buy some eggs.

Harrison and others urged Davis to leave his family behind and ride for Florida at once. The President gave his "positive promise" to leave as soon as he had eaten supper, and to travel at least ten miles before halting for the night. The debilitated Harrison then directed the placement of the wagons and tents for the camp and lay down on the ground. Worn out by sickness, he fell into a sound sleep, expecting the President to keep his word. Though aides had convinced Davis that he should leave Varina and his own escort behind on more than one occasion, none of these plans for his escape had succeeded. Even after his impulsive ride across country to rescue Varina and his subsequent departure in response to her pleas, the Davises had courted disaster by passing and repassing each other on the roads. Now, at nightfall of May 9, the President again delayed his departure.

Colonel Johnston returned from the village with a basket of fresh eggs, bearing a now-familiar rumor: Confederate army stragglers planned an attack on the camp during the night. Davis then said he would delay his departure for about two hours to see whether the marauders came. The President had his horse tethered to a tree near the roadside, saddled and bridled, with holstered pistols strapped in place. He then entered Varina's tent.

If there was conversation between them, it was brief. Davis ate supper with his wife and soon afterward complained of "a bilious feeling." Then, despite promises that he would leave camp, the President lay down, fully clothed, on a cot and fell asleep. There was no one to protest this fateful decision—though Reagan, Johnston, Wood and Thorburn sat beside a nearby campfire until a late hour, hoping for a summons to depart. They finally fell asleep themselves.

Maggie Howell and the Davis children slept in a tent adjacent to that of the Davises. All others of the party slept in the open. Captain Wood, one of the last men to fall asleep in the grove, noted that the camp had been carelessly made, with few of the usual security measures taken. Wood reported that Captain Campbell and his scouts had camped some distance in advance, and there were no guards posted in the rear, "from which direction alone we might expect danger." Camp security had been Harrison's responsibility, but his illness had caused him to neglect the customary precautions.

Quiet fell over the camp. Mists filled the thickets of the creek valley and the light of the fire grew dim. Long before dawn Jim Jones, the servant, who was on guard, stirred the fire and began heating water in a pot for the washing of Winnie's diapers.

U.S. cavalrymen rode through the sodden Georgia countryside all night, approaching the Davis camp on separate roads. These riders were part of the large cavalry force which U.S. General James H. Wilson had led on a 1,000-mile march through Alabama, Mississippi and Georgia, leaving behind a path of destruction more than thirty miles wide. In the pattern of Sherman's more famous March to the Sea, Wilson's foray had cowed Southern civilians, "dealing them terrific blows." The riders had taken Selma and Montgomery, Ala., and Columbus and Macon, Ga., by the time news of Appomattox reached General Wilson.

The flamboyant twenty-seven-year-old general, now based in Macon, sent his troopers fanning out through southeast Georgia. They had seized Henry Wirz, the Swiss-born physician who was director of the infamous Andersonville prison where so many Federal prisoners had died of disease, malnutrition and starvation, and Wilson was confident that they would soon capture the Confederate President. His 15,000 horsemen, already stationed throughout Georgia, had stretched a cordon from Atlanta to Tallahassee, Fla., along the western line of the search area. More menacingly for the Davis party, two of Wilson's columns were riding eastward from Macon headquarters, probing the south central area of Georgia. The Davis party had camped near the heart of this region.

Wilson had planned shrewdly. Though he had not yet learned of President Johnson's offer of a reward, the general acted on his own initiative, offering $100,000 for the capture of Davis and $25,000 each for lesser Confederate officials, a lure calculated to spur hundreds of soldiers and hangers-on, including ex-Confederates, to join the chase. Wilson also held forth the promise of a further, irresistible, prize: "Several million dollars of specie reported to be with him will become the property of the captors."

Armed with the report of Captain Yeoman of the 1st Ohio, who had ridden with the fugitives—and excited by rumors of some $15,000,000 in gold Davis was thought to be carrying—the two Federal columns rode confidently out from Macon, closing in on the President and his party. They consisted of about 150 horsemen of the 1st Wisconsin Cavalry, led by Lieutenant Colonel Henry Harnden, and another detachment, of the 4th Michigan, under Lieutenant Colonel Benjamin Pritchard.

Pritchard's party of the 4th Michigan, mustered mysteriously in light marching order with three days' rations, had been dispatched without bugle calls or other customary ceremony. These men knew little of their mission—and it was only after two days of hard riding that Pritchard revealed that they were on the trail of Jefferson Davis, who was thought to be guarded by 500 Texas cavalrymen. (In fact the President's party was only about sixty strong, including women, children and servants. Captain Campbell's ten Kentucky cavalrymen, a handful of soldiers from assorted units, armed teamsters and a few officers with side arms provided the protection for Davis and his family.)

Within twenty-four hours the 4th Michigan moved fifty-one miles, then camped in a pine woods during the severe thunderstorm.

Lieutenant Colonel Benjamin D. Pritchard, who led this band, was in civilian life a lawyer from Allegan, Mich., who had made his way through Hiram College and the University of Michigan working as a farmer, carpenter and teacher. He had been severely wounded at the battle of Chattanooga and promoted for bravery.

Pritchard's Michiganders and Harnden's 1st Wisconsin troopers, acting independently and under separate orders from Wilson, met in the village of Abbeville at about 3 P.M. on May 9. The Wisconsin column, which had been reduced in order to cover a wider area, was now only seventy-five strong, but Colonel Harnden, eager to outrace his rivals to the quarry, rejected Pritchard's warning that his force might be too weak to overcome the Confederate guard. Harnden moved off on a roundabout route to Irwinville. Both columns rode through the night, on separate roads leading toward Irwinville.

At dusk Pritchard learned that a party with tents and wagons had gone down the Abbeville-Irwinville road during the afternoon. Since he knew that Harnden's troopers had no wagons, Pritchard realized that Davis must be near at hand. Some Michigan scouts located the Confederate camp soon after midnight, and by 2 A.M. Pritchard's men had moved stealthily into position for attack.

In the President's camp only Jim Jones was astir when Colonel Thorburn and his Negro servant rose and left the sleeping camp. Thorburn took the road to the south, riding briskly once his eyes became accustomed to the darkness. The Colonel had been planning for the President's escape from Florida during the past month, and was now bound for the Indian River, where a small boat was awaiting Davis.

As he neared the village of Irwinville, Thorburn blundered into a Federal party, which opened fire and followed, under the impression that President Davis was escaping. Thorburn shot the foremost of his pursuers, who fell from the saddle, and then, with his companion, outdistanced the enemy troopers. Thorburn was on his way to safety across the Florida border.

Shortly after this encounter, Pritchard's Michigan troops dashed into the President's camp, at first meeting no resistance. But within a few moments the rear guard of this band was attacked by unidentified riflemen—dismounted men who fired from behind trees. The dawn roared with heavy volleys and orange spurts of gunfire flickered in the valley mist.

Jim Jones turned from the campfire and ran for the tents. He aroused Burton Harrison with a warning that the Yankees had come and then dashed ahead to warn the President. Harrison was astounded to learn that Davis was still in the camp.

The President, who was already awake, thought the firing had come from raiders seeking gold. Fully dressed, he leapt up and called to Varina, "Those men have attacked us at last. I'll go and see if I can't stop the firing. Surely I'll have some authority with the Confederates."

But Davis raised the tent flap and saw several bluecoat troopers in the camp and realized that he had been mistaken. The enemy had found him at last. He called to Varina, "Federal cavalry!"

Captain John Taylor Wood ran up and told Davis that he should escape during the confusion.

Davis called to Jim Jones, ordering him to take his horse into the swamp, which was less than a hundred yards away. Varina screamed as Jones unhitched the mount, begging the President to flee. Davis hesitated, and as he recalled it later, "lost a few precious moments before yielding to her importunities." In the darkness of the cold, damp morning he snatched a sleeveless raglan rain cape which he thought was his own—it was, in fact, Varina's. When he was unable to find his hat, Mrs. Davis took a shawl from her shoulders and impulsively threw it over his head.

Colonel Pritchard, who had by now galloped to the center of the camp, hurriedly posted sentries at the three tents by the roadside. He shouted down to a civilian who appeared before him—Burton Harrison.

Pritchard pointed across the creek, where the heavy firing still crackled. "What does that mean? Do you have men with you?"

Harrison, who thought the teamsters were resisting the enemy, said, "Of course we have. Don't you hear the firing?"

Pritchard flashed him an angry glance and led a troop of riders at a gallop across the stream and out of sight. The only Federal soldier left in the camp was a sentry near the Davis tent. Harrison saw Varina emerge and speak to the Federal and realized that she was attempting to persuade him to move away.

Harrison approached the soldier and to his surprise was able to lead him into the road a few yards distant. At that moment President Davis appeared and, Harrison said, "walked away into the woods to the eastward."

From the tent, Varina sent her mulatto maid Helen after her husband with a bucket, in hope that they would pass unnoticed, as if he and Helen had gone to the stream to get water.

Davis had moved about fifty feet from his tent when a Federal trooper galloped up to him, leveled his carbine and shouted, "Halt!"

Varina, who had expected some reckless move from her husband, had run from the tent into the open with surprising speed. She was just in time. The President shouted his defiance at the Federal rider, dropped his cloak and shawl and lunged forward, expecting, as he said later, that the soldier would fire at him and miss, and that he might then throw him from the saddle with an old Indian trick, putting a hand under the trooper's foot and flinging him off on the opposite side of the horse.

Varina threw her arms around Davis. "Shoot me if you wish," she called to the trooper.

"I wouldn't mind a bit," the bluecoat replied.

This, at least, was the President's version of the capture, which was corroborated by Varina, with minor differences in detail.

But Captain Wood, who watched from a few yards away, saw things differently. He felt that Varina's hysterical reaction at the crucial moment ruined the President's opportunity to escape. The Davis children had now emerged from their tent, sobbing, and terrified black servants screamed. As Wood was to recall it: "Then Mrs. Davis by her appeals—the children by their crying, the servants by fear and howling destroyed all."

Several of the Federal soldiers who took part in seizing Davis offered still more versions of the events in the camp. Lieutenant Julian G. Dickinson and Private Andrew Bee, the latter a Norwegian who spoke broken English, both claimed to have been first to recognize Davis—and said he had deliberately disguised himself in woman's clothing in an attempt to escape.

Dickinson declared that the Davis servant, Helen, had begged him, "Please let me and my grandmother go to the brook and wash ourselves."

Bee claimed that he had realized instantly that the "old woman" wore a man's boots beneath the cloak, and said he had called out a warning to the fugitive, "Sheff Davis, you stay dare . . . See, that Sheff Davis himseff."

Bee also paid tribute to the President: "Anybody who think Sheff Davis a coward should have seen him. He turned right square around and came towards me fast . . . " And it was only Varina's quick move that prevented Davis from challenging Bee's marksmanship and attempting to throw him from his horse.

The controversy that was to rage over whether Davis had worn a disguise was complicated by the testimony of another Federal observer who had encountered the Confederate President during the confused moments of his capture. Captain James H. Parker, who claimed that he had recognized Davis at first glance, denied that the captive had sought a cowardly way to escape: "I defy any person to find a single officer or soldier who was present at the capture . . . who will say upon honour that he was disguised in women's clothes . . . His wife . . . behaved like a lady, and he as a gentleman, though manifestly chagrined at being taken into custody." And Parker, as he said, was qualified to judge: "I am a Yankee, full of Yankee prejudices, but I think it wicked to lie about him."

Within a few days, as Parker evidently foresaw, the northern press was to proclaim: "Jeff Davis Captured in Hoop Skirts". . . "Jeff in Petticoats," and cartoonists were to stir laughter for months to come at the expense of Davis. Even the government was to stoop to fraud in perpetuating the myth that Davis had worn one of Varina's dresses.

Federal troops now began returning to the camp.

After a few moments of skirmishing, Colonel Pritchard suspected that his men were being fired upon by the Wisconsin troops, and when he halted his riflemen his suspicions were confirmed. The Federal parties had been firing on each other at close range in the confusion. Two Michigan troopers were dead and an officer was wounded. Three of Harnden's Wisconsin men were wounded.

Once the firing ended between the Federal troops, Colonel Pritchard returned to camp and learned for the first time that Davis was a captive. He went to the tent and shouted to the ex-President in abusive language, but soon regained his composure. Davis faced him with dignity, as Pritchard said, and "proudly pled for his family and his aides," urging that they be allowed to go on their way. Pritchard refused.

"My orders are to take everyone to Macon."

"God's will be done," Davis said, and led Varina to her tent.

He was taken to a log near the center of the camp, where he sat, closely guarded while the camp was looted. The President was searched and his currency was taken, including Vizetelly's fifty-pound note. John Reagan was robbed of the heavy burden of his gold—$5,500 in coin, as well as his sheaves of "Liverpool Acceptances." Colonel Johnston lost not only his $1,500 in gold, but, more distressing to him, the pistols which his father, General Albert Sidney Johnston, had worn when he was fatally wounded at the battle of Shiloh. Burton Harrison lost $110 in gold, but foiled the looters by dumping the contents of his haversack into a campfire—official papers, personal letters, and a picture of his fiancée, Connie Cary. Governor Lubbock resisted so fiercely that he managed to save his $1,500, which was well hidden in his saddlebags, but was robbed of his gold watch, $50 in gold, and his horse. Captain John Wood also managed to save his gold in some way, and was soon to escape the enemy net through an ingenious ruse.

The Federals swarmed through the camp, plundering the tents and wagons, breaking into trunks and flinging clothing onto the ground. Gold and jewelry were taken from Varina and Maggie Howell. Troopers scattered Bibles and prayer books in the grass, and even carried off Piecake's baby garments as souvenirs. Varina lost most of the clothing in her trunks, including a hoopskirt she had never worn, but she retained her composure and made no protest. Frank Lubbock was impressed by her bearing and "womanly fortitude."

When the President complained to Pritchard that the troops were stripping his family of many personal belongings, the colonel promised to parade his men as soon as he had secured the camp, buried the dead and loaded the wounded in wagons. At that time, he assured the President, any stolen valuables would be returned.

Davis continued to watch calmly, "without the tremor of a muscle . . . with flashing eagle eyes undimmed," as Lubbock said.

The President maintained his dignity despite harassment by Federal troops, though he did call to an enemy soldier after watching the looters for a time, "You're an expert set of thieves."

The heart of the Confederate capital, gutted by fire on the night of April 2-3, 1865. Looting civilians and retreating soldiers set off the blaze just as Jefferson Davis and his cabinet fled the city. *(The Library of Congress)*

Richmond Falls

St. Paul's Episcopal Church, which survived the fire. Davis was at worship here when the dispatch from Robert E. Lee warned that the city must be evacuated. *(The Library of Congress)*

Judah P. Benjamin, Secretary of State.
(The New York City Public Library Picture Collection)

John C. Breckinridge, Secretary of War.
(The Library of Congress)

The Cabinet . . .

These six men fled with Jefferson Davis as the Confederacy collapsed, but only Benjamin and Breckinridge escaped via Florida and Cuba after hair-raising adventures. Benjamin, "the Brain of the Confederacy," went on to a distinguished career as a British lawyer. Breckinridge, a former Vice-President of the United States, finally returned from exile to his home in Kentucky. George Davis, after brief imprisonment, returned to practice law in Wilmington, North Carolina.

George Davis, Attorney General.
(George Rountree, III)

Stephen R. Mallory, Secretary of the Navy. *(The Library of Congress)*

John H. Reagan, Postmaster General. *(The Library of Congress)*

. . .*in Flight*

The brilliant Mallory, who created ironclad ships, submarines, and torpedoes from scanty resources, was arrested as a "pirate." The Texas politician, Reagan, though not one of the President's inner circle, was the only minister who remained with Jefferson Davis to the end. Trenholm, an invalid during the flight, received the most lenient treatment from the victorious Federal government. All three men were released after serving brief prison terms.

George A. Trenholm, Secretary of the Treasury. *(The Library of Congress)*

Prominent among the adversaries of Jefferson Davis were the officious veteran generals Johnston and Beauregard, who continued to challenge his authority up to the moment of final surrender. *(Johnson: The Valentine Museum, Richmond, Virginia; Beauregaud: The Library of Congress)*

The Opposition

Confederate Vice-President Stephens's extreme views on States' Rights were a constant menace to the Davis administration. Contemporaries said of the tiny, deformed Stephens that his only distinguishing trait was that "he had a good opinion of himself" and that he would not be content until he had edited the text of his own obituary. *(The Library of Congress)*

The artist Frank Vizetelly of *The London Illustrated News* was the only journalist to accompany officers of the Confederate government in their flight, and his drawings provide the sole pictorial record of this historic event. *(The Library of Congress)*

"Newsreel"

Davis leaves his escort in the village of Washington, Georgia, just five days before his capture. It is apparently Vizetelly himself who is pictured saying farewell to the Confederate President. *(The Library of Congress)*

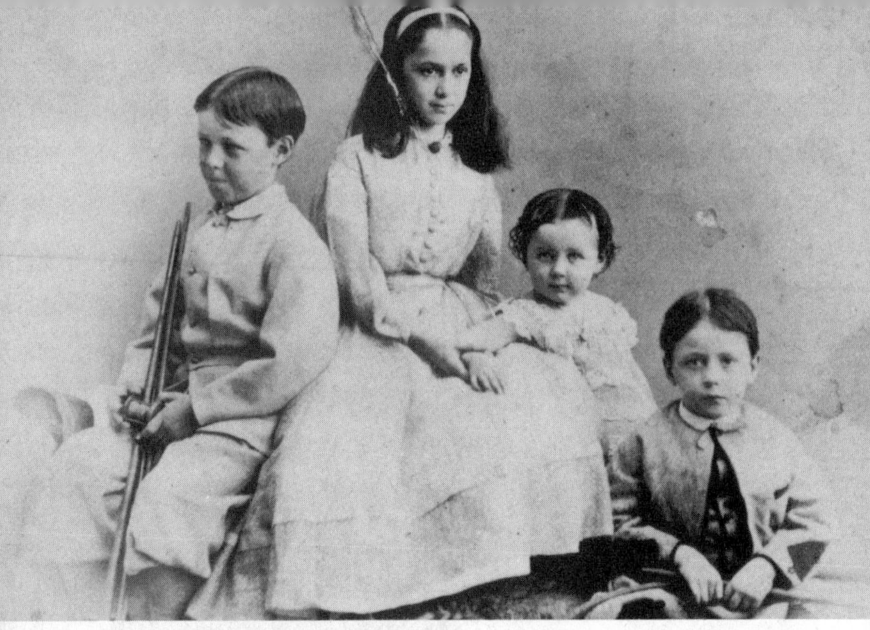

The children of Jefferson and Varina Davis. From left, young Jeff, Maggie, Varina Anne (also called Winnie and "Piecake"), and Billie. The boys died in postwar epidemics and Winnie of malaria in New York City at the age of thirty-three. Only Maggie, who married Addison Hayes (later Hayes-Davis), survived to rear a family and perpetuate the Jefferson Davis line. Photographed in Montreal, circa 1867. *(The Library of Congress)*

Children in War

"Jim Limber," a playmate of the Davis children, was rescued by the family in Richmond from a cruel father and "adopted." The small boy was taken away by Federal authorities before Davis was imprisoned and never saw the family again. *(Museum of the Confederacy, Richmond, Va.)*

Sara Anne Dorsey, who took Jefferson Davis into her home during the writing of his memoirs and acted as his secretary, stirred Mrs. Davis to jealous wrath. Mrs. Dorsey left her entire estate to Davis. *(Nora Avery, courtesy Beauvoir, Biloxi, Mississippi)*

Rivals of Varina Davis?

Virginia Tunstall Clay, never a beauty but always a belle, was prominent in the society of both Washington and Richmond. Gossips linked her name with Jefferson Davis's in an alleged postwar romance.
(William R. Perkins Library, Duke University)

The report that Jefferson Davis was wearing his wife's clothing when captured occupied Northern cartoonists for months. The Currier and Ives version of the garbled accounts was typical. *(Boston Public Library)*

Yankee Laughter

General Edward L. Molineux, commander of the U. S. garrison in Augusta, Georgia, was the last ranking Federal officer known to have a substantial amount ($30,000) of Confederate gold. The whimsical Molineux said he once tried to chip a gold bar which came into his possession, but was foiled by his "sharp conscience or his dull knife." *(Will Molineux)*

The cold, dank cell in the depths of Fort Monroe as it appeared after restoration in 1967, the centennial of Jefferson Davis's release. A broad moat lay beneath the barred windows and two U. S. soldiers paced beside the prisoner's cot day and night. (The Daily Press, *Newport News, Virginia (Buddy Norris))*

Prison Years

Dr. John Craven, a remarkable self-trained physician from Newark, New Jersey, saved the life of Jefferson Davis and prompted a major shift in public opinion about the Confederate ex-President in both the North and the South. *(Museum of the Confederacy, Richmond, Va.)*

Eдward M. Stanton, U. S. Secretary of War. *(The Kunhardt Collection)*

President Andrew Johnson. *(The Kunhardt Collection)*

The vindictive Stanton and his adversary Johnson both sought to saddle Jefferson Davis with guilt for the war itself and complicity in the assassination of Abraham Lincoln. Only after two years did public opinion in the North force them to free Davis from prison.

The Enemy

General Miles, a twenty-six-year-old former crockery clerk, the jailer of Fort Monroe, had Davis placed in irons and inflicted many petty tortures upon him. Miles later became Commander-in-Chief of the U. S. Army and directed campaigns against Indian tribes in the West. *(The New York City Public Library Picture Collection)*

The Ultimate Zealot

Edmund Riffin, who is alleged to have fired the first shot of the Civil War against Fort Sumter, committed suicide soon after Jefferson Davis was imprisoned. Riffin's final cry of defiance: "I hereby declare my unmitigated hatred of . . .the perfidious, malignant, and vile Yankee race."

(Museum of the Confederacy, Richmond, Va.)

Freedom at Last

Bearing the marks of his two-year ordeal, Jefferson Davis poses with his wife Varina in Montreal in 1867, shortly after his release from prison. Davis complained that his self-imposed exile was "vegetation rather than life."

(Museum of the Confederacy, Richmond, Va.)

Frail Survivors

Old friends and fellow prisoners, Jefferson Davis and Clement Claiborne Clay in Memphis after being freed from Fort Monroe, Virginia, through the efforts of their wives (circa 1867). *(William R. Perkins Library, Duke University)*

A Belle in her Final Glory

Virginia Clay-Clopton, at ninety, more handsome than in her youth—a formidable dowager, suffragette, author, and society queen who refused to concede that her reign had ended. Photographed in Washington, D. C., circa 1915. *(William R. Perkins Library, Duke University)*

Dixie's Aging Knight

Robert E. Lee within nine months of his death, the devoted president of Virginia's Washington College. The education of young southerners, Lee said, was the "self-imposed task" to which he would devote his last years. Photographed by Miley (December 1869 or January 1870).

(Lee Chapel, Washington and Lee University, Lexington, Va.)

The Lee monument, Richmond, Virginia. A rare photo of its unveiling, May 29, 1890, before a crowd estimated at 100,000. *(The Valentine Museum, Richmond, Va.)*

Symbol of an Era

The ninety-year-old bronze became an enduring symbol of Southern —and national—pride. *(Virginia Department of Conservation, Richmond, Va.)*

"You think so, do you?" was the only reply.

Neither captors nor captives seemed to reflect that the treatment of Davis was remarkably mild under the circumstances, considering the view of Northerners that he bore a major share of guilt for the bloodiest war in American history. Yet Davis, when he was goaded to wrath by minor excesses of jubilant soldiers, responded as if they had committed unspeakable atrocities. When he saw food snatched from a fire and gobbled by soldiers as it was being cooked for the breakfast of his children, the President leapt to his feet and raged at Colonel Pritchard, in indignant but futile protest. Davis quickly subsided, but his sense of outrage was still strong years later when he recalled these "annoyances such as military *gentlemen* never commit or permit."

Colonel Pritchard failed to qualify as a military gentleman, for he not only failed to search his men for stolen goods, as he had promised; he himself confiscated Varina's fine carriage horses, which had been gifts from admirers in Richmond.

While the looting continued, Captain Wood made his escape by subterfuge. Abandoning his clothing and saddlebags, Wood mingled with the enemy soldiers, studied their faces to choose a gullible victim, and asked one trooper to accompany him to the edge of the swamp so that he might relieve himself. The bluecoat hesitated but finally did so. After standing in the underbrush for a few moments, the Federal called to Wood, "I'm going back to camp. You come on when you're ready."

Wood halted him. "I'm not going back. I'll give you half of what's in my purse if you'll let me stay here."

The soldier agreed, and Wood gave him two $20 gold pieces and crouched in the swamp for three hours, enduring "the most painful position." Wood heard all that was said in the camp during the pilfering of Confederate possessions, but though soldiers who came to the stream for water passed within a few yards of him, the captain escaped observation.

He waited until bugles sounded, wagons rolled and the enemy moved the Davis party from the campsite. Wood saw the departure of his uncle, "The President started off on one of his carriage horses followed by his staff and a squadron of the enemy. Sad fate."

. . .

No sooner had the camp been cleared than Captain Wood emerged cautiously from the swamp—and caught sight of a friend, one Lieutenant Barnwell, who had also been hiding in the underbrush. Barnwell went his own way, leading two horses, and Wood made his escape. He was bound for Florida.

10

"He must be executed"

COLONEL PRITCHARD herded his captives along the road toward Macon early on the morning of May 11. Reagan, Harrison, Johnston and Lubbock led the procession, followed by the ten Kentucky troopers of the Davis escort, all of them plodding along in two columns.

The President and his family rode in the ambulance, where Maggie Howell sobbed for hours, upsetting the children, who also began to weep. Davis remained silent throughout.

The procession passed numerous Confederate soldiers along the way, and though few of them glimpsed their former leader, jubilant Federal officers were quick to tell them of the capture. One bluecoat called to the Rebel troops in a gloating voice, "Hey, boys, we've got your old boss back here in the ambulance—we've got old Jeff Davis and his whole band of rebels and are taking them to Macon."

Officers of the Michigan escort were delighted by the "inevitable reply" from the Confederates to this sally: "Hang him! Shoot him! . . . We've got no use for him. The damned Mississippi Mule got us into this scrape. Hope you'll hang every man in Mississippi and South Carolina."

Though this fierce response was reported by enemy officers who were anxious to portray Davis in the worst possible light, it was probably an accurate reflection of the attitudes of many Southern veterans, especially those who were small farmers, tenants, laborers or clerks. Davis had already experienced a variety of reactions to his appearance along his route—now hailed as a hero and then shunned as a pariah—but these catcalls must have come as a shock to him. In the reeling Confederacy, with its military and economic system in ruins and its slave-based society vanishing in the moment of defeat, white survivors were overcome by uncertainty and despair. To these people, however loyal they had been as Rebels during the war, the President was the visible symbol of ruin and failure. It was hardly surprising that some disillusioned, hungry, unpaid soldiers gloated over his capture.

Davis, it seemed, was to end his career as a false prophet, despised and reviled by many of his people. The popular Northern parody, "The Sour Apple Tree," the first line of which was "Hang Jeff Davis on a sour apple tree," was not anathema to everyone in the Confederacy.

Pritchard reported capture of the presidential party to General Wilson, who telegraphed Edwin Stanton. The North erupted in spontaneous celebration. As yet there was no mention of the woman's clothing Davis had worn when he was taken.

Varina Davis, who was not usually slow to assert herself, made no complaint of their treatment for two days—until May 12, when the caravan halted near a Federal camp where a band was blaring out "Yankee Doodle" and enemy soldiers were whooping in celebration. It was only now that captives and captors alike learned of the $100,000 price on the head of Davis and of the charge that he was involved in Lincoln's murder. Primitive communications had failed to spread the news through the isolated rural region of central Georgia.

The soldiers in this camp hooted at Davis, and Varina found Captain Charles Hudson of the wagon guard especially offensive. Though there was no violence, news of the charge against the President had put his captors into an ugly mood.

Varina conceded that Colonel Pritchard tried to cause them "as little unnecessary pain" as was possible, and she was later to forgive him. She never forgave his troops, and twenty-five years later she found it distressing to recall "the horrors and sufferings of that journey."

Pritchard, overjoyed by his good fortune, passed one of the reward notices to Davis, who read it, as Burton Harrison said, with no emotion "other than scorn." When he saw Johnson's name on the sheet, Davis said, "The miserable scoundrel . . . knows it is false. Of course, the accusation will fail—but now these people will be willing to assassinate me."

On May 13, after three days on the road, the band reached Macon, where the captives were halted for an hour on the outskirts of town under heavy guard. As the fearful children clung to their father, Davis tried to calm them by reciting psalms, while soldiers were shouting at him in language Varina thought "unfit for women's ears." When Colonel Pritchard reappeared with a brigade of Federal troops, the newcomers also shouted at Davis "in the rudest manner."

The returning captors were hailed for their bravery in seizing Davis, but Henry Potter, an officer in the 4th Michigan who did not accompany the raiders, scoffed at this as "all nonsense." Many men of the unit, he said, had not fired a shot during their service. He added with a hint of envy, "but the fact that they gobbled up old Jeff will be enough to put their names in history."

Potter talked with Davis, whom he expected to be hanged, and with Varina, who must have spat defiance at the victors, for Potter found her "haughty & insulting, as any woman I ever saw—if she is a lady I failed to discover it." Though he felt little pity for her, he was moved by the sight of the "pretty & innocent" children who were, he thought, so soon to become orphans.

There was a notable change in atmosphere when the prisoners reached Wilson's headquarters in the Lanier Hotel. Davis entered between files of Federal troops, who smartly presented arms. He accepted the salute as "an expression of the feeling brave men show to a fallen foe." More surprises were in store. The Davises were given a spacious room, where dinner was brought to them on a covered tray. They were moved at the sight of some hastily plucked, short-stemmed roses on the tray. With tears in his eyes their Negro waiter said, "I couldn't bear for you to eat without something pretty from the Confederates." Varina took this as a mark of affection from an ex-slave to strangers who had been slave owners, amidst the ruins of a doomed Southern culture. She pressed one of the blooms as a reminder of the gesture of the naïve old black man who had reached across racial barriers to proffer his friendship.

Davis and Wilson talked after dinner, the general in "a courteous, obliging" mood as they discussed West Point and mutual friends in the U.S. Army. The young general, a native of Shawneetown, Ill., was descended from soldiers; one grandfather had fought in the

Black Hawk War, in which Davis had served, and the other had been a German veteran of the Napoleonic wars. After graduating near the top of the West Point class of 1860 and entering the war a few months later, Wilson had won a reputation for aggressive leadership and risen rapidly in rank. His cavalry had helped to isolate John Hood's Rebel army during the bloody battle of Franklin, Tenn., and later slashed through Alabama to overwhelm the fierce Nathan Bedford Forrest and force his surrender at Selma.

When Wilson mentioned the proclamation issued over the name of President Johnson, Davis repeated, "There's one man who knows it is false—the man who signed it. Johnson knows I preferred Lincoln to himself." Davis said he expected no mercy and predicted that a vengeful Federal government would prosecute him as a traitor.

Though no one knew where Davis was to be imprisoned, Wilson was ordered to send him northward. Offered his preference of transportation, Davis chose the sea route, which would be more comfortable for Varina and the children. Wilson agreed—but the party was forced to travel far to avoid broken rails, from Macon via Atlanta to Augusta, whence they would sail down the Savannah River to Savannah itself, where they would board a coastal steamer.

By now Clement Clay and his wife, Virginia, were also captives. They had paused in La Grange at the home of Georgia's Senator B. H. Hill, where they met Secretary Mallory and his wife and two other Confederate senators. The group was unaware that Davis had been captured, and, after hearing the news of Appomattox, the La Grange refugees assumed that they were in no danger from the enemy—until Virginia learned from a railroad conductor that Federals were in Macon and that huge rewards were offered for the arrest of Davis and Clay—her husband apparently because his recent mission to Canada had somehow linked him with Lincoln's murder in the minds of Washington officials.

Virginia hurried to the home of the Hills to find her husband calmly reading one of his favorite books, Robert Burton's *Anatomy of Melancholy.* She noted that Clay blanched when he heard the news, but he remained silent when the group broke into excited chatter, urging him to flee. "Fly from what?" Clay asked.

"From death, I fear," said Senator Semmes of Louisiana.

Mallory pointed out that the reward would tempt almost any Confederate soldier to betray him.

"But I am innocent of any conspiracy," Clay said. "I will surrender at once."

Virginia broke into sobs and begged him to flee, but Clay was adamant. He sent a telegram to General Wilson in Macon, saying that he was on his way to headquarters to turn himself in. The Clays were soon aboard a train en route to a reunion with Davis and other captives.

The Clay and Davis parties joined in Macon just as their train was ready to depart. Varina and her husband were already seated, on opposite sides of the aisle, when the Clays entered. The senator sat beside Varina, and Davis rose to embrace Virginia. "This is a sad meeting, Jennie," he said. She sat at his side, noting that his face was shockingly pale and drawn.

The coach filled with soldiers and a sergeant bawled an order. Musket butts thundered on the floor. "In the dull thud," Virginia Clay said, "I realized for the first time that we were indeed prisoners, and of the nation!" The train jerked into motion.

General Wilson, who watched stolidly through the uproar, seemed "somewhat saddened" when the train left—not for Davis, but as if he sensed in the departure of the captured President an ebbing of the excitement of the chase and capture, and of the war itself, which had become the chief concern of his life. Like thousands of men caught up in the national disaster which had brought so much death and destruction, the general apparently mourned the end of it as the passing of a great adventure.

The long ride over rough, recently repaired tracks left the Davis party "haggard and ill," and only the children slept through the night. As the train rocked on, Virginia Clay noted, the air in the car was "of the foulest," and the passengers suffered.

Crowds of civilians, drawn by the surprisingly rapid spread of news, greeted the train at each station, and approached Davis closely. The prisoners were guarded so carelessly that many Southerners upbraided Davis for "surrendering to what they considered certain death." Federal officers gave so little thought to an attempted escape that numbers of men and women were permitted to board the train; some of them begged Davis to allow them to overpower the few guards and rescue him. He refused, with a strained smile.

Once during the day someone tossed a small purse of gold coins through a coach window into Virginia Clay's lap, but Davis promptly handed it back to the man who had thrown it.

There were stops during the night, one at the remote village of Crawfordville, where the Confederate Vice-President Alexander Stephens boarded the train, a tiny figure swathed in a bulky overcoat despite the spring warmth. In February, when Abraham Lincoln had met him at an ill-fated peace conference aboard a ship in Hampton Roads, Va., Lincoln had said of Stephens as he removed his wrappings that he was "the biggest shuck and the littlest ear you ever did see." "Little Ellick" had been seized at his home in Crawfordville, where he had waited since the failure of the conference. Davis, who had not seen Stephens in the interim, did not glimpse him this night.

Stephens had left Richmond, he said, "in no ill-humor with Mr. Davis, or with any purpose of opposing the administration in any way, but because I could not sanction a policy which I thought would certainly end in disaster." His disclaimer was misleading, for Stephens had denounced Davis as "timid, peevish, obstinate and neither a statesman nor a genius." The strong-willed, self-assured little man had been affronted by Davis's failure to consult him on wartime policy.

Stephens had been a leader of opposition to Davis within the Confederacy. His theories of the sacred rights of the states, loftily intellectual, if impractical, had often conflicted with Confederate policies and with the realities of war. Stephens had voted against Georgia's secession and had campaigned for peace and reconciliation throughout the war. He regarded each state as a nation, and went further: "A citizen of the state has no allegiance to the Confederate States government . . . and can owe no military service to it except as required by his own state." In recent months he had castigated Davis in a long speech in which he declared: "Tell me not to put confidence in the President. . . . The most ill-timed, delusive and dangerous words that can be uttered are, 'Can you not trust the President?' "

Since he had been in almost total disagreement with the Davis administration, Stephens had spent most of the war in Georgia, ceaselessly writing and declaiming his opinions and prophesying ruin for the Confederacy. Though less bitter than some critics of Davis, his thin voice was seldom stilled during the war, raised always in defense of the constitutional rights of Georgia and other Southern states. He was incapable of compromise. A critic had said of him that Stephens had "only one distinguishing trait—he had a good opinion of himself." Another declared that Stephens would not die satisfied until he had corrected the proof of his own obituary.

His frailty and emaciation had made Stephens the butt of jokes and apocryphal tales. Richmond had laughed over the story of the wife of a newly elected official who called at the Stephens home and asked a black butler for Mrs. Stephens.

The butler stared. "Ma'am," he said, "Mr. Stephens ain't married. My God! Did you ever *see* him?"

Even in his better days the Confederate Vice-President had been a pathetic figure: "lean, yellow, care-worn, his back bent forward almost into a hump, one shoulder higher than the other, small arms and wasted legs. . . . His face . . . withered and twitching, his scanty hair on his shoulders in disorder . . . his restless eyes blazed with excitement. His voice . . . was sharp, shrill and squeaky."

Tonight, as he clambered aboard the little train as a prisoner of war, Stephens was "slim as a skeleton . . . nothing but skin, bone and cartilage . . . so feeble as to be hardly able to move about." The Confederate gnome weighed less than ninety pounds.

When they reached Augusta, Davis and Varina were driven to the riverside wharves in a "jimber-jawed, wobble-sided barouche drawn by two raw-boned horses," through streets warm with sunlight and fragrant with scents of flowers. Maggie Howell and the Davis children and their two nurses followed in a carry-all. Virginia and Clement Clay rolled along at the rear of the procession in another aged vehicle, passing through "an alien crowd," as Virginia said. People on the walks hooted derisively at the passing captives.

One Federal soldier shouted to a forlorn Confederate soldier in the crowd, "Hey, Johnny, we've got your President!"

The tattered Rebel called back, "And the Devil's got yours!"

Other captives joined the President here: General "Fighting Joe" Wheeler and officers of his staff. This miniature warrior, a humorless, dignified, earnest adversary, had fought the enemy to the last, a zealot to his cause. Wheeler's valor had astounded his staff, one of whom complained, "it overruns itself"; Wheeler was said to have fought flies with the same ferocity he had shown in fighting Sherman's advancing horde in the final weeks of the war. The intense young general betrayed his restlessness even now—but he had resolved to become a model prisoner for the moment, and to work for the restoration of the union.

As the party rode toward the riverfront, with Davis in the leading carriage and Alexander Stephens not far behind, a nine-year-old boy peered through the blinds of the Presbyterian minister's manse. He was Woodrow Wilson, the future President of the United States. The passage of the defeated leaders of the Confederacy, hauled along by their conquerors, was a scene he would remember.

The other prisoners and their families joined Davis at the Savannah River docks, where Federal soldiers herded all of them aboard a small, dirty harbor tug for the downstream trip to Savannah. The crude vessel lacked furnishings and had no cabins. Davis, who was suffering from intense pain in an eye, perched atop a stack of valises, while Virginia Clay, who was still at his side, bathed his temples with eau de cologne. Vice-President Stephens looked so wretched that Varina, forgetting bygones, settled him atop one of their mattresses and gave him a share of the plain but hearty supper she had bought from the boat's cooks—using some of the last of her meager hoard of coins. Both the President and Vice-President seemed to recover during the night. Davis went on deck in the early morning and there, for the first time in three months, spoke with Stephens.

The morning was warm, clear and sunny, with a fresh river breeze sweeping the deck as the tug fell downstream. Stephens had awakened refreshed, and after "a rough soldier's breakfast" had gone to the rail of the deck.

The President managed a civil greeting, but did not smile. The two spoke briefly, exchanging only a few words, and, as Stephens recalled it, "these were commonplace." Federal guards watched and listened attentively as the Confederate leaders met and quickly parted. War-long differences between them were too great to permit reconciliation or a show of warmth. Davis felt a sense of outrage at the opposition of Stephens, especially during recent months, when the tiny Georgian had spoken openly in criticism of the Davis administration, defending his cherished theory of state sovereignty even in the face of enemy invasion.

Today, however, Stephens felt a tug of sympathy for his stubborn, unforgiving chief: "Much as I disagreed with him," Stephens said, "and much as I deplored the ruin which, I think, his acts helped to bring upon the whole country, as well as on himself, I could not but deeply sympathize with him in his present condition."

The two leaders of the Confederacy realized that they faced charges of treason and would be tried—and that there was a rising cry for their execution. The Northern people were being prepared for this now that Davis had been captured. Within a few days the influential *Harper's Weekly* was to declare, "Treason is the highest crime known to the Constitution. . . . Jeff Davis must be tried for treason. If convicted, he must be sentenced. If sentenced, he must be executed . . . treason against the United States is not a political difference of opinion, but a crime whose enormity will not remit the legal penalty."

At Port Royal, near Savannah, the prisoners were transferred to the *William P. Clyde,* an oceangoing sidewheel steamer, and during these moments a tug came out from the city, crowded with jeering Federal soldiers and "their painted companions," who shouted obscenities at Davis until he disappeared into his cabin. Davis still did not know his destination, but assumed that he was being taken to Washington for imprisonment and a possible trial for treason.

The Davis children looked back tearfully as they boarded the ship, for they now had to part with their playmate, black Jim Limber, who had been their inseparable companion. Jim had "fought like a tiger" when he realized that he was being left behind, and ceased his frantic resistance only when overpowered by Federal soldiers. As a farewell gesture at this particularly painful parting, Virginia Clay tossed the little boy a twenty-five-cent piece from her almost empty purse. Davis later wrote to an old friend, the Federal general Rufus Saxton, and asked him to look after the boy and see to his education. Many years afterward Varina was to read a report in a Boston paper saying that Jim had complained that he would bear to his grave stripes given to him by the Davis family. Mrs. Davis could not believe that he had made the charge, "for the affection was mutual between us, and we had never punished him."

The *Clyde* churned away on its northward journey.

Newspapermen converged on Macon, Ga., eager for details of the most sensational story emerging from the Confederate collapse. Colonel Pritchard had been sent northward to accompany Davis to prison, but other officers and men who had taken part in the chase were interviewed. It was Wilson, however, who took over the publicizing of the President's capture.

After Wilson was told by Pritchard that Davis had worn a woman's clothing when captured, the story was rapidly embellished. General Halleck, who heard the news in Richmond, telegraphed Stanton, "If Jefferson Davis was captured in his wife's clothes, I respectfully suggest that he be sent north in the same habiliments."

General Wilson, eagerly accepting the attention drawn to him and his command, reported to Stanton that "the device adopted by Davis was even more ignoble than I reported at first." Davis, Wilson claimed, had worn a woman's bonnet as well as a dress, and also carried a weapon, a wicked-looking Bowie knife. The Northern press made much of this and cartoonists depicted Davis completely disguised in feminine regalia, until the story became accepted as factual. P. T. Barnum offered the government the substantial sum of $500 for Davis's dress, and, unable to acquire that, was soon displaying in his popular shows a figure of Davis wearing a hoopskirt some soldier had stolen from Varina's trunk. Thousands of children who saw this at Barnum's Museum never forgot the sight.

Wilson had trapped Davis through his stratagems and the skills of hundreds of veteran troops trained in tracking and intelligence work—but he had failed to apprehend Judah Benjamin or John Breckinridge, who, though less important as fugitives than the President, were eagerly sought by pursuers directed from Washington. These two Rebel leaders were now well along their way down Florida's "underground passage," desperate to reach a haven of safety beyond the reach of the implacable Edwin Stanton.

11

"This is not like being Secretary of State"

BENJAMIN and Breckinridge, resolved to escape the fate of President Davis, fled southward as if their lives were at stake. Both men endured hair-raising adventures on their way to freedom.

Within a few days after leaving the Davis party on the Savannah River, the disguised Benjamin ("Monsieur Bonfals") and his friend Colonel Leovy reached the relative safety of the sparsely settled state of Florida, where Leovy left for his home in New Orleans. The Secretary, Leovy thought, was never "so great as during that time of adversity," when he traveled in disguise and discomfort, living on the plainest fare, sleeping in log huts "with all his plans shattered and without definite hope for the future." Amid all this, Leovy said, Benjamin's "superb confidence and courage raised him above all; and he was the great, confident, cheerful leader that he had been in the days of his greatest prosperity."

Benjamin changed his disguise. He now became "Mr. Howard," a South Carolina planter in search of homesteads for himself and his neighbors. He persuaded a farmer's wife to make him ill-fitting clothes from the same homespun her husband wore, found rough, much-used harness for his horse, and continued his way southward through central Florida, avoiding settlements and towns. He learned that the Atlantic coast was heavily patrolled by Federal boats in search of escaping Confederates, so he turned toward the Gulf coast. He usually traveled by night, and since he covered only about thirty miles between sunset and dawn, his journey was long.

At times, Benjamin recalled later, he made his way only with the aid of miracles. One blazing hot day, riding a mule alone through palmetto scrub, he was confused by a maze of tracks which led in many directions. Rather than risk asking advice in the neighborhood, he tethered the mule and went to sleep in the underbrush.

He was awakened by a shrill cry, "Hi for Jeff!"

Benjamin, following the sound, saw a parrot in a tree. Reasoning that the bird had escaped from a house and that its owner was a loyal Confederate, Benjamin tossed pebbles at the parrot until it flew homeward. There, indeed, Benjamin discovered a farmer who was a Confederate sympathizer, and who dared to help him on his way.

Other Southern loyalists appeared to guide Benjamin through the trackless hammock country of the interior to the Florida west coast. Major John Lesley of Tampa, who was familiar with the wild region, led Benjamin to the Manatee River and found refuge for him in an imposing Greek Revival mansion on a sugar plantation. Benjamin was welcomed to the house by another fugitive, Captain Archibald McNeil, a former Confederate commissary officer.

When Federal troops appeared without warning, Benjamin and McNeil dashed into nearby thickets, followed, to their dismay, by McNeil's dog. But though Federal soldiers walked within a few feet of them, men and dog remained hidden quietly until the Yankees gave up the search and returned to their gunboat.

Benjamin was then taken to the home of Captain Fred Tresca, a Frenchman who had sailed a freight sloop along the Gulf coast before the war and had then become a fearless blockade-runner in the region. Tresca agreed to sail Benjamin southward along the coast, through the Keys and thence to the Bahamas. The captain enlisted the aid of a Confederate Navy veteran, H. A. McLeod, and led Benjamin to the home of another waterman of the neighborhood, Captain John Curry, who provided a boat for the journey. The craft was the *Blonde,* a sixteen-foot yawl which had lain hidden for two years in a deep creek, and was only now raised for Benjamin's use. The fugitive Secretary offered Tresca and McLeod $1,500 in gold "to expose their lives to the very great hazard" of sailing him down the coast, through the Keys and thence north by east to the Bahamas.

The three were carried overland to the shore of Sarasota Bay by the Reverend Ezechiel Glazier, who had been a member of Florida's Secession convention, and on June 23 they set sail for the South.

The heavily burdened *Blonde* made her way through the maze of inlets, bays and estuaries of the sparsely settled coast, past slow dark rivers that emptied into the Gulf: the Caloosahatchee, the Peace and the Myakka. As the yawl neared the broad, sheltered bay of Charlotte Harbor, Tresca caught sight of a Federal gunboat; a small boat was being lowered to pursue the *Blonde.* Tresca and McLeod maneuvered the yawl into Gasparilla Pass and hid the boat under a growth of mangroves, where the three men lay in the cramped hull, tormented by swarms of huge black mosquitoes. The Federal gunboat came so near that the fugitives heard the voices of their pursuers. But, as McLeod recalled it, "We kept quiet, so quiet indeed that above the voices of our enemies, and the taunting song of the mosquitoes, against whose attack we were quite helpless, rose the hollow sound of our beating hearts." Though the gunboat soon steamed out into the Gulf, Benjamin and his companions waited until late at night before building a small fire to breakfast on freshly caught fish, bacon and coffee. They remained on Gasparilla Island for two nights.

The *Blonde* moved warily southward, past Sanibel Island and the future site of the city of Naples. For two weeks they sailed on toward the Keys, pausing occasionally for water, or to fish or dig turtle eggs on the beaches.

Once more they encountered the enemy and this time could not avoid detection. Another gunboat sighted the *Blonde* in open water and steamed menacingly toward her. Ordered by Tresca to don the cook's cap and apron and busy himself in the galley, Benjamin smeared his face and arms with soot and grease and played his role so convincingly that Yankee sailors who boarded the yawl were soon satisfied. The Federals departed, but one of them left with a long glance at the plump cook and a remark that amused Benjamin for days: "It's the first time I ever saw a Jew at common labor."

By the end of the first week in July, after threading their way past hundreds of small islands, the fugitives reached Knight's Key. Here Tresca was able to obtain a larger, more stable, sailboat and dispose of the *Blonde,* which he feared was too fragile to challenge the open sea.

Tresca now sailed into the Atlantic, steering to the northeast for the British possession Bimini, some 125 miles away. They scudded swiftly along for the first two days, but when squalls blew up as the third night approached, Tresca and McLeod took in the sails, unstepped the mast and let out their anchor, preparing for a blow. The imperturbable Benjamin, who had said he hoped to see a waterspout, soon got his wish. "A very heavy, livid cloud" descended and two large spouts churned toward the small craft. The men heard the "furious whirl" of water within the spouts as they swayed over the sea, and realized that they would be swamped instantly if the spouts reached them. The full blast of the squall struck at the last moment, diverting the waterspouts, which passed within a hundred yards of the boat, "tearing up the whole surface of the sea . . . whirling it furiously into the clouds, with such a roar as is heard at the foot of Niagara Falls."

Water fell in sheets. McLeod bailed desperately with a tin pan and Benjamin aided him by using his hat. In the midst of this Benjamin grinned at the sailor. "McLeod, this is not like being Secretary of State." McLeod never forgot the corpulent Secretary's aplomb during the voyage: " . . . he enlivened the tedious hours and lessened the strain on our nerves by his cheerful spirit and humorous speeches." Though, as McLeod said, any man would have been frightened by the squall, Benjamin was "an awfully nervy man."

The fugitive's courage seemed to stem from his scorn for the enemy. As he wrote his sister, Benjamin preferred to risk death in attempting to escape rather than endure the "savage cruelty" he expected the Federals to inflict upon any Confederate leader who fell into their hands.

As Benjamin and his guides huddled against the driving rain, a third waterspout bore down upon them. This one, too, was checked by the force of a squall; the storm ended abruptly, and within a few moments the small boat was skimming toward safety over the long swells of the Bahama Sea.

Tresca and McLeod put Benjamin ashore in the Biminis on July 10, but his adventures were not over. He took passage for Nassau in a small sloop loaded with sponges and towing a skiff. The vessel sank thirty miles from land and foundered so swiftly that Benjamin and the native crew barely had time to scramble into the smaller boat.

Benjamin recalled, "In the skiff, leaky, with but a single oar, with no provisions save a pot of rice that had just been cooked for breakfast, and a small keg of water, I found myself at eight o'clock in the morning, with three Negroes for my companions in disaster, only five inches of the boat out of water." Even he realized that they were lost unless the sea remained perfectly calm—and their luck held until late afternoon, when they were rescued by the *Georgina,* a lighthouse vessel.

Back ashore, Benjamin met Tresca and McLeod and persuaded them to sail him to Nassau in a chartered sloop. Though head winds, calms and squalls kept them at sea for six days, Benjamin reached Nassau "contented and cheerful under all reverses." A few days later, taken to Havana by a British steamer, he was hospitably received by a colony of Southern refugees. One of these was General Edmund Kirby Smith, who had just arrived from Vera Cruz, Mexico, after the disbanding of his Trans-Mississippi armies.

Misfortune dogged Benjamin even on his departure for England. He sailed aboard a British steamer on September 6, but near St. Thomas the vessel burst into flames and only after a desperate battle by passengers and crew was it able to limp back into harbor. Two days later Benjamin sailed for England once more, this time on an uneventful voyage that led him to a new life.

John Breckinridge, who had led his small band southward from Washington, Ga., in hope of overtaking President Davis, made his own way to Florida in the face of obstacles as forbidding as those overcome by Benjamin. The Secretary of War traveled with few companions—his sons Cabell and Clifton and his cousin W. C. P. Breckinridge; General Basil Duke, young James Clay, the grandson of Henry Clay; Colonel James Wilson; a black servant called Tom Ferguson, and "a few others" who acted as guards.

Breckinridge assumed a simple disguise by merely shaving his familiar drooping mustache and ordering his companions to call him "Colonel Cabell." The party dwindled rapidly. General Duke and W. C. P. Breckinridge left to surrender to Federal officers and return home to Kentucky. The general then sent his son Clifton and James Clay homeward, and led his remaining party toward Madison, Florida. It was an emotional parting as he entrusted the twelve-year-old Clifton with a prized sword and a letter to a friend in Kentucky. Clifton had always been his father's favorite.*

*These two boys were captured near Macon on May 10. A Federal soldier who took the handsome sword from Clifton later named his own son Breckinridge. The letter, which never reached its destination, contained Breckinridge's comment on his service as Confederate Secretary of War, "Should my friends ever know my part in the occurrences of the past three months, I venture to think it will give me an increased claim on their confidence and regard." Clifton Breckinridge took his parole in Macon and made his way home.

On May 10, the day President Davis was captured at Irwinville, Ga., Breckinridge camped within ten miles of that village, unaware that his chief had been taken prisoner.

On May 14, resting near the Florida border in hope of meeting Davis, Breckinridge learned of the President's capture. He dismissed the last few troopers of his escort and rode into Florida with Cabell, Colonel Wilson and Tom Ferguson. They soon reached the town of Madison, where they were joined by Captain John Taylor Wood, and learned details of the President's capture and of Wood's own ingenious escape.

Both Wood and Breckinridge were anxious to disappear into the Florida "underground passage": the Secretary of War had been branded as a traitor, and marked for hanging by the legislature of Federally occupied Tennessee; he was soon to be indicted for treason by a grand jury in Washington, D.C. Wood, as commander of the deadly Rebel raider *Tallahassee,* was being hunted as a "pirate" whose depredations were second only to those of Admiral Raphael Semmes.

From Madison, Breckinridge sent his son Cabell homeward, hoping to spare him the torment of mosquito bites, to which the boy was dangerously allergic. Cabell rode off to Tallahassee to be paroled and his father continued southward. With Wood and Wilson and Ferguson, he crossed the Suwannee River at a ferry used by Judah Benjamin only two days earlier. Breckinridge and his men left the Suwannee on May 17, riding through dry, barren scrub, vexed by "countless and intolerable" mosquitoes, as they made their way past Collins, a lonely stagecoach station on the Santa Fe River, and into Gainesville.

In this town Breckinridge met Colonel J. J. Dickison, "The Swamp Fox of The Confederacy," who advised him to change his intended direction and make his way across the Florida peninsula to the east coast, rather than seek safety on the heavily patrolled Gulf coast as Benjamin had done. Breckinridge agreed.

After a slow, arduous march across the interior under the guidance of Lieutenant William McCardell, the party reached the St. Johns River, where they found a boat provided by Dickison. Three ex-soldiers were to man the oars in times of contrary winds: Sergeant Joseph O'Toole, Corporal Richard Russell and Private P. Murphy. Breckinridge inspected the boat dubiously—she was only seventeen or eighteen feet long, a small sailing cutter which had once served as a lifeboat on a captured Federal gunboat.

The overloaded boat, riding so low in the water that she almost sank beneath the party of seven, set off to the southward up the St. Johns, with the three soldiers at the oars. They were forced to row against the current for two days, anchoring in midstream by night to avoid clouds of mosquitoes on the banks. Breckinridge found the St. Johns "the most crooked and bewildering stream I ever saw," and even the veteran Captain Wood, their helmsman, was frequently led astray by false channels.

Private Murphy left them on May 29, a day when Captain Wood and Sergeant O'Toole walked several miles across the sandy countryside, hoping to find a wagon that would transfer their boat some thirty miles eastward to the Indian River, a tidal estuary that ran roughly parallel to the north-south course of the St. Johns along the coast. With the aid of one George Sauls, an illiterate but cunning Florida "Cracker," they made the portage by carrying the boat on a rickety farm cart drawn by two oxen, and on the last day of May emerged on the Indian River. Just to the eastward, across a narrow barrier of dunes, lay the Atlantic, the pathway to safety.

On June 3, when they neared Jupiter Inlet, the party laboriously hauled the boat fifty yards across the sand and launched her in the ocean. "What a relief it is," Captain Wood said, "to get out of the swamps and marshes of the Indian River into the blue waters . . . and the freedom from mosquitoes; what enjoyment to us, who have been punctured and bled for the past two weeks." Wood turned the vessel to the south, hugging the coastline. They landed near dawn at the future site of Palm Beach, where they rested, swam in the sea, found fresh water inland and dug green-turtle eggs for breakfast. At dusk Wood turned the boat out to sea on a course for the Grand Bahamas some seventy miles away, but they were soon forced back to the coast by contrary winds.

The Breckinridge party had a close call the following day, when a Federal troop transport halted to investigate the fugitive party and lowered a small boat full of men armed with cutlasses and pistols. Wood and the two soldiers, O'Toole and Russell, sailed out to meet the enemy as Breckinridge watched apprehensively from a hiding place ashore.

Assuming the speech of a Florida fisherman, Wood explained to the Federals that they were fishing, hunting and salvaging materials from wrecked ships. The captain played the role of a rustic so convincingly that the enemy party turned back and the steamer disappeared.

On June 6, still held to the coast by contrary winds, Wood decided to turn southward toward Cuba, rather than await favorable breezes which might carry them the shorter route to the Bahamas. Within a few hours they met another small boat, a sloop which was beating its way northward. Wood and Breckinridge at first feared capture, but when the newcomers veered away Wood suspected that they were escaped convicts from the Dry Tortugas. Captain Wood resolved to capture the sloop, which was larger and more seaworthy than his lifeboat. After a long row in a calm, they overtook the vessel, which hove to when Wood fired a pistol shot across her bow.

The sloop's three men, obviously intimidated by the sight of Breckinridge's bearded and bedraggled crew, submitted to being disarmed when the general and Captain Wood boarded their boat. Breckinridge threatened his captives with hanging, but then relented: "The war's not over for us," he said. "You're our prisoners and your boat is a prize. You're deserters and pirates—but under the circumstances we'll take your paroles and exchange boats with you."

The relieved escapees willingly agreed, accepted $20 in gold offered by Breckinridge to seal the bargain, and sailed on northward in the lifeboat.

Wood discovered that the sloop sailed well, though she was slow, and turned her southward, now confident that they could escape by sailing a direct course to Cuba.

Their course would take them past Fort Dallas, a limestone ruin on the site of the future city of Miami, thence past Elliott Key, about twenty miles south of Fort Dallas, where they gathered food for the crossing to Cuba. Here Breckinridge shot two pelicans and a heron. Tom Ferguson cooked the birds, but after Breckinridge had eaten one bite of pelican he hurried wordlessly into the underbrush and quickly returned. "His tone and expression," Wood said, were testimony enough that pelican was inedible.

They sailed on, past Key Largo, where Wood turned the boat into the open sea, hoping to sail across the Gulf Stream to safety in Cuba.

The first night out opened with a severe electrical storm, and near daybreak, when the inept Colonel Wilson was at the helm, the fugitives narrowly averted disaster. O'Toole and Russell, both seasick, lay in the bottom of the boat. Breckinridge and Tom Ferguson dozed and Captain Wood was sitting forward when a sudden wave broke over the bow, half filled the boat and swept Wood overboard. Breckinridge saw that Wilson was steering "as stiff as a stanchion," holding like grim death to the tiller and the sheet as the boat heeled dangerously.

"Let go the rope!" Breckinridge shouted, and when the startled helmsman did so the boat righted herself at once. Wood reappeared, having caught a loose line as he was swept sternward. The captain then took the helm and would not relinquish it for the next twelve hours. They were off on a sea passage as perilous as that endured by Judah Benjamin a few days earlier.

The wind, freshened into a gale, swept the sloop along over giant seas, some of them twenty feet high. Wood almost lost hope of reaching land—he had never felt such danger in his nineteen years at sea. Breckinridge watched in amazement as Wood kept the "egg-shell" afloat—but the captain finally gave up his attempts at steering. The sloop bobbed and lurched at will, driven before the wind. O'-Toole and Russell bailed furiously and the frightened Tom Ferguson huddled beside Breckinridge.

By now they were without food. All the men were blistered and dehydrated. Breckinridge stood guard over the water keg, rationing an occasional sip to each of the thirsty men.

Soon after dawn, when the sea had calmed, the sloop sailed near a U.S. merchant ship, the brig *Neptune* out of Bangor. Breckinridge boldly called for water: "They stared very hard at us, but no explanations were demanded or given." Despite his misgivings the Yankee skipper lowered five gallons of water and a dozen hard ship's biscuits. It was his generosity, Breckinridge thought, that saved their lives.

On June 10, safely across the Gulf Stream, the fugitives sighted the keys off the Cuban coast and realized that they were safe. Two days later they heard church bells from the town of Cardenas, and were soon ashore. The escapees were fed and clothed by families of the Confederate colony, serenaded by a Cuban crowd, and entertained at a gala banquet. Soon afterward, Breckinridge found an enthusiastic welcome in Havana, where he was offered a house if he agreed to make his home there.

Attorney General George Davis, who had been the first Cabinet member to resign during the flight, left Charlotte, N. C., for the South once he had arranged for the care of his children. After a brief visit in Camden, S. C., with his brother, the Reverend Thomas F. Davis, the blind bishop of South Carolina, the fugitive moved through upland South Carolina and Georgia into Florida. Carrying only the clothing in his saddle bags and traveling under the name of "Hugh Thompson," he eluded all Federal patrols.

In early June he stopped at the farmhouse of a cousin, Mrs. Thomas Hill Lane, about twenty miles from Lake City, Fla. His identity was so carefully guarded that Mr. Lane, who had never met Davis, was at first unaware of who his visitor was.

George Davis left Gainesville in mid-June, hid for a time in Ocala, and moved into the wilderness of west central Florida, which he found "the very verge of civilization and clean beyond good morals and religion." For three months he wandered in this region, seeking to avoid detection, in search of someone who might help him escape the country. Still in disguise, he stopped at isolated farmhouses in the scrub, where he was taken in without question and offered "rude but warm hospitality." He found no means of leaving Florida by boat, and knew nothing of the passage of Benjamin or Breckinridge to safety. At last, in September 1865, when he had begun to despair, George Davis found an Italian seaman in New Smyrna who was soon to sail for Nassau.

Attorney General Davis had no money, and since he dared not reveal his identity, the captain said he must work for his passage. Davis was dismayed by the sight of the boat which awaited him: "When I saw the craft in which he proposed to make the voyage, I was amazed at the rashness of the undertaking," he said. He knew the dread reputation of the Gulf Stream between Florida and the Bahamas in the hurricane season: " . . . fancy the attempt to cross it during the equinox in a little boat about 20 feet long and seven feet wide, with rotten sails and a leaky hull!"

But the Italian was resolved to sail and Davis refused to be left behind. "With good luck," the captain said, "we'll make Nassau in five or six days."

In fact they were thirty-three days "beating about the coast, sometimes on the open sea and sometimes in the bays and among the reefs and keys." Often half starved, they survived "numberless anxieties, difficulties, troubles and hardships and dangers." The passage was so confused and violent that Davis, laboring as a deckhand, had no idea of their whereabouts and could keep no track of the passage of time.

Balked by the heavy storms of late September and early October, the Italian sailed down to Key West, where he planned to take the shortest sea route to Cuba. Here Davis heard that Alexander Stephens, John Reagan and George Trenholm had already served terms in Federal prisons and had been released. Reasoning that his term would be no longer than those served by his colleagues, George Davis decided to surrender to the Federal government. He was in Key West, awaiting northward passage for this purpose, when he was arrested and shipped to Fort Lafayette in New York Harbor, where he was imprisoned for less than three months.

Secretary of the Navy Mallory, who had no intention of attempting to escape, had joined his family in the home of Senator Benjamin Hill in La Grange, Ga., when a band of Federal soldiers burst in at midnight and rushed off with him, though he was only "half-dressed." Mallory was charged with "treason and setting on foot piratical expeditions."

The Secretary discovered that his contributions to modern naval warfare while building the small Confederate Navy had outraged public opinion in the North. His work in the development of the torpedo and submarine and the devastation among U.S. merchant shipping by daring Rebel sea raiders had singled him out for denunciation as an outlaw. Some embittered Northerners demanded that Mallory be hanged for his activities.

Secretary of the Treasury George Trenholm, after leaving the Davis party near Charlotte because of poor health, made his way to Abbeville, S. C., where he arrived after Federal troops had occupied the town. He was not arrested, but was allowed to take his family to Columbia, S. C., where he was placed under "constructive arrest" and allowed to go to his home town, Charleston.

Admiral Raphael Semmes, who had left Greensboro, N. C., after his carefully worded surrender on May 1, rode southward in a baggage wagon, accompanied only by young Raphael, half a dozen officers and two or three servants. By the end of May the party reached the Semmes home in Montgomery, Ala., where the admiral's family had assembled. The admiral declared that his conscience was clear and that he could see nothing in his wartime career "with which I have to reproach myself as unbecoming a man of honor and a gentleman

. . . I rendered this service without ever having treated a prisoner other than humanely . . . and without ever having committed an act of war . . . which was not sanctioned by the laws of war. Yet my name will probably go down to posterity in the untruthful histories that will be written . . . as a sort of Blue Beard or Captain Kidd. . . . The President treats me as an outlaw, unworthy of amnesty. I have nothing to say. If I am deemed unworthy to be a citizen, I can remain in my native land as an alien."

Semmes expected to salvage no more than $5,000 of his fortune, but resolved to retire to a farm to spend his old age. He was not to be permitted to realize his dream.

Several other Southern leaders who had played roles in the flight of Davis and the Cabinet were imprisoned. North Carolina's Governor Zebulon Vance, who had gone to his home in Statesville after being assured by General John Schofield in Greensboro that there were no orders for his arrest, was seized on May 15 and sent to Washington under guard; he was soon released, returned to North Carolina, and was once more to become governor of the state—the first to succeed himself in that office.

General Robert Toombs, who had once served as Confederate Secretary of State, vowed that he would not be captured, and when Federal soldiers appeared at his home in Washington, Ga., on May 12, he escaped by a back door and rode off on a wandering trail to safety. After spending months in hiding in rural Georgia, he asked his wife to inquire whether he would be paroled if he surrendered, but President Johnson ordered that he be imprisoned if captured. That was enough for Toombs, who sailed first to Cuba and then to Paris, whence he finally returned home via Canada. After some months he called on President Johnson in Washington but did not request clemency then or later. When asked why he had not sought a pardon, Toombs said, "Pardon for what? I have not pardoned you all yet."

PART

4

THE PRISONER

"With all the archives of our government in the hands of your government, do they despair of proving him a rogue, falsifier, assassin and traitor—that they must in addition guard him like a wild beast, and chain him for fear his unarmed hands will in a casemated cell subvert the government?... He is not held for the ends of Justice but for those of torture.... Is no one among you bold enough to defend him?"

—VARINA DAVIS TO HORACE GREELEY, BEGGING AID FOR HER HUSBAND.

12

"Oh, the shame! The shame"

LONG before his companions had met their varied fates, Jefferson Davis had been imprisoned under conditions which outraged the Southern people and blinded them—permanently—to the fact that the policy of the conquerors toward Confederate leaders was essentially lenient. Alone among those who had played leading roles in the rebellion, Davis was to be imprisoned for a long period and given unusually harsh treatment. His travail at Fort Monroe became a climactic event of the war and created major shifts in public opinion, north and south.

The voyage of the President's party northward from Savannah aboard the *Clyde* was stormy and several passengers were seasick. All of the prisoners were watched with care: Davis and Alexander Stephens and Clement Clay, John Reagan, Burton Harrison, William Preston Johnston, Frank Lubbock, General Wheeler and his staff, and the President's young brother-in-law, Jefferson Davis Howell. Like the prisoners themselves, Varina Davis and her children and Virginia Clay were uncertain of their status and knew nothing of where they would be taken.

President Davis suffered an attack of neuralgia and spent hours on deck, often pacing with Piecake in his arms, looking frail and ill, but composed. A New York *Times* reporter noted that "he seems to be the observed of all observers" as Federals sought to plumb the mystery of the strangely reserved man who had led the Confederacy and came so near destroying the Union.

The little steamer toiled along under the close guard of the

U. S. S. *Tuscarora,* whose gunners were kept on alert. The captives were amused to learn that the enemy feared an attack by the Confederate ram *Stonewall,* reported to be still at sea. The cautious guards removed emergency axes from the bulkheads to prevent an uprising by the captives, but security was otherwise so lax that the soldiers usually went below to meals, leaving muskets stacked on the deck. General Wheeler urged Davis to attempt an escape, "Let's grab the guns. The ten of us would soon be masters of this situation." Davis refused to listen.

His friends observed that the President sought to avoid the appearance of grief aboard the ship, though some of them believed that he was on his way to the gallows. Davis's efforts at normal conversation left a lasting impression of his aplomb with General Wheeler: "President Davis showed not the slightest trepidation, but reviewed the situation as calmly as if he had no personal interest in it. He discussed the war, its men and incidents, in the same dispassionate way that a traveller might speak of scenes and incidents in some foreign land."

The *Clyde* left the open sea and turned in through the Virginia Capes into the Chesapeake on May 19, as if she were bound up the bay for Washington, where Davis expected to be taken. Instead, the ship anchored in Hampton Roads within sight of the grim bulk of old Fort Monroe. The captives waited aboard, ignorant as to the cause of delay. On May 20, with no announcement as to their destination, most of the prisoners were told to prepare for immediate departure—but Jefferson Davis and Clement Clay were to remain behind. Davis went on deck to say farewell to his old friends and associates.

He embraced Burton Harrison tearfully; the young secretary was in fact bound for Washington, where Edwin Stanton hoped to wring from him evidence of Davis's guilt in the death of Lincoln. Among the others departing was Jefferson Davis Howell, who, though already paroled, was soon to be jailed simply because he was the President's brother-in-law. There were also General Wheeler and his staff, William Preston Johnston and Frank Lubbock, who were destined for prison in Fort Delaware, near Philadelphia. Alexander Stephens and John Reagan were taken away as well—bound for damp cells at Fort Warren in Boston Harbor.

There was a fond farewell between Davis and Reagan. For years the Texan retained a vivid memory of their parting and later said of

Davis, "I loved him as I never loved any other man." The frail Stephens, who expected to be hanged, approached Davis at the last moment with a woebegone expression. He held out his tiny hand, which Davis clasped wordlessly before he turned away. Some warmth of feeling passed between them but it was not affection. As Stephens wrote long afterward, "I was not very friendly and in no way chummy with Mr. Davis, but I wish to say that he was the bravest and most courageous man I ever knew."

Of the fates planned for these men Davis knew nothing. He and Clement Clay knew no more of their own future. They could only surmise that they were held aboard the *Clyde* for later transfer. There was no explanation as to why they were anchored at Fort Monroe.

For two days longer, without a hint as to what their captors planned for them, the Davis family and Clement and Virginia Clay waited aboard the ship. They saw a bustle about the fort as workmen moved in and out, but expected the *Clyde* to get up steam at any moment and sail up the Chesapeake into the Potomac and thence to Washington, the most likely place for the confinement of state prisoners.

There was a fresh commotion at the fort on May 22, when a ship from the north eased into the dock, and several bluecoated officers emerged. Soon afterward a double line of Federal soldiers formed from the docks to the walls of the fort. With only ten minutes' warning Davis and Clay were taken from the *Clyde* and hurried ashore amidst the wailing of women, children and servants. At the first warning of this Little Jeff ran to his mother in terror. "They say they've come for Father. Beg them to let us go with him." Davis embraced Varina. "It's true," he said, "I must go at once." Looking into her stricken face he whispered, "Try not to weep, they will gloat over your grief."

An observant Federal official noted that Davis was flushed, and wore an expression of "hauteur," but Varina, who felt the violent tremors of his thin body as she held him, realized that the flush was due to a high fever, and his "hauteur" was in fact a proud, defiant concealment of his distress. She was calm until he was gone—then wept, receiving no comfort from Virginia Clay, who said firmly, "I should die before they should see me shed tears." At this moment it seemed that it was Mrs. Clay who was the President's kindred spirit and that Varina was merely a distraught onlooker.

Little Jeff looked after his father in tearful belligerence. "I'll kill every Yankee in the country when I grow up," he shouted.

Varina watched Davis move onto the wharf between the blue lines, walking feebly but with a quick, light step. A young Federal officer wearing the stars of a brigadier general gripped the President's stringy arm as if he feared that he might even now make a dash for freedom. Varina remembered the moment later: ". . . as we looked, as we thought, our last upon his stately form and knightly bearing, he seemed a man of another and higher race, upon whom 'shame would not dare to sit.' " She nourished a bitter memory of the abrupt parting forced by the enemy: "With a refinement of cruelty worthy of savages we were not told we were to meet no more." She begged for permission to send a note, or even a verbal message, to her husband, but was brusquely refused.

As the figures of the prisoners and their guards diminished in the distance ashore, those on the ship could see Davis leading the way into the fort, still clasped by the general. Clay followed, led by Colonel Benjamin Pritchard, who was included in the ceremony to honor his role as the captor of Davis. A strong guard of bluecoats brought up the rear.

Davis now had his first glimpse of the interior of the fort since he had visited it as Secretary of War, many years before. On that occasion a fireworks display had emblazoned his name in the sky, linked with that of President Franklin Pierce. Virginia Clay, who had been with him at that time, had a vivid memory of the visit and must have recalled it as Davis went from sight.

The massive walls of "The Gibraltar of the Chesapeake" were more than thirty feet high and fifty feet thick in the area of the casemates. A line of sentries barred the road to the fort. The only entries were three drawbridges raised and lowered by windlass to span a moat that was eight feet deep. This moat was 125 feet wide below Casemate No. 2, where Davis was to be kept. In the outer cell of his casemate were an officer and two soldiers; the officer was under orders to see the prisoner at least once every quarter hour. Two more guards were posted outside the door, and the key was kept only by "the general officer of the guard."

The flanking casemates were occupied by off-duty guards and other sentries were posted on the opposite bank of the moat and on the ramparts overhead. All told, more than seventy guards were constantly on watch. Two of these, among the most trustworthy, were to pace beside the cot in the Davis cell, day and night.

Neither verbal nor written communication with the famous prisoner was to be permitted. Guards were forbidden to respond to Davis or to speak in his presence. In case of illness, the doctor was to be accompanied on visits by the duty officer. The lamp in the Davis cell was kept burning all night so that the prisoner could be kept under observation, even while taking a sponge bath or using the small portable toilet.

These remarkable security measures had been taken on orders from Secretary of War Edwin Stanton, who still sought, by whatever means, to implicate Davis in the Lincoln murder plot. The unstable Stanton, who seemed to see conspiracies on every hand, may have suspected that General Sherman might aid Rebel leaders in an attempt to free Davis, and was resolved to make such a rescue impossible.

Stanton had sent two men to ensure the safety of his prisoners: Henry Halleck, the Army's chief of staff, whose retailing of Richmond gossip had circulated reports of vast riches in the Confederate treasure trains; and Charles A. Dana, the Assistant Secretary of War, who bore a secret order for even harsher security measures to be taken against Davis and Clay.

In addition, Stanton had chosen, with the aid of General Grant, a special jailer to keep watch over the two important prisoners of state. This officer was Brigadier General Nelson A. Miles, a twenty-six-year-old former crockery clerk from Boston. Stanton had rejected West Point-trained officers on the theory that they would be sticklers for military etiquette in the treatment of the prisoners. When Stanton asked for a veteran devoted to duty and iron-fisted discipline, Grant sent him General Miles, who had risen rapidly in rank because of gallantry in combat. The boy general, Grant promised, "will by no possibility permit the escape of the prisoners."

The New York *Herald* approved the arrangements: "Davis can never escape . . . He is literally in a living tomb . . . Napoleon at St. Helena was [not] subjected to greater surveillance. . . . No more will Jefferson Davis be known among the masses of men. . . . His life has been a cheat. His last free act was an effort to unsex himself and deceive the world. He is . . . buried alive."

Both Federal authorities and the *Herald*'s editors failed to realize that the possibility of escape from the fort never entered the President's mind. He hoped for a prompt trial as a Secessionist, confident that he would clear his name in court and legitimize the cause of the fallen Confederacy.

Once he had seen Davis safely into his cell, Miles left and the iron door clanged behind him. As the two guards paced, Davis inspected the cell briefly and stooped to peer through the bars of the embrasure, across the moat to the masonry wall towering beyond. There was a heavy scent of stagnant water.

The prisoner turned to one of the soldiers, "Which way does the embrasure face?"

There was no reply. Davis raised his voice and repeated the question, but the guard remained silent. As if he thought the soldier deaf, Davis turned to his companion and repeated the question once more. He then understood that the men had heard but were forbidden to speak. Despite the presence of the constantly pacing men, his confinement was to be solitary.

At night Davis was brought a chunk of bread and a gray slab of boiled beef on a tin plate. The only utensil was a wooden spoon —no knife or fork was allowed, lest the prisoner slash his wrists or throat and spoil the hanging Stanton had planned for him. Davis did not eat. He sat on his cot reading the Bible—the sixteenth psalm, which included the verse, "For thou wilt not leave my soul in hell; neither wilt thou suffer thine Holy One to see corruption."

At dusk on May 23 Captain Jerome Titlow, the fort's officer of the day, entered the cell with a burly blacksmith, under orders from Miles to shackle Davis. They found the President seated on his cot, still reading his Bible. The bread and beef brought to him the night before lay untouched in the tin plate at his bedside. Davis called in a weak voice, "Well?"

Titlow, perhaps inadvertently, violated orders by responding. "I have an unpleasant duty to perform, sir," he said. The smith took the clanking chain from his assistant. Davis leapt from the cot when he saw the shackles and clutched his throat, "now appearing to swell with indignation and then to shrink with terror."

"My God! You've not been sent to iron me?"

"My orders, sir." The wrought-iron shackles were more than half an inch thick, linked by a heavy chain.

Davis looked wildly about the cell. "Monstrous," he said. "Captain, I demand to see the commanding officer—shackles for a weak old man—here, with all these guards?"

"It's no use," the captain said. "His orders, and mine, come from Washington."

"He can telegraph," Davis said. "There's been some mistake. There's been no such outrage in history. Beg him to telegraph and wait for a reply."

Titlow said his orders were peremptory. "I cannot delay," he said. "For your own sake I advise you to submit. As a soldier, you know, Mr. Davis, that I must carry out my orders."

The old man shouted in a rising voice, "These are no orders for a soldier! They're for a hangman! No soldier should accept them. The world will ring with this disgrace, I tell you! The war's over. The South is conquered. America is my only country. I plead against this degradation for the honor of America!"

Davis spread his arms. "Kill me!" he said. "Kill me!" He strode the cell in agitation and finally paused to place one foot on his chair. Titlow, assuming that the prisoner had submitted, ordered the smith to shackle Davis, but as the soldier knelt to rivet an ankle iron in place, the wiry Davis knocked him to the floor. The infuriated smith sprang to his feet with upraised hammer. Titlow stepped between them and Davis flattened himself against the wall, awaiting an attack.

"No," the captain said. "This is madness. Don't force me to violence."

"I'm a prisoner of war," Davis said. "I've been a soldier. I know how to die. Kill me! This thing will not be done so long as I have strength to resist."

Titlow called in four men from the adjoining cell. Davis sprang forward and seized the musket of the first man, but the soldiers flung the thin body onto the cot. Even now Davis resisted, kicking off the blacksmith with a supreme effort—a "show of unnatural strength," Titlow said. At last the four men overcame the prisoner and held him as the smith hammered a rivet through the shackle on one ankle and fastened the other with a huge brass lock ("the same as in use on freight cars," Titlow said). Davis lay for a moment "as if in a stupor," then sat and dropped his shackled feet to the floor, held his face in his hands and sobbed, rocking to and fro. "Oh, the shame! The shame."

Orders for the shackling had come from Edwin Stanton, borne

by Charles Dana—but it was General Miles who decided that they should be carried out. Stanton had given a discretionary order, but Dana had urged that the shackles be applied at once. He was overruled by General Halleck, and then contented himself with leaving an order for Miles to apply the leg irons whenever he saw fit. As soon as they had seen Davis into his cell, Halleck and Dana left the fort. Miles carried out the order immediately.

The young brigadier general of volunteers, who yearned for a regular commission as a means of escaping the life of a clerk, was eager to please both Charles Dana and Secretary Edwin Stanton. Already he exhibited the driving ambition which would make him commander-in-chief of the U.S. Army, and win him acclaim as a hero of the Indian wars on the plains of the developing west.

The second day of Davis's shackling brought into his cell for the first time an unusual medical officer, Lieutenant Colonel John J. Craven of New Jersey, a kindly man who was to record most of what is known of the imprisonment of Jefferson Davis. He also saved the ex-President's life, foiled the efforts of Miles to hold the prisoner incommunicado and forced a major change in government policy toward state prisoners.

Craven was a slender, handsome officer of forty-two, with courteous urbane manners. He wore the full sideburns and mustache then fashionable with U.S. Army officers. When not attending patients, Craven pursued his hobbies—gathering rare insects, fish and herbs for the Smithsonian Institution and for his own collections.

Dr. Craven had also been a carpenter, inventor, naturalist, sanitarian, family physician, army surgeon, industrial chemist and successful businessman. As a youth he had been befriended by Samuel F. B. Morse, with whom he worked in the early experiments in telegraphy. Craven developed the first successful underwater cable by preparing a gutta-percha covering on his kitchen stove—but was denied the fruits of his invention by the U.S. Patent Office, which found nothing unique in his concept. Craven also worked with the inventor Samuel Colt in developing a "torpedo" for blowing up ships.

After studying medicine with a doctor and attending lectures, Craven had begun his own medical practice in 1856. He was serving as coroner in Newark when war broke out and he was named surgeon of the First New Jersey Regiment—a position he lost when the local medical society protested his lack of a diploma. The resolute Craven took his case to Washington, to Abraham Lincoln himself, who ordered that Craven be given an examination for brigade surgeon. The doctor not only passed the test but survived a subsequent hearing before the Secretary of War as well. He had filled several important medical posts during the war before being assigned to Fort Monroe and the care of Jefferson Davis.

Craven was startled to find the old man chained in irons, and was alarmed by his physical condition: "Mr. Davis presented a very miserable and affecting aspect, his eyes restless and fevered, his head shifting from side to side for a cool spot on the pillow. His pulse was full and at ninety, tongue thickly coated, his extremities cold and his head troubled with a long-established neuralgic disorder." Davis was so emaciated that his skin chafed against the slats of the cot, which was covered by a wafer-thin pad.

Craven saw that the President's "intense cerebral excitement was the first thing needing attention," and that evening he carried tobacco to the prisoner. Davis lit his pipe, the only object other than his clothing and Bible he had been permitted to take from the *Clyde.* "This is a noble medicine," he said. "With this I hope to become tranquil."

Craven also provided a more comfortable mattress, but Miles ignored his plea that the shackles be removed. It was only when newspaper reporters at the fort learned of the leg irons and published details that the jailer relented. These stories, widely reprinted, aroused such indignation even in the North that the powerful political leader Thurlow Weed, with his infallible ear for the slightest stir among the electorate, wrote Stanton that the shackling had been "an error and an enormity . . . wholly unnecessary severity. If a mistake has been made I am sure it was made without authority and I pray that you will immediately correct it." Stanton did so. Miles removed the leg irons on May 28, after Davis had suffered them for five days.

When Craven went to the cell the next day the grateful Davis wept, crediting him with his relief. The doctor turned the talk to treatment and urged him to take exercise to regain strength and circulation in his legs. But Davis could think only of Varina's reaction to news of his shackling. "Oh, my poor wife, my poor, poor girl! . . . I wish she could have been spared this knowledge . . . I can see the hideous announcement with its flaming capitals . . . how much her pride and love will both be shocked."

Davis did not seem to foresee the response of the Southern people to the news of his harsh treatment by Stanton, but it was inevitably more dramatic than the reaction in the North. His people identified themselves with their leader in his suffering, and many of his former critics were silenced. Overnight the ex-President's reputation was transformed. The image of a new hero began to rise, and that of the scapegoat to fade.

John Reagan was to write his old chief, "The great mass of our people regard you as suffering in your own person for and on account of them." The poet Sidney Lanier, a Confederate veteran who had also been imprisoned, went further. "If there was guilt in any there was guilt in nigh all of us. . . . Mr. Davis, if he be termed the ringleader of the rebellion, was not so by virtue of any instigating act of his, but purely by the unanimous will and appointment of the Southern people. . . . The hearts of the Southern people bleed to see how their own act has resulted in the chaining of Mr. Davis, who was as innocent as they. . . ."

13

"Ankle deep in gold and silver"

DURING the capture and imprisonment of Jefferson Davis and his companions, the chase for the imagined El Dorado of Confederate gold and silver became frantic, spurred by gossip among Southerners as well as by the telegrams from the overwrought Stanton to his officers. The Georgia backwoods, so lately the scene of a manhunt, were now witness to a spectacular gold rush by both Confederates and Federals.

The Virginia bank tellers, led by Judge W. W. Crump, had continued their anxious journey into Washington, Ga., after passing the caravan of Varina Davis, and deposited their funds in the vault of a local bank on May 3—the same day that the President had arrived in the town. Crump spent the night in the home of Judge Garnett Andrews, the father of young Eliza Andrews, the alert diarist of the Confederacy's last days. The two judges conferred anxiously about the danger to the Virginia bank funds, since lawless bands of Confederates filled the town, and Federal troops were expected at any moment. Crump sought a meeting with the President to discuss the problem but apparently did not see him, and no decision to transfer the money was reached. The coin remained in the Washington bank.

On May 5, the day after Davis had fled the place, Federal troops entered the town and confiscated all Confederate property, but the resourceful Judge Crump, though stripped of his authority over the money, hurried to Norfolk, Va., where he somehow made arrangements for transfer of the funds to their rightful owners in Richmond.

On May 8 two bank officials sent by Crump reached Washington, Ga., and appealed to Judge Andrews for help. The judge was able to persuade the commander of the local garrison, one Captain Lot Abraham of the U.S. Army, to release the private funds, and also to provide guards for their secret shipment to Richmond.

It was on May 24, when President Davis was ending his first day in shackles, that these funds of the Virginia banks were stealthily removed from the vault, loaded into wagons and sent northward under a few Federal guards. These men were disorganized, however, their force was under strength and they were evidently shadowed by desperadoes from the start. Despite precautions, word of the shipment of coin spread through the countryside. Rebel army stragglers in the town believed that the money belonged to the official Confederate treasure—and that it was being spirited off by Northern leaders.

Rebel veterans watched as the five wagons creaked out of town on their northward journey, and, because of their familiarity with the road, surmised that the caravan would camp for the night at the home of the giant Methodist minister, Dionysius Chenault, near the Savannah River. The Confederates, most of them Tennessee and Kentucky cavalrymen, made plans for a night attack on the wagons. News spread through the neighborhood and reached the home of young Otis Ashmore, who was later to become a historian of the epic journey of the treasure trains. Ashmore's father dressed and armed himself to join the raiders, but was dissuaded by Mrs. Ashmore, who feared for his life. Other Wilkes County residents probably rode with the troopers that night.

Just as the Rebel veterans had predicted, the Federal guards arrived at the home of the Reverend Chenault near sundown and asked permission to camp. Chenault welcomed them into his enclosed horse lot, which was protected by a fence with a double gate. The Federal guards drew their five wagons into a defensive circle for the night, apprehensive of a raid. After guards and teamsters had cooked and eaten supper they remained awake, keeping an uneasy watch on the campfires of straggling Confederate troops in the vicinity.

Later in the night, when the rising moon gave a clear view of the lot, the Federal guards saw a horseman pause outside their gates. The unidentified man wore a blue U.S. Army blouse—he was later thought to have been in disguise. The stranger studied the wagons and the small force of sentries for a few moments and then disappeared. The aroused guards and teamsters became more alert, but fell asleep after an hour or so, worn by the hard travel of the day.

They were aroused long after midnight by a chorus of shouts and curses as a band of unknown riders galloped through the gates and began to plunder the wagons. The outnumbered Federal guards did not fire a shot, and the teamsters fled into the woods. Guards were quickly trussed and the raiders helped themselves to the treasure. Boxes and bags were broken open and coins spilled to the ground. Eliza Andrews, who seems to have anticipated the attack after listening to the urgent conversations between Judge Crump and her father, reported soon afterward, ". . . men waded ankle deep in gold and silver. The raiders filled their haversacks and their pockets. They tied bags of gold to their saddles. They went away so heavily laden that they were compelled to throw away much of their booty by the wayside."

The well-known Confederate general, Edward Porter Alexander, responded to this news by rounding up former members of a local battery and riding from Washington to rescue the stolen treasure—with mixed results. He seized about $110,000 from the culprits (at least $80,000 from one man), but he was not always successful. Some determined veterans defended their booty with drawn pistols and refused to give up the money even when Alexander explained that these were private funds, and not Confederate property, so that only a portion of the stolen money was returned to the Washington bank vault by the general.

Despite Alexander's exertions, many raiders had ridden from the scene and were never apprehended. Lewis Shepherd, a Tennessean from General Vaughan's brigade who was a witness, claimed that two men took $120,000 in gold to Kansas City, where they opened a business and became "men of large wealth." Others, Shepherd said, used their loot to become "cattle kings" and wealthy entrepreneurs in Texas and California. However reliable these tales, most of the Richmond bank funds disappeared from recorded history, and their fate led treasure hunters to search the locality well into the twentieth century.

The Federal soldiers stationed in the area, angered by news of Alexander's seizures, were not content to leave this bonanza to the Confederates. Freed from restraints, the bluecoats embarked on a spree of gratuitous cruelty and vandalism.

The commander of the Federal garrison in Washington seized the funds placed in the bank vault by General Alexander, arrested the bank officers and redoubled the efforts of search and seizure. Not surprisingly, the lure of golden riches brought out the worst in the raiding troops as they coursed through the countryside. Some of the Federals looted the home of the Reverend Chenault. These men shot a pet dog known as "Jeff Davis," stole a small amount of gold and several watches, and strung the 300-pound minister to a tree limb by his thumbs in an effort to force him to reveal the hiding place of more gold. Two other men of the household, tortured in the same way, broke under the strain; one of them fainted and for a time was presumed dead. The Chenault women were stripped and searched by a black slave girl—the informer who had told false tales of hidden gold on the plantation. The family was imprisoned in Washington, and only the persistence and skill of Judge Andrews accomplished their release and the return of the Chenault coins and watches, ending an ordeal that was "forever emblazoned in their minds"— as Chenault's daughter Mary Anne Shumate said: "It took a sight more [than was returned to us] to pay counsel and other expenses, so after all we were robbed by the Yankee government instead of our robbing anybody." Mary Anne later told a colorful story about the missing money: "The Yankees got a good deal of it, but there were oceans more of it scattered all over Wilkes and Lincoln counties, besides what was carried off. Some of it was hid about in swamps and woods, some was buried in the ground, and there is no telling how much has been forgotten and not found again."*

Bluecoat squads combed the neighborhood for weeks, "questioning and intimidating" other families, leading many residents to bury even their legitimately held personal funds for fear of confiscation. It was only with the departure of the Federal troops that the bizarre wartime history of the Richmond bank funds came to an end, an almost incredible series of events: a Federal commander approving transfer of the money to legitimate owners in Richmond, the looting of the wagons by Confederates, the attempted recovery of the stolen wealth by General Alexander's men, and finally the impulsive pillaging by the army of occupation.

*The fate of the missing bank funds stirred controversy and litigation for almost thirty years, until 1893, when the U.S. Court of Claims awarded the Bank of Virginia less than $17,000, declared $78,000 to have been subject to confiscation as Confederate property and surmised that at least $250,000 had been stolen.

During their looting of other houses close to the Chenault farm, near the banks of the Savannah River, Federal forces came upon remnants of the official Confederate treasure as well. The chest of jewelry left at the home of Mrs. J. D. Moss by General Breckinridge was seized by the invaders—a cask filled, as Mary Shumate said, with the "bracelets, necklaces and rings . . . and silverware of all kinds" contributed by Southern women to the Lost Cause. "I never saw such a splendid collection of silver and jewels as was in that box," Mrs. Shumate recalled. This hoard was carried into Washington, with the addition of jewelry confiscated from the Chenault family—but a few weeks later, after a change of Federal commanders in the town, Mrs. Chenault was allowed to select her belongings from the chest. Apart from this, no report of the fate of this portion of the Confederate treasure was ever made.

Much of the money disbursed by Captain Micajah Clark when he closed accounts at Washington also found its way into Federal hands. Major Raphael Moses, who was given $40,000 to help feed returning Rebel soldiers, turned over $10,000 to the Quartermaster Department in Washington—just before the Federals arrived to confiscate all funds. Under great difficulties Major Moses carried his remaining $30,000 to Augusta and gave it to General Edward L. Molineux of the Federal garrison, upon his promise to feed returning Confederate soldiers and help the sick in local hospitals. Otis Ashmore, who made an early investigation of the fate of Confederate treasure, reported that Molineux entrusted this $30,000 to "one Adams of Massachusetts, then acting provost marshal of Augusta," and concluded that "very little if any part of the funds carried to Augusta was ever used to feed Confederate soldiers."

The larger sum of $86,000 in gold bullion and gold coin given to James A. Semple, the "trusted naval officer" who was expected to carry it to safety, simply disappeared. Ashmore concluded after a long study that though Semple may have concealed it in the false bottom of a carriage and attempted to ship it out of the country, he was unable to do so. Ashmore wrote, "It probably fell into the hands of the Federal troops, who were scouring the country in every direction." In that case, this small fortune disappeared into private hands.

Only one portion of the official Confederate treasure remained intact: the $25,000 residue of funds entrusted to President Davis on his journey southward from Greensboro, N. C. These gold coins, still under the protection of Captain Micajah Clark and the presidential wagon guards, were already deep inside Florida. This treasure trove, too, provoked a squabble at its final disposition.

Made wary by reports of Federal troops prowling the region of upper Florida, Captain Clark and the Van Benthuysens traveled back roads. On May 19, stunned by news of the capture of President Davis, Clark halted near Gainesville at the plantation of Senator David Yulee and left there the baggage and official documents entrusted to him by Davis.

Clark then proposed a division of the remnants of the treasure. He told the others that he would pay them for their services, and ship the remainder of the $25,000 to England, to await orders from Davis and Secretary Reagan, who had authorized him to supervise the treasure. If they were unable to ship to England, Clark said, he would use the money to finance the defense of Davis and the Cabinet when they were brought to trial.

This proposal set off a heated argument between Clark, the Acting Treasurer, and the President's cousin, Watson Van Benthuysen—who insisted that the money had been turned over to him as a quartermaster fund. Van Benthuysen said that since the Confederate government had ceased to exist, he would dispose of the money as financial agent in charge.

Van Benthuysen persuaded the five Maryland officers and his two brothers to support him, and Clark was forced to surrender control of the gold. Van Benthuysen proposed that one-quarter of the fund, about $6,250, be set aside for Mrs. Davis and her children.* The balance of the money should be divided equally among the party.

Though Clark bowed to the will of the majority, he took the precaution of obtaining a written statement from Watson Van Benthuysen, endorsed by the rest of the men, as proof that he had sought to perform his duty as Acting Treasurer. As Captain Van Benthuysen reported, he paid to each of the nine men, including Captain Clark, 400 gold sovereigns, valued at $4.85 each, or $1,940 per share.

*Discrepancies in the reported values of the funds were due to abnormal fluctuations of currency in the unsettled times, particularly reflected in values of such foreign gold coins as sovereigns. At the then-current rate, Mrs. Davis's share was worth from $6,250 to $6,790. Jefferson Davis was to spend years in a futile attempt to collect such a sum from Watson Van Benthuysen.

He also gave each of the nine $55 for traveling expenses, paid a scout and a presidential guard $250 each, five Negro servants $20 each and devoted $250 to "miscellaneous." By this accounting, a total of $18,930 had been divided among the baggage guard party, the final survivors of the hectic flight of Confederate officialdom from Richmond into the Deep South. As Clark reported (and no one denied), Watson Van Benthuysen kept 1,400 gold sovereigns for Mrs. Davis.

After dividing the gold, Clark and Van Benthuysen and their band scattered, the Marylanders and the Van Benthuysens to surrender to Federal officers and take oaths for parole. Clark attempted to return to Washington, Ga., to retrieve the letter books and message books he had left in the town a month earlier, but found the place so heavily garrisoned that he feared to enter.

Clark then rode northward, stopping briefly in Abbeville, S. C., to destroy some unimportant documents among the presidential papers which had been left with Mrs. Leovy. He preserved only those communications from congressmen, Cabinet members and other high officials, as well as important army records. Clark continued northward to Baltimore and was not molested on his journey.

A Negro teamster of the Clark party carried news of the divided treasure and the President's belongings to a Federal garrison nearby, and his garbled tale of buried gold attracted Captain O. E. Bryant, who marched out with a squad of black troops and located the baggage. To his surprise Bryant found the trunk and chest in a shed, "unguarded even by a lock." But he found no golden hoard of coins or ingots. The trunk was packed with clothing, four pistols, and a homely collection of personal effects—smoking and plug tobacco, toothbrushes, a simple ring, some spectacles, six boxes of cigars, $20,000 in Confederate bills, and portraits of Mr. and Mrs. Davis and of General Lee. The trunk contained a few valuable documents: the letters from the Cabinet members written at Charlotte, approving the first surrender agreement between Sherman and Johnston. There was also a key to the Confederate secret code which had been used in official communications.

14

"Watch and wait for the morning"

IN these traumatic days, with news of Appomattox and other surrenders followed by tales of their President's flight, capture and humiliation, the people of the South were moved by conflicting emotions. Thousands vowed to leave their homes rather than live under Yankee rule.

Judge John Perkins, a congressman from Louisiana, took extreme, but not unique, action: he burned to the ground his stately bayou plantation mansion with its priceless collections of porcelains, paintings and statuary, as well as his barns, cotton presses and crops. The judge then fled into Mexico, which became the most popular haven for the Confederate fugitives.

Uncounted numbers of families, lured by the relative freedom on the frontier, flooded into Texas in a movement which was to make the Lone Star State the region's most populous by 1880. The outflow continued in every direction until, as a contemporary wrote, "In some of the Cotton States it looked as if more white men were to be lost thus than had been lost in battle."

The impetus for these abrupt migrations lay in the profound shock of a people who had been conditioned to expect victory. Though Confederate ruin had not surprised government officials and perceptive soldiers, to white civilians at large the demise of the Old South came as a clap of thunder from a clear sky. Joel Chandler Harris, who was to create the character of Uncle Remus, was then a boy in a remote Georgia village. He wrote later: "The last trump will cause no greater surprise and consternation . . . than the news of Lee's surrender caused in that region. The public mind had not been prepared. . . . Almost every piece of news printed in the journals . . . was colored with the prospect of ultimate victory; and then the curtain came down and the lights went out . . . [Southerners] were confronted with conditions that had no precedent or parallel in the history of the world. It is small fault if their minds failed at first to grasp the significance and the import of these conditions, so new were they and so amazing."

Alert Southern promoters were quick to capitalize on the public mood of the region. Newspapers fostered emigration schemes, and one New Orleans entrepreneur contracted to send 1,000 white Southerners annually into Brazil. Thousands more merely joined the enemy, moving into the North to find work in the burgeoning cities, to escape racial tensions—or to exchange the thin, exhausted farmlands of Dixie for the rich black soil of the Midwestern plains. The phenomenon of out-migration, which began to appear during the southward flight of Jefferson Davis, was to send some 8,000 to 10,000 Southerners to Central and South America (to Mexico, Brazil, Venezuela and British Honduras) and to Cuba, Jamaica, Canada, Egypt and Japan.

Many of these unrepentant Confederates left their native land for no other reason than resentment of Federal efforts to force ex-Confederates to take an oath of allegiance. Though the oath was neither punitive nor restrictive, old Rebels felt that they were being treated as aliens in their home country; they hotly denied that they had been treasonable—or done anything other than resist what their leaders depicted as oppression. The Jefferson Davis doctrine that the Confederacy had merely defended the Constitution against its despoilers was widespread in the region. Many veterans were to die without taking the despised oath.

These attitudes were hardened by the numerous signs that most Northerners were unforgiving, and insisted upon saddling the South with war guilt: Andrew Johnson had taken office by declaring, "I hold that robbery is a crime; rape is a crime; murder is a crime; treason is a crime and crime must be punished. Treason must be made infamous and traitors must be impoverished."

On Memorial Day, Federal troops stood guard around graves of Southerners in Arlington Cemetery to prevent anyone from placing flowers there. Northern resentment prevented the burial of Confederate dead on the Antietam battlefield until the public health was endangered by "skeletons, rooted up by the hogs and blanching in the open fields."

A Federal grand jury in Norfolk, Va., returned indictments of treason against Robert E. Lee and Jefferson Davis—and if convicted they might expect death by hanging.

Friction and occasional violence spread through the region as Federal authorities sought to force the oath upon former soldiers and officials—even those who had surrendered and been properly paroled, with guarantees that they would not be disturbed further if they ceased resistance to the Federal government.

One of these troubled young veterans was Captain George Wise, the brother of the lieutenant who had carried to Davis news of Lee's impending surrender during the President's halt in Danville, Va.

Captain Wise had a typical experience when he was called before a provost marshal in Richmond, who told him that he must take the oath.

"Why must I take it? I will not. My parole covers the ground."

"You fought under General Lee?"

"Yes. And surrendered with him, and gave my parole. To demand this oath of me insults me and my general."

"I'll make a bargain with you, Captain," the Federal said. "Consult General Lee and abide by his decision." It was clear that the enemy, as well as defeated Southerners, instinctively thought of Lee as the leader of the late Confederacy. With Jefferson Davis in his prison cell, the revered commander of the Army of Northern Virginia had become the symbolic hope of the Southern people.

Wise found Lee in his Richmond home, pale and weary, but willing to see any veteran who was having trouble with the enemy. Wise held out a copy of the oath. "They want me to take this thing, General. My parole covers it and I don't think it should be required of me. What should I do?"

"I would advise you to take it," Lee said. "It's absurd that it should be required of my soldiers, for, as you say, the parole practically covers it. Nevertheless, take it, I should say."

"General, this is submission to an indignity. If I must continue to swear the same thing over at every street corner, I'll move to another country where I can at least keep my self-respect."

After a moment of silence Lee said sadly, "Don't leave Virginia. Our country needs her young men now."

When Captain Wise told his father that he had taken the oath the fiery ex-governor roared, "You've disgraced the family!"

"General Lee advised me to do it."

"Oh, that alters the case. Whatever General Lee says is all right, I don't care what it is."

Northern newspapermen also sought Lee's views on the plight of the South and the political dilemma facing the nation. "I'm no politician," Lee said. "I'm a soldier—a paroled prisoner."

Though it was not publicly known, Lee was even then seeking a pardon from President Johnson. Since General Grant had assured him that Confederate officers would not be tried for treason after his surrender at Appomattox, Lee had approached the conquering general through an intermediary, Reverdy Johnson of Maryland. Grant sent a verbal message of full support, and urged Lee to apply for a pardon.

Lee did so in mid-June 1865, less than a week after he had been indicted for treason. He made application for pardon by sending it through Grant, asking for "the benefits and full restoration of all rights of privileges" of American citizenship. He explained to Grant that he did not seek to avoid trial, but reminded him of the protection guaranteed by his parole. Grant at once urged Johnson to pardon Lee, and to go further and dismiss all indictments against paroled prisoners of war in the South. Grant's position embarrassed the administration. Prosecutors who hesitated to challenge the integrity of the general's paroles simply suspended proceedings against the accused traitors, though they did not remove them from the dockets. Lee, like Jefferson Davis and other leaders, was to be left in limbo. The government might reopen its case against Lee and his associates at any time.

A basic problem was that the nation was at a loss as to how to bring the devastating conflict to an end. There would never be agreement as to whether the warring sections had fought a Civil War or a War Between the States, and for generations bitter controversy would rage as to what penalties and reparations, if any, should have been exacted from the vanquished.

When General Lee was pressed for his opinion by a newspaper he managed mild criticism of the North with his plea for harmony: "The South has for a long time been anxious for peace. In my earnest belief, peace was possible two years ago, and has been since. . . . They [Southerners] have been looking for some word . . . of compromise and conciliation from the North upon which they might base a return to the Union, their own views being considered. . . ."

Lee made a plea for moderation toward the South, saying that oppression would keep alive the spirit of resistance. "If a people see that they are to be crushed, they sell their lives as dearly as possible."

The general said emphatically that he deplored plans of families of any Southern state to emigrate, "especially at a time when the region needs rebuilding, and so many young Southerners have been killed or disabled."

The general made it clear that he was not to join the diehard Rebels. He spoke of North and South as "we," and urged the restoration of peace and prosperity, as if he were anxious to forget the war and end sectional animosities.

But he also spoke courageously of the plight of Jefferson Davis, the first Southern leader to do so: "What has Mr. Davis done?" Lee asked. "What has he done more than any other Southerner that he should be singled out for persecution? He did not originate secession, is not responsible for its beginning; he opposed it strenuously in speech and writing."

Though Lee had accepted the verdict of the battlefield and realized that Davis would never do so, the general was not ashamed of the Confederacy or of his own role in the war. He would always resent the vengeful attitude of men like Edwin Stanton, Attorney General Joseph Holt and General Nelson A. Miles. It became increasingly clear that Americans on both sides of the Mason-Dixon line shared his view that war-born hatreds should be curbed.

But it was equally clear that thousands of young ex-Confederates would reject his advice to remain at home and suffer the armed occupation that was to come. Some of these inconsolable Johnnies drifted out of the country singly, or by twos, threes or dozens. Rarely, there was an organized band to march across the border with the hope of finding a new and better world.

On July 4, as Davis and Clay sweltered in their cells, and the Federal garrison whooped and paraded and fired muskets to mark Independence Day, a final scene in the collapse of the Confederate empire was enacted on the banks of the Rio Grande, some 2,000 miles to the southwest of the Chesapeake capes.

With a scorching wind stirring a dust storm at their backs and a tattered battle flag going before, a file of Rebel troops wound through cactus scrub toward the Mexican border at Eagle Pass. Those on foot, moving with the tireless stride of veteran infantry, kept pace with cavalrymen who rode in advance, leading pack mules. Ten new French guns, thickly covered in dust, followed the marchers, and a train of twelve-mule wagons brought up the rear.

Though other refugees had joined in the past few days, the column was no more than 500 strong, and the troops were the last organized body remaining in the field from the once-vast western armies of the Confederacy.

They were halted at the shallow stream by their commander, a slight, erect officer from whose trooper's hat a black ostrich plume streamed in the wind. This boyish black-bearded Rebel brigadier general was Jo Shelby, commander of the Iron Brigade whose riders had terrorized enemy-held areas of the Trans-Mississippi throughout the war. Twenty-four horses had been killed under this daredevil leader, who had won fame as a guerrilla, bushwhacker and raider. The senior U.S. cavalry chief, Major General Alfred Pleasanton, who had fought Jeb Stuart in the east and Shelby in Missouri, had said, "Shelby was the best cavalry general of the South. Under other conditions he would have been one of the best in the world."

Today he was leading into exile the largest body of troops who were to desert their homeland in a concerted flight from U.S. rule.

Shelby called an order and a trooper rode into the Rio Grande, carrying a stone about which he had wrapped the battle-worn Confederate flag. The soldiers bared their heads and came to attention. A bugler sounded a mournful call and the horseman tossed the stone into the brown water. The flag sank slowly from sight.

The column splashed into the stream and crossed into exile, into a harsh, hostile land that was to test them more cruelly than war. Jo Shelby, one of the rare Confederate generals who never surrendered, was on his way to the court of the Emperor Maximilian, an Austrian archduke sent by Napoleon III to collect debts and to revive a French empire in America.

Shelby was followed onto the Mexican shore by distinguished companions: Governors Charles S. Morehead of Kentucky and Henry W. Allen of Louisiana, and the Texas ex-governors, Pendleton Murrah and Edward Clark. There was also a swarm of army officers from other commands: Generals John B. Clark, Jr., and Sterling Price of Missouri, Danville Leadbetter of Alabama, William

P. Hardeman of Texas. Among the others were Generals John Bankhead ("Prince John") Magruder, Hamilton P. Bee, Monroe Parsons, Trusten Polk and George Flournoy. Numerous colonels and other field officers had joined—all of them willing to sacrifice home, property and prospects of reunited families to escape enemy control and avoid the despised amnesty oath.

They were not the first who had gone—Edmund Kirby Smith had already surrendered and fled, his defiance tempered at last by desertions, mutinies and partisan squabbling. His troops had simply left him, seizing all government property except for a few mules and wagons, which Smith sent "to the brush." As an observant Union officer wrote of the dissolution of the Trans-Mississippi Department where Davis had hoped to carry on the war: "The thing is going to pieces so fast that one cannot count the fragments." Kirby Smith had left it behind and slipped across the Rio Grande, almost alone, "mounted on a mule and dressed in shirt sleeves with a silk handkerchief tied around his neck 'a la Texas' and armed with revolver and shotgun."

Kirby Smith and Shelby's band were but a few among the thousands who had gone, or were now going, to Mexico. There were also Generals Cadmus M. Wilcox of Tennessee, T. C. Hindman, Jubal Early of Virginia, William Preston of Kentucky, Alexander T. Hawthorne of Arkansas, A. W. Terrell of Texas, and John McCausland, who had led his Confederate raiders to burn Chambersburg, Pa. Among the politicians were Isham G. Harris, ex-governor of Tennessee, Senator Louis Wigfall of Texas, Congressman John Perkins of Louisiana, and the internationally famous Commodore Matthew F. Maury of Virginia. The New York *Daily News* reported a stream of migrants into Mexico: Judge W. G. Swan of Georgia, a former Confederate congressman, who led twenty families; General John S. Williams, who led sixty Tennesseans; and, it was reported, 150 families in western Virginia were preparing to join the crowds. Among the bands were small-town mayors, blacksmiths, carpenters, farmers, peddlers, coopers. Most of them were bound for Maximilian's new Confederate colonies—in particular a village oasis in the jungle country called Carlota, where Shelby and his men hoped to find a life of ease. There were some who dreamed of banding with French reinforcements to invade Texas and renew the war on the Yankees.

Around campfires on foreign soil men of Shelby's Iron Brigade sang songs celebrating their swift raids through Missouri, which had won them notoriety during the war:

> *Ho boys! Make a noise!*
> *The Yankees are afraid!*
> *The river's up, hell's to pay,*
> *Shelby's on a raid!*

Shelby's path led through country held by the fierce native troops of Benito Juárez, the rightful leader of the Mexican people and now commander of the resistance movement against Maximilian. Though Juárez was supported by the U.S. government, General Shelby hoped to pass peacefully through this territory. But his column marched on the alert, ready to fight at a moment's notice.

Few Confederate gray uniforms remained in this motley band, but the wagons bore thousands of British Enfield muskets, with 40,000 rounds of ammunition. There were stocks of bacon, salt pork, rice, dried fruits and preserves—and Kentucky bourbon whiskey—enough to sustain a long campaign. The French cannon were well supplied with shot and shell.

When the Rebels were about fifty miles inside Mexico, the Juáristas came, seeking to buy cannon. Shelby sold them without hesitation; they were growing heavy on the trail, he said. When he was asked later how he dared place his guns in the hands of so desperate an enemy, Shelby replied in astonishment, "Why, we still had our small arms!"

Within a matter of hours a dispute broke out between the Confederates and the barefoot Juáristas, allegedly over the ownership of some horses. There was a sharp little skirmish, during which Shelby retook his guns, and immediately marched on into the interior.

Thereafter, for six exhausting weeks, foraging for food, fighting Indians, slipping past suspicious French forces, Shelby led his party through the rocky wastelands and into Mexico City. His greeting by Maximilian and the Empress Carlota was friendly enough, but Shelby was shocked to learn that organized military units were unwelcome; the new Mexican empire sought peaceful settlers. Shelby was forced to disband his little army.

Hundreds of other ex-Confederates were now coming into Mexico, lured by dreams of a new freedom—but for survivors of the Iron Brigade the tropical sanctuary had already lost much of its charm.

Shelby himself made his way to Carlota, near Vera Cruz, planning to grow coffee or cotton and help in building Maximilian's Mexico. The campaigns of the western front under the banner of the Lost Cause seemed long ago and far away.

The domestication of the old bushwhacker chief in his colony was an example lost upon his restless veterans. Some joined the French army—fifty of them the elite Third Zouaves, an African regiment—some stole away to aid Juáristas in the north. Others marched to the Pacific, to remain in California or sail for the Sandwich Islands or Japan. Still others disappeared to prospect for gold in the Sierra Madre or left for Brazil or British Honduras.

It was much later when Jefferson Davis learned of the movement to Mexico and other countries, but he was distressed by the news. Though he agreed in general with Robert E. Lee that all Southerners should remain at home, he hoped that they would not remain there submissively. He expected the South, in some unforeseen way, to rise again, "The night may be long, but it is the part of fidelity to watch and wait for the morning."

A migration of quite another kind had begun in the South among the five million blacks of the region. Hardly noticed by the leaders of the old Confederacy, it would become one of the most spectacular shifts of population in American history, and one of the most significant.

The first reactions of former slaves to the reality of Confederate collapse were tentative and confused as they faced unprecedented upheavals in their lives. One observer watched in amazement the sudden activity among freed slaves through the countryside: ". . . gangs of Negroes were passing and re-passing restlessly, moving to and fro, some with bundles and some with none . . . their restless and uneasy movements were perfectly natural. They had suddenly come to the knowledge that they were free, and they were testing the nature and limits of their freedom. They desired to find out its length and breadth. It was extraordinary, but not perilous."

There were also signs of future migrations which were to disperse black families from the isolated rural South into cities throughout the nation. The first step was from the backwoods farms into Southern cities. The majority were to remain docilely in place, tending fields of white landlords, but the pioneers of the new movement were already showing the way. A Northern visitor to South Carolina in the summer of 1865 was so fascinated by the spectacle of the incipient migration that he rode out to watch on a moonlit country road as streams of Negroes went past, "each carrying his bundle and making his way to Charleston and the coast, where freedom was supposed to be freer, perhaps."

15

"We cannot convict him of treason"

In the isolation of his cell, denied visitors or correspondents, Jefferson Davis knew little of the fate of the Confederate treasure, the archives or his family—or of the stirrings of the New South. The whitewashed walls of his casemate enclosed his world.

Hot, humid weather came early to tidewater Virginia, but though his discomfort increased and he seemed to grow weaker, Davis was much more concerned for his wife and children than for his own condition. Dr. Craven felt that his anxiety for Varina was endangering the President's health. But Miles would give him no news of his family, or of his plans for them.

As Davis feared, Varina had been harassed by Federal soldiers from the moment her husband left the *Clyde.* She and Mrs. Clay were guarded by women who, as Virginia Clay said scornfully, were "garishly dressed, rouged, powdered and befrizzled with huge chignons, bustles of the largest size, high-heeled shoes, conspicuous stockings, and gay petticoats." When these formidable guards insisted upon searching the wives of the prisoners, Varina sobbed with rage and humiliation, but Virginia Clay laughed and ridiculed their jailers, playfully twirling a small pistol (which apparently had not been found on her when she was captured) as the search went on.

Colonel Pritchard came aboard, greeted Varina courteously, and asked for her waterproof cape. She gave it to him at once, with the thought of disproving the claim that this garment which her husband had snatched up at the time of his capture was "essentially a woman's coat." The cape was soon to be shown in the North as part of the Davis "disguise." Later, when soldiers opened her trunks and seized other clothing, including her shawl, Varina broke into tears once more. She revived only after Virginia Clay suggested that she give the bluecoats both their shawls, to confuse their efforts to assemble the complete costume worn by Davis in his so-called disguise.

General Miles boarded the *Clyde* for a look at Varina. She was astonished to see that he was so young, hardly more than a boy. She found him "disrespectful," but concluded that he knew no better, and was thus unaware that his manner was offensive. Miles would tell her nothing of the President's health. Instead, he confronted her accusingly: "Davis announced Mr. Lincoln's assassination the day before it happened and I guess he knew all about it." Though she knew they were false, the words chilled her. She feared for her husband under care of this stern young man; she judged that he would be merciless. Miles brusquely refused to tell Varina where she was to be sent, and then left the ship. He telegraphed Charles Dana in Washington soon afterward, ". . . Both he [Davis] and Clay are well. The females were sent to Savannah today."

As the *Clyde* prepared to sail, Varina saw a British warship nearby and made a vain attempt to escape. She scrawled a note to the vessel's captain, begging for passage to England, explaining that she had been "reduced to poverty" by the Federals. "They have burned our two plantations and stolen our property. . . . I cannot pay my passage. . . . May God . . . fill your heart with pity." The British skipper never saw her plea. The note was intercepted and the *Clyde* sailed for Savannah, where Varina and her family could be kept under watch by the Federal garrison in that city. Except for the faithful Robert Brown, all her servants had left Mrs. Davis, and now her mother, Mrs. William Howell, came to help with the children. In distress, Varina complained that she had been sent against her will to Savannah, where she had never been before, and that she was destitute, "Left with no other support than the small sum which the cupidity of the enemy . . . failed to ferret out and steal."

As her husband had anticipated, Varina read an account of his shackling in a Savannah newspaper and was prostrated by grief and anxiety. She shut herself in her room, sobbing and screaming hysterically, and was quieted only when a doctor gave her an opiate. She remained under sedation for a week, but even later she could not resist the temptation to pore over accounts of her husband's plight, shuddering as she read graphic descriptions of his failing health. On June 1, frantic with worry, she wrote to Dr. Craven and managed to slip the letter past her guards and into the mail.

She told Craven that she was prompted to write him by reading "the terrible newspaper extras issued every afternoon, which represent my husband to be in a dying condition." She pleaded with him to respond to her: "It seems to me that no possible harm could accrue to your government from my knowing the extent of my sorrow. If you are only permitted to say that he is well, or he is better, it will be a great comfort to me, who has no other left."

There was no response from Dr. Craven; General Miles had forbidden him to communicate with Varina.

About this time Davis complained bitterly to Craven of the ceaseless watch kept on him by guards, under the glaring lights, "To have a human eye riveted on you in every moment of waking or sleeping, sitting, walking, or lying down, is a refinement of torture on anything the Comanches or Spanish Inquisition ever dreamed. . . . The lamp burning in my room all night shooting its rays . . . into my throbbing eyeballs, one of them already sightless from neuralgia, is torture of the most intense agony."

Miles did not relent in this matter, but on June 17, after Davis complained that he could not sleep while sentinels paced beside the cot, the general ordered the two soldiers on duty in the cell to stand while keeping watch over the prisoner.

Davis was gratified, but as he told Dr. Craven, the order imposed hardships on the sentries, who must stand like statues throughout their watches. Craven found that such thoughtfulness toward others was characteristic of Davis.

It was on this hot Sunday morning, on a farm hardly one hundred miles to the west, at a Virginia plantation house called Redmoor, that old Edmund Ruffin ended his life. The aging firebrand of Secession had delayed for weeks, until he had convinced himself that suicide in his case was an affair of honor. He made a final diary entry, asking forgiveness of his children, and absolving himself of guilt:

> I hereby declare my unmitigated hatred to Yankee rule—to all political, social & business connection with Yankees—and to the Yankee race. Would that I could impress these sentiments, in their full force, on every living southerner, & bequeath them to everyone yet to

> be born! May such sentiments be held universally in the outraged & down-trodden South, although in silence & stillness, until the now far-distant day shall arrive for just retribution for Yankee usurpation, oppression, & atrocious outrages—& for deliverance & vengeance for the now ruined, subjugated, & enslaved Southern States! . . .
>
> I hereby repeat . . . my unmitigated hatred . . . to the perfidious, malignant, & vile Yankee race.

He then placed in his mouth the barrel of a fine silver-chased rifle and pulled the trigger with a forked stick. There was a sharp crack, for only the percussion cap had fired—but the willful old man hurried off a second shot, and when his son found him a moment later Edmund Ruffin was dead, sitting straight as a ramrod, the symbol of defiance he had proclaimed at Fort Sumter.

Two days later his son Edmund wrote his own sons, "The Yankees have killed your Grandfather."

Otherwise the passage of the arch-Secessionist drew little attention in a Confederacy still caught in the spasms of death and transfiguration. If Jefferson Davis learned of Ruffin's death in his prison cell, the observant Dr. Craven failed to record it.

In Washington, in the heat of this early July 1865, the government hanged the conspirators in Lincoln's murder, among them the boardinghouse keeper Mrs. Mary Surratt, who was almost certainly innocent. The execution of the aging woman whose crime had been in renting rooms to conspirators set off indignant protests in the northern press, and thereafter the public thirst for vengeance against all Rebels appeared to abate.

But there was still a clamor for the execution of Davis. Speaker of the House of Representatives Schuyler Colfax (who was soon to be exposed as a grafter) told the House that if justice were done, Davis would be "hanging between heaven and earth as not fit for either."

But ex-President Franklin Pierce, who was now corresponding with Varina, assured her that her husband would not be tried, since the government's case rested upon "wicked fabrications from the perjured lips of the lowest on earth."

Pierce referred to a bizarre "professional perjurer" by the name of Charles A. Dunham, who, under the alias Sanford Conover, offered—in return for a handsome fee—to produce witnesses who would swear that Davis had plotted with them to have Lincoln murdered. Judge Advocate General Joseph Holt, who was as gullible as he was vindictive, accepted Conover's tales, and for some weeks hoodlums and drifters were smuggled into Washington and rehearsed in false testimony by Conover. But their unlikely tales were so transparently untrue that the Bureau of Military Justice exposed them.

One witness, William Campbell (actually Joseph A. Hoare, a New York "gas-fixer") gave away the scheme. "This is all false," he said. "I must make a clean breast of it; I can't stand it any longer."

Campbell testified that Judge Holt, anxious for proof of Davis's guilt after payment of the $100,000 reward, asked for any testimony that might convict him: "Conover wrote out the evidence," Campbell said, "and I learned it by heart." He was paid $625, of which Holt had given him $500. Another "witness," Dr. James B. Merritt, was paid $6,000.

After Campbell had confessed, Conover fled but was captured and imprisoned. Only then was the fanatic Holt forced to abandon his effort to send Davis to the gallows.

From the moment of Conover's exposure, Davis was no longer in danger of prosecution for conspiracy in Lincoln's death—but Edwin Stanton, though he ceased to fill the newspapers with insinuations, made no public acknowledgment of defeat, and defendants were left in ignorance as to the status of the charges against them.

The Davis case became more vexing to Secretary Stanton and the Radicals in other ways. The trunk full of personal and official letters left at the David Yulee plantation in Florida by Captain Clark had arrived in Washington, where War Department officials scanned every sheet without finding evidence to incriminate the Confederate President. During the summer's heat, while Stanton and the Cabinet still debated as to how the case should be tried, Chief Justice Salmon P. Chase urged Stanton to forget the problem: "If you bring these leaders to trial, it will condemn the North, for by the Constitution, secession is not rebellion." He added that it was absurd to try to prove in court that Davis had been the chief of an armed uprising, since that had been common knowledge. "Lincoln wanted Jefferson Davis to escape," Chase said. "And he was right. His capture was a mistake. His trial will be a greater one. We cannot convict him of treason. Secession is settled. Let it stay settled."

. . .

Meanwhile, at Fort Monroe, the condition of Jefferson Davis continued to deteriorate, so rapidly that Miles himself ordered Dr. Craven to make an emergency visit to the cell. Craven reported Davis "in a very critical state," more despondent than ever, without appetite, and his slow pulse denoting "deep prostration of all the physical energies." Craven was alarmed least Davis die in the cell, without trial, the victim of cruel treatment by Miles and the War Department. Davis suspected that the government was eager for him to die behind bars, to save embarrassment "to those in power." He said sharply to Craven, "If death without trial is the object of the Washington people, I wish they would take a quicker means of dispatching me." Davis repeated his hope that he would live to vindicate the justice of the Confederate cause and the constitutionality of the rights of states to withdraw from the union they had created.

Dr. Craven continued to insist that Davis be permitted to leave his cell for short walks within the walls of the fort. He rejected the claim by Miles that the old man would attempt escape: "If all the doors and gates of the fort were thrown open he would not leave. The only duty left to him—his only remaining object—is to vindicate the action of his people, and his own actions as their representative, by a fair and public trial."

To the wonder of the prisoner, Miles appeared at the cell door a few days later and told Davis he was to be allowed an hour of exercise on the ramparts each day. Davis was eager to begin, but his enthusiasm waned when Miles and the Officer of the Day held his arms as they walked, with four guards pacing closely behind. Miles said he would accompany him on every walk. Davis concealed his distaste for the young officer, but was unable to walk far. He shuffled along, breathing deeply of the fresh air and staring seaward. Dr. Craven noted that though the old man's carriage was as proudly erect as ever, "his step had lost its elasticity," that he halted frequently to pant for breath, and was forced to return to his cell within half an hour.

A few days later Davis met Clement Clay walking along the ramparts, and saw his own plight more clearly in the stooped form of his old friend. Clay seemed to have aged many years. The prisoners halted briefly and exchanged a few words in French. Their guards, who did not understand, separated them at once and forbade further conversation.

Davis learned that Varina and their children were in Savannah, and was disturbed by tales that they were being harassed by their captors: Federal troops had bribed four-year-old Billie to sing in public, "Hang Jeff Davis on a Sour Apple Tree"; two women from Maine who saw Little Jeff in the hotel lobby had threatened to whip him because his father was "such a villain"—and a Negro sentinel had pointed a rifle at the boy and threatened to shoot because he had called him "Uncle."

Varina, probably with the aid of Confederate sympathizers, sent the older children to Canada, where they would be shielded from annoyances. She herself was forced to remain in Savannah. She kept Winnie with her, but sent her mother and the devoted Robert Brown to care for the children in the North. Brown protected Little Jeff at every opportunity. When a white man on their ship cornered the boy and made insulting remarks about his father, Robert interrupted.

"Do you consider me an equal?" he asked.

"Certainly," said the Northerner.

"Then take this from your equal." Robert knocked the man down with his fist, and was exonerated by the ship's captain, to whom the crestfallen passenger complained.

Under increasing anxiety because she could learn nothing of her husband's condition, and dependent upon contributions of friends and loyal ex-Confederate families for support, Varina seemed to be in danger of a breakdown. An unexpected stroke of good fortune lifted her spirits and gave her confidence for the future. Judah P. Benjamin, who had arrived in London in August 1865, wrote to tell Varina that the Confederate agent there, C. J. McRae, had placed some $12,500 to her credit, representing final salary payments to "your noble husband, my unhappy friend." Suddenly, she was to have a small fortune at her disposal.

Benjamin, who was on the verge of a spectacular second career at the British bar, never returned to America.

Varina was now beginning to keep her hopes alive with a surreptitious correspondence, writing to acquaintances and men of influence in the North to plead for help in freeing Davis. Her first success was with Horace Greeley, who had made stinging attacks on the ex-President of the Confederacy but who was attracted, as usual, by a lost cause. Greeley persuaded George Shea, a prominent New York attorney, to inspect Confederate archives which had been smuggled into Canada. When these showed that Davis had insisted upon humane treatment for Federal prisoners during the war, steadfastly resisting pressure to retaliate against them for alleged mistreatment of Confederate captives in the North, Greeley wrote editorials favorable to the ex-President. Soon afterward Shea was joined by another New York attorney, Charles O'Conor, who also worked as a volunteer, assembling evidence for the expected trial of the now-celebrated prisoner. O'Conor wrote Davis an open letter saying that though he had no Southern associations or sympathies, he would be happy to serve as his attorney in the interest of justice. Stanton permitted the prisoner to see the letter and write a reply—but refused to deliver Davis's response to O'Conor, on the ground that the ex-President was "not in civil custody." But though O'Conor was unable to see his client, he remained ready to represent him. O'Conor declined a fee of $20,000 offered by the State of Mississippi, saying that he had volunteered for the sake of his country, and not for personal gain.

Even the radical Abolitionist leader Thaddeus Stevens offered to represent Davis and Clay. "They are public enemies. . . . But I know these men. . . . They are gentlemen and incapable of being assassins."

Varina was cheered by such developments, and by newspaper reports that Johnson's Cabinet was discussing the Davis case; it appeared that there was sharp disagreement in Washington as to how to proceed against the Confederate leader. Many months passed while the government's agents went "mousing among the archives," as Varina said, seeking incriminating evidence against Davis.

In September, by what seemed to her a miracle, Varina had a letter from her husband, who was now permitted to correspond with her, on family matters only, with all letters to be cleared through the Attorney General. Even these bland exchanges seemed to firm Varina's resolve. She learned that General Miles had relented and now allowed Davis to have wine, brandy, liquor and "dainties," even a knife and fork. The government had dropped the pretense that the prisoner might kill himself.

In early autumn, when the feeble Davis seemed near death, Craven again urged Miles to move the prisoner from the damp cell where mold grew on his shoes and even on crumbs Davis saved for a mouse he had tamed. Miles agreed, and the prisoner was moved to a new room in a former officers' quarters. Though it could be observed through bars from three sides, the new room was airy and spacious, and had a fireplace. Davis was still forbidden any clothing except what he wore, which he could change only at the whim of Miles. But he now was allowed to bathe and use his portable commode behind a screen, hidden from the eyes of watchful guards.

Dr. Craven was astonished by the patient's vitality and the breadth of knowledge he displayed during their conversations. Davis sometimes quoted Milton on his blindness, or Edmund Burke, or talked of the works of Izaak Walton, or Hogarth's drawings—but he also spoke of oyster culture, optics and acoustics, modern and ancient warfare, statuary, loggerhead turtles, engineering. Davis was also willing to talk of the war, and said he had made it a rule to express no regret over the inevitable: "Success is virtue and defeat, crime." He talked for hours each week on the right of Secession, as if preparing for a constitutional debate. He heaped scorn upon the government's methods of prosecuting other Confederate officials.

Davis was upset by the execution of the lone U.S. "war criminal," the physician Henry Wirz, commander of Andersonville prison in Georgia, where so many Federal soldiers had died. Wirz was doomed from the moment of capture, for Northerners could not forget his purported remark during the war, "I am killing more Yankees than Lee at the front." Nor was there any forgetting the photographs of the camp's pathetic survivors, sickening images of men whose bodies had been reduced to living skeletons by the ravages of starvation, exposure and disease.

Before he was hanged in Washington, Wirz was offered freedom if he would implicate Jefferson Davis in the management of Andersonville. The prisoner refused indignantly. "I would not become a traitor to him or anyone else to save my life." He denied having known Davis, "either officially, personally or socially."

Davis knew nothing of the attempt to wring false testimony from Wirz, but he denounced the hanging and said evidence against the prison chief had been falsified. To Dr. Craven, Davis insisted that it was U. S. Grant who bore the guilt for Andersonville's tragedies, since he had refused to exchange prisoners. This war of attrition, Davis said, had caused overcrowded prisons and had deprived both Confederates and their prisoners of food and medical care. Davis said Wirz died "a martyr to conscientious adherence to truth."

By now the cold of November penetrated the prison rooms and one day when Dr. Craven found Davis shivering in a thin coat, he ordered a new one for him from Washington. Some Confederate sympathizers, who learned of this, paid the tailor to make a much more expensive garment, and a handsome black pilot-cloth overcoat soon arrived at the prison. Miles knew nothing of the gift until Horace Greeley's New York *Tribune* reported: "Jeff. Davis' new overcoat was sent down to Fortress Monroe today. The garment is an expensive one in accordance with Davis' fine taste in matters of dress and is paid for."

Miles, who was already irritated by the warm friendship that had developed between Davis and the doctor, called Craven before him and demanded an explanation. The physician said he had merely provided a warm coat for a sick prisoner in need. But Miles was not content. He discovered that the coat had cost $125—a staggering price—and that unknown parties had come to the tailor's shop to pay for a much finer coat than Craven had ordered. Craven insisted that he knew nothing of the affair, beyond his order for a simple, inexpensive coat.

A few days later Miles ordered conversation between Craven and Davis restricted to professional matters. The doctor protested this as a "cruel and unnecessary order," since the long daily talks, filled with brilliant monologues by Davis, had helped the prisoner to keep his sanity. The order also brought to an end Craven's diary, in which he had recorded his visits with Davis, commenting on his health, conversation, treatment and reactions to his imprisonment.

On Christmas Day, 1865, Miles dismissed Craven from his post, and replaced him with a physician of supposedly "sounder" political outlook: Dr. George Cooper, whom Miles described as "the blackest of Black Republicans," a term used to describe hard-core radicals and Abolitionists of the party. Davis was stricken by the loss of his friend, and at first was dismayed by Cooper's stern, gruff manner—but he soon found that his new physician, too, was generous and humane in spirit. Within a few days Cooper, also, had succumbed to the prisoner's personable manner and rapidly became his advocate before Miles. It was not long before an alarming report on Davis's health by Dr. Cooper reached the press. The outraged Miles complained to his superiors that he was merely carrying out orders for the treatment of Davis—and laid his new troubles to Dr. Cooper, who, he now said, was "entirely under the influence" and "stronger mind" of Davis. Further, Miles said, Cooper's wife was a "secessionist."

Inspired by the two doctors, press reports in many states were now reflected in public protests in Washington. Some women from Baltimore took President Johnson a petition signed by several thousand people, demanding that the Confederate chief be freed. A committee of Italian-Americans from New York presented Johnson with a similar petition signed in Milan.

These stirrings further raised Varina's hopes, but she now realized that she must exert herself to the limit if she was to free her husband from Fort Monroe. Virginia Clay had already demonstrated how this could be done.

16

"The President is bailed!"

IT had been the ingenuity and spirit of Mrs. Clay that first inspired Varina to attempt to aid the imprisoned President through correspondence with men of influence. No sooner had the *Clyde* left Fort Monroe, in fact, than Virginia had begun her assault upon the Federal hierarchy in behalf of Clement Clay—with the aid of a sympathetic stranger. Before the ship docked in Savannah she had written half a dozen impassioned appeals to friends in Washington, as well as to prominent lawyers whom she knew only by reputation, including Horace Greeley's New York friends, Charles O'Conor and George Shea.

Virginia also wrote, in her naïveté, to Joseph Holt, the grim Judge Advocate General who was now insisting upon the hanging of Davis and Clay, his erstwhile friends. Virginia Clay did not suspect that the charming young lawyer she had known in prewar days had become a vengeful radical, embittered by wartime hatreds. Holt must have read in amazement Mrs. Clay's mention of "that happy & hallowed time when you esteemed my husband as all that was noble, true & brave," her remembrance of his "angelic wife," and her plea for a fair and impartial hearing.

Virginia was puzzling over how she would get these letters from the *Clyde* to the men who might help her husband when good fortune almost literally dropped the solution into her lap. A Federal soldier tossed a note into her cabin: "I will mail your letters. Trust me." She passed the envelopes to the soldier with a gold coin for postage. When the ship touched at Hilton Head, S. C., her appeals went into the mail without the knowledge of Federal officers. Later in the day the gold coin was tossed back through a porthole to land on Virginia's berth. Her offensive had begun.

While Varina Davis settled in Savannah with her family, Mrs. Clay was allowed to go to Macon, where she had encouraging replies from the lawyers, who assured her that Clay was not likely to be tried, much less hanged. Joseph Holt did not respond to her plea.

Virginia wrote to ex-President Pierce and Horace Greeley to protest Clay's "cruel and inhuman" treatment at Fort Monroe and begged them to intercede. Though her letters were forceful, she wrote with a grace and sparkle—even coquetry—that Varina Davis lacked. Mrs. Clay also appealed to Andrew Johnson when she became impatient with the easy assurances of distant lawyers. And when the President did not reply to her, Virginia wrote her Washington friend Ben Green to urge Johnson to suspend the ban on travel by "arch rebels" so that she could come to the capital.

Green advised her to invade Washington even without consent: " 'Tis said that the President likes the opportunity of granting personal favors direct to the parties on their own application—That he don't like intermediaries—and that the ladies never fail with him."

To Virginia, who had now returned to the Clay farm near Huntsville, Ala., the prospect of trying her wiles upon the President was irresistible. Friends and relatives warned that she would fail, but the self-assured Mrs. Clay prepared for the journey. Though she was penniless, she persuaded a Huntsville merchant to lend her $100, and to sell her on credit the silk cloth to make a new dress. Then, accompanied by Major William Echols and two other friends from the neighborhood, she was off on the long trip to Washington by train.

She was greeted in the capital by friends, most of whom were Southerners also seeking pardons or other favors from Andrew Johnson. She visited some lawyers, and then U. S. Grant, who not only gave her a sympathetic and courteous hearing, but also wrote the President, reminding him that Clay's voluntary surrender had indicated his good faith. Grant ended with the recommendation that "C. C. Clay, now a state prisoner, be released on parole."

Armed with this note, Mrs. Clay then bearded Johnson at the White House, taking with her the beautiful Adele Cutts Douglas, the widow of Stephen A. Douglas. Virginia Clay began an emotional appeal to Johnson, begging to see her husband before he died. Mrs.

Douglas burst into tears and dropped to her knees at the President's feet, urging him to relent. She motioned Virginia to kneel beside her, but Mrs. Clay refused. She had poured out her heart to him, but could not bring herself to kneel before Johnson, whom she scorned as a turncoat and poor white. Not even to free Clement would she humiliate herself.

Johnson was relieved to see the women leave. He made no promises, but sent them to see Edwin Stanton.

The Secretary of War, who was known as "The Black Terrier," was a short, powerful man, whose coarse black beard reached down to his chest. He wore thick rimless spectacles and spoke with an asthmatic wheeze.

Stanton listened with ill-concealed impatience until Virginia finished her appeal, and said righteously, "I am not your husband's judge. . . . Neither am I his accuser!" Stanton's obsession with the case had its basis in his legal training—he thought only of bringing Clay and Davis before a court to answer for their crimes as rebels and conspirators.

The discouraged Virginia went to New York seeking more help, and was astonished to find Southerners thronging the city's hotels. "Hospitalities without number were proferred," she wrote her husband. "And, would you believe it, thousands of dollars!" Many of the downtrodden victims of the war, she saw, had recovered overnight. She got promises of support from the lawyers O'Conor and Shea and from Horace Greeley, and then returned to Washington to besiege the White House. At Christmas, to her inexpressible joy, Andrew Johnson issued an order permitting Virginia to visit Clement Clay.

On her first visit to her husband's cell she poured out the story of her adventures in the North, and left with him a sheaf of papers and notes. These scattered documents were the first information that either Clay or Davis had seen of the government's charges against them.

Virginia soon gained from President Johnson unlimited permission to visit Clay, but that was not enough for her. And in April 1866, having won the support of Thaddeus Stevens and other Radical Republican leaders who had succumbed to her charm and persistence, Virginia returned to the White House, confident that she could free Clement Clay from prison.

This time she spoke fearlessly to Johnson, accusing him of truckling to his belligerent Secretary of War. "Who's President?" she demanded. "You, or Stanton?" Johnson wrote an order for the release of Clement Clay.

Clay agreed to sign an amnesty oath in return. Virginia hoped that he would join her in Washington but he refused. "I am too enfeebled by my long & painful confinement to bear the excitement . . . & I am too anxious to see my dear old parents. . . . Let us hurry to them."

Mrs. Clay carried her husband to Alabama in triumph, and though he was in the chronically poor health that he was to suffer the rest of his life, the friends and neighbors who greeted him at the home of his father were pleasantly surprised: "We hardly expected to see him looking so well as he does. The trouble, harassment and deprivation of prison life have, however, left visible marks . . . and his head is sprinkled with premature gray."

Clay's exultation over his freedom was tempered by the death of his father soon after the homecoming. He and his wife then began a long, desperate struggle to save the Clay properties amidst the ruins of the Southern economy and in face of greedy carpetbaggers who had already begun gathering like vultures to prey upon helpless white landowners.

Varina Davis, though heartened by the release of Clay, knew that her own task in freeing her husband was a much more formidable one. She realized that Davis would never sign an oath in order to regain limited citizenship as offered by the government. And, though the case of Clement Clay had not been insignificant, Varina was aware that her husband's was much more vital to Washington officials. Jefferson Davis was the symbolic victim whose blood was sought by Edwin Stanton, Joseph Holt and their allies. President Davis had been the real quarry of the massive manhunt mounted from Washington, and he was still the focus of Radical Republican efforts to fix blame for the catastrophic war.

As the only remaining state prisoner behind bars, Davis was ostensibly held on the original charges—complicity in Lincoln's murder and treason to the government. But there was no hint from Washington as to when he would be tried. In the spring of 1866, a congressional committee proposed a special court for the trial, headed by the celebrated Judge Francis Lieber. After studying more than 270,000 Confederate documents, seeking evidence against Davis, this court discouraged the War Department: "Davis will be found not guilty," Lieber reported, "and we shall stand there completely beaten."

In face of this, government prosecutors began shifting their charge to treason alone, and it was this charge on which the U.S. grand jury in Norfolk, Va. (which included white and black illiterates), returned indictments against Davis and Robert E. Lee. O'Conor and Shea were exuberant. The volunteer lawyers for Davis were confident of victory.

By this time Varina, who had been granted permission to visit her children, was in Canada. She had hardly arrived when she heard a rumor that Davis was near death. She telegraphed President Johnson: "Is it possible that you will keep me from my dying husband?" Johnson sent permission for her to visit Fort Monroe.

She arrived at the prison on May 3, accompanied by Piecake and Maggie Howell. She was horrified by Jefferson's "shrunken form and glassy eyes. . . . His cheek bones stood out like those of a skeleton." She noted that his walking across the cell brought on labored breathing; his voice was barely audible.

She found his mattress crawling with bedbugs, such a heavy infestation as to create a foul odor in the room. The unsuspecting Davis, who "could not imagine what annoyed him at night," naïvely insisted that he suffered from some skin disorder, and not from the bites of lice. His food, she thought, was adequate, though served in an unpalatable manner. Davis could eat but a single oyster for dinner one night for fear of stomach pains. She noted other shortcomings: Davis used a horse bucket for water, his chair had one short leg that caused it to teeter, his tablecloth was a copy of the New York *Herald*. Despite all, she found her husband calm and "bitter at no earthly person"—though he did express mild contempt for General Miles and the petty tortures the jailer had devised for him.

Miles grudgingly permitted Varina to visit the cell for short periods, but in the evenings, she complained, "If the General came over to the guardroom and found us cheerfully talking together, whether at 7, 8, or 10 o'clock, he left the room and sent an order for me to go home." One day when Varina was with her husband, Miles came and said "something so insulting" to Davis that he flung himself upon the bars in fury, shouting, "But for these you should answer to me now." Miles drew back.

Gifts from admirers began to arrive at the prison for Davis, to the indignation of Miles, who resented even the oysters sent occasionally by Dr. Cooper's wife. When he learned that some women in St. Louis had sent a dressing gown to Davis in a package addressed to Varina, he accosted her: "This fort shall not be made a depot for luxuries and such delicacies as oysters for Jeff Davis. I shall have to open your packages and see that this is not done."

Varina turned upon him with blazing eyes: "I am not your prisoner. You would not find yourself justified by the laws in infringing on my private right." The astonished Miles muttered, "I guess I couldn't," and said no more of the parcels.

Varina had developed a hatred for Miles which would lessen only in the mellowness of her old age. "A beast," she wrote. "A hyena, and only 26 years old."

Soon afterward, like Virginia Clay before her, Varina took her case to the White House. She went with misgivings, since she was aware that Andrew Johnson had nurtured a hatred of Davis for more than twenty years. This animosity traced to a speech on the Mexican War made in the Senate by Davis, when he had referred scornfully to tailors as opposed to soldiers—a reference Johnson took as a calculated insult and a slur upon his former profession and station in life. Johnson thereafter spoke scathingly of Davis as a member of "a swaggering, bastard aristocracy."

Varina was taken by surprise as she entered Johnson's office, for the President greeted her with grave, almost obsequious, courtesy. His black eyes glistened in their deep sockets, and his rugged face suggested candor and unflinching courage. But Varina knew him to be narrow and dogmatic in his opinions (he had voted against establishment of the Smithsonian Institution on the ground that public funds should not be spent on improvements, however laudable their purpose). But now Johnson greeted Varina as if she were an ally. "Our hope," he said, "is to mollify the public to Mr. Davis."

"But there would be no need for mollification, if you had not proclaimed that my husband was an accessory to Mr. Lincoln's murder. . . . I'm sure you did not believe it."

"No," Johnson said. "I did not. But I was in the hands of wildly excited people."

Something in the President's manner won Varina's grudging sympathy. Though she did not realize it, Johnson was on the verge of an impeachment trial, the climax of a Republican feud which had grown from the stormy secret relationship between the Democratic President and the increasingly insolent Edwin Stanton. Varina had a glimpse of the stress and turbulence which lay behind the White House façade.

Johnson was telling her of his problems as a Democratic President under domination of a Republican administration and Republican Congress when Senator Thaddeus Stevens burst in and began scolding him, as Varina reported, "in such a manner as would have been thought inadmissable to one of the servants."

When the disrespectful Stevens had left the room Johnson said, "You see a little of the difficulty under which I labor." He suggested that Davis ask for a pardon in writing. Varina replied that her husband would never consent to that. Unable to win concessions from Johnson, she returned to Fort Monroe.

Public opinion in the North began to turn even more strongly against Edwin Stanton and his policies, and against Miles in particular—due largely to the publication of a book by the deposed Dr. Craven which gave intimate details of the imprisonment of Davis and revealed Miles as an insensitive brute.

Anxious to write a book about Davis and his imprisonment, but aware of his shortcomings as an author, Dr. Craven had gone to New York to consult an army friend, Colonel Charles G. Halpine. This journalist, a facile writer of sensational articles, had also won a reputation as a humorist with his books of army tales—written under the pseudonymn Private Myles O'Reilly.

Halpine had led a notable career. After writing for newspapers in Dublin and London, he had arrived in New York ten years before the war and had served as private secretary to both P. T. Barnum and Senator Stephen A. Douglas. He had also become Washington and foreign correspondent and then associate editor of the New York *Times.*

Craven turned over to Halpine his diary and notes covering about seven months of the imprisonment of Davis, letters on the overcoat incident and two of his official medical reports.

In return for a fee, Halpine organized these scanty materials into book form and within a brief period—from nine days to three weeks, by various accounts—delivered the manuscript to his publisher, George Carleton. Craven was paid an advance of $2,000. *The Prison Life of Jefferson Davis,* bearing Craven's name, appeared in June 1866, and became a best seller despite the carping of some Northern critics, who deplored its sympathetic view of Davis.

Not only was the book rich in details of Davis's imprisonment —it argued for his release. If he were guilty of plotting against Lincoln's life, or of authorizing cruel treatment of Union prisoners (of which the government had declared him innocent by inference), then he should have a fair and open trial. But if his only guilt had been rebellion, then a magnanimous nation should set him free to wield his influence as a responsible leader of the postwar South.

The book created a clamor in the North for the release of Davis, this time joined by Gerrit Smith, a prominent philanthropist who had been an Abolitionist leader and an uncompromising anti-Confederate. Smith signed a petition to Johnson demanding the release of Davis: "We have neither moral nor legal right under the Constitution to put on trial under the Constitution, those whom we have recognized as belligerents and under the protection of the law of war. . . . The South, in her vast uprising, reached the dignity and rights of a party to a civil war."

Publication of Craven's book evoked an equally striking shift of public opinion in the South, where it served to unify further the vanquished people behind a leader they had so recently seen vilified. When they learned from Craven's story the melodramatic details of the shackling of the prisoner, Southern patriots were moved to wrath that surpassed their former indignation. This account was persuasive, the more so since it was testimony by a staid army doctor who was a Yankee in the bargain. (The role of the sensationalist Halpine in sketching the imprisonment of Davis was unknown to the public and would long remain so. The ghostwriter was to die in 1868 from an overdose of chloroform taken "to relieve insomnia.")

In face of the new sentiments among influential Northern politicians and others, Andrew Johnson moved to alleviate the sufferings of Davis: he ordered General Miles mustered out of the volunteer army. Miles protested vehemently that he had done no more than his duty and that he had been slandered by "the disloyal press." He begged to be allowed to remain at Fort Monroe until Davis was removed for trial, but Johnson was adamant and Miles was relieved. His disgrace was temporary indeed, for the regular army accepted him as a colonel and the former crockery clerk soon began a meteoric rise to fame within the service.

Davis and Varina celebrated the departure of the tyrannical young jailer and welcomed his successor, the humane General Henry

S. Burton, who quickly gave Davis freedom of the fort and allowed Varina to accompany him on his walks in the open air. But even these concessions merely intensified Varina's depression over the delays by the government. She turned to Horace Greeley once more, and this time he responded with an editorial that might have been written for an audience of one in the White House.

Davis had spent eighteen months in prison, the editor reminded, and the $100,000 reward for his capture had been paid.* Government efforts to try the prisoner were so inept that "Congress President and Chief Justice were in a complete muddle on the subject." Greeley urged the immediate release of Davis and called on Johnson to retract his charge that the prisoner had been involved in the assassination of Lincoln. It would be unwise and unjust, Greeley argued, to release a state prisoner with "the brand of murder on his brow," especially when the charge was unproven. The *Tribune* added:

"A great government may deal sternly with offenders, but not meanly. . . . We feel confident that magnanimity toward Davis . . . will powerfully contribute to that juster appreciation of the North at the South which is the first step toward a beneficial and perfect consolation."

Determined to act while public response to Greeley's editorial was at its peak, Varina went to Baltimore to seek the aid of John W. Garrett, President of the Baltimore & Ohio Railroad, who was said to favor the release of Davis.

She had found the right man. Garrett and Edwin Stanton had long been friends, ever since Stanton had served as a young attorney for the railroad in the Midwest. Varina's plea to Garrett was simple: Davis would die unless he could be released soon. She explained that she already had allies in Washington, and that Secretary of the Treasury Hugh McCullough had promised his aid in the attempt to free Davis.

Garrett was so impressed that he went to Washington a few days later, determined to win Stanton's approval. The Secretary was

*The reward had been paid belatedly after brisk political maneuvering in Congress by delegations from Michigan and Wisconsin. With the aid of Ohio, Wisconsin triumphed in the final hours of the session of 1868 and won a settlement which paid $3,000 each to General Wilson, Colonels Pritchard and Harnden and Captain Yeoman of the First Ohio, leader of the spies who rode with Davis. The balance was divided among about 100 men of the First Ohio, 70 men of the First Wisconsin and 120 men of the Fourth Michigan. Colonel Pritchard advised his Michigan men not to accept their share, but this protest was in vain.

so ill that he was receiving no visitors, but Garrett drove to his home, sent in his card and was admitted.

When Garrett said forthrightly that he had come in behalf of Davis, Stanton flushed with anger and declined to talk of the matter, but Garrett forced him to listen: "At least two members of the Cabinet are willing. The court would approve. But Davis's health is your chief concern. If he dies in prison you'll find that most unpleasant— shall we say inconvenient—for the government."

Garrett added that President Johnson was waiting for Stanton's approval. After a brief, heated discussion, Stanton surrendered to the logic and humanity of Garrett's appeal, and said he would no longer offer an objection to the release of Davis. Garrett then approached Horace Greeley, who had already agreed to join Cornelius Vanderbilt and Gerrit Smith in posting a bond of $100,000. Charles O'Conor, the volunteer attorney, promised to go to Washington to arrange final details. It now appeared that Davis might be a free man within a few weeks.

Despite her elation at these signs of approaching triumph, Varina had suffered a painful, trying time in Baltimore, where she had all but three of her teeth extracted. She also had an eye inflammation and was quite ill for several days. She would not appear in public, she said, even in her husband's behalf, until her dental plate was finished. Meanwhile, she wrote him, she was in such pain from "the killing of nerves, and punches and plugging" that she could hardly think. Of the loss of her teeth she said, "I can live just as well without them, however unlovely I shall appear. I do hate it, however." Just before she prepared to return to Fort Monroe she wrote wistfully, "Little Winnie must make much of her old toothless mother . . . and Maggie must make believe I am indispensable to her. As to you, I must demand a great deal of petting in return for the thinking I have done about you."

Varina returned to the fort at the end of April, having accomplished more with her artful schemes and barrage of correspondence than had all of the distinguished lawyers who had rallied to the defense of her husband. Though Davis remained skeptical of chances of release after so many disappointments, Varina began packing for his return to freedom.

Ex-President Franklin Pierce, who came to visit his old friend at the time, was also optimistic—the government, he predicted, would not dare to try Davis for treason and risk a vindication of secession in the courts. The Constitution, Davis and Pierce agreed, justified the Confederacy and its defense of the rights of states, which were the parents of the nation. Davis told Pierce that he planned to go to Canada when he was released, so that he could see his older children for the first time since his flight. Pending a court ruling, he could make no further plans.

Already his freedom was at hand. The attorney Charles O'Conor had sent Burton Harrison to the court in Richmond with a writ of habeas corpus, and Harrison arrived at Fort Monroe with the executed document on May 10. A Federal court hearing was to be held in Richmond immediately, and the President would be released from prison—or held to face trial for treason. It was precisely two years since he had been captured in the South Georgia woodlands.

Davis and Varina, accompanied by Harrison and Dr. Cooper, sailed up the James River on a U.S. steamer, hailed by people along the route who waved from the banks or from plantation landings.

A newspaper reporter commented on the prisoner's appearance on his arrival in Richmond: "A full beard and mustache conceal the ravages made by sorrow and suffering . . . but his countenance, although haggard and careworn, still preserves the proud expression and the mingled look of sweetness and dignity for which it was ever remarkable." His hair was now silvered but his face was bright, and Davis seemed "every inch a king." The leader who had fled Richmond in disgrace, cursed by many of his people, had returned a hero—despite a defeat which had brought ruin to his region.

A crowd gathered later at the old Spotswood Hotel, where the Davises were given the same room they had used six years earlier, when Davis had arrived as President of the new nation. Davis was notably calm throughout the informal reception which ensued.

Burton Harrison wrote, "No stranger would suppose for an instant that the quiet gentleman who receives his visitors with such graceful elegance and dignity is the state prisoner . . . whose trial for treason against a mighty Government today attracts the interest of all mankind." His dignity did not prevent Davis from kissing the women who came, Harrison noted, and "he kissed the prettiest again on their departure."

There was an air of tension the next morning as Davis prepared for court, for it was feared that even if the President was released by the military without further complications, the U.S. Judge John Underwood might send the prisoner to a local jail to be held for later trial. Davis dressed in new finery for the occasion, in a black suit flecked with gray and with green kid gloves, a costume mysteriously acquired overnight. The ex-President entered the courtroom with "a proud and lofty look," so a reporter said. The room in the old Customs House was all too familiar to the prisoner—it had served as his presidential office throughout the war. He was alone with his attorneys and well-wishers who had come from afar. Varina had remained in the hotel room, where she joined a number of Richmond women in prayer for the defendant.

Davis was joined by six attorneys—Charles O'Conor and Judge George Shea of New York and William B. Reed of Philadelphia, with three prominent Virginia reinforcements, Judge Robert Ould, John Randolph Tucker and James Lyons. George Davis, the former Confederate Attorney General, was also there to lend support.

Among distinguished Northerners in court were the Abolitionist leader Gerrit Smith and Augustus Shell, who represented Commodore Cornelius Vanderbilt. The arrival of Horace Greeley caused a stir as people craned their necks to see the bizarre figure who was one of the most famous of living Americans. Greeley peered through thick glasses which sat askew on his nose. His black silk cravat was rumpled and his pink face and skull glowed beneath a fringe of yellowed hair. (Greeley had been fired from a newspaper because the owner wanted "only decent looking men in the office.") Though he had come to help pay bail for Jefferson Davis, Greeley was known as an uncompromising Republican. Men still repeated his quip, "While not every Democrat is a horse thief, every horse thief is a Democrat."

When Justice Underwood accepted the writ of habeas corpus and declared that Davis was no longer under jurisdiction of the army, the audience waited anxiously for fear he would remand the prisoner to jail to await trial in civilian courts. O'Conor announced that the defense was ready for immediate trial, but William M. Evarts, the U.S. Attorney General, replied that the case could not be heard at that term. Underwood then ruled, to the relief of the uninformed audience, that Davis was eligible for bail (which had been agreed upon secretly in advance). The judge set bail at $100,000, and ten men, led by Greeley, Gerrit Smith and Shell, advanced to sign their names to the surety bond. Davis was then released by the marshal.

The room echoed with shouts and applause. A man yelled from a window to the crowd in streets outside, "The President is bailed!" Cheers rolled across the city's hills, and the clamor subsided only when Davis made his way to his carriage and arrived at his hotel, where a watchful crowd fell silent and someone shouted, "Hats off, Virginians!" Some 5,000 men uncovered their heads. Davis joined Varina in their suite, where they knelt to pray with the little German minister, Charles Minnigerode.

Varina and Harrison took him away that night, on a ship for the North, but other crowds awaited him in New York, visitors eager to speak or shake hands—and many more came to stare curiously at the frail figure whose trials had become so familiar to them.

Though Davis had every reason to believe he would not be further molested by the Federal government, his case was not to be dismissed until almost two years afterward, in February 1869. He was free in the interim, with the proviso that he must hold himself ready to appear in court within forty-eight hours, upon notification.

The ex-President was destitute and homeless, physically and emotionally spent and entering upon old age without prospects of employment or a new career. Yet he had triumphed. From the moment that he had struggled against Edwin Stanton's brutal blacksmith at Fort Monroe, Jefferson Davis had become a martyr of the Lost Cause, a role he never lost. He was not slow to assume the mantle that ill-advised Northern policy had thrust upon him: "The consolation which I derived from the intense malignity shown to me by the enemy was in the hope that their hate would, by concentration on me, be the means of relieving my countrymen." He was also aware that most Southerners now found in him a symbol of their continuing sufferings.

Davis prepared to enter voluntary exile in Canada, where he was to remain until the government called him back into court.

PART

5

THE PHOENIX

"The war being at an end, I believe it to be the duty of everyone to unite in the restoration of the country."

—ROBERT E. LEE

17

"*Preserve the traditions of our fathers*"

DAVIS emerged into a world already being transformed at fantastic speed. The New York City in which he paused for a few days was changed almost beyond recognition. War had not slowed the flow of immigrants—more than 250,000 had come in 1865 alone. Tenements to house the newcomers were rising everywhere. Only ten years after Appomattox the city's population was to exceed one million.

One-fifth of the nation's people were now foreign-born. Other cities staggered under the burden of the influx—Philadelphia soon had 750,000 people and Chicago, 300,000. Stimulated rather than retarded by the unprecedented war effort, the North and Midwest had entered a new era of development. The movement westward had never ceased. Wagon trails pushed into new areas across the plains and ignited a series of bloody Indian wars that were to drag on until near the close of the century. The first transcontinental telegraph line had opened in 1861.

During the war, Kansas, West Virginia and Nevada had entered the Union, and Colorado, the Dakotas, Arizona, Montana and Idaho approached statehood as Territories. Nebraska had become a state only a few weeks before Davis left his prison. Completion of the first cross-country railroad was only two years in the future. Alaska had been purchased from Russia, and Midway Island in the distant Pacific had been occupied.

The South that Davis had known and loved was also in the throes of change, rising from the ruin that had fallen upon cities, towns and countryside. Desolation seemed to be a spur to energetic Southerners as well as the hordes of newcomers from the North and Midwest, who were drawn by the promise of revival of trade in the conquered region. Within a month after Sherman had left Atlanta in flames, the city was again served by railroads, a post office had opened, a mayor and aldermen had been elected (with $1.64 in their treasury), a salt factory, grocery store and newspaper were in operation. Amidst ruins, rubbish and streets deep in mud, the city entered a frantic boom. On Peachtree Street lots brought the unheard-of price of $40 per front foot; rents were soaring.

An English visitor, Sir John Kennaway, hardly knew "whether to wonder most at the completeness of the ruin which had swept over Atlanta, or at the rapidity with which its restoration was being effected."

The revival of devastated Charleston, S. C., had already begun by the time of Lee's surrender; workmen there were swarming over scaffolds about charred buildings when guns were being stacked at Appomattox.

In Memphis, more than 1,900 new dwellings were underway before the year 1865 came to an end. Under the stimulus of a booming cotton market (whose prices reached 50 cents per pound), the city's wharves were crowded night and day with stevedores and huge drays. Hundreds of portable sawmills, brought down from the North, began cutting in the vast forests of the region, and Memphis became a leading lumber center.

Chattanooga, which was indebted to the war for "half its eight thousand inhabitants and all its notoriety," had become a center of heavy manufacturing whose plants made a spectacular nighttime show beside the Tennessee River, with the "lurid glare upon the black waters of sparks and flames sent out from the chimneys of a rolling mill busy day and night in turning out railroad iron to replace the waste of war." This industry was launched by General John T. Wilder, an Indiana brigadier who had noted the plentiful coal of the region during the war and returned to operate coal mines, coke ovens and pig-iron furnaces.

A kindred enterprise in Bibb County, Ala., was headed by General Josiah Gorgas, who turned from development of Confederate ordnance to building iron works in middle Alabama, the forerunner of a vast industrial complex centered in Birmingham, "the second Pittsburgh."

The cotton textile industry revived overnight. By the spring of 1866, mills at Columbus, Ga., which had been destroyed in one of the last cavalry raids of the war, were back in operation. Seven small cotton mills in upland South Carolina were repaired. A year later, the industry was to have 32,000 spindles at work.

By the time that Jefferson Davis became a free man, the Southern railroads, which Sherman and others had destroyed so completely, were running again. Southern ports from Galveston to Norfolk, Va., were filled with foreign shipping. Agriculture languished in ruins in some states, but business everywhere, in towns large and small, flourished surprisingly. Though the new activity was frequently led by migrants from the North and Midwest, native Southerners played key roles—men like P. G. T. Beauregard and William Mahone, former generals who became railroad builders. Many active and able men, rising from the ranks of small farmers and poor whites, were to create a large middle class in the region and lend it a new vitality.

There were, to be sure, thousands of unfortunate Southern families to whom the promises of the new day were scarcely visible. Long years of economic dependence lay ahead for the South, and restrictive policies such as discriminatory freight rates would penalize the region—but for the first time the foundations of an industrial economy had been laid.

In numerous, if undocumented, cases, iron-willed victims set out to overcome all obstacles: a North Carolina woman pulled a plow herself, driven by an eleven-year-old son. An armless Georgia veteran returned to his desolated farm and hitched himself to a plow, which was driven by his wife. Not all Georgians were so resolute; some families lived on roots and berries, and the weaker perished.

The new poverty cut across class lines. The Reverend General William Pendleton, Lee's old artilleryman, was mistaken for a farm laborer as he plowed, followed by a daughter who dropped seed corn into the furrow behind him. Another ex-general saved his Mississippi farm with a loan from a Northern bank—at sixty percent interest—and paid his debt in cotton. General Wade Hampton, refusing the offer of a house from the state of South Carolina, worked as a carpenter with some ex-slaves to rebuild his burned home.

Many refused to despair of the uncertain future, and could manage a grin when the popular humorist Charles H. Smith said through his character Bill Arp, "Well, I killed as many of them as they did of me, and now I'm going to work."

No Southerner went to work more effectively than Robert E. Lee. Though he had spent his life in uniform, Lee sought civilian employment and began his own effort to restore national unity. The old commander, impoverished and homeless and suffering from a heart ailment diagnosed as angina, was besieged by insurance companies and other enterprises which were eager to capitalize on his fame. When Lee rejected these blandishments, he was approached by several struggling colleges who saw in him the hope of solvency during the troubled times.

The general declined an offer from the University of the South at Sewanee, Tenn., because it was a church school, and another from the Virginia Military Institute, which was state-supported. He succumbed to tiny Washington College in Lexington, Va., which had been founded and endowed by the first President but was then almost in ruins from depredations of Federal troops. Its few buildings were dilapidated and its library and laboratories had disappeared. A four-man faculty and a student body of forty remained on the campus. Lee was offered a salary of $1,500 per year, plus fifteen percent of tuition fees. He accepted the modest offer almost at once, though his only previous experience as an educator had been as superintendent at West Point. In August 1865, only five months after Appomattox, he had ridden his gray Traveler to Lexington to assume his new duties.

In words that drew the attention of thoughtful Americans everywhere Lee outlined his motive in undertaking this new career. "I have a self-imposed task which I must accomplish. I have led the young men of the South in battle. I have seen them die in the field; I shall devote my remaining energies to training young men to do their duty in life." He went further. It was his obligation, he said, "to educate Southern youth into a spirit of loyalty to the new conditions and the transformation of the social fabric which . . . resulted from the war." As to his role as college president in the defeated South: "It is particularly incumbent upon those charged with the instruction of the young to set them an example of submission to authority."

The general exhorted students in the same vein: "Obedience to lawful authority is the foundation of manly character."

Lee's modesty and sincerity of purpose were revealed in other ways. Almost as soon as he appeared on Lexington's streets on the familiar gray horse, crowds gathered and cheered him with raucous rebel yells, which so disturbed the general that he turned back abruptly and disappeared into the home of a friend; he was determined that he would not lend himself to spontaneous, partisan Confederate rallies while the town was under martial law. He would not seek to revive the Confederacy, nor permit himself to be idolized.

The college trustees soon discovered that he was a firm adversary, for when they proposed to invite a crowd of thousands to his inauguration, for which bands would play followed by young girls, dressed in white, "bearing chaplets of flowers, [who would] sing songs of welcome"—Lee rebelled. He refused to participate in such a "grand holiday." He was sworn into office in a second-floor physics classroom before a few college officials, accepted a ring of keys to the campus buildings and went into his new office.

On the same day Lee signed an oath of allegiance to the United States, a document he had not included in his earlier application for pardon, since he was not aware that it was required. Though Lee was careful to send the document through the customary channels, its receipt was never acknowledged from Washington. Lee concluded that the government was merely following its policy of keeping him in ignorance of its intentions to prosecute, and inquired no further. This oath signed by the South's leading soldier was to have a curious history in later years.

In his new role at Washington College, Lee did as much to win the hearts of the Southern people as he had with his wartime sacrifices and exceptional military talents. His modesty, his rejection of riches and assumption of an obscure role for the sake of the South, all became part of the Lee legend. His quiet resolve created no sensation at the time, but the general's leadership reformed the college in ways that set a pattern for regional development. The moribund endowment grew rapidly and began to produce revenue. Lee built a chapel and restored the old buildings. Within five years there was a faculty of twenty-three and a student body of almost five hundred, most of these war veterans. Lee's salary grew to $5,000 per year.

More significant for the South was Lee's overhaul of the curriculum, which had emphasized Greek, Latin and moral philosophy. The general added engineering, law, agriculture, commerce, modern languages and journalism. His object was to "provide the facilities required by . . . our young men who, looking to early entrance into practical pursuits of life, need a more direct training to this end." Lee hoped that the new Washington College would help to "call forth the genius and energies of our people" and prepare them to "develop the resources and promote the interests" of the South. Obviously this was not, as the Chicago *Tribune* had feared it might be, "a school run principally for the propagation of hatred to the Union." Instead, it was becoming a model for a new era. As a leading historian of the period declared:

"Lee became the embodiment of the spirit of the New South. It was a South which, following Lee's example, would abandon its past, forsake its rural folkways, and discard the romantic notions and the constitutional theories which had led to disastrous defeat—to build a new society on a Northern model."

This was in direct contrast to the attitude of Jefferson Davis, who derided those "men who once led the Southern movements" and were now "degrading themselves, gaining power and place." He could not have been speaking of Lee, but the ex-President did deplore the direction in which the general would lead the South. Davis urged all Southerners "to preserve the traditions of our Fathers, and to keep in honorable remembrance the deeds of our Brothers." As to bowing before the conquerors, the ex-President said, "it will not be possible for me to join the throng who hurrah for the pillagers and houseburners who invaded our homes."

By now Davis had gone to his exile in Canada, hooted at by crowds as he passed through the New England states by train. As the first flush of triumph over his release began to recede, Davis found that his limited freedom brought no surcease from troubles. He was almost penniless and with no prospects of employment. His Mississippi plantation had been taken over by the Freedman's Bureau and given to his ex-slaves; it would be years before it was returned to him.

After a reunion in Montreal with his children, Varina's mother and three of the Howell brothers, Davis found life in the city almost unbearable. Varina said he became "wild with nervousness" amidst the stir and noise about him. The voices of visitors in his house resounded "like trumpets in his ears." He avoided crowds and sought to remain incognito when he went out.

Soon after his arrival in Canada, Davis was comforted by a

letter from General Lee, who was distressed that he had been unable to help him:

"You can conceive better than I can express the misery which your friends have suffered from your long imprisonment. . . . To none has this been more painful than to me, and the impossibility of affording relief has added to my distress. Your release has lifted a load from my heart. . . ." Lee said he prayed daily that Davis might be shielded from "all future harm" and that his remaining years should be "triumphantly happy."

The Davis family found little happiness in Canada. Though unaccustomed to household work, Varina cooked on a wood stove, mopped floors and did all the work once left to her slaves. She saw her husband sink into "an appalling lassitude" and felt that this was the result of his pending trial, which hung over him constantly, leaving Davis "floating uprooted."

Varina sought to divert him by urging that he write his memoirs, a prospect that excited him momentarily. Davis read his wartime dispatch and letter books, which Maggie Howell had smuggled across the border in her trunk, but was quickly discouraged. He leafed through the familiar documents only until he came upon a copy of the telegram he had sent to Lee from Danville on April 9, 1865, the day of the surrender at Appomattox:

"You will realize the reluctance I feel to leave the soil of Virginia and appreciate my anxiety to win success north of the Roanoke. . . ."

The sight of this message aroused such painful memories that Davis closed the books and paced the floor in distraction.

"Let us put them by for a while," he told Varina, "I cannot speak of my dead so soon."

He was not to resume the task until ten years later.

Davis did consent to an occasional outing, and was exhilarated during a brief trip to Toronto and Niagara, where friends and Southern supporters cheered at sight of him. But there were also hostile critics. Varina took him to a performance of *The Rivals* in Montreal, where the orchestra played "Dixie," and Davis bowed gravely to the whooping audience. But as he left the place an unknown man pressed a note into his hand, and the ex-President's pleasure in the evening drained away as he read the message: "Andersonville."

Northern newspapers deplored Montreal's enthusiastic public reception of the paroled state prisoner. The New York *Tribune* declared testily, "The fuss made over the arch rebel on this occasion proves that the Canadians are in a very bad condition of mind. They won't recover their equanimity until they are formally annexed to us."

There were persistent reports of a plot to assassinate Davis, and though he spoke of it to Varina, the ex-President made light of the tales "that there exists a conspiracy in the States to murder me. . . . I have been assured by letters of various dates and from various places. . . . There is a proverb that threatened men live long. I hope to be an example of it."

Alarmed by the dwindling of his resources, Davis moved his family from Montreal to the village of Lennoxville in eastern Quebec, where the boys were put into school. Varina wrote a friend, "We found housekeeping too expensive and have gone to boarding and are tolerably comfortable." Davis disagreed. He disliked their cheap hotel that catered to itinerant circus performers and traveling salesmen, and found the experience "vegetation rather than life."

Davis wrote urgently to Watson Van Benthuysen in an attempt to collect the money the captain had claimed on behalf of Varina and her family when the last of the Confederate treasure had been divided in Florida, but apparently managed to obtain only $1,500 of the debt of more than $6,000.

In November 1867, Davis was forced to return to Richmond for a court hearing—this time without Varina, whose mother was critically ill in Canada. General Lee, also under indictment, appeared in the capital and the ex-President and his former field commander met for the first time since the hectic flight from Richmond. There was no report of their discussion but it was evidently friendly. Davis had made no public criticism of Lee, though the general seemed to feel that the President had not approved of his surrender at Appomattox.

Lee himself had refrained from all criticism of Confederate leaders since the war, and was especially circumspect in his comments on the performance of Davis as Confederate President, even on his stubborn refusal to surrender after Appomattox, which had cost lives that might have been saved. Lee did concede in private conversation that Davis was "of course, one of the extremest politicians"—and the general believed that "the war was only created by a poor set of politicians . . . that it was by no means a necessity and could easily have been avoided." But even in intimate conversations

Lee did not place blame upon Davis; he felt that the inflexible Republican politicians had brought on war.

The general also revealed to close friends significant disagreements he had with the President during the war. He once said, "I told Mr. Davis often and early in the war that the slaves should be emancipated, that it was the only way to remove a weakness at home and to get sympathy abroad, and to divide our enemies, but Davis would not hear of it." Lee said he thought highly of Davis, but blamed him for failing to conciliate his opponents: "Mr. Davis' enemies became so many as to destroy his power and to paralyze the country. . . ."

These matters remained dormant as the two old friends faced the Federal indictments. Lee was called to testify, uselessly, about wartime movements of his army which were familiar to all, in order to establish proof of "armed resistance." Davis was not called, and his hearing was postponed once more.

Varina, whose mother had died in Canada, met Davis in Baltimore and persuaded him to take a long journey through the South, his first public appearance before his people since the close of the war.

They sailed first to Cuba, where they withdrew from a Havana bank a modest sum deposited by friends for the education of the Davis children, and then left for the South. The ex-President was moved to tears when they entered a New Orleans hotel lobby to find it packed with cheering Southerners, both friends and strangers. At each stop, as their train carried them into Mississippi, the Davises were hailed with the same enthusiasm. The now-familiar ordeal of Fort Monroe had stirred most Southerners and the sight of the thin figure of their old leader sent crowds into almost hysterical displays of emotion.

But Davis saw the rural South in ruins as he passed on his way, and the endless landscape of neglected fields and houses depressed him—though he found hope in the determined efforts of many landowners to work their own farms:

"The desolation of the country . . . made my visit sad, but the heroic fortitude with which our people bear privation, injustice and persistent oppression fills my heart with pride. It cannot be that so noble a race and so fine a country can be left permanently subject. . . .

"I start this morning for Richmond, but it is probable the trial will again be postponed. Having robbed me of everything I had, my enemies do not now allow me the poor privilege of going to work."

But there were moments when Davis forgot his troubles. Their train was once boarded by some pretty girls who brought flowers and made speeches of welcome. In his wartime tradition the ex-President claimed a kiss from each girl. When Varina was teased about this she replied,"Oh, they're not always pretty girls. He has to kiss the ugly old women, too, and then I get my revenge."

On his way to court in Richmond, Davis heard that the House of Representatives had voted to impeach Andrew Johnson, opening a furious political struggle in Washington. The squabble had begun when Johnson, stung by the insubordination of Edwin Stanton, forced him from the Cabinet. The Secretary of War resisted to the end by barricading his office, where he lived behind a cordon of guards, defying all efforts to oust him. Stanton inspired the impeachment action, charging the President with "high crimes and misdemeanors," which included liberal grants of pardons and a refusal to confiscate estates of Southern landowners—not to mention the illegal dismissal of his Secretary of War in defiance of a Tenure Act passed by Congress. As the Radical Republican Charles Sumner said, Johnson had gone over to the enemy. "A. J. is now a full-blown rebel . . . in spirit he is as bad as J. D."

In the midst of this uproar, the government again declined to press its case against Davis, and his trial was postponed indefinitely.

The Radicals failed to impeach Johnson by a single vote in the Senate, where four immovable Republican moderates stood firmly against all threats of political ruin to side with the President. Though Davis was still subject to call from the court, Johnson's survival signaled the waning of Radical influence, and his lawyers assured the ex-President of the Confederacy that the end of his travail was in sight.

Davis returned to Canada, but a few weeks later, desperate to find some way to support his family, he took Varina and the children to England, with the uncertain prospect that he might launch a new career as a cotton broker in Liverpool. He made an ineffectual effort to find a place with a commission house, and then with an insurance company in Liverpool. Not surprisingly, he failed even in this emergency, for he sought to find work only through intermediaries. His pride and dignity, as he confessed, would not permit him to "ask employment by personal application."

In London, Davis had a reunion with his old friend Judah P. Benjamin, who was on his way to new fame and fortune. Befriended from the start by Benjamin Disraeli, who was also of Sephardic descent, the Confederate immigrant had made a wide circle of acquaintances among titled Britons and already had a brisk practice in international law. He was also author of a definitive work on contracts known as "Benjamin on Sales" *(A Treatise on the Law of Sale of Personal Property),* which was to become a standard work familiar to lawyers and students of many nations until well into the twentieth century.

The Davises spent the next few months in England and France, entertained by expatriate Southerners and wealthy natives who had sympathized with the Confederacy, but the ex-President's financial problems were becoming so desperate that he was forced to return to America, where he had accepted the presidency of the Carolina Insurance Company, with headquarters in Memphis. He left Varina and the children behind.

He arrived to be welcomed by exhilarating news. Andrew Johnson, nearing the end of his term, issued a proclamation of general amnesty for ex-Confederate leaders on Christmas Day, 1868. Jefferson Davis was no longer a prisoner on bail, under threat of further imprisonment or execution. As Varina said, he was at last "safe from the clutches of the Yankees."

This significant turn of events was the first major step toward true reconciliation between the warring sections. It marked the final decline of Radical power in the sharply divided Federal administration, a decline due less to the act of the lame-duck President than to the short-sighted policies of Edwin Stanton. But for his order to shackle Jefferson Davis and the public outcry inspired by Dr. John Craven, Stanton would almost certainly have succeeded in imposing a much harsher, more vengeful, policy upon the South. The nation was fortunate for Stanton's blunder—for if he had hanged the Confederate leader, true reconciliation would have been impossible for many years to come. An embittered South would never have completely forgotten or forgiven.

But even the amnesty offered by the courageous Johnson failed to satisfy Davis, who still lived only to justify before the world the right of secession. He longed to see the North exposed as guilty of an illegal, unjustifiable war. But he was now obliged to abandon these concerns and begin a new career as a businessman.

In November 1869, Davis settled in Memphis as president of the Carolina Insurance Company at the comfortable salary of $12,000 per year. Temporarily, at least, he was freed from the anxieties of his precarious hand-to-mouth existence.

Varina was not with her husband. She remained in Europe for two years to be near her children while they were in school—but also because she was reluctant to return to a South torn by racial strife and overrun by the Ku Klux Klan and the Knights of the White Camellia, who sought to preserve white supremacy through violence and terror.

In the spring of 1870 the Southern people were given another opportunity to express their devotion to a Confederate hero—and to reveal the depths of their growing pride in the Lost Cause: General Lee left Lexington for his only postwar tour. Though he was sent by doctors who prescribed a warmer climate for his pains of angina, Lee found himself surrounded at every stop by crowds which greeted him reverently, almost as if he were a divine apparition.

With one exception Lee declined to speak to those who gathered, standing silently as his train halted in stations along the route. Frequently he kept to his seat, ill and weary and nonplussed by the attention he drew. "Why should they care to see me?" he asked. "I am only a poor old Confederate."

When he refused to emerge, the people sent gifts into the train, trays of food and baskets and garlands of flowers. His daughter Agnes, who was at his side all the way, said, "Even soldiers on the train sent in fruit, and I think we are expected to die of eating."

Lee failed to understand the emotions of those who strained for a glimpse of his worn face. "He's mighty like his pictures," people said at each stop. Many observers thought of God when they glimpsed the old general. One young woman cried, "We had heard of God, but here was General Lee!"

The journey carried Lee to the graves of his daughter Annie, at a remote spot in North Carolina, and of his father, Light-Horse Harry Lee, on Cumberland Island, Ga.—but the trains also wound through Raleigh, Greensboro, Salisbury and Charlotte, N. C., and ruined Columbia, S. C., thence through Augusta and Savannah, Ga. By small boat Lee went into Florida, to Jacksonville and up the St. Johns River, where John Breckinridge had passed toward freedom five years earlier, and to the village of Palatka, where he met his old chief commissary, Colonel Robert G. Cole. Here, for the only time in his life, Lee ate a strange, large citrus fruit which Cole said he raised only to amuse his friends—it had no commercial value. Since it grew in clusters on his trees, he called them "grapefruits."

At a stop in Charleston, S. C., on his way home, Lee was unable to deny crowds who gathered, led by patriotic delegations, fire companies, military units and bands. The general asked the former Confederate Treasurer, C. C. Memminger, to respond for him, but the excited crowd would not hear of it. Lee finally said a few words and then, pleading illness, disappeared. The brief comment was sufficiently conciliatory to impress the N. Y. *Herald,* which praised him: "It is pleasant to witness the dignified and temperate course of General Lee in the midst of these heart-felt ovations . . . it is pleasant to find the name of Lee connected with words and acts of fraternal reconciliation." But nothing could tempt Lee to speak again as he rode homeward.

By the time he reached Richmond the general was near exhaustion. When the talented young sculptor from Virginia, Edward Valentine, measured Lee for a statue and explained that he would need to come to Lexington for the modeling, Lee said, "You had best make the visit at once."

Jefferson Davis visited his wife in Europe in the summer of 1870, expecting to bring her back with him, but returned without her once more. The ex-President of the Confederacy was at sea on his homeward voyage from England when Robert E. Lee died in Lexington, Va., at the age of sixty-three. It was barely four months since the general had returned from his memorable tour.

General Lee's five rewarding and highly publicized years as college president had enhanced his reputation, but it was only after his death that the Rebel general began his rise to the pantheon of American heroes. Within hours after his simple funeral, a group of his influential friends met in Lexington to form the Lee Memorial Association. It was the opening of a campaign unique in American history, a vigorous and enduring effort that was to enshrine Lee as a national, rather than a regional, hero. He was to be ranked with George Washington and Abraham Lincoln.

Lee died amidst cold October rainstorms that lashed the rivers of the Shenandoah Valley into torrents. Several old friends kept watch beside him as the general neared his end. Colonel William

Preston Johnston, now professor of history and English literature at the college, refused to leave the dying man. It was Johnston, the veteran of the flight with Jefferson Davis, who left future publicists the theme of a creed which was absorbed into Lee's legendary reputation:

"Never was more beautifully displayed how a long and severe education of mind and character enables the soul to pass with equal step through . . . the gloom and shadow of approaching death. The . . . self-contained composure, the obedience to proper authority, the magnanimity and Christian meekness that marked all of his actions, preserved their sway, in spite of the inroads of disease. . . ."

But Lee's last thoughts were not of Christian forbearance, but of the terrible campaigns he had fought. As his mind wandered, he became once more the aggressive general who had said, "It is well that war is so terrible. We should grow too fond of it." He was also the proud veteran who had once told his wife, "Ah, Mistress Lee, we gave them some hard knocks, for all our rags!" Now, in his dying moments, he imagined himself in the midst of his war against the Union: "Tell Hill he *must* come up," he said with surprising clarity. And then, in the early morning of October 12, he breathed his last quiet words: "Strike the tent."

Lee's abbreviated funeral reflected his wishes. He was dressed in a simple black suit and there was a minimum of military pageantry. Cadets of the Virginia Military Institute fired a salute, and some old soldiers joined the hastily-arranged procession. The gray Traveler stepped slowly behind with the general's empty saddle on his back. College officials and students composed most of the file which marched to the graveside service in the cemetery, since the flood had made roads all but impassable, and many Virginians had been unable to attend.

Marse Robert's distinguished career ended on a curious and homely note, for he was apparently buried in his stocking feet. The local undertaker, C. M. Koones, had lost his supply of coffins when James River torrents washed them from his wharf, and a hurried search for a replacement ensued. Two volunteers, C. G. Chittum and Robert E. Hillis, braved the rampaging currents in a small boat to rescue a coffin which was wedged amidst undergrowth on an island. Hauled across the river for Lee's burial, the coffin proved to be so short, Chittum said, that the general's body could be stuffed into it only with difficulty, and Koones buried it without the shoes. This improvisation, so lacking in dignity, was not revealed to the Southern people at the time of the funeral and remained a well-kept secret for two generations.

The Lee Memorial Association, in its meeting of that afternoon, announced its intention "to guard the sacred dust," and began at once to plan a mausoleum on the campus—where Lee was eventually to lie beneath Edward Valentine's striking recumbent marble statue. More was to come out of this meeting. Before these admirers (mostly college faculty members) were done, they would dispatch fund-raisers throughout the country, and to France and England, gathering contributions to perpetuate the memory of Lee—and of Washington & Lee University.

Such unabashed solicitation would have displeased Lee, but it would not have surprised him. The press announcement of his arrival on the campus had spoken, in fact, of "the holy work" he had undertaken. One minister hired by the college as a fund-raiser had campaigned so blatantly through northern newspapers to raise Lee's salary that the incensed general had urged his trustees to call off the reverend solicitor "to prevent my being presented to the country in so reprehensible a manner."

The movement to honor Lee's memory could not be contained. It spread rapidly beyond the campus, notably to Richmond, where a competing group hoped to claim Lee's body as its own. Jefferson Davis gave early impetus to the new effort to keep the general's memory green.

The ex-President learned of Lee's death as his ship arrived in New York, where he found a committee from Richmond awaiting him at the dock. Davis agreed to give an address at a memorial service in the old Confederate capital a few days later—his first public address since the war's end. He used this occasion to make a contribution to harmony between factions in the postwar South.

The Richmond audience responded to its first glimpse of Davis with a roar that signaled a revival of Southern pride in Confederate accomplishments, as well as a warmth of feeling for Davis never expressed before his imprisonment. The Richmond *Dispatch* reported the phenomenon:

"As Mr. Davis walked to the stand every person in the house rose to his feet, and there followed such a storm of applause as seemed to shake the very foundations of the building, while cheer upon cheer was echoed from the throats of veterans as they saluted one whom they delighted to honor."

It was not the response of a downtrodden people.

Davis spoke of his friendship with Lee:

"Robert E. Lee was my associate and friend in the Military Academy, and we were friends until the hour of his death . . . when he was a soldier and I a congressman . . . when he led the armies of the Confederacy and I presided in its Cabinet. We passed through many sad scenes together, but I cannot remember that there was aught but perfect harmony between us. If there ever was a difference of opinion it was dissipated by discussion, and harmony was the result. I repeat, *we never disagreed.*"

This was not the time for the ex-President to recall his adamant refusal to name Lee as Commander-in-Chief until Congress forced the change upon him.

Davis did not mention his political differences with Lee in the postwar period, nor his own refusal to accept the Cause as a lost one. He also ignored conflicts of opinion between the famed field commander and his President at crucial moments during the war itself.

Davis praised Lee's modesty, "I never in my life saw in him the slightest tendency to self-seeking." This was a thinly veiled reference to the difficulties he had faced in dealing with those egotistical commanders, Joe Johnston and Beauregard.

After a pause the frail President asked, "Of the man, how shall I speak. . . . His moral qualities rose to the height of genius. . . .

"Here he now sleeps in the land he loved so well, and that land is not Virginia only, for they do injustice to Lee who believed he fought for Virginia alone. He was ready to go anywhere on any service for the good of his country. . . . Here the living are assembled to honor his memory and here the skeleton sentinels watch over his grave.

"This day we write our words of sorrow with those of the good and great throughout Christendom, for his fame is gone over the water."

Not even the most fervent members of the Lee Memorial Association could have hoped for a more auspicious opening of this movement to enshrine the Commander-in-Chief.

18

"Alas for frail humanity!"

FROM his hour of high communion with Confederate faithful in Richmond, Jefferson Davis went forth to defend the cause of the short-lived nation he had led to defeat, and to justify his stewardship of its valorous struggle. Davis was to spend most of his remaining years doing battle for his reputation. The engagements were not always of his own choosing.

The first skirmish, in fact, was launched, fought and concluded by the enemy, and passed without a word from the ex-President.

The *Louisville Commercial,* a notably partisan journal representing Northern opinion and interests, assailed Jefferson Davis on July 15, 1871, in one of the most sensational news stories of the era. It was a bold, direct and confident attack upon his moral character from the camp of the enemy.

Davis was living alone in Memphis at the time. Varina had returned from Europe and joined her husband briefly, but was soon off to Baltimore, where their sons were in school, and where Davis hoped she would find relief from the oppressive humid heat of Memphis. Varina, who still complained of vague ailments, was told by her doctor that her afflictions were merely "nerves." Davis advised her to consult a homeopath in Baltimore.

In the midsummer heat of July, while Varina probed the mysteries of homeopathy, scandal was first heard about the personal life of her husband. According to the *Commercial,* at least, "certain circles in Memphis" began gossiping about an alleged assignation between Davis and an unidentified woman in a Pullman car of the

Memphis & Charleston Railroad, during a trip from Memphis to Sewanee, Tenn.

The gossip soon found its way to the front page of the *Commercial,* presented with a heavy-handed humor designed to devastate its victim:

". . . On Tuesday evening at 6:30 [July 11] the Venerable Davis, the insurance president, left the Peabody Hotel in Memphis and took a sleeping car. . . . The distinguished ex-President . . . was kind enough to honor with his protection and fatherly care the handsome wife of a gentleman who boarded at the Overton Hotel. About a dozen persons were in the sleeping car, to all of whom the form of the ex-President was familiar."

Under the watchful eyes of his fellow passengers, Davis asked that his berths be made up at 8:15 P.M., a lower for the woman, an upper for himself.

"We approach the subject with hesitation. The berths were prepared. The lady retired to the lower couch, and the form of the distinguished ex-President, partially disrobed, was seen to ascend in a dignified manner to the upper berth.

"The train rolled on. . . . The passengers chatted and the minutes passed rapidly. Strange to say, the curtains which hid the form of the distinguished ex-President from the gaze of his fellow passengers, were seen to sway and bulge outward.

"A form descended cautiously from the upper berth, and dropped into the lower one. . . . "

Someone called Mr. Hess, the Pullman conductor, who "approached, in solemn silence . . . pulled aside the curtain with a trembling hand, and

"O, horror!

"O shades of departed chivalry and purity!

"Alas for frail humanity!

"The distinguished ex-President of the Southern Confederacy and the President of a Southern life insurance company was occupying the berth with the married lady under his chivalric protection.

" 'Mr. Davis, you cannot be permitted to do this, sir you must take another berth, sir.' "

Davis, so the report said, refused to budge: "It's none of your business, sir . . . I have paid for these berths, and will occupy which one I choose." While Hess protested in vain, "The lady discreetly turned her face away. . . . "

Hess called his superior, a Mr. Miller, the train conductor, who spoke more sternly and ordered Davis to take another berth at once. Then, according to the *Commercial,* Davis "retired with deep disgust, and elevated his venerable form (in shirt and drawers) to the upper berth."

After chiding Davis for having been vanquished by two railroad conductors, the *Commercial* gleefully reported that the ex-President had added to "the enormity of breaking the established rules" the "crime" of traveling on a pass issued by the railroad.

The conductors, so the newspaper said, reported the incident to the assistant superintendent, a Mr. Ryan, who reported in turn to the superintendent, a Mr. Anderson. The exposé ended with additional flourishes in its mock-heroic style, finally suggesting that the outraged husband of the affair might go gunning for Davis.

The story created a sensation, particularly in Memphis, where "several hundred extra copies" of the *Commercial*'s July 15 edition were sent at the request of news dealers.

In any case, Davis did not protest the publication of the tale then or later.

Even in an era when the Northern press customarily flayed leaders of the old Confederacy at every opportunity, the detailed report by the *Commercial* bore such an air of authenticity that it seemed to be unassailable, with its citations from witnesses and precise date.

But if the "exposé" had been an elaborate hoax designed to discredit Davis and the Confederacy, its effect was short-lived. The story was to remain almost forgotten for more than a hundred years, and evidently did not reappear in print. No biographer of Davis mentioned the alleged incident. But there was more to come.

Soon after the *Commercial* published its story, there was further gossip to the effect that the woman involved in the alleged escapade on the Pullman car was Virginia Clay. The tradition was to remain a persistent, albeit oral, one for generations. Unsupported by printed or other publicly disseminated charges, the gossip might have been dismissed as fanciful assumptions based upon the well-known close relationships of the past. Some friends, however, may have suspected that there was a basis for such rumors. The marriages of both the Davises and the Clays were showing certain signs of stress.

Varina Davis's mood had become testy. After a minor disagreement with her husband over his interest in the affairs of Mary Stamps, an attractive young relative, she apologized by mail. "I am ashamed of a letter I wrote you a few days ago—a seeming mad letter full of highstrikes. However, I erred on the side of love."

Virginia Clay had exhibited signs of dissatisfaction with her lot. Her husband had settled to a solitary life on his farm, eighteen miles from Huntsville, but Virginia, seeking a more active social life in the town, boarded with a friend for a few years and later moved into an apartment in an office building owned by her husband. She evidently saw Clement only on his infrequent trips into town—and between her travels.

Virginia was once absent from Huntsville for a period of five months, during which Clement Clay had written her, "I am trying to prepare our log cabin for your reception. . . . If it were possible for you to love me & enjoy my company as I love you & enjoy yours we might be happy in our seclusion."

Matters did not improve. Virginia, who made frequent visits to Memphis during this time, was consumed with jealousy and anger when she saw other families enjoying the prosperity of the reviving city. And she responded to Clay's plaints with an impassioned outburst of frustration: "I feel lonely and sad and poor. . . . Tho' I try to smile thro it all. When I see luxurious homes . . . and trousseaux from Paris, and think of my lot, my home and my one black silk dress —I do not need in addition one word from you or any other one to realize my situation."

At the time of the purported escapade on the Pullman car, Virginia Clay was forty-six and Davis just past his sixty-third birthday. Many who knew him well judged the habitually cold, reserved Confederate leader to be incapable of the warmth which would lead him into such an affair, but several witnesses, it must be admitted, had taken note of the ex-President's lively interest in pretty women.

Only older friends of Davis might have recalled an incident from his youth when, as a soldier on the western frontier, he had offended his commander—and future father-in-law, old Zachary Taylor—by his attentions to an alluring Indian girl. The escapade, in fact, had so incensed the future President Taylor that he had sought (in vain) to dissuade his beautiful daughter Sarah Knox from marrying Davis (though the old man was to change his mind after Davis had fought bravely in the Mexican War).

And there was obvious warmth in the letters Davis wrote

to Virginia Clay in the months and weeks before the *Commercial* made its allegations. Late in 1870, after a visit to Huntsville, the ex-President wrote Mrs. Clay in a rather intimate tone: "The hours dragged by wearily after you left me at the station, for the contrast with your sweet home was a strong one.... What a pity that I cannot like the good children have a fairy godmother to fulfill all wishes and banish regrets for what might have been. . . . Let me hear from you as freely as your convenience will permit and . . . put on the envelope, 'personal.' . . ."

He had written again on Valentine's Day, 1871, "It has been long since I heard from you. . . . It seems strange that we should be so near and yet so far. . . . Do you go to New Orleans this month? How happy it would make me to meet you there. . . ."

By July 1871, Virginia had returned to Memphis, where she learned that Davis was soon to make a trip to Sewanee. She made plans to accompany him, but was unable to complete them in the absence of her husband, whom she expected in Memphis shortly. When Clement Clay failed to arrive on schedule, she wrote to him in Huntsville, on July 1, "I am disappointed at yr. deferred return. Aside from the pleasure of yr. presence, I wanted to run up for a few days to Sewanee. It wd. not do for me to accompany Mr. D. without you, wd. it? I mean, with others, of course?"

It was the contention of the gossips that she had done so without awaiting her husband, or insisting upon chaperones.

Whether Varina Davis learned of the purported affair—or, if so, what her reaction was—remain matters of conjecture. Later scholars were left to their own conclusions as to whether Davis and Virginia Clay had been lovers, or were outrageously libeled by the hostile *Commercial* and declined to issue denials for reasons unknown.

Though the attack by the *Commercial* was the only one of a salacious nature, there were others in different vein, all apparently part of a widespread attempt to disavow the ex-President, or to abuse him and ruin his reputation. Some of these, assailing his brief career as political leader of the Lost Cause, came from prominent ex-Confederates, most notably Joseph E. Johnston and Pierre G. T. Beauregard, whose memoirs charged that the war had been lost through the misguided policies followed by Davis.

One of Johnston's accusations was that Davis and his original Secretary of the Treasury, C. C. Memminger, could have provided ample funds for the hard-pressed Confederacy to fight the war simply by shipping the South's huge cotton crop to England before the Federal blockade closed Southern ports. By taking that step, Johnston claimed, Davis could have armed half a million troops and funded a treasury richer than that of the United States.

Davis replied acidly that Johnston was "an ignoramus," and pointed out that the 1861 cotton crop was gone before it could have been acquired from private hands and shipped abroad, even if the Confederacy had had the vast merchant fleet necessary to carry it.

Such charges from his disgruntled former generals were the more irritating to Davis since they were more prosperous than he was in the postwar era (Beauregard stirred scandal by directing a lottery in Louisiana). By 1874 the Carolina Insurance Company had failed, and Davis had lost not only his position as President but also the hard-won $15,000 he had invested in the firm. This blow was severe and he was unable to find another place in the months following. A British insurance firm declined to hire him as its American representative for fear of a boycott in the North.

Davis then became head of a visionary scheme to ship goods from the Mississippi Valley to Europe through New Orleans, an effort that failed when prospective British backers refused to support the project, despite the grandeur of its name: The International Chamber of Commerce and Mississippi Valley Society. Davis spent a few months prospecting for mines, was drawn into plans to build a railroad, and rejected an offer to become President of Texas A. & M. College.

Pride still prevented his making a systematic search for employment, as he wrote to Varina: ". . . we can fast, we can toil in secret, but we *cannot* crawl in public." While he was in this mood, and with his need for income more acute than ever, he was asked to write his memoirs by the New York publisher, Appleton & Co. This seemed a heaven-sent opportunity to justify his support for and leadership of the Confederacy—and to respond to his critics at length. Appleton offered an advance which would enable him to hire an assistant to collect material, and there was hope of substantial royalties, in view of the intense national interest in the inner workings of the late Confederacy and the remarkable man who had directed them throughout its life. Davis had visions of providing comfort for his family during his last years.

He began searching for a place where he could settle for the long task of writing his book and found a secluded spot on the Mississippi Gulf coast, on a pleasant 600-acre plantation known as Beauvoir. The place seemed to be ideal—comfortable, inexpensive and with the prospect of inspiring company. Unfortunately, it was to stir Varina to fits of jealous rage.

Beauvoir was the home of Mrs. Sarah Anne Dorsey, a vivacious and ambitious woman from a wealthy family who had become a successful novelist under the nom de plume Filia. She was well known in British literary circles and was a collector of celebrities. Jefferson Davis had known Mrs. Dorsey and her family for many years—and she and Varina Davis had been schoolmates in their youth. When she learned that the ex-President was writing his memoirs, Mrs. Dorsey offered him a small house on her plantation, a retreat perched above the shore of the Gulf, surrounded by orange groves and vineyards and plantings of flowering shrubs and magnolias.

Varina was again in Europe, in such poor health that doctors advised her against travel. Davis settled at Beauvoir in a "cottage pavilion," which the widow had remodeled for his use. At his insistence she permitted him to pay rent, but it was only $50 per month, which included board for Davis and Robert Brown, his servant. Sarah Dorsey also found room for a researcher—Major W. T. Walthall, late of the Confederate Army, who was soon hurrying through the region, gleaning material from former officers. Mrs. Dorsey became secretary to Davis. The author dictated to her for several hours daily in a room cooled by Gulf breezes. Meals were brought from Beauvoir's kitchen, and Major Walthall provided a flow of material to bolster the memory of the ex-President.

Mrs. Dorsey's pages of manuscript grew into formidable piles as the weeks passed, and this literary idyll was undisturbed until Varina learned of it from a newspaper article. She wrote Davis in distress:

"I see . . . that you have called your book 'Our Cause.' I have so often hoped, though so far away, that you would find it necessary as a matter of sympathy to tell me of its plan and scope, and of its progress—but I know I am very far off and—'other things.' "

Seeking to make peace, Sarah Dorsey invited Varina to join them at Beauvoir. The injured wife would have none of it. As she wrote to Davis, "I am sorry not to have written Mrs. Dorsey—but I do not think I could satisfy you and her if I did . . . I do not desire ever to see her house. . . . When people here ask me what part of your book she is writing . . . I feel aggravated nearly to death."

It was clearly Sarah Dorsey, and not her husband, whom Varina was determined to avoid. She sailed for home without advising him of her coming, for fear that he would meet her in New York and try to persuade her to join him at Beauvoir. When Davis did invite her to the plantation she refused, and went instead to Memphis, where she moved in with their daughter Maggie and her husband.

Davis did his best to make amends. He appeared in Memphis in late October 1877, to beg Varina to move to Beauvoir. He endured her petulant behavior for ten days—she was "extremely cool in private"—and gave up his attempt only when she told him flatly that she would never live under the same roof with Sarah Dorsey.

The depressed Jefferson Davis returned to Beauvoir alone, leaving Varina with Maggie, who had married J. Addison Hayes, a young Memphis banker. Also in the household was young Jeff Davis, who had failed his course at the Virginia Military Institute and was now also working in a bank. Jeff was the last of the Davis sons; eleven-year-old Billie had died of diphtheria in 1874. Though Davis missed his family, he was determined to complete his book and felt that Beauvoir was indeed the right place for him to work.

During their association, Mrs. Dorsey discovered that Davis had virtually no income and sold Beauvoir to him for $5,000, payable in three installments. She also secretly made a will leaving him her entire estate.

The widow sought to convince Varina that she should settle at Beauvoir, and when her letters brought no reply, Mrs. Dorsey resolved to go to Memphis in hope of persuading her old friend to relent. When she learned of this, Varina wrote, "There is only one thing, my dear husband, that I beg of you. Do not—please do not let Mrs. Dorsey come to see me. I cannot see her and do not desire ever to do so again. . . . Let us agree to disagree about her, and I will bear my separation from you as I have the last six months and hope for better times, the history being once over."

If this reaction was colored by memories of the alleged Pullman car incident, they remained unspoken, but the depth of Varina's resentment was striking.

Later biographers theorized that Varina's confidence of her place in her husband's affections was so complete that she could not suspect him of having an affair with Sarah Dorsey. But gossips of the day interpreted Varina's prolonged absence as aloofness, and there was much speculation about the relationship between Jefferson Davis and his attractive landlady and patron, as they worked in such intimate circumstances to complete his book.

Some of this gossip may have reached Varina's ears, for she appeared suddenly and unexpectedly at Beauvoir.

In the hope of luring Mrs. Davis to her home, Mrs. Dorsey had planned a party in her honor. Though at first her refusals had been emphatic, Varina changed her mind without warning. She arrived unannounced at the plantation house, only a few moments before the first guests were to arrive for the party. Sarah Dorsey greeted her effusively, but something set off Varina's explosive temper and she lashed out at her hostess, screaming and sobbing uncontrollably. She then ran from the house into the woods, but Sarah Dorsey followed and managed to placate her distraught guest of honor before others arrived. During the party, no one suspected that the mercurial First Lady of the Confederacy had so recently recovered from a tantrum. She "reigned with queenly dignity" over the gathering of prominent guests from the region.

Surprisingly enough, Varina remained at Beauvoir, where she, too, became a paying guest. She resumed her familiar role as amanuensis to Davis, supplanting Mrs. Dorsey, and as the weeks passed and her confidence and serenity returned, Varina grew fond of her old friend Sarah. Their reconciliation seemed to be complete.

Numerous visitors began to appear at Beauvoir, most of them old Confederate officers who answered calls to aid Davis in the task of writing his book. The author found some of their testimony frustrating and complained of the difficulty of persuading ex-officers to tell him, "in a manner to be used, the truth as known to them orally." These visitors, he said, refused to appear on the record for fear of offending the enemy—"that miserable spirit of harmonizing now endemic," as the ex-President put it.

In fact, Davis received generous help from scores of former associates and could hardly have completed his work without them. In the stacks of fresh material arriving almost daily from correspondents, Davis found valuable offerings from such men as Treasury Secretary Trenholm, General Jubal A. Early, Commissary General Isaac St. John, and J. William Jones, the energetic Baptist preacher from Lexington, Va., who had assumed control of the Southern Historical Society and made it into a potent influence.

Judah P. Benjamin was another who offered help. He wrote from England of Joe Johnston and his "*nervous* dread of losing a battle" which had cost the Confederacy dearly. But Benjamin begged to be excused from the airing of other old quarrels, whose memories he said he had buried.

While Davis was deeply involved in his attempt to justify his administration and the Confederate cause, his son, young Jeff, died of yellow fever during a Memphis epidemic. Only the two girls, Maggie and Winnie, were now left to the Davises.

Mrs. Dorsey moved to New Orleans in early 1879, leaving the Davises behind. She was ill with cancer and believed that she had but a short time to live—and also felt that Varina's resentment of her had revived and was distracting Davis from his efforts to complete the book.

Sarah Dorsey was soon dead. Only then did Davis discover that he was her sole heir as well as her executor. The will praised Davis extravagantly at its conclusion, "I do not intend to share in the ingratitude of my country towards the man who is in my eyes the highest and noblest in existence."

Davis not only owned the home in which he was to spend the rest of his life—he had been left three plantations in Louisiana as well. Even so, the surprised heir was by no means a wealthy man. Like most Southern plantation owners of the Reconstruction period, Mrs. Dorsey had suffered severe losses. Labor problems beset her farming operations, and the most productive of her plantations in Louisiana now returned only $2,500 per year. The ex-President also had inherited Mrs. Dorsey's debts. In fact, the value of the estate at that time, including Beauvoir, was estimated at only $10,000.

Davis made steady progress on his book, but when he had completed the manuscript of the first volume his publishers sent a writer, the personable Judge W. T. Tenney, to Beauvoir to help improve the text. Appleton had evidently been surprised to find that the chief subjects of the work were the attacks upon Johnston and Beauregard and an interminable discussion of the Confederacy as the lawful heir of the American Revolution. All efforts to divert the President from these themes were in vain—about 200 pages of the first volume were devoted to linking his own views with those of the founding fathers.

When it was over at last, the work had dragged on for three years, exhausting both Davis and his wife. Varina had remained at his side until the end, taking dictation for long hours each day, contributing precise recollections of wartime events when his memory failed him, and adding such distinction as the work could boast. When they finished after a trying night of labor, at the hour of 4 A.M., Varina wrote to Maggie with a burst of optimism, "Well, dear love, the book is done and coming out—'Whoop-la!' "

The two massive volumes of *The Rise and Fall of the Confederate Government* appeared in 1881, but its high price and lifeless prose prevented a large sale. There was little to interest most readers in this account of the Confederacy and its spectacular war for survival. Davis had not attempted a personal version of the internal affairs of his regime, and there was thus no hint of the intriguing personalities involved. Davis did not dwell upon the causes of Confederate collapse, nor suggest that he might have borne part of the blame.

Instead, Davis insisted that the Southern people had lost their will to resist during the last year of the war (though he had denied this during early phases of his flight in 1865). His memoirs brought little acclaim to their author, and his account of the Southern cause was eclipsed by those of other participants, which were published in growing numbers. Davis's exhaustive defense of Secession became tiring, and failed to express his views as clearly as he had in a brief earlier statement: "The war proved secession to be impractical. It did not prove it to be wrong."

Even in the South, however, there were critics who denounced *The Rise and Fall* as biased and incomplete. To these people Davis replied, "The other side has written . . . their side of the case. We wish to present ours also . . . I would distrust the man who had served the Confederate cause and was capable of giving a disinterested [unbiased] account of it." His defiant spirit had not waned.

Reviewers in the North largely ignored the volumes, the publisher provided scanty promotion and Davis received little income from his effort. Indeed, he became embroiled with Appleton in litigation that would drag on until after his death.

The most sensational result of the publication was the bitter reaction of Joseph E. Johnston. The officious little general, who had so long nursed his grudges against the President, created a climactic quarrel between ex-Confederate leaders when he charged that Jeff Davis had stolen Confederate gold. Still seeking to discredit his old antagonist, Johnston had revived the long-forgotten gossip.

The general told a Philadelphia reporter, Frank A. Burr, "on good authority" that the treasure train which had fled Richmond at the time Davis and his Cabinet began their move southward had actually contained $2,500,000 in gold and silver—of which only $179,000 had been accounted for.

When Burr asked what had become of the missing money, Johnston gave a knowing smile. "That I am unable to say. Mr. Davis has never given a satisfactory account of it, and what is a strange thing to me, the Southern people never held him to an account of it."

In the face of angry protests from Davis supporters both North and South, Johnston made evasive and spiteful statements rather than an explanation or apology. He at first claimed he did not know Burr, and when challenged by the reporter, Johnston said he had been "beguiled into the conversation," which he did not "take to be an interview."

His lame and evasive responses to all queries concerning his charges cost Johnston the respect of many friends, but though Davis seemed to have the better of the argument the ex-President remained silent throughout the controversy, as he had in face of the *Louisville Commercial*'s attack.

Several old Confederates defended Davis against Johnston, particularly Captain Micajah Clark, who had been Acting Treasurer at the time of the collapse. Clark wrote an extensive account of the treasure's disbursal and added, "No gold was found on the President when captured, for he had none. He could have received it only through me and I paid him none." In a rebuke to Johnston, Clark added, "The old Confederates brought nothing out of the war, save honor; for God's sake and the precious memory of the dead, let us preserve that untarnished and defend it from slanderous insinuations."

This controversy, like others that had raged over the head of the ex-President, soon subsided, and outwardly at least, the intended victim continued his sequestered life as if he had heard none of the vituperative exchange.

Despite the commercial failure of his book, Davis continued his literary career at Beauvoir. His theme was still a defense of the Confederacy and his role as its leader. He wrote on such topics as Robert E. Lee, including only his "sunny memories" and avoiding all criticism at the suggestion of Varina; and on Andersonville and prisoners of war. As to his own guilt for the sufferings of Federal soldiers at Andersonville, he claimed, "it was not starvation . . . but acclimation, unsuitable diet, and despondency which were the potent agents of disease and death. . . . These it was not in our power to remove."

The President did not seem to be distressed by his isolated life nor by his impoverished condition. His health improved. He was so fond of Beauvoir that he thought of it as home. To General Josiah Gorgas, who was now at the University of Alabama, he wrote, "The air is soft, in winter especially the sea breeze is invigorating. The oranges are shining golden on the trees and our pine knot fires roaring in the chimneys and in their light I try to bury unhappiness."

Visitors were impressed by the apparent energy of the old man: ". . . elegant in manner, unbent by age, and his conversation of rare interest . . . a beautiful speaking voice . . . distinguished and remarkable in his appearance."

Varina, who was with him constantly, realized that their guests were deceived by her husband's feigned air of vigor. Doctors came frequently to Beauvoir, treating him for his eye disorders, gastric pains and malaria. Varina also treated him continually, with hot cloths for neuralgia, with doses of calomel and soda and "Dover's Powder" for other, often vague, ills. She was careful to keep him out of drafts, but, despite precautions, he suffered frequent attacks of bronchitis. She was depressed by his condition. "I do not know what is the matter with my head or with the world at large when Mr. Davis is ill, but I get so worried up I do not get anything right." She saw that Davis was growing perceptibly weaker each day and felt herself "powerless to do more than smooth his path."

19

"My ambition lies buried"

DURING his last years, with his daily life peopled by the vivid ghosts of the past, Jefferson Davis had little contact with the modern world which burgeoned about him. Younger, more pragmatic men wielded control of Southern politics and had begun to build upon the ruins of defeat. The old man failed to realize how little he knew of the roles of the new political opportunists who would direct the South in the years ahead.

Reconstruction came to a dramatic end with the Compromise of 1877, when the Republican presidential candidate Rutherford B. Hayes bargained his way to the White House by promising to withdraw the last Federal troops of occupation from the South. Of the complex political maneuvers which lay behind this historic turn of events, Jefferson Davis seemed to know only what he read in an occasional newspaper.

Election night 1876 found Samuel J. Tilden, a Reform Democratic governor of New York, leading the Ohio ex-general (and three-time governor) by a wide margin in popular votes, and an almost decisive total in the electoral college. It was only when an anxious worker at Democratic headquarters revealed to the Republican N. Y. *Times* that his party was ignorant of the balloting in distant Southern states that the Republicans perceived that victory could still be theirs. Telegrams went to the three Southern states still occupied by troops, whose votes were processed and controlled by Republican Returning Boards:

> Hayes is elected if we have carried South Carolina, Florida and Louisiana. Can you hold your State? Answer immediately.

Within a few days Republican newspapers were claiming victory, for Tilden had been counted out in the capitals of South Carolina, Florida and Louisiana. What took place in secret during these few days was a major victory for Southern Democrats at the expense of their national party, for the new leaders struck one of the most amazing bargains in American political history. In a cynical game of give-and-take, these white Southern leaders agreed to allow Hayes to snatch the votes of the three disputed states—fraudulently or otherwise—in return for concessions.

First, Hayes would withdraw the last Federal troops from the South, but was willing to concede more: henceforth, local Democrats would control Federal patronage in their regions. Internal improvements in the South, including a transcontinental railroad along a southern route, would be financed by Federal subsidies. Since it would have been difficult to present the outcome of these complex negotiations to the Southern people as a victory without the symbolic withdrawal of the troops, it was this result which was most apparent, and the full significance of the Compromise of 1877 was never well known, despite the durability of the bargain.

Jefferson Davis himself was obviously unaware of what was taking place at this time, for he wrote to Varina from New Orleans on December 9, 1876, at the height of the negotiations, "The excitement over the fraud in counting the vote in Louisiana is intense here, but they have become accustomed to injustice and will suffer long." A few days later, on a return trip to New Orleans, Davis wrote Varina once more, revealing his continuing ignorance of the historic deal being struck:

"I will not weary you with details of our political muddle, as it is commonly called, but will give you my hopeful opinion that Tilden will be our next President. The scenes through which we are passing would be ridiculous if less tragical, and may well induce those who doubt the capacity of man for self-government to say I told you so."

It was not long before bluecoat columns left the last occupied Confederate capital, Columbia, S. C., and once they left, Davis's old friend Wade Hampton became governor of the state and white voters regained control. After twelve years of often corrupt and oppressive rule since the death of Lincoln, the white South was free. Its people had endured the "long night" whose coming had filled Jefferson Davis with foreboding.

Future historians were to view the bargain between Hayes and white Southern leaders as callous and corrupt, since it dashed the hopes of the region's five million blacks for equality and doomed them to another half century of servitude reminiscent of the days of slavery. The experiment, some Northern scholars were to say, had been "Reconstruction that did not reconstruct," a failure to cope with the pattern of racial injustice which had plagued Americans since early in the seventeenth century. If there was blame for this to be borne by bargainers, Northern politicians who had sacrificed goals of racial equality deserved an equal share. The political trades of 1877 were evidence that race prejudice flourished on both sides of the Mason-Dixon line.

Davis certainly welcomed the dawn of the new era, but by deliberate choice did not become part of it during his brief remaining days. Although he had been hailed a hero at every public appearance since his release from prison, the ex-President seemed to be reluctant to face the Southern people. Except for a few business trips he seldom left Beauvoir, and it was evidently in the solitude of the countryside that he could "bury unhappiness." But near the end he had a change of heart.

It was his old home state of Mississippi which first lured the ailing Davis from retirement and almost literally forced upon him the adulation of his people. The ex-President was greeted with "the wildest enthusiasm" by a joint session of the Mississippi legislature in the spring of 1884: "Cheer after cheer went up, handkerchiefs waved, and the grand old man knew that he was appreciated by his own people." It was his first appearance before a legislative body in almost twenty years.

Davis, unlike Robert E. Lee on his lone foray into the Deep South, unhesitatingly accepted the opportunity to make a speech, a dignified, thoughtful statement for the first few moments. But he could not refrain from a cry of the defiance he had nurtured for so long:

"It has been said that I should apply to the United States for a pardon, but repentance must precede the right of pardon, and I have not repented. Remembering . . . all which has been suffered, all which has been lost, disappointed hopes and crushed aspirations, yet I deliberately say, if it were all to do over again, I would do again just as I did in 1861."

He was halted by applause. And then, as if to reassure listening politicians who feared giving offense to the North, Davis made a plea of a sort he had previously avoided. It was almost as if the conciliatory voice of Robert E. Lee were echoing in the chamber:

"Our people have accepted the decree. It therefore behooves them, as they may, to promote the general welfare of the Union, to show to the world that hereafter, as heretofore, the patriotism of our people is not measured by lines of latitude and longitude, but is as broad as the obligations they have assumed and embraces the whole of our ocean-bound domain."

It was a startling reversal of position which he never sought to explain. He may have made this call for national harmony in the mellowness of old age with its intimations of mortality, or because his intelligence was at odds with the emotions which had wracked him for so long—or perhaps out of admiration for the example of such die-hard old Confederates as Wade Hampton, who was now actively helping to build the New South and seeking to forget old hatreds.

It was two years later when the old man ventured forth again to receive public acclaim. An insistent committee from Montgomery, Ala., came to Beauvoir to ask him to be guest of honor when Alabama laid the cornerstone of a monument to its Confederate dead—one of the first of thousands to come, granite and marble sentinels which were to stand in virtually every courthouse square in the South. The Alabama ceremony was to be held near the spot where Davis had been sworn in as President of the Confederacy twenty-five years previously.

With announcement of his forthcoming visit to Montgomery, Davis was besieged by other Southern cities. He accepted invitations from Atlanta and Savannah, the first to honor his friend the late Senator Benjamin Hill, and the second to unveil a monument to General Nathanael Greene, a hero of the American Revolution who had spent his last years on the Georgia coast—and under whom Davis's father had fought against the British.

Young Winnie accompanied her father to Montgomery, for the Alabamians had convinced him that only the cheers of the welcoming crowds on such occasions could reveal to her the depths of the affection in which he was held. Cannon salutes greeted them in the city and crowds pressed their carriage so closely that they were delayed in reaching their hotel. A fireworks display blazed in the dusk: "Welcome, Our Hero!"

The President was kept up late greeting crowds that surged into his rooms. One of his visitors was Virginia Clay, still handsome and vivacious.

For two days crowds roared and bands played, and on the second day Davis gave his address near the old Capitol for the cornerstone ceremony. Most of those who gathered before him were strangers; all of the members of the Congress which had elected him President were dead.

Of the monument, he said it would commemorate "the deeds of Alabama's sons who died that you and your descendants should have the inheritance your fathers in the War for Independence left you. . . . The war between the states was *not* revolution, as sovereigns never rebel."

Once more, however, he urged the audience to "promote the welfare and happiness of their common country," but his audience seemed to hear what it wished to hear. The crowd cheered itself hoarse, more cannon salutes were fired, and President Davis was mobbed at another reception. The New York *World* reporter was more interested in the President's durability than in the developing Southern psyche. "How this old man, who is fast nearing his eighty years, has stood the exertions of the past two days is a mystery to everyone. . . . Yet he seems well and in the best of spirits. This welcome has evidently given him a new lease on life."

Davis was then off in another special train, through "one prolonged ovation," to Atlanta and Savannah, where there were similar uproars. The celebrated Southern orator Henry W. Grady welcomed Davis to Atlanta, "Never king inhabited more splendid palace than the millions of brave hearts in which your dear name and fame are forever enshrined."

Moving on to Savannah, Davis rode in a car smothered in flowers and festooned with mottoes, one of which proclaimed, "He Was Manacled for Us." In Savannah, while eulogizing General Greene, Davis went further than before with a call of defiance to the

North. He had learned, he said, that some Savannah businessmen not only wished to avoid "offending the Yankees," but had tried to placate Northern capitalists by pretending to believe that the Confederate cause had been wrong. Of this reported disloyalty to the cause Davis said, "In 1776 the Colonies acquired State sovereignty. They revolted from the mother country. . . . Is it a lost cause now? Never. . . . The independence of these States . . . which Nathanael Greene . . . helped to win for Georgia, can never die."

The "inflammatory" remark was sent to Northern newspapers, and friends advised Davis to soften the impression he had made. The old man offered a halfhearted apology during a banquet in Savannah: "There are some," he said, "who take it for granted that when I allude to State sovereignty I want to bring on another war. I am too old to fight again, and God knows I do not want you to have the necessity of fighting again." Reporters dutifully took down his clarification—but even now Davis could not resist one more challenge to the enemy. After a pause he added, "However, if that necessity *should* arise, I know you will meet it as you always have discharged every duty you felt called upon to perform."

This provoked an outcry from several newspapers in the North, where every statement of the ex-President was taken seriously and public opinion had been conditioned to expect Southern acceptance of the war's verdict, if not a burden of guilt. Even the friendly New York *World* reporter who was following Davis saw a threat in the enthusiasm with which the South had greeted the ex-President on this tour, "All the South is aflame, and where this triumphant march is to stop I cannot predict."

Still, there were signs that some perceptive Northerners saw that this was not so much a threat to national harmony as a declaration of Southern pride in Davis and his cause. The Lowell (Mass.) *Sun* expressed this: "Jefferson Davis suddenly emerges from his long retirement, journeys among his people and everywhere receives the most overwhelming manifestation of heartfelt affection, devotion, and reverence. Such homage is significant, startling. And it is useless to attempt to deny, disguise, or evade the conclusion that there must be something great and noble and true in him and in the cause to evoke this homage."

The Lowell editor might have been forgiven for his assumption that this display of homage was the natural reaction of a proud people to the sight of their former leader; but there was something unique in the fresh chorus of rebel yells for Davis. The Southern people at large clung to the attitudes they had held in prewar days: their region and their people were somehow superior to others in America, and conquest by their inferiors did not alter the case. This persistent notion owed much to the spirit of Jefferson Davis, and—for all his apparent humility and concern for national harmony—to that of Robert E. Lee.

Davis returned from his triumphs happy but exhausted. He came down with an attack of bronchitis, and twenty-two-year-old Winnie had a bout with measles. There were few other outings for the aged chief, but these, too, evoked powerful reactions from those who heard his weakening voice.

In the autumn of 1887 he was greeted by a crowd of 50,000 in Macon, Ga., about one-tenth of them Confederate veterans. Davis narrowly missed serious injury when the column of veterans lost their heads in their enthusiasm, broke ranks and rushed their old chieftain, seeking to grasp his hand. One man wrapped a faded battle flag about their hero. Davis buried his face in the folds to conceal his tears.

The excitement was too much. Davis was staggered by a chest pain, and, as Varina said, "The brave heart that had not quailed under imprisonment and vilification, gave way under the weight of his people's love and almost stopped beating."

Doctors were alarmed, and there were reports that Davis was dying. But he was back at Beauvoir a few days later, clinging to life with an iron will. Though he said he would make no more speeches, he did appear once more before a group of young men in his neighborhood. With the intention of urging them to accept national unity, the ex-President began his talk to the youthful leaders with, "Friends and fellow citizens. . . ." He hesitated and corrected himself, "Ah, pardon me, the laws of the United States no longer permit me to designate you as fellow citizens, but . . . I feel no regret that I stand before you a man without a country, for my ambition lies buried in the grave of the Confederacy."

He returned to his speech, and for the first time urged without equivocation that young Southerners pledge themselves to reunion. "The past is dead; let it bury its dead, its hopes and its aspirations. Before you lies the future—a future full of golden promise; a future of expanding national glory, before which all the world shall stand amazed. Let me beseech you to lay aside all rancor, all bitter sectional feeling, and to take your places in the ranks of those who will bring about a consummation devoutly to be wished—a reunited country."

It was a prophetic voice, but it was hardly recognizable as that of Jefferson Davis, who had kept alive for so long the tenets of a cause which had nearly destroyed the Union.

Davis survived his eightieth birthday by only a few months. After long outdoor exposure in a cold November rain during a trip to his Brierfield Plantation, he developed a respiratory infection and was taken to New Orleans in serious condition, which doctors diagnosed as acute bronchitis, complicated by malaria. On December 5, 1889, soon after a quiet announcement to Varina that he had no fear of death, Jefferson Davis breathed his last.

In Atlanta, Henry W. Grady was aroused with the news about 2 A.M., and began writing an editorial for his *Constitution.* "This morning is another page in the history of the world. Jefferson Davis is dead! . . . he will be mourned in millions of hearts today."

Newspapers in the North were hardly less laudatory in their comments.

Charles A. Dana, who had carried the order for the shackling of Davis to Fort Monroe, wrote an editorial in the New York *Sun:* "Even among those who looked upon him with least sympathy it was felt that this man bore defeat and humiliation in the high Roman fashion. . . . "

The comments of other newspapers in the city made it obvious that Davis had outlived many of the animosities he had generated in the North.

The *World* said: "The death of Jefferson Davis ends a most remarkable chapter in history. . . . He was the chosen chieftain of the new Republic which . . . battled for its existence with a heroism the memory of which is everywhere cherished as one that does honor to the American character and name. . . . He sacrificed all for the cause he cherished, and he alone of all the South has borne the cross of martyrdom.

"He was a man of commanding ability, spotless integrity, and controlling conscience. . . . He was proud, sensitive, and honorable in all his dealings. . . . A great soul has passed."

The *Times* joined this chorus:

"The South loves his memory as it should love it and as the people of every patriotic country should and ever will respect it. . . .

"Jefferson Davis will live longer in history and better than will any who have spoken against him." (Including, apparently, previous editors of the *Times* who had demanded his execution in 1865.)

In one sense the conquered South had triumphed by imposing upon the victors its version of the legitimacy of the Confederacy and its divisive war. Even in the camp of the enemy the Lost Cause was seen as a noble one.

After a state funeral which drew more than 150,000 people to New Orleans, Davis was buried in a temporary grave in Metairie cemetery.

20

"No infidelity to the Union"

JEFFERSON Davis had been in his grave only a few months when, in the spring of 1890, the South once more gave itself over to the enshrinement of a Confederate hero—this time in Richmond, Va., where a towering equestrian statue of Robert E. Lee was unveiled. For almost twenty years groups of women, old soldiers, school children and church congregations had painfully accumulated the fund now translated into majestic bronze.

Even the smallest Southern town was sooner or later invaded by a bewildering number of agents from: the Lee Memorial Association, the Lee Monument Association, the Ladies' Lee Monument Association, and Lee Memorial Episcopal Church at Lexington, Washington and Lee University and the Southern Historical Society.

Public squabbles among the rivals raged for years. But there was also competition within Richmond itself. Only a few days before the men had organized, a few women launched the Ladies' Lee Monument Association, which included matriarchs from several influential families from tidewater Virginia. They were only a handful but they were resolute, and they surpassed all the men in raising funds, with an immediate appeal to churches throughout the South—$3,000 came from Savannah alone. For fifteen years the women's group refused to join the men's association and went its own way, steadily adding to the fund. General Jubal A. Early of the Richmond group went so far as to send a spy to learn the women's secrets. But the dowagers survived and it was not until 1886, when all but two members had died or moved out of Virginia, that the Ladies' Lee

Monument Association was persuaded to combine its efforts (and its substantial treasury) with the men's Lee Monument Association of Richmond.

It was many years before the fund reached $15,000. And it was 1886, when the end was in sight, before the Ladies' Association, in one of its final acts, offered $3,000 in prizes for the best models of an equestrian statue of Lee. Though the cash prizes went to others, it was the work of a Frenchman, Marius Jean Antonin Mercié, which caught the eyes of the Richmond judges, and after submitting two more models he won a contract for the immense statue of the hero. Lee's boots, saddle, hat and uniform were sent to the sculptor, whose previous work included bas-reliefs at the Louvre, "Young David" in Luxembourg Palace, and "Genius of the Arts" in the Tuileries. The Confederacy took him for its own and remained in a state of excitement during his years of work.

A granite pedestal forty feet high was designed by a French architect, one Pujot, and Richmond marked the laying of its cornerstone in 1887, an occasion which drew thousands of veterans and other patriots from the South at large. Into the cornerstone went: a history of the Monumental Church, statistics of the City of Richmond, records of R. E. Lee Camp of the United Confederate Veterans, Masonic records, Confederate and U. S. money, a square and a compass made from a tree that grew over the grave of Stonewall Jackson, the Lee family tree, Chamber of Commerce reports, souvenirs of the Fredericksburg battlefield, a picture of Lincoln in his coffin, several visiting cards, a program of the cornerstone ceremonies, Richmond newspapers and other publications, including a book by Carlton McCarthy, *Detailed Minutiae of Soldier Life in the Army of Northern Virginia.*

Colonel Charles Marshall, the Baltimore lawyer of Lee's wartime staff who had written the general's celebrated farewell order was orator of the day and spoke on "The Secret History of the Army of Northern Virginia." He said of the statue-to-be: "It will perpetuate no infidelity to the Union as it was, and will teach no lesson inconsistent with a loyal and cheerful obedience to the authority of the Union as it is." There was dissent from Colonel Elliot Shepherd, editor of the New York *Daily Mail,* who protested that Lee was a traitor unworthy of such honor. This drew an impassioned response from a Richmond judge: "We therefore ask that you will relent in your wrath, fold the ensanguined garment, realize that the war is over, allow the holiest emotions of humanity to find a place in your bosom, permit us, the citizens of a common country, to obey the promptings of loving hearts and do honor to the memory of that great and good man, General Robert E. Lee."

The city got its first glimpse of its new historic treasure on May 7, 1890, when four huge wooden crates arrived. A contractor was hired to assemble the work, but Richmonders were determined to move the heavy statue themselves. Loaded on oversized wagons, the dismembered sculpture was hauled through the city by school children, young women, aging veterans and others, all pulling on ropes —more than a mile of rope—as they towed the bronze burdens to their resting place. Major B. W. Richardson, the eighty-year-old president of the Richmond Blues, was first to seize a line—but 10,000 others followed him. Veterans who arrived belatedly and could find no places were provided with fresh rope—and one group became so excited that when their rope was cut at the end of the march, they circled the site once or twice before realizing that they had been freed.

Small boys carved their names on the statue through slats of the packing cases; the ropes were cut up and sold for souvenirs; the watching crowd, estimated at about the size of the pulling crews, lined the streets and crowded the fields, with many men and boys perching in trees and on telegraph poles. "Very few colored persons," it was noted, were among the volunteers who drew the wagons. Someone got a peek at the features of Lee's head, which was "about the size of a half-barrel," and was to tower some sixty feet above ground when erected. The sight through the packing case boards as reported by a local newspaper was reassuring:

"He was handsome as a youth; he was better looking still when he was in the old army; but the perfection of his manly beauty was reached in the Confederate service. Then he was at the apex of his mental and physical power. So Mercié has endeavored to picture him . . . a model soldier and man, a hero whose fame will forever gild our history's pages."

The statue, which weighed twelve tons, was riveted together on a wooden platform, and, concealed under heavy drapes, was raised on the pedestal in time for the unveiling ceremony on May 29, 1890, a spectacle attended by crowds estimated at 100,000.

Lee had been dead for almost twenty years, but there were still living two full generals, eight lieutenant generals, thirty-one major generals, and about 160 brigadiers of the Confederacy. Many of these appeared in the four-mile parade, which required two and a half hours to pass a given point. The older generals rode in carriages. Among the celebrities were Generals James Longstreet, John B. Gordon, Jubal Early, Wade Hampton, Edward P. Alexander, Joe Wheeler and scores of other famous men.

Providing a touch of irony that the more knowledgeable of older veterans could appreciate, Joseph E. Johnston, Lee's old rival and detractor of Jefferson Davis, had been chosen to unveil the statue—he was the oldest living general.

Several Confederate widows, including Mrs. Stonewall Jackson and Mrs. George Pickett, drew the attention of the crowd.

Chief marshal was the old commander's nephew, an ex-governor of Virginia, General Fitzhugh Lee. Also on hand were Robert E. Lee's children, Mildred and Agnes, Custis, Rooney and Robert E. Lee, Jr.

It was, as an observer said, "the largest crowd of distinguished people in Virginia history." A visiting Louisianian declared, "Virginia's great heart is in her throat today."

Lively notes were provided by a street band from New Orleans which had been imported by the Washington Artillery of that city. A popular number was the ragtime tune, "Down Went Mr. Ginty," and a less-welcome one was "Marching through Georgia," which was played but once. Colonel Archer Anderson, an orator of the day, gave the address, which ended: "Let this stand as a memorial of personal honor that never brooked a stain, of knightly valor without thought of self, of far-reaching military genius unassailed by ambition, of heroic constancy from which no cloud of misfortune could ever hide the path of duty.

"Let it stand as a great public act of thanksgiving and praise, for that it has pleased almighty God to bestow upon these Southern states a man so formed to reflect His attributes of power, majesty and goodness.

"Let this man, then, teach to generations yet unborn, these lessons of His life. Let it stand, not as a record of civil strife, but as a perpetual protest against whatever is low and sordid in our public and private relations."

Joe Johnston then rose, with a veteran who had lost a leg standing stiffly on one side, and another veteran who had lost an arm on the other side. The old general pulled a cord and the statue was unveiled. There was silence for a moment, then a roll of cheering rebel yells. Cannon fired, musket volleys roared, hats were tossed into the air. Many old soldiers wept, declaring that the image of "Marse" Robert on Traveler was perfection itself. A sham battle between aging mounted troopers followed, a fury of charge and countercharge which rang with saber blows and shouts that roused memories of fields lost and won so long ago.

The bronze memorial was left alone at last, identified for posterity only by its inscription, "LEE."

The imposing statue became one of the most visible symbols of the Confederacy's reviving pride in its war heroes and gave further impetus to the proliferation of military statuary in the region. It also inspired veterans' organizations, which now began a rapid expansion. The sight of the mounted "Marse" Robert was enough to send visiting survivors of the gray legions into nostalgic frenzies and fetch forth a quavering of rebel yells—a reaction which would have dismayed the gentle peacemaker of Washington College.

The infant United Confederate Veterans group, which had grown from state organizations, held its second South-wide convention in Richmond in 1891, when the Lee statue was a major attraction. Inspired perhaps by this reminder of the chieftain who had *almost* won their war, some delegates to the UCV convention helped to give the movement a new vigor and spirit which were to mark its career down to the final parade.

The Southern phoenix began to soar in the opening session of this Richmond convention, though its first moments bore no such promise. Several speakers labored their way through dull recitations of some aspect of the war or problems of the veterans. There was a lingering air of guilt and apology in the attitudes of these men—almost as if they were conscious of a hostile audience in the North. The listening veterans may have shared some of that awareness: they had been defeated in a long and bloody war, oppressed by an unscrupulous regime during Reconstruction and frequently taunted by conquerors who insisted that slavery, and not States' Rights, had been the root cause of the war.

These were not men to muse about such matters. As the speeches droned on, the UCV delegates began to nod. But there was one whose boredom gave way to anger. Delegate Chiswell (Buck) Langhorne, late of the 11th Virginia Infantry, who became increasingly restless as the dreary recitals continued, longed to change the atmosphere of the session. He had quite another concept of the proper fare for these old soldiers, hungry for a revival of the vivid memories of the grand adventures of their youth.

Langhorne had begun his postwar career as a tobacco auctioneer in Danville, where he had won a certain fame as the originator of the singsong chant which was to become so familiar in the auction houses of the region, the theme song of the colorful tobacco industry. Langhorne, who was now on his way to wealth as a railroad builder, was the father of the celebrated Langhorne sisters—one of whom became Lady Astor and another the Gibson Girl, symbols of style and elegance on both sides of the Atlantic.

The irrepressible Langhorne endured the pompous speeches for a time, but then rose to interrupt a solemn passage with a burst of song:

"Oh! I wish I was in the land of cot-ton. . . . "

The crowd came to its feet, bellowing "Dixie" and yelping the rebel yell until the hall resounded with triumphant, defiant cries. The wake was transformed into a celebration of Rebel pride in the Southern heritage. Memories aroused by the roar of the country auctioneer Langhorne awoke wartime memories and revived the pride they had always felt in their army. In such a mood their war became idealized, if not sanctified. Whatever their views on slavery or any other issue, none of these old soldiers could conceive of their cause as having been a disreputable one. Memories that surfaced in that hour became a familiar part of the lore—and folklore—with which Southern writers and orators rallied the heirs of Confederate traditions and lambasted the foe which had Overcome, but never Defeated, the gray legions. An abiding theme of the postwar publications of war memoirs by old Confederates was that it was Too Damned Bad they had failed, and that it was only fate that had deprived them of victory.

Men who had been steeped in the romances of Sir Walter Scott and the Arthurian legend, as literate Southerners had been, could lose themselves in such illusions. A body of belief grew up about the Invincible Lee and his army, and from the believers came the inevitable sigh of "What Might Have Been." This grew into a tradition as durable as the perennial study of the campaigns of the fratricidal war itself. Spontaneously, it seemed, men from all parts of the South, and from generation to generation, asked themselves the tantalizing questions:

If Beauregard had pursued the panicstricken enemy in its flight into Washington from the field of Manassas/Bull Run. . . . If Albert Sidney Johnston had not bled to death from his minor wound, when victory seemed to be within his grasp at Shiloh. . . . If the *Monitor* had not appeared as if by magic to challenge the *Merrimac* at the mouth of the Chesapeake. . . . If "Stonewall" Jackson had survived the tragic volley from his own men at Chancellorsville. . . . If Lee's order of concentration before Antietam had not been used as a cigar wrapper, found by the enemy. . . . If Great Britain had recognized the Confederate States. . . . If Jeb Stuart had not been tardy, or Longstreet insubordinate, at Gettysburg. . . .

The twentieth-century historian Bernard DeVoto, who had little patience with the South's romantic concept of the Civil War and of its own unique regional character, conceded the power of the appeal of the Lost Cause. The defeated Confederacy, he protested, was in a fair way to win the renaissance as the nation prepared to mark the centennial of the conflict. DeVoto identified the heart of the Confederate mystique:

"The whisper of a great Perhaps. . . . Almost . . . four hours in Hampton Roads . . . a shot in the spring dusk at Chancellorsville . . . Spindrift blown back from where the high tide broke on Cemetery Ridge. A passionate *if*! sleeps uneasily in the grandsons' blood."

Epilogue

MANY survivors of the Confederate collapse lived long, useful lives in the postwar era, and some went on to new distinction in their interrupted careers.

Alexander Stephens, the most exasperating critic of Jefferson Davis, withstood his several ailments to serve nine years as congressman from Georgia, after his first election in 1873. The frail former Vice-President of the Confederacy wrote several books, one of which, *A Constitutional View of the War Between the States,* gave the war its most popular name in the South, and became known as the most able defense of the Confederate position.

Stephens was elected governor of Georgia, and died in office in 1883, at the age of seventy-one.

Officers of the Confederate Cabinet who accompanied Davis on his epic flight also found new prominence, none with more success than Judah P. Benjamin, whose rise to fortune and a position as Queen's Counsel in England became an epic tale of the Confederate hierarchy's recovery from adversity. Without money, he had lived simply at first, eating in cheap restaurants and earning his way by writing editorials on international affairs for the *Daily Telegraph.* But all the while he was studying at Lincoln's Inn to begin a new career in the law, thirty-four years after admission to the Louisiana bar as a fledgling lawyer. At fifty-five, he created a sensation in the Inns of Court. "The young men who came up from Oxford and Cambridge," the London *Times* said, "saw a grizzled man old enough to be their father, who had, after four years of the fiercest fights, unremitting labor, and the exercise of great power, just escaped with his life, and now sat quietly down to qualify himself to earn his bread."

Benjamin also became a clerk in a leading law firm, and so impressed his superiors that requirements for lengthy training were soon to be waived, and the ex-Secretary of State of the Confederacy became a much-honored barrister, bewigged and splendid in knee breeches, white stockings and buckled shoes. His income as one of the leading members of the profession was about £15,000 (the equivalent of about $200,000 to $250,000 in 1985 values).

Judah P. Benjamin retired in 1883, after seventeen years of unbroken success in the courtrooms of England. He had served long as Queen's Counsel, and though never appointed, had been considered for a judgeship. His retirement was marked by a rare farewell banquet in the Inner Temple Hall, presided over by the Attorney General, with speeches by the Lord Chancellor and other notables. Benjamin's gracious, moving response was long remembered in British legal circles. In declining health he moved to Paris to be near his still-beautiful wife and their daughter and died in that city the following year, 1884. Benjamin's life, said the London *Times,* had been as various "as an Eastern tale . . . and he had carved out for himself not one, but three histories of great and well-earned distinction."

John Reagan, the lone Cabinet member who had been at the side of Jefferson Davis to the last, returned from his brief imprisonment to his home in Palestine, Texas. He found his house wrecked beyond repair and began his new career on a nearby farm. As one of the most popular Texas politicians, he quickly returned to action. He played a leading role in writing a new state constitution and was elected to Congress in 1875, one of the vanguard of Confederate leaders returning to Washington. He served as chairman of the House Committee on Commerce for ten years, and remained in the House until he entered the Senate in 1887. Later chairman of the Texas Railroad Commission, an important factor in developing the vast western reaches of the state, Reagan retired to private life in 1903. He died two years later, deeply mourned by the people of his adopted state. The Texas legislature attended his funeral in a body.

The brilliant Secretary of the Navy, Stephen R. Mallory, returned to his home in western Florida to find his law library stolen or destroyed, and was forced to rebuild his practice without many of his most treasured assets.

Immediately after his release from prison, Mallory began urging his fellow Floridians to submit to Federal authority "to evoke order from chaos." To make his own peace he sought to efface his wartime reputation as a "pirate" by recalling his resistance to Secession during his service as a U.S. senator, and his firm refusal to approve an early attack on Fort Pickens in Pensacola Harbor by his hotheaded neighbors.

Mallory lived quietly with his wife, the daughter of Don Francisco Moreno, who had once been known as "King of Pensacola." Only seven years after he left prison, in 1873, Mallory died in Pensacola, leaving a son who served in Congress with distinction for many years.

Secretary of War John Breckinridge, who sailed to England after his escape to Cuba, spent his time in England and Canada until the end of 1868, when Andrew Johnson issued his amnesty proclamation and made it safe for old Confederate leaders to return home. Breckinridge was soon back in Kentucky, where he was warmly welcomed and expected to resume his political career. Refusing all such offers, the former Vice-President became a successful railroad lawyer and practiced in his home town until his unexpected death in 1875.

The Confederate Attorney General George Davis returned to Wilmington, N. C., after release from prison, to resume a prosperous law practice. He became counsel for the Atlantic Coast Line Railroad during its formative years and served on a state commission which restored North Carolina to solvency after the excesses of the carpetbagger era, but did not otherwise enter public life. He died in 1896.

Secretary of the Treasury George Trenholm, after his pardon in 1866, returned to his cotton brokerage business and partially restored his international trade. Elected to the South Carolina legislature in 1874, he led the fight of whites against black incumbents and their carpetbagger allies, with some success. The strenuous service impaired his already delicate health, and Trenholm died shortly after leaving office, only a year before Reconstruction came to an end in his state.

Burton Harrison, the faithful secretary to Davis who shepherded both the President and his wife during their flight, married the winsome Connie Cary in 1867 and the couple moved to New York, where Harrison practiced law. They traveled widely, and Connie, who wrote a number of popular novels, plays and essays, became a well-known literary figure, as well as the mother of two sons who became prominent.

Harrison's son Francis became Governor General of the Philippines, and his brother Fairfax served as President of the Southern Railway System. After the death of her husband, Mrs. Harrison moved to Washington, where she was a prominent social figure until her own death in 1920.

Frank Vizetelly, the British artist who had shared the hardships of the retreat from Greensboro, N. C., to Washington, Ga., with Jefferson Davis, died on the distant field of another civil war. Soon after leaving the small Georgia town, Vizetelly sailed for England, where the London *Illustrated News* published a series of his drawings called "Last Days of the Confederacy."

In 1883, Vizetelly went to Egypt to cover the uprising of the Mahdist movement against Egyptian rule in the Sudan. An army of 10,000 men, led by Colonel William Hicks of the British Army, marched into an ambush at the village of Kashgil in January 1883, and was annihilated by the Mahdi, except for one man. For months rumors were heard in Egypt and in London that the lone survivor of the massacre had been Vizetelly, but the lone white survivor, it developed, was a German scientist. The fate of Vizetelly was unknown, but he was presumed to have died in the butchery at Kashgil.

Five years later, in 1888, the artist was honored as one of seven British correspondents who had lost their lives while following the expansion of the Empire in Africa.

The Missouri firebrand, General Jo Shelby, who had led his tiny army into Mexico with such high hopes, was back home within two years, frustrated in all his aims. The Emperor Maximilian had been executed, the Confederate colonies, including Carlota, were declining to ruin and the grand experiment was over. Shelby and his men had been doomed from the start. The lands they had bought at inflated prices had been confiscated from their owners, jungle growth soon reclaimed fields where they hoped to grow grain and vegetables, bandits raided the towns and wiped out their wagon trains.

Shelby had begun by sending for his wife and children, whom he had not seen for four years—he was fiercely determined that the Shelbys, at least, would never return to the United States.

But Mexico was more than he had bargained for. Three months later Shelby wrote, "One thing is certain, we must all get away from here or I will be damned if we don't starve—there is no joke about it."

Shelby settled near Aullville, Mo., where he established a hemp farm, became involved in two thriving short-line railroads, operated a coal mine which was worked by a crew of fifty and opened a store in Lexington, Ky. Unlike most of his comrades who led embittered, impoverished lives in this period, Shelby embraced the Union. He became a U.S. marshal in Kansas City and recanted his Confederate faith. "I am ashamed of myself," he told a friend shortly before his death. Shelby's conversion was so complete that he voted Republican in his last years.

Shelby died in 1897 at the age of sixty-seven, still mourned by his old soldiers, despite his defection to the enemy cause.

Edwin M. Stanton was one of the first actors in the fiery drama of the war's aftermath to pass from the scene. The controversial Secretary of State finally evacuated his barricaded office after impeachment proceedings had failed against Andrew Johnson, and for six months recuperated from the stress of his stormy career in Washington. He resumed the practice of law on a limited scale, but because of poor health remained relatively inactive for the rest of his life.

When the furor of Andrew Johnson's impeachment trial had subsided, Stanton admitted that the beleaguered Democratic President had done his best to implement the enlightened Reconstruction policies of Abraham Lincoln—and that, as President, Johnson had every right to remove his Cabinet members as he saw fit.

He also revealed anxiety about his role in the hanging of Mrs. Mary Surratt with the conspirators in Lincoln's death, for he swore to secrecy a government prosecutor in the case, John A. Bingham of Ohio, exacting from him the promise never to divulge his knowledge of the backstage maneuvers which had led to the conviction and execution of the woman.

A supporter of U. S. Grant in the presidential campaign of 1868, Stanton was nominated for the Supreme Court by the victorious general. He accepted, but died in December 1869, before he could take his seat. His death was due to "an asthmatic ailment." But a rumor was circulated immediately that Stanton had cut his throat (as his brother had done)—and that Mrs. Stanton had ordered the coffin sealed to prevent observation of the self-inflicted wound. Stanton was buried in Georgetown.

. . .

Ex-President Andrew Johnson took up politics anew after leaving the White House, but though still popular in Tennessee, was defeated in his first race for a seat in Congress. Still a powerful, rabble-rousing speaker, he made vigorous attacks on his old enemies. He assailed Grant's policy in governing Louisiana during Reconstruction and belittled the general's hope of running for a third term. In defending his own presidential career, Johnson declared that it had been Edwin Stanton, and not he, who "railroaded" Mrs. Surratt to her death. Johnson charged in a public speech that Stanton had committed suicide because of his burden of guilt in the Surratt case—and that the Secretary of War had deliberately withheld a petition of clemency prepared for the unfortunate woman. Still fighting to clear his name and establish a record as Lincoln's heir in the reconstruction of the South, Johnson won a Senate seat from Tennessee. He died of a paralyzing stroke in July 1875, after serving but a few months.

Nelson A. Miles, dismissed from his post at Fort Monroe, became military commander of North Carolina during early stages of Reconstruction but soon was sent to the West, where he was in command of army troopers in virtually every campaign of the bloody wars for the Great Plains. It was Miles who drove Sitting Bull into Canada and dispersed the bands of Crazy Horse, Spotted Eagle and Broad Trail, who were among the most talented military leaders of the Western tribesmen. Miles also captured Chief Joseph of the Nez Percé and Geronimo—and was still in command in the West at the time of the battle of Wounded Knee Creek, a massacre shameful in the annals of U.S. military history.

Miles married a niece of General William T. Sherman, but his domestic life was constantly interrupted by his military duties. He put down the violent Pullman strike in Cleveland, Ohio, with his troops, became commander-in-chief of the army in 1895 and fought in the Spanish-American War. He retired from the army in 1903 as a lieutenant general, and wrote two books dealing with his career. Miles sought to vindicate himself for his role at Fort Monroe with a magazine article, "My Treatment of Jefferson Davis," but he found a tartar in Varina, who challenged his version of her husband's captivity. Miles was dismissed by the unforgiving Mrs. Davis as "a vulgarian, a boor . . . risen from the depths of ignorance and brutality. . . . No man was ever more heartily despised by those under him."

Miles died of a heart attack while attending a circus in Washington in May 1925. He was eighty-six years old.

Virginia Clay lived a long, active life after the war. Clement Clay died in 1882, and Virginia waited five years before she remarried. Her new husband was Judge David Clopton of the Alabama Supreme Court, an old friend. Clopton died in 1892 and Virginia returned to the Clay farm, and a struggle to save it from creditors. Though she now seemed content to live in the cottage she had once scorned, the aging queen of Alabama society was by no means a recluse. She was a leader in the cause of women's suffrage, made speeches, wrote articles for newspapers, attended reunions of Confederate veterans and became honorary life president of the United Daughters of the Confederacy.

The chief occupation of Virginia's late years was the writing of her memoirs, which she dictated to Ada Sterling, a New York journalist. She had prepared for this by keeping a diary and a scrapbook, the latter crowded with newspaper clippings concerning the Confederacy and Reconstruction.

Virginia's lively recollections of the past were published in 1904 as *A Belle of the Fifties,* "by Mrs. Virginia Clay-Clopton." The book gave no hint of the alleged tryst with Jefferson Davis on the Pullman, nor of any other spicy romance in the author's life. She left few clues for those who sought to substantiate reports of an affair with Davis. Her diary and scrapbook, which found their way into the archives of a university library, fascinated researchers nonetheless. Portions of the penciled diary had been erased with care, and since the diary book for 1871 is missing, there are no entries for the months following the reported Pullman car incident.

Virginia Clay-Clopton lived for eleven years after publication of her book, enjoying a reputation as an author and as an ornament of prewar society in Washington. Aglow with a regal beauty she had lacked in youth, she passed through her eighties in genteel poverty. Virginia's ninetieth birthday was celebrated by a party in Huntsville on January 16, 1915, when the handsome old lady appeared in a black velvet dress trimmed with duchesse lace, wearing a corsage of pink roses. Six months later she was dead, after a brief illness.

Varina Davis also lived to see most of her wartime contemporaries pass on. Though her own health caused her constant anxiety, she worked untiringly through the years to preserve the memory of her husband and his associates. Her correspondence expanded—she now signed herself as V. Jefferson-Davis—and she began writing a book that might depict her husband in human terms such as he had not attempted in his own work. Despite complaints ("Dear me, I'm so tired and miserable") Varina pushed ahead, and by the end of 1890 her *Memoir of Jefferson Davis* was complete, an imposing (if biased and wandering) two-volume work that ran to almost 1,600 pages.

During these months of labor Varina fended off creditors with the aid of an old family friend who sold some of her husband's property to help keep up Brierfield Plantation. She now realized that she could not afford the $6000 annual maintenance costs of Beauvoir. Winnie, the actual owner, was offended by an offer of $90,000 from a hotel company, which she rejected—the property was later sold to a veterans' organization for $10,000, and survived as a popular historic site.

Varina was rescued from her financial plight by her late husband's relatives, the friendly Pulitzers, whose New York *World* paid Varina and Winnie $1,500 a year each for weekly articles—a bonanza, since their annual income had been only $1,000. Varina was to follow this career in New York until her death, living in rather precarious comfort in a succession of hotels. She did not escape criticism from loyal Confederates, many of whom bitterly denounced her as a traitor and defector.

The extended *Memoir* itself, though it was overly laudatory, was crammed with anecdotes and presented revealing pictures of both Davis and Varina. The well-known critic Kate Field challenged Varina's account of the ex-President's imprisonment as overdrawn. "Certainly Mr. Davis never went so far as this, and he was not at all given to underestimating his sufferings for the lost cause. Mr. Davis was sensible enough to recognize the reasonableness of his treatment." Miss Field spoke for many Northerners in her judgment that Varina's protests were twenty-five years too late—but it was clear that the critic knew few of the details of the prison experience, or of the ex-President's barrage of complaints over his treatment at Fort Monroe.

Most reviewers of the *Memoir* were friendly enough, but the book did not win a public. The publisher Belford became bankrupt and few copies were distributed. Varina and Winnie must earn their living from other sources.

Unexpectedly, Varina emerged as a leader of society and queen of a small Confederate salon which flourished during the nineties. The former First Lady was often to be seen at the theater or the opera or driving in Central Park, always wearing a flat widow's cap, and looking for all the world like Queen Victoria, with her heavy cheeks and drooping lids. The quick wit and sparkling conversation that had impressed her friends in wartime Richmond drew minor literary figures and a faithful coterie of Southerners to her.

In 1893 the widow became the center of another furor in the heart of the ceremony-prone South: the body of Jefferson Davis was to be moved from New Orleans to its permanent grave. Varina must choose between Mississippi, where he had lived for so long, his birthplace in Kentucky, or Virginia, where he had spent four years of trial. Even Georgia pressed a claim for the ex-President's body.

Leaders in Virginia conducted the most aggressive public campaign, reminding Varina of the number of great men already buried in the state: Washington, Jefferson, James Monroe, James Madison —all Presidents; such Revolutionary patriots as Patrick Henry and George Mason, and the great Confederates Lee and Jackson, J. E. B. Stuart, George Pickett, John Pegram, A. P. Hill.

Varina chose Virginia, and in May 1893, almost exactly thirty-two years after Davis had gone to Richmond to lead the doomed Confederacy, his body was returned there. The South made a state occasion of the slow, roundabout journey. A special train moved at a funereal pace through the country, past bonfires at remote stations, halting occasionally for local ceremonies.

Varina joined the procession in Richmond and made the drive to Hollywood Cemetery for the brief military funeral. She did not emerge from the carriage until the final moments, when the casket was lowered; she stood by it sobbing amidst a small group of aged veterans, who were also in tears.

The funeral drew little or no criticism in the North. A New Orleans newspaper noted the changing times: "Ceremonies like these have lost all political significance, and the sensible people of the North see nothing to criticize in our showing respect, devotion and admiration for our heroes."

There was complaint from Mississippi: Varina was accused of selling her husband's body to the highest bidder, of having deserted the South to live in luxury in New York. Mrs. Davis was so incensed that she wrote a friend in Mississippi, "How could they think that after all the sacrifices I have made for the South, born, bred in it, and indissolubly connected with it, indeed feeling daily the weight of the prejudices of our enemies against us—how could they suppose I did not love it? . . . I think I have earned the confidence and love of the Southern people." She explained at length her limited financial means, saying that she and Winnie, who had been living in the Marlborough Hotel for $1,200 a year, were moving to avoid increased rates.

Varina's last years in New York were comfortable, if not always happy. Winnie died of complications of malaria at the age of thirty-three, and was buried beside her father in Richmond, where the rest of the family was to lie.

Varina vacationed yearly at Narragansett Pier, often with the Pulitzers, or with other friends in Vermont. In the city, though she now moved with difficulty, she still attended the opera and morning musicales at the old Waldorf Astoria.

Near the end of her life she disposed of her most precious possessions, photographs, clothing, weapons and other articles once owned by her husband—all of these, numbering in the hundreds, were sent to Confederate museums in the South.

Varina died in October 1906, in an unfamiliar room in the Majestic Hotel overlooking Central Park, where she had moved a few days earlier. She, too, was buried with military pomp in Richmond, after a service at St. Paul's, where the fateful message had come to her husband on April 2, 1865.

A Richmond newspaper, recalling her arrival in the city more than forty-five years earlier, declared, "Today, Mrs. Davis came back to Richmond . . . an old woman long widowed and bereft, who has been waiting these years for death. The Confederacy has gone, the hopes clustered so thickly and brightly about it have faded and gone, the dreams are vanished. The vast majority of the glorious, strong young men who answered the President's call . . . died on the field or have been borne away by . . . time. . . . But a few worn and aged veterans remain to represent them. . . . She was one of the last living mementoes of the Confederacy, one of the very last to die."

A sense of continuity unusual in American history was lent to the stirring events of the war and its final days by the heirs of vanquished Confederates. During the 1920's and 1930's, "Robert E. Lee Week" was celebrated at White Sulphur Springs, West Virginia, one of the general's favorite haunts during his last years. In 1932 Lee's old cottage was opened, and guests at a lawn party ate frozen watermelon, a delicacy the general had often served to guests. Mrs. Woodrow Wilson led a grand march to the Lee Ball. Later in the week there was a "Traveler's Round-robin Tennis Tournament," and the Lee biographer Douglas Southall Freeman lectured on the stately Virginia mansion in which Lee had been born: "Stratford: A Landmark in American Genetics."

Lee's statue remained a focus of Richmond life even in these years. An unprecedented crisis arose when municipal authorities discovered that a swarm of bees had entered a small hole in Traveler's belly, and there were fears that the entire statue might fill with honey and topple to the paving below. An elite emergency team of apiarists, metal-workers and welders was summoned, a hole was cut in the bronze belly, the honey was removed, the errant bee swarm ejected and the monument was preserved for posterity.

Old soldiers saluted the figure of Lee with regularity until the last of them had gone, and the habit was then assumed by Dr. Freeman, who paid his respects with a firm, professionally military gesture on his daily passage by the likeness of the "great gentleman" he so much admired. "I wouldn't think of driving past without saluting," he said. Freeman continued to publish his narratives of the campaigns of the Army of Northern Virginia, dramatic works which launched a renaissance in the study of the war. Given fresh impetus by the astounding success of the epic romance of the war by Atlanta's Margaret Mitchell, *Gone With the Wind,* intense interest in the divisive conflict continued unabated until the years of its centennial celebrations.

The last participant in the Civil War lingered on the American scene for almost a century after the secession of the Southern states. The soldier generally recognized as "the last man" among the four million who had fought was Walter Williams, a forager for General John Hood's Texas command, who died in Houston on December 19, 1959, at the age of 117. He had outlived the last Union veteran, Albert Woolson of Duluth, Minnesota, by about three years.

In the week of Williams's death, the nuclear submarine *Robert E. Lee* was launched, while troops in Confederate uniforms stood at attention to the strains of "Dixie."

During the same year General U. S. Grant III, a grandson of

Abraham Lincoln's most successful commander, precipitated a minor international crisis during a visit of Russia's Premier Nikita Khrushchev to Washington. Security officers posted near the Soviet leader's quarters collared General Grant when they saw grenades, muskets and swords unloaded on the sidewalk—and desisted only when convinced that the weapons, all of Civil War issue, were to be displayed on television by the general. Grant was a veteran lecturer to a public whose appetite for Civil War lore seemed to be insatiable. There were numerous other signs that the war was not over.

In 1960, Washingtonians noted a change in Mount Olivet Cemetery, where Henry Wirz, the commander of Andersonville prison, had been buried after his execution. Beside the simple stone with its weathered legend "Wirz," a new marker had mysteriously appeared, reading, "Captain, C. S. A. Martyr." This was thought to have been the contribution of an anonymous Confederate sympathizer from South Carolina.

In 1961, as the centennial's ceremonies opened, the U.S. government finally returned to the descendants of Jefferson Davis the raglan cape and woman's shawl he had worn when captured. Only then, with the release of the garments by the National Archives, was the deception of Edwin Stanton and his aides revealed—for they had allowed the nation to suppose that Davis had been fully clad in woman's dress.

Ten years later, in 1971, General Lee's faithful war horse Traveler was back in the news. In response to a patriotic clamor, officials of Washington & Lee University reinterred the skeleton of the animal—which had been on display in the cellar of the Chapel, an adjunct to the marble recumbent statue of Lee. For more than sixty years it had served as a tourist attraction.

Traveler had survived his famous master by only two years, dying of tetanus after stepping on a nail, despite the ministrations of the same two physicians who had attended Lee in his final illness. Though buried on the University grounds, Traveler had been exhumed for display thirty-five years after his death at the suggestion of a publicist for the college.

Visitors saw not only the whitened bones of Lee's favorite horse —also in the glass case was displayed a replica of the miniature skeleton of a prehistoric horse, providing whimsical young interpreters with the opportunity to explain to visitors: "This is Traveler's skeleton when he was a very young colt, and this . . . "

Traveler's bones deteriorated over the years, perhaps as a result of a curious form of Washington & Lee student graffiti—freshmen dutifully signed their names on the skeleton in the belief that this would prevent their flunking a course. In any event it was concluded that Traveler's bones were no longer appropriate to the Lee Chapel. As the campus newspaper, *Ring-Tum-Phi,* declared, "To display a skeleton among the Lee family memorabilia is a grotesque and macabre idea. The next logical step would be to exhume General Lee and place him in the saddle." At this time the moldering bones were removed to storage, Traveler's head was detached, and Lee lay thereafter in solitary grandeur.

The reburial of Traveler's bones in 1971 terminated a crosstown rivalry almost a century old, for the Virginia Military Institute continued to display proudly its own historic skeleton—that of General Stonewall Jackson's Little Sorrel, who was on exhibition complete with his skin.

In the year 1975, just one hundred and ten years and three months after Appomattox, Congress restored American citizenship to Robert E. Lee—as a result of the accidental discovery of the wayward oath of allegiance the general had signed in 1865.

Lee had not received a reply to his application for the reason that it somehow appeared on the desk of Secretary of State William Seward. The Secretary assumed that it would have been routed to him only for information, and that the application must have been acted upon and recorded elsewhere. Seward then passed the document to a friend as a souvenir, and the oath gathered dust in an unidentified Washington office for many years until it found its way into the National Archives.

It was 1970 before the oath was found, wrapped in a bundle of State Department papers. Thus prompted, Virginia Senator Harry F. Byrd, Jr., introduced a resolution to restore Lee's citizenship. President Gerald Ford finally signed this into law on August 5, 1975.

Three years later, in 1978, Jefferson Davis was similarly welcomed back into the Union, apparently because of the example of the return of General Lee—and with an ironic disregard of the ex-President's refusal to ask forgiveness during his lifetime.

A Note on Sources

Flight into Oblivion, the only previous work on the pursuit of Davis and his Cabinet, won a devoted readership over the years after publication by a small Virginia press in 1938. Though the narrative by the late Alfred J. Hanna is rather limited—it does not treat the imprisonment or postwar lives of Davis and his officers—its underlying research was an invaluable guide in the composition of this account.

Dr. Hanna made use of the important collections of Davis papers and of those of John Breckinridge, Judah Benjamin, John T. Wood, Burton Harrison, Stephen R. Mallory, John Reagan, F. R. Lubbock and Tench Tilghman, as well as accounts left by less-prominent participants.

The chief defect of Hanna's book is a lack of unity, but the accuracy of its chronology was also challenged in considerable (if chiefly minor) detail by Dr. Nora M. Davis of South Carolina. Her article in *Proceedings of the South Carolina Historical Association,* 1941, inspired a challenge to Hanna from the late Monroe F. Cockrell of Chicago, a banker and amateur Civil War historian. A lively correspondence between the two is in the M. F. Cockrell Papers, Manuscript Department, Perkins Library, Duke University, Durham, N.C. Dr. Hanna acknowledged that Dr. Davis had found numerous errors in his text, including some dates. This little-known controversy was studied, but its outcome had little effect upon the present volume, which does not include such detail. The originality, charm and generally sound background of Hanna's book make it of enduring interest to readers and scholars alike.

Though prominent among sources cited in the notes to this volume, the papers of Jefferson Davis should be given further emphasis. Scattered items collected by Davis himself in writing his *Rise and Fall of the Confederate Government* are in Confederate Memorial Hall, New Orleans, and were first used by Dunbar Rowland in his definitive ten-volume work, *Jefferson Davis, Constitutionalist . . .* Jackson, Miss., 1923. This work, of limited circulation, is known chiefly to historians.

Davis's letters from prison are at Transylvania College, Kentucky, and those of Varina Davis to her husband in this period are at the University of Alabama. Other papers are in the Museum of the Confederacy, Richmond, Va.; The Mississippi Department of Archives and History, Jackson, the Virginia State Library, Richmond, and the Library of Congress. An extensive collection on Davis in the New York Public Library, gathered by Walter L. Fleming for a projected life of Davis, was used by Robert McElroy in his two-volume biography of Davis. McElroy's work is basic to a study of the Confederate President.

Hudson Strode, the most recent biographer, made full use of these papers, and brought to light many previously unknown private letters in his edition of the correspondence of Davis.

Of special value to this book were the C. C. Clay Papers at Duke University, including several letters unknown to Davis biographers; and the papers of veterans of the 4th Michigan Cavalry, at the University of Michigan, particularly those of Orlando E. Carpenter, Lauren Ripley, Albert Potter and Julian Dickinson. These manuscript sources apparently escaped the notice of earlier writers on the capture of Davis and his party.

Interpretation of the influence of the dramatic events of the Confederate collapse upon postwar attitudes was greatly enchanced by these works:

Cass Canfield, *The Iron Will of Jefferson Davis,* N.Y., 1978; Thomas L. Connelly, *Will Success Spoil Jeff Davis?,* N.Y., 1963; and *The Marble Man: Robert E. Lee & His Image in American Society,* N.Y., 1977; Clement Eaton, *The Mind of the Old South,* Baton Rouge, 1967; Douglas S. Freeman, *The South to Posterity,* N.Y., 1939; William B. Hesseltine, *Confederate Leaders in the New South,* Baton Rouge, 1950; Burton Kendrick, *Statesmen of the Lost Cause,* N.Y., 1939; Arthur S. Link and Rembert W. Patrick, *Writing Southern History,* Baton Rouge, 1965; Grady McWhiney, *Southerners and Other Americans,* N.Y., 1973; W.C. Nunn, *Escape from Reconstruction,* Fort Worth, 1956; Andrew F. Rolle, *The Lost Cause,* Norman, Okla., 1965.

Bibliographical Notes

1 "Now . . . they will repent"

Details of life in Richmond from John B. Jones, *A Rebel War Clerk's Diary,* Vol. 2, Phila., 1866; Varina H. Davis, *Jefferson Davis . . . a Memoir,* Vol. 2, N.Y., 1890; T. C. DeLeon, *Belles, Beaux & Brains of the Sixties,* N.Y., 1907; Burke Davis, *To Appomattox,* N.Y., 1959.

The medical problems of Jefferson Davis are cited in W. A. Evans, *Jefferson Davis, His Diseases & His Doctors,* Aberdeen, Miss., 1942, p. 7; and in Frederick W. Gray, M.D., and Chester D. Bradley, M.D., "The Medical History of Jefferson Davis," *Virginia Medical Monthly,* Vol. 94 (Jan. 1967), pp. 19–23.

The effects of age upon the appearances of Davis and his wife were described by Mrs. H. L. Clay, 1/17/1865 in family correspondence. C. C. Clay letters, "Confederate Notables" collection, National Archives.

General sources on Jefferson and Varina Davis throughout are his *Rise & Fall of the Confederate Government,* Vol. 2, N.Y., 1881; her *Memoir;* Robert McElroy, *Jefferson Davis, The Unreal & The Real,* Vol. 2, N.Y., 1937; Hudson Strode, *Jefferson Davis,* Vol. 3, N.Y., 1964; and Ishbel Ross, *First Lady of the South,* N.Y., 1958.

Comments on Robert E. Lee are drawn from Armistead L. Long, *Memoirs of Robert E. Lee,* N.Y., 1886; Lee's story of his visit to the tobacco-chewing Confederate Congress is by George T. Lee in *South Atlantic Quarterly,* July 1927, pp. 236–37; and the general's comment on Davis is from John B. Gordon's *Reminiscences,* N.Y., 1903.

The theory that the Confederacy was doomed by aggressive field tactics is advanced by Grady McWhiney, *Southerners & Other Americans,* N.Y., 1973, p. 105 ff.

His opinion that Davis had a "screw loose" and was otherwise unfit for office was advanced by Henry A. Wise in letters to Dr. A. Y. P. Garnett, the President's personal physician, 11/17 and 11/26, 1863.

Burton N. Harrison's accounts of the final days in Richmond and the President's flight, all invaluable to historians, appeared in several forms, and ultimately in *The Harrisons of Skimino,* Fairfax Harrison, ed. Privately printed, N.Y., 1910.

The departure of Varina Davis is drawn from her *Memoir,* Vol. 2, p. 575 ff.

2 "We should abandon our position to-night"

Davis on the eve of departure is described by John H. Reagan in his *Memoirs . . . ,* N.Y., 1906; Frank R. Lubbock, *Six Decades in Texas;* and the *Rise & Fall,* Vol. 2, by Davis and *Memoir,* Vol. 2, of Varina Davis.

The Richmond *Whig*'s picture of panic in the city's streets appeared 4/4/1865; Alfred Hoyt Bill's *The Beleaguered City,* N.Y., 1946, and B. Davis, *op. cit.,* collate accounts of numerous witnesses, including W. A. Tomlinson, Mann S. Quarles and Walter Philbrook; the most complete of the unsatisfactory reports on the Confederate treasure as it departed Richmond is in William H. Parker, *Recollections of a Naval Officer,* N.Y., 1883; James Morris Morgan's *Recollections of a Rebel Reefer,* Boston, 1917, also offers some information on the composition and handling of the hoard of gold and silver at this stage.

The unrealistic summary of remaining Confederate troop strength was offered by Davis in *Rise & Fall,* Vol. 2, p. 699. Details of his move of household goods were written to his wife on 5 April, from Danville. (See Strode's *Jefferson Davis, Private Letters,* N.Y., 1966, for this and subsequent correspondence between the two.)

Clement and Virginia Clay material from Ruth K. Nuermberger, *The Clays of Alabama,* Lexington, Ky., 1958; Clement C. Clay Papers, Manuscript Division, Perkins Library, Duke University; C. C. Clay's comment on the deep reserve of Davis in letter to Senator William L. Yancey, 1863 (undated), cited by Clement Eaton, *Jefferson Davis . . .* N.Y., 1977, pp. 267–68.

The stay of Varina Davis in Charlotte is recorded in James M. Morgan's *Recollections* and in Harrison; *op. cit.*

The courage and generosity of Abram Weill in aiding Mrs. Davis were acknowledged by the President, who gave the host the gold-headed cane he had used during his final speech in the Senate. Robert D. Meade, *Judah P. Benjamin,* N.Y., 1943, p. 316.

3 "Blow her to hell"

Richmond *Times* citation, 4/22/1865.

Admiral Semmes left his graphic account in *Memoirs of Service Afloat . . .* Baltimore, 1869. The order to burn tobacco in Richmond, issued by Robert E. Lee 1/15/1865, is cited by McElroy, *op. cit.,* p. 451—an order which contributed to the destruction of the heart of the city, but one seldom acknowledged by Southern sympathizers.

Captain Sulivane's account of his departure and the destruction of Mayo's Bridge is in *Battles & Leaders of the Civil War,* Vol. 4, pp. 725–26. (*B&L* hereafter.)

Colonel Blackford's description of the chaotic retreat of civilians and military men is in his *War Years with Jeb Stuart,* N.Y., 1945, pp. 282–83.

Mrs. Pember's testimony is found in Phoebe Yates Pember, *A Southern Woman's Story,* N.Y., 1879. The account of George Bruce is from his *The Capture and Occupation of Richmond,* n.d., n.p.

The story of Edmund Ruffin is drawn largely from Betty L. Mitchell, *Edmund Ruffin,* Bloomington, 1981; Avery Craven's earlier *Edmund Ruffin, Southerner,* is regarded as definitive.

4 "a fire bell in the night"

The flight to Danville was recorded by Davis in *Rise & Fall,* and by Reagan, Mallory and Lubbock in their memoirs. Minor contributors were Captain M. H. Clark and Robert G. Kean (see Notes, Chapter 6). Revealing sketches of Cabinet members are in Rembert W. Patrick's *Jefferson Davis & His Cabinet,* Baton Rouge, 1944; and Meade, *op. cit.,* offers a penetrating analysis of the personality of Judah Benjamin. Reagan's career is also studied in W. F. McCaleb, "The Organization of the Post Office Department of the Confederacy," *American Historical Review,* VII, pp. 67–74, N.Y., 1906. The comment on Benjamin's easy social graces is from DeLeon, *op. cit.,* p. 91; and the domestic difficulties of the Benjamins are clarified by Meade's citation (*op. cit.,* 123–26, 393) from the diary of Gabriel Manigault and an interview with Benjamin's niece, Alma Kruttschritt, of New York.

Davis's reluctance to delegate authority is from William L. Katz, *Teachers' Guide to American Negro History,* Chicago, 1968, pp. 71–77.

The story of John S. Wise and his encounter with the trains of Confederate fugitives is found in his *The End of an Era,* Boston, 1902, p. 444 ff.

Danville's brief career as temporary capital is recorded by narratives cited above, and *The Official Records of the War of the Rebellion,* 1881–1901, Wash., D.C., 70 vols. (Hereafter *O.R.*), Ser. 1, Vol. XLVI, Pt. 3, p. 1393 ff; Edward Pollock, *Sketch Book of Danville, Va.,* Danville, 1885; Danville *Weekly Register,* 4/7/1865; and in *Confederate Veteran,* Vol. 19, p. 377 ff.

The highly informal accounting for the Confederate treasure and the Treasury's operations in Danville are based upon a later account by Captain Micajah H. Clark, detailed in A. J. Hanna, *Flight into Oblivion,* Richmond, 1938, pp. 90–92. (See Notes, Chapter 8, below: "You're Southern gentlemen, not highway robbers.")

The exchange between Davis and Raphael Semmes is reported by W. Adolphe Roberts in *Semmes of the Alabama,* Indianapolis, 1938, pp. 236–37.

The demands from the Northern press for revenge are from *Harper's Weekly,* 4/15/1865; New York *Times,* 4/12/1865; and New York *Tribune,* 4/13/1865.

Lincoln's visit to Richmond, observed by U.S. Admiral David Porter, is described clearly by McElroy, *op. cit.,* pp. 460–61.

The departure of John Breckinridge from Richmond and his journey through the ranks of Lee's army to Danville are described by W. C. Davis in his *Breckinridge* . . . N.Y., 1974; see also *Southern Historical Society Papers,* Vol. III, p. 102; Breckinridge–Jefferson Davis, 4/8/1865, in B. N. Harrison Papers, Library of Congress. W. C. Davis, *op. cit.,* summarizes this journey, pp. 502–08.

John Wise, *op. cit.,* p. 446, describes his report to Davis and the Cabinet in Danville.

Clement Clay's departure is recorded in *American Historical Review,* Vol. XLIV, July 1939, an account declaring that Clay "turned pale as a sheet" upon learning of Lee's surrender.

Colonel Blackford, *op. cit.,* described Lee's tearful return to his troops after surrender, pp. 294–95.

The glimpse of the Lincolns returning to Washington is from Adolphe de Chambrun, *Impressions of Lincoln and the Civil War,* N.Y., 1952.

There is some doubt that Davis and his party escaped capture by only five minutes as they entered Greensboro; some sources set the burning of the vital trestle at one hour after the train's passage. H. K. Weand, in "Our Last Campaign . . . "; Charles H. Kirk, *History of the 15th Pennsylvania Volunteer Cavalry,* Phila., 1906; *O.R.,* Vol. XLVI, Series 1, Pt. 3, pp. 393–94; and *Southern Historical Society Papers,* Vol. XXV, p. 270, offer views of the incident.

5 ***"We could rally our forces"***

Three of the companions who fled with Davis and left accounts of the epic journey were unanimous in declaring Greensboro cold and inhospitable. (Mallory, *op. cit.;* Harrison, *op. cit.;* and Captain John T. Wood, in his *Diary,* Vol. 3, Southern Historical Collection, UNC Library, Chapel Hill.) These accounts were hotly challenged by local citizens—immediately by one "Athos" (probably the Confederate Major James R. Cole), who declared, "It is a . . . slander upon the chivalry of the town to say . . . that no home was offered to Jefferson Davis . . . I know of my own personal knowledge that several invitations were extended to him, but for some reason he declined . . ." Other local traditions mention several houses in which Davis was purported to have stayed during his five-day visit. In this narrative the reports of the Davis companions are accepted as generally accurate—though they may have overstated the case.

Even more incendiary was the charge of Harrison, *op. cit.,* p. 232, that Governor John M. Morehead sought to coerce Secretary Trenholm into exchanging gold for Morehead's bonds and currency, then nearly worthless. Morehead's daughter Letitia, upon reading such accounts in 1901, said she was "*furious*" and denounced them as "false slanders." She insisted that President and Mrs. Davis had been in the town together, and were offered the hospitality of the Morehead home, Blandwood, but that Davis refused, fearing Federal retaliation upon the family. Mrs. Letitia Morehead Walker's several lapses of memory and her response (Charlotte *Observer,* 1905) at such a late date have caused historians to dismiss her protests. But Morehead's great-great-granddaughter, Mrs. Mary Lewis Edmunds of Greensboro, maintains persuasively, "It is hard to believe that any host, particularly Governor Morehead, known for his tact, kindness, and hospitality, would force himself into a guest's sick room and try to bully him! . . . How could Morehead have expected to get the gold from Trenholm? I'm sure that Trenholm, sick as he was, could not have personally carried the gold to Blandwood."

In any case, a small body of literature presents the local side of the matter: William B. Bushong, *History of Blandwood,* Greensboro, 1979; Burton A. Konkle, *John Motley Morehead and the Development of North Carolina,* 1922; Ethel S. Arnett, *Confederate Guns Were Stacked at Greensboro,* Greensboro, 1965; The Reverend Jacob Henry Smith, *Diary,* microfilm, Southern Historical Collection, UNC Library, Chapel Hill.

Movement of the Confederate treasure through Greensboro is reported in W. H. Parker, *op. cit.,* p. 355.

A full account of the difficult negotiations between Davis and his two generals is in "Davis and Johnston," *Southern Historical Society Papers,* Vol. XX, pp. 95–108.

Robert E. Lee, Jr., left his account in *Recollections and Letters of Robert E. Lee,* N.Y., 1904.

Captain John Taylor Wood, whose *Diary,* though terse in style and occasionally inaccurate, is indispensable, came into his own in Greensboro. As the President's most competent, forceful associate, he might have led the party to safety, given the opportunity. His singular life is rendered in Royce Shingleton, *John Taylor Wood . . . ,* Athens, Ga., 1979.

Sketch of Breckinridge from W. C. Davis, *op. cit.,* pp. 20, 23, 32, 254 ff.

The failure of Southern negotiators to consider slavery as an issue in framing terms for peace stemmed from the view that the Confederacy had fought over the constitutional issue of state sovereignty, to defend themselves against a strong central government. Jefferson Davis in particular clung to this view. He believed that defense of slavery by the South was coincidental, "an inferior aspect of the conflict."

Mrs. Davis later, lacking other means, sent Abram Weill a pitcher from her family silver service as a token of appreciation, and wrote in her *Memoir,* "This acknowledgement . . . is . . . a relief to my heart, which has borne his goodness in grateful memory for 25 years." Mrs. Edward Loewenstein of Greensboro, N.C., Weill's great-granddaughter, owns the pitcher as well as a letter from Mrs. Davis written at Weill's death, praising his "exceeding kindness to me and mine at much risk to himself and his family . . . as long as I shall live he has left me his grateful debtor." (Varina Davis–Carolina Weill, August 31, 1902.)

Mrs. Mary B. Chesnut's comments on Mrs. Davis are found in her familiar *A Diary from Dixie,* Ben Ames Williams, ed., Boston, 1949.

Semmes reported desertions in Greensboro, *op. cit.,* pp. 219–20; David P. Conyngham's report comes from his *Sherman's March . . .* N.Y., 1865, p. 393.

Ethel Arnett, *op. cit.,* describes the rioting and looting by Confederate soldiers (and some civilians) in Greensboro.

The oft-described final Cabinet meeting of the Lincoln administration is presented here from Gideon Welles, "Lincoln and Johnson," *Galaxy Magazine,* Vol. XIII, pp. 522–27 (no access to file of magazine); and from Benjamin Thomas, *Abraham Lincoln,* 1952, pp. 516–17.

The departure of the Davis party from Greensboro is reported in *Southern Historical Society Papers,* Vol. IX, pp. 542–43; Mallory's account is in "The Last Days of the Confederate Government," *McClure's Magazine,* Vol. XVI, p. 242; Harrison's in *The Harrisons of Skimino,* Fairfax Harrison, ed., N.Y., 1910, p. 239.

Sketch of Frank Vizetelly from W. Stanley Hoole, *Vizetelly Covers the Confederacy,* Tuscaloosa, Ala., 1957, p. 141 ff.

6 "I cannot feel myself a beaten man!"

The strikingly relaxed, outgoing Davis, enjoying life in his fugitive's camps, is depicted in Mallory's *Diary,* Vol. 2, p. 80.

Zebulon Vance gave his own version of his meeting with Davis, cited in Clement Dowd's *Life of Zebulon B. Vance,* Charlotte, N.C., 1897, pp. 485–86.

The skirmish which saved the railroad bridge at the Yadkin River crossing was recalled by Henry Mills of Stanly County, N.C., a participant; in Charlotte *Observer* (n.d.), 1907, quoted by James Brawley, Salisbury *Post,* 3/4/1979.

Varina Davis, *op. cit.,* pp. 627–29, tells the story of the Salisbury visit of her husband, and the anecdote of the fearful child; from an unidentified but contemporary letter.

The party's stop in Concord was verified by Meade, *op. cit.,* 408n, through Dr. Paul Barringer, Charlottesville, Va., nephew of Victor B. Barringer.

William Johnston, who had been an unsuccessful candidate for governor of North Carolina against Vance, served as mayor of Charlotte and became a railroad builder after the war. Files, Charlotte *Observer,* courtesy Jack Claiborne, associate editor.

The erroneous quotation of Davis by Bates appeared in the New York *Times,* 5/31/1865.

Numerous comments on the death of Lincoln have been attributed to Davis, including one recorded by Mallory: "I certainly have no special regard for Mr. Lincoln, but there are a great many men of whose end I would much rather hear than his. I fear it will be disastrous to our people, and I regret it deeply." A. K. McClure, a prominent magazine publisher from Pennsylvania, quoted Davis as saying in 1875, "Next to the destruction of the Confederacy, the death of Abraham Lincoln was the darkest day the South has ever known."

The sermon at St. Paul's church by Everhart, and Davis's reaction, are described in Harrison, *op. cit.,* p. 243; added comments, perhaps by Everhart, in the *Church Intelligencer,* Charlotte, 5/4/1865.

Basic sources for final negotiations between Johnston and Sherman, and the ineffectual efforts of the distant Davis to influence their course, are Davis, *op. cit.,* Vol. 2, pp. 678 ff.; Sherman, *op. cit.,* Vol. 2, p. 326; and Johnston, *op. cit.,* p. 404 ff.

The remarkable letter, Jefferson Davis to Varina Davis, from Charlotte, was dated 23 April, Strode, *Jefferson Davis, Private Letters.*

The departure of George Davis from the caravan was noted in Lubbock, *op. cit.,* p. 566.

Raphael Semmes's story of his parole appears in W. Adolphe Roberts, *op. cit.,* pp. 240–41.

For Breckinridge and Kean and the Confederate archives in Charlotte, see

Edward Younger, ed., *Inside the Confederate Government: The Diary of Robert Garlick Kean . . .* N.Y., 1957, p. 207.

7 "Why are you still in the field?"
William Preston Johnston reported the President's chagrin at being greeted with such high confidence in Abbeville, S.C.

Senator Orr's bitter comment was made in a letter to F. W. Pickens, 4/29/1865, cited by John K. Aull, Columbia (SC) *State*, 9/20/1931.

The young Benthuysens, who were Brooklyn-born, had been reared in New Orleans. Their aunt was the wife of Joseph Davis, the President's brother.

The scene of Davis and three of his Cabinet members playing marbles with the Springs boys is described by Katherine W. Springs, *The Squires of Springfield*, Charlotte, N.C., 1965, pp. 235–36 (based on Mallory's account in "Pen & Ink Sketches," otherwise unidentified).

Trenholm's letter of resignation, dated 4/29/1865, appears as a copy in the Edwin M. Stanton Papers, Library of Congress. The jesting over Reagan's assumption of the role of Secretary of the Treasury was reported by Lubbock, *op. cit.*, p. 565.

Sherman's disdain for Stanton's gossip of the Confederate "millions" is revealed in his *Memoirs*, Vol. II, p. 372.

Orders to Palmer's troopers and their route southward may be found in *O.R.*, Ser. 1, Vol. XLIX, Pt. 1, pp. 545–47.

The Boston *Transcript* quotation, edition of 1/5/1865.

General Grant's admonition that Confederate officers were not to be harmed, expressed to Robert Bingham, is cited in McElroy, *op. cit.*, Vol. 2 p. 468.

The crossing of the Catawba River is described in Tench Tilghman, *Diary, April–May, 1865*, cited in Hanna, *op. cit.*, p. 58.

Comments on Bragg by Davis are in McWhiney, *op. cit.*, pp. 93, 99–100, and his opinions of other leading Confederates are detailed in this valuable work.

Senator Orr's sally on the Davis-Bragg relationship appears in a letter from Dr. J. H. Claiborne of Petersburg, Va. to his wife, 3/29/1864 (Claiborne papers, Univ. of Va. library).

The comment by Gorgas on Davis as an administrator is cited in McWhiney, *op. cit.*, p. 85.

Breckinridge and Bragg are compared as to personal appearance in Eliza F. Andrews, *Diary of a Georgia Girl . . .* ed. Spencer B. King, Jr., Macon, Ga. 1960, p. 169. (Hereafter Andrews, *Diary*.)

See Palmer's final movements in pursuit of Davis in *O.R.* Ser. 1, Vol. XLIX, Pt. 1, p. 346 ff.

Varina's long letter to her husband, including a warning about General Bragg, is dated 4/28/1865, Strode, *Private Letters.*

Edmund Kirby Smith and his domain are sketched by Andrew F. Rolle in *The Lost Cause, The Confederate Exodus to Mexico,* Norman, Okla., 1965, pp. 38–51 and *passim.*

Sketch of Virginia Clay is drawn from C. C. Clay Papers, esp. her scrapbooks; Nuermberger, *op. cit.;* and Chesnut, *op. cit.*, p. 285.

Parker, *op. cit.* pp. 351–52, describes movement of the treasure to and from Abbeville; and in *Southern Historical Society Papers,* Vol. 21, pp. 304–12, this author adds further details. Robert M. Willingham, Jr., in *No Jubilee . . . ,* Washington, Ga., 1976, p. 192, notes that five of Parker's young guards refused to leave, and remained on duty. John F. Wheless made his report in *Southern Historical Society Papers,* Vol. 10, p. 137.

For Varina's arrival in Washington, Ga., see Andrews, *op. cit.,* date of April 30, 1865 (pp. 190 ff.) for the President's sojourn in the town. Varina's own account of the flight omits the final phase around Washington and Irwinville, Ga., and substitutes the narrative of her husband.

The "final" meeting of the Confederate Cabinet in Abbeville is described in Duke, *op. cit.;* Lubbock, *op. cit.;* and several other writers. *Battles & Leaders,* Vol. 4, pp. 764–65, has a summary; see also *Southern History Assn. Publications,* Vol. 5, pp. 291–92; 296–97. There is no agreement as to where the "last" meeting was held, and the claimants for the honor range from Danville, Va. through Greensboro and Charlotte, N.C. to Fort Mill, Abbeville, S.C. and Washington, Ga. The last session attended by all members of the Davis Cabinet was held in Charlotte; the quorum was steadily reduced in subsequent sessions during the flight.

The transfer of the gold and silver from the railroad cars at Abbeville added to the air of confusion surrounding the journey of the treasure. Basil Duke, in his *Reminiscences*. . . (Reprint of 1969, Freeport, N.Y.), p. 388, noted that there were so many guards at the train "that some of them might have appropriated a considerable sum and the others have not been aware of it." Duke never knew the exact amount of the treasure he was guarding on the last leg of the flight, but he personally searched the box cars by candlelight in Abbeville, gathering stray coins. Even afterward, he reported, an officer discovered a small box containing from $2000 to $3000 in gold coins which had been overlooked.

The Richmond *Whig,* then issued as a Union paper, commented on the Davis flight 4/25/1865; the Augusta *Constitutionalist* and the Edgefield *Advertiser* were quoted by John K. Aull, Columbia *State,* 9/13/1931.

The New York *Times* urged on the Federal pursuers on 5/1/1865.

8 "You're Southern gentlemen, not highway robbers"

Mallory's resignation to Davis, dated 5/2/1865, is in Harrison papers, Library of Congress; his protest that he felt further resistance useless is in his *Diary,* Vol. 2, p. 79.

It is unlikely that a completely satisfactory account of the fate of the Confederate treasure will be written. Otis Ashmore's account in *Georgia Historical Quarterly,* Vol. 2, pp. 119–33, accepted as the most reliable, does not include the scene of the looting of the money wagons. The account by C. E. L. Stuart, a rather shadowy figure, appeared in Benson J. Lossing's *Pictorial Field Book of the Civil War,* Vol. 3, p. 577. The author was unable to locate the work cited, Stuart's "History of the Last Days and Final Fall of the Rebellion." Though Lossing is not always reliable, his voluminous historical works include unique and valuable material, and an assessment of the worth of Stuart's testimony is difficult.

The scene of Breckinridge and the unruly troops is sketched by W. C. Davis, *op. cit.,* p. 521, though without mention of looting.

In addition to Ashmore's article, which reviews testimony of witnesses, Willingham, *op. cit.,* reviews the entire affair as it occurred in Georgia, and cites a number of local sources. Captain Micajah H. Clark's account, accepted as most nearly authoritative, appeared in *Southern Historical Society Papers,* Vol. 9, pp. 542–56; that of Paymaster John F. Wheless is in the same papers, Vol. 10, pp. 138–41; Captain W. H. Parker, who is quoted by Ashmore, wrote an additional account in *Southern Historical Society Papers,* Vol. 21, pp. 304–12. A bibliography covering the transfer of all funds from Richmond into Georgia is in *Publications of the Southern Historical Association,* Vol. V, No. iii, pp. 188–227; (previous articles on the subject appeared in the same volume—No. i, pp. 1–34; No. ii, pp. 95–150).

Though Captain Clark's "complete" accounting appears in Hanna, *op. cit.,* p. 92, balancing the books at $327,000 received and disbursed, Ashmore's careful study concluded that some $43,800 was unaccounted for. Several omissions are obvious, and witnesses who had knowledge of details offered conflicting statements.

Captain Clark wrote of the matter as late as January 16, 1882, in the Louisville *Courier-Journal.* Walter Philbrook and others were quoted in the New York *Times* in the spring of 1865 (April 12; May 1 and 28; June 1), and in January 1882.

Varina Davis placed Benjamin's departure from Davis in the "Vienna Valley," a few miles from Washington, Ga. (Letter to Francis Lawley, 6/8/1898, Pierce Butler Collection, Tulane Univ. library). Benjamin was carrying $1500 in gold, drawn from the Confederacy's "Secret Service" fund in Richmond on April 1; he presumably used this in his escape. (Manuscript Division, Perkins Library, Duke Univ.) Colonel Leovy's role in this escape is detailed in *Lousiana Historical Quarterly,* Vol. XIX, p. 965.

The plea from Varina Davis to her husband, urging that he "cut loose" and flee, is found in Strode, *Private Letters,* under "May 1865" (n.d., n.p.).

The President's "wish" to be captured is discussed in Patrick, *op. cit.,* pp. 354–55.

The movements of Breckinridge, as he prepared to leave the Presidential column near Washington, are found in W. C. Davis, *op. cit.,* p. 522.

Distribution of the final substantial amounts of the treasure in Washington, Ga. is described by Clark in accounts cited above. (For final disposition, see Notes, Chapter 13.)

The story of Varina Davis traveling as "Mrs. Jones" is given in Dunbar Rowland, *Jefferson Davis, Constitutionalist* . . . 10 vols., Jackson, Miss., 1923, Vol. 7, p. 819 (citing Burton Harrison's "Narrative").

9 "God's will be done"

Lieutenant Yeoman's account (which has been challenged by other Federal soldiers) appeared in *Four Years in the Saddle. History of the First Regiment of Ohio Volunteer Cavalry,* W. L. Curry, compiler, Columbus, 1898, p. 248 ff. Yeoman's claim to a portion of the $100,000 reward drew the ire of Michigan troopers who actually captured Davis.

The "disguise" adopted by Davis was noted in Wood's *Diary,* Vol. 3, May 4, 1865; the account of Davis for this period is in his *Rise & Fall,* Vol. 2, pp. 700–05. The President's reckless decision to join his wife, on the basis of a rumor that her camp was to be attacked, is described in Patrick, *op. cit.,* p. 356, among numerous other sources. Except for this delay, Davis would almost certainly have escaped abroad—as Lincoln had hoped he would.

See Harrison, *op. cit.,* pp. 253 ff.; Harrison sent proofs to Davis, who made numerous corrections, as he frequently did when Harrison presented writings about the flight.

Wood's criticism of the lack of security in the camp at Irwinville is in his *Diary,* Vol. 3, 10/5/1865.

Federal reports on the capture of Davis and his party are in *O.R.,* Ser. 1, Vol. XLIX, Pt. 1, p. 515 ff; and pp. 530–32; and in Pt. 2, pp. 556, 665. A full report by General Wilson is in *Senate Document 13, 39th Congress, 2d Session,* reported 1/31/1867; this also includes reports of Colonel Harnden of the 1st Wisconsin, Colonel R. H. G. Minty, commander, Second Cavalry Corps, and others.

See "The Capture of Jefferson Davis," a pamphlet accompanying Bill No. 1277, 40th Congress, 2d Session. A Report by the Committee of Claims. (Problems of distribution of the $100,000 reward. A valuable source on the capture itself.)

Also consulted: *Record of Service of Michigan Volunteers in the Civil War, Vol. 34, Fourth Michigan Cavalry;* James Green, *The Life and Times of General B.D. Pritchard,* Allegan, Mich., 1979; Lauren H. Ripley, 4th Mich. Cavalry, "Personal Reminiscences of the Flight and Capture of Jeff Davis," typescript, Bentley Historical Library, Univ. of Michigan; diaries and letters of Henry Albert Potter and diary of Orlando E. Carpenter, typescripts, Bentley Library.

Pritchard, who led the Michigan troopers, became the leading citizen of Allegan after the war, practiced law and served as State Treasurer, but declined offers to run for governor and for Congress. His share of the reward for the capture of Davis was $3,000. Pritchard died in 1905.

Claude B. Denison, the Adjutant of the 4th Michigan Cavalry, wrote "The Capture of Jefferson Davis" for The Military Order of the Loyal Legion of the United States, Michigan Commandery, War Papers No. 10—an account consistent with the versions of Jefferson and Varina Davis.

Major Confederate sources are Jefferson Davis, *Rise & Fall;* Varina Davis, *Memoir;* Burton Harrison, *op. cit.;* Francis R. Lubbock, *op. cit.;* John T. Wood, *op. cit.;* W. T. Walthall, "The True Story of the Capture of Jefferson Davis" in *Southern Historical Society Papers,* Vol. 5, pp. 97–126 is detailed and accurate, and cites correspondence with Lubbock, Raphael Semmes, Colonel W.P. Johnston and George Davis; the definitive discussion of Davis's "disguise" is an article by Chester D. Bradley, M.D. in the *Journal of Mississippi History,* August 1974, pp. 243–68.

The current text is a synthesis of the accounts of participants most directly involved, striving for clarity of the brief action during the capture, and attempting to illuminate the enduring controversy which followed. (Actual participants were few. As Burton Harrison wrote, "I have not found there was anyone except Mrs. Davis, the single trooper at her tent, and myself, who saw all that occurred and heard all that was said at the time. Any one else who gives an account of it has to rely upon hearsay or upon his own imagination." Cited in McElroy, *op. cit.,* p. 513. This view, of course, was challenged by Julian Dickinson, Andrew Bee and James H. Parker of the Federal forces.)

10 "He must be executed"

The reported Confederate heckling of Davis is from Ripley, *op. cit.,* pp. 40–41. Other incidents on the road to Macon, under Federal guard, are described by Varina in *Memoir,* Vol. 2, pp. 641 ff.

Henry A. Potter's critical view of Varina is in his letter to his father, 5/19/1865, Bentley Library, Univ. of Michigan.

The story of the solicitous Negro waiter is given by Varina in *Memoir,* Vol. 2, p. 643n.

Virginia Clay's recollection of her husband's surrender is from *Belle of the Fifties,* p. 246 ff; the train ride from Macon to Augusta is described by Mrs. Clay, *op. cit.,* p. 248 ff; her sketch of Davis at this time is found on p. 68. Other detailed observations by Mrs. Clay are in the C. C. Clay Papers, Manuscript Division, Perkins Library, Duke University, especially in her Scrapbook No. 2 (1886–93), consisting chiefly of undated, unidentified newspaper clippings.

Sketch of Stephens from *Dictionary of American Biography;* E. Ramsey Richardson, *Little Aleck, a Life of Alexander H. Stephens;* Myrta L. Avary, *Recollections of Alexander H. Stephens;* Patrick, *op. cit.,* p. 40 ff. The apocryphal story of the butler's denial that Stephens was married is from Morgan, *op. cit.,* p. 203. The sketch of the physical appearance of the Confederate Vice-President in earlier days is from John Peyton, *The American Crisis,* London, 1867.

Woodrow Wilson's glimpse of the captive Confederate leaders is recorded in William B. Hale's *Woodrow Wilson,* N.Y., 1912, p. 30.

Virginia Clay, *op. cit.,* described her treatment of Davis's headache, pp. 59–60.

The call for the execution of Davis by *Harper's Weekly* appeared in the edition of 5/27/1865.

Varina Davis, *op. cit.,* p. 645n, recalled the parting with Jim Limber and his later betrayal.

Many Southerners, hearing rumors of the "disguise" worn by Davis at his capture, defended him by recalling heroes of the past who had sought to escape danger by wearing female attire: Charles II after Woodstock, the Young Pretender after leaving Flora Macdonald—even King Alfred dressed as a cowherd, Richard the Lion-Hearted as a pilgrim, and Abraham Lincoln entering Washington in a "Scotch cap and cloak." Such defenses were anathema to Davis, who protested that he would never have stooped to such deceit as "unbecoming a soldier and a gentleman." (McElroy, *op. cit.,* pp. 517–18.)

11 "This is not like being Secretary of State"

Benjamin's journey through Florida is fully described by Hanna, *op. cit.,* Meade, *op. cit.,* Pierce Butler, *op. cit.,* and by Louis Gruss, "Judah Philip Benjamin," *Louisiana Historical Quarterly,* Vol. XIX, p. 965. The parrot story told by Benjamin was found by Butler in "Lawley Manuscripts," otherwise unidentified. (Meade, 320.) Fred Tresca and H. A. McLeod described their roles in Lillie B. McDuffee, *The Lures of Manatee,* Nashville, 1933, p. 158; also see Galveston *Daily News,* 5/27/1894.

Despite his testimony, Benjamin's route through north-central Florida is difficult to trace, since he went alone much of the way, through sparsely settled country, avoiding towns and settlements. His progress from Tampa onward is clearly defined and documented.

The squalls and water spouts described by Benjamin from his hair-raising sea voyage appeared in a letter to his sister Rebecca.

There is a minor controversy about the identity of the boats used by Benjamin. Hanna, *op. cit.,* p. 200, names the *Blonde,* the first, smaller, vessel; Meade, *op. cit.,* p. 322 identifies this craft as the second, larger, boat found in the Keys. Meade offers full citations, but this text follows Hanna, long the dean of Florida's local historians.

The companion adventure of John Breckinridge in escaping was first told in a letter to his son Owen, written from the British steamer *Shannon* and mailed in London in July 1865. The account, presented as a diary, appeared in the *Register* of the Kentucky State Historical Society, October 1939, edited by A. J. Hanna.

The diary of John T. Wood, though helpful, was so sparse as to contribute little drama to the hegira. It was Wood to whom Breckinridge owed his life and safe arrival in Cuba. Wood himself went to Nova Scotia, where he settled as a shipper and insurance agent. He flew a Confederate flag from his office building until his death. Fortunately, Wood expanded his diary into a narrative of the escape, which appeared in *Century Magazine,* November 1893, pp. 110–23.

The flight of George Davis is sketched in Hanna, *op. cit.,* p. 219 ff; Davis left an account in a letter to his son Junius, November 14, 1865; see also Samuel A. Ashe, *George Davis,* Raleigh, N.C. 1916 and W. W. Davis, *The Civil War & Reconstruction in Florida,* pp. 53, 351–52.

Stephen Mallory's recollections, which appeared in several versions, are in typescript, Southern Historical Collection, Univ. of N.C. Library, Chapel Hill; see also Hanna, *op. cit.,* p. 242 ff. Hanna consulted an unpublished thesis by Occie Clubbs, "Stephen Mallory, the Elder," at the Univ. of Fla.

Raphael Semmes's *Memoir* and W. Adolphe Roberts, *op. cit.,* were sources for the homeward journey of the general-admiral. Semmes later taught at the future Louisiana State Univ., and edited a Memphis newspaper, but was driven from these posts by the hostile influence of Andrew Johnson. He practiced law in Mobile with his son, and died in 1877, at the age of sixty-seven.

The defiance of Robert Toombs and his fate in these days are recorded in Patrick, *op. cit.,* pp. 87–89 and 359.

12 "Oh, the shame! The shame"

The surprising leniency of the U.S. government in the treatment of Davis and his Cabinet is discussed in Patrick, *op. cit.,* pp. 363–65.

The imprisonment of Davis is detailed in Strode's *Jefferson Davis,* p. 226 ff; in McElroy, *op. cit.,* p. 524 ff, and, more recently and in greater detail, by Dr. Chester Bradley, especially in "Dr. Craven and the Prison Life of Jefferson Davis," *Virginia Magazine,* Vol. 62, p. 60. Most valuable of all is John J. Craven, *Prison Life of Jefferson Davis,* N.Y., 1866. The most vivid account was left by Captain Jerome Titlow, who supervised the shackling of Davis; letter to Titlow's son, preserved in the Confederate Museum, Richmond. Titlow died in 1912 in the Minnesota Soldiers' Home, Minneapolis.

See also the accounts by Davis himself, *op. cit.,* and by Varina Davis, *op. cit.,* p. 647 ff. In virtually all sources, Davis is depicted as long-suffering in face of gross and cruel mistreatment. The lone dissent came from Clement Clay, who wrote his wife, "Mr. Davis is petulant, irascible, and offensive in manner to officers . . . though they say he is able, learned, high-toned and imposing in manner." Cited by Virginia Clay-Clopton, *op. cit.,* pp. 288–89.

The comment of Sidney Lanier on the "guilt" of Davis and his enshrinement in the hearts of the Southern people is found in his *Tiger Lilies,* p. 120.

13 "Ankle deep in gold and silver"

The scene of the looting of the Virginia bank funds is drawn from Otis Ashmore, The *Georgia Historical Quarterly,* Vol. 2, December 1918, pp. 171 ff; a somewhat different version is found in Eliza Andrews, *op. cit.,* pp. 269 ff. See also Willingham, *op. cit.,* p. 195 ff. Ashton Chapman, a Wilkes County, Ga. native, wrote in The Charlotte *Observer,* February 2, 1941 in considerable detail, citing several documents, as well as the account left by Eliza Andrews. The narrative of Lewis Shepherd is cited by Ashmore.

For the fate of the bank funds see report of House Committee on Claims, 49th Congress, 1st session, 1886, and subsequent Joint Resolution. (Cited by Ashmore, *op. cit.,* pp. 185 ff.)

The author failed to discover traces of the $86,000 given to Semple, and the $30,000 given to U.S. General E. L. Molineux by Major Moses. Molineux, of Brooklyn, N.Y. reported June 17, 1865, in a family letter, that he had captured millions in Rebel property in and around his Macon headquarters—and that $275,000 of this was in gold and silver bars (probably none of which was a part of the official Confederate treasure). The whimsical Molineux wrote, "I tried hard to chip off a piece of gold, but my conscience was too sharp or my knife was too dull, I don't know which." Letter owned by Will Molineux of Williamsburg, Va., the general's great-grandson.

The disbursement of the last of the official treasure in Confederate hands, the $25,000 remainder of the money carried by President Davis and his party, is reported in Clark's various accounts, as cited, and in a diary of Tench F. Tilghman, edited by A. J. Hanna in *Florida Historical Quarterly,* January 1939. See reprint, *The Confederate Baggage Train Ends Its Flight in Florida,* by A. J. Hanna, n.p., n.d.

Those belongings of Davis found by a Federal patrol near the Yulee plantation were kept in government offices in Washington until 1874, when some of them were returned to Davis.

14 "Watch and wait for the morning"

The story of the diehard Judge Perkins is told by Sarah Dorsey, *Recollections of Henry Watkins Allen,* N.Y., 1866. For an able presentation of Southern postwar attitudes, see Andrew F. Rolle, *The Lost Cause: The Confederate Exodus to Mexico,* Norman, Okla., pp. 8 ff; also see Robert S. Henry, *The Story of Reconstruction,* Indianapolis, 1938, pp. 26 ff. The quotation from Joel C. Harris also appears here, p. 28.

General Lee's postwar life is eloquently chronicled in Charles Bracelyn Flood's *Lee: The Last Years,* Boston, 1981. For Lee's application for a pardon, see pp. 62–3.

The story of Shelby's men is told in Rolle, *op. cit.,* pp. 3–4 and pp. 57 ff. For another version of the crossing of the Rio Grande see W. C. Nunn, *Escape from Reconstruction,* Fort Worth, 1956, p. 34 (citing John N. Edwards, an early Shelby biographer).

The opposition of Davis to Confederate migration is expressed in Rowland, *op. cit.,* Vol. 7, p. 69.

The restless stirring of the freed Negroes at the end of the war is described in Henry, *op. cit.,* p. 29, quoting Sidney Andrews of Massachusetts, a reporter for "radical newspapers in Boston and Chicago."

15 "We cannot convict him of treason"

Varina Davis, *op. cit.,* Vol. 2, p. 648 ff, tells her experiences on shipboard at Fort Monroe, and cites testimony of Dr. Craven, Captain Titlow, and Davis himself as to her husband's life in prison.

The death of Edmund Ruffin is fully described in both Mitchell, *op. cit.,* and Avery Craven, *op. cit.*

The Sanford Conover story is told in Rolle, *op. cit.,* pp. 286 ff. Edwin Stanton's role in the execution of Mrs. Surratt is shown, from Stanton's point of view, in Benjamin P. Thomas and Harold P. Hyman, *Stanton . . . ,* N.Y., 1962, p. 432. Despite the conclusion of these writers, there is evidence that Stanton did play a villain's part in "railroading" Mrs. Surratt.

Judah Benjamin's letter to Varina Davis, notifying her of money held for her account in England, was dated 1 September 1865. (Cited in Strode, *Jefferson Davis,* Vol. 3, p. 265.)

Thorough accounts of government legal actions against Davis, and their suspension, appeared over a span of many years. George Shea explained his willingness to defend Davis and discussed many aspects of the case in *Southern Historical Society Papers,* Vol. 37, pp. 244–52; George S. Boutwell's "Why Jefferson Davis Was Never Tried" is in *ibid.,* Vol. 38. pp. 347–49. The most able later study is "The U.S. vs. Jefferson Davis," by Ray F. Nichols, *American Historical Review,* Vol. 3, No. 2, January 1926, pp. 266 ff. Other discussions include "The Trials and Trial of Jefferson Davis," a paper read before the Virginia Bar Association 1900, and published by this organization.

The alleged guilt of Henry Wirz and the Confederate government in mistreating prisoners at Andersonville was hotly denied by Varina Davis, *op. cit.,* pp. 537 ff. (She devoted an entire chapter to the defense, citing correspondence of Davis, Grant and others, newspaper accounts, and messages of Davis to the Confederate Congress.)

16 "The President is bailed!"

Mrs. Virginia Clay-Clopton, in *op. cit.,* p. 300 ff. tells her own story of her husband's imprisonment and her successful campaign to free him. She includes voluminous correspondence not to be found elsewhere. Her account is supplemented in her Scrapbook No. 2, Duke Univ. Mss. Dept., chiefly through unidentified newspaper clippings.

Varina Davis gave her account of her effort to free her husband in her *Memoir* in somewhat scattered form, and frequently in the words of others. In Vol. 2, p. 768 ff. she tells briefly of her encounters with Andrew Johnson and Edwin Stanton.

Some have claimed that Richard Taylor, the ex-President's brother-in-law, was actually responsible for persuading Johnson to free Davis. Rolle, *op. cit.,* p. 191.

Thomas and Hyman, *op. cit.,* sought to revise the conventional view of Stanton's role in the postwar era, denying that Stanton conspired against Johnson, and presenting the Secretary of War as honest and forthright. In the opinion of these historians, Stanton's reputation as an intemperate, vindictive partisan traces from his quarrel with President Johnson.

The remarkable Colonel Charles Halpine, Dr. John Craven's "ghost" for *The Prison Life of Jefferson Davis,* is discussed by two hostile critics, William Hanchett and David Rankin Barbee. Hanchett's *Irish Charles G. Halpine in Civil War America,* N.Y., 1970, and Barbee's "Dr. Craven's Prison Life of Jefferson Davis'—an Exposé," *Tyler's Quarterly,* April 1951; pp. 282–95, find the Halpine-Craven book dishonest. This view was convincingly challenged by Dr. Chester Bradley, Newport News, Va. in correspondence with Hanchett and in the *Virginia Magazine of History and Biography,* Vol. 62, January 1954. Bradley, a former curator of the Jefferson Davis Casemate Museum at Fort Monroe, has made valuable contributions to the understanding of the capture and imprisonment of Davis, and of Craven's book and its influence.

Payment of the reward for the capture of Davis, and the political maneuvers in Congress by the Michigan and Wisconsin delegations on behalf of army veterans, are clarified by Lauren H. Ripley of the 4th Michigan Cavalry in his *Personal Reminiscence,* typescript, Bentley Historical Library, Univ. of Michigan.

The motivation of prominent Northerners, including Abolitionists, in defending Davis and providing bond for his release is clear from a statement of Horace Greeley to Varina Davis, "I will sign his bond though it will cost me a Senate seat, the *Tribune* circulation, and kill the sale of my last volume on the history of the war. I will do it because it is right." Gerrit Smith, another signer of the bond, felt that the North bore a heavy burden of guilt for the war, a guilt rooted in attitudes toward slavery. "The North did quite as much as the South to uphold slavery," he said. "She did it wickedly because more calculatingly. Slavery was an evil inheritance of the South, but the wicked choice, the adopted policy, of the North." (Cited in McElroy, *op. cit.,* Vol. 2, pp. 567, 588.)

17 "Preserve the traditions of our fathers"

Myrta L. Avary, in *Dixie after the War,* N.Y., 1906, recounts numerous stories of hardship in Southern families, including those of men and women who hitched themselves to plows to make a crop in 1865. Pp. 155–63.

Flood, *op. cit.,* pp. 99–100, describes Lee's installation as President of Washington College, and traces his subsequent career. Thomas L. Connelly, in *The Marble Man: Robert E. Lee and His Image in American Society,* N.Y., 1977 studies Lee's final years (and the memorialization of the general thereafter) from a detached and "irreverent" point of view.

The historian who saw Lee as "the embodiment of the spirit of the New South" was Henry Steele Commager, in his introduction to *The Blue & The Gray,* 2 vols., N.Y., 1955.

The attempted collection of the debt from Watson Van Benthuysen by Davis is partially recounted in Hanna, *op. cit.,* p. 265. (Citing the Burton Harrison Papers, Library of Congress.)

The scene of Davis kissing pretty girls on a train during his Southern tour is from "Nannie Davis Smith narrative," McElroy Papers, New York Public Library. (Cited by Ishbel Ross, *op. cit.,* p. 305.)

The granting of amnesty to Davis by President Johnson was received with joy in the South, but the "turncoat" Tennessean's reputation was not altered in the ex-Confederacy. The ex-General Carl Schurz, speaking for Northern intellectuals, said of the amnesty proclamation and the decision to drop the trial of Davis, "There is not a single example of such magnanimity in the history of the world, and it may be said that in acting as it did, this Republic was a century ahead of its time." (Cited in McElroy, *op. cit.,* Vol. 2, p. 594.)

Lee's tour of the Carolinas is described in Flood, *op. cit.,* pp. 231 ff.; and in Marshall Fishwick, *Lee After the War,* N.Y., 1940, p. 198 ff. Flood also wrote feelingly of the last hours of Lee.

The movement to erect monuments to Lee is well and amusingly told in Connelly, *op. cit.,* pp. 27 ff.

The story of Lee's burial in his stocking feet is drawn from *Washington & Lee Alumni Magazine,* Jan. 1927, p. 8; and from Charles H. Chittum, *The Story of Finding the Coffin in Which Gen. Robert E. Lee was Afterwards Buried.* Lexington, Va., 1928 (?).

Though Davis insisted in his Richmond eulogy of Lee that the two never differed, the two leaders were clearly at odds in their views of the proper Southern attitude toward the Northern conquerors. Davis never accepted Lee's embrace of the new order. Their positions had lingering effects beyond the borders of the old Confederacy. As the late historian William B. Hesseltine said, in *Confederate Leaders in the New South,* Baton Rouge, 1950, "It was a conflict with many manifestations. Men divided along the lines of Davis and Lee in religion, in politics, and in economics. Eventually, in both the South and the nation as a whole, a working compromise was found between the antagonistic ideologies; but the struggle itself left a long legacy in the life of the South."

18 "Alas for frail humanity!"

The story of the alleged Pullman-car incident is found on page 4 of the Louisville *Commercial* of July 15, 1871. Microfilm, Library of Congress. Except for comments in newspapers cited in the text, the author was unable to find mention of this report. Two weeks after the first publication, the *Commercial* listed other newspapers which had challenged the story, including the Frankfort (Ky.) *Yeoman.* The editor of the *Commercial* defended the story in strong terms, pointed out that he had given "names and dates," and noted that Davis had not denied the facts: "He may not be able to deny them, or he may feel that he has no need to deny such a story. We have no desire to do him an injustice in any way, and, if the tale prove groundless, will make every amend in our power, but we will not retract it because papers which know nothing about it say it is a slander."

The tradition that Virginia Clay was on the Pullman car with Davis should be accepted as no more than tradition, since proof is obviously impossible. The author heard the story more than twenty-five years ago from a Civil War historian and obtained a copy of the *Louisville Commercial*'s story. It was only after a study of the C. C. Clay papers at Duke University that written evidence argued strongly that the couple might indeed have been together on the train from Memphis to Huntsville on the night of July 11, 1871.

Davis wrote his daughter Maggie from Memphis, June 29: ". . . Some of my friends at Sewanee . . . have urged me to visit them on the 12th of July, their commencement, and if it should be practicable I will do so and go thence to Maryland." He wrote again, to his wife, the following day, saying that his friend Bishop Green had sent an "urgent request" that he attend the Sewanee exercises, and Davis said, "If I can get away in time I will go." Strode, *Jefferson Davis, Private Letters,* pp. 351–52. Strode declared, "Davis did go to Sewanee and delivered the commencement address."

It was only a day after Davis wrote Varina about this that Virginia Clay wrote her husband, to say that she wanted to accompany Davis on the trip. (Her letter, in the C. C. Clay papers, is dated July 1, 1871; the two warm letters from Davis to Virginia Clay, in the same collection, are dated September 14, 1870 (?) and February 14, 1871.)

Archivists at the University of the South find no evidence that Davis was on the campus for the 1871 commencement (but report he was there the following year).

Though the C. C. Clay papers include Virginia Clay's diaries for several years, there are no volumes for 1870 or 1871—and some of the others have been carefully erased in some passages. Her scrapbook, crowded with newspaper clippings, has one notably uncluttered page. A small engraving clipped from a newspaper or magazine, depicting an illicit meeting of lovers, is accompanied by a few lines of doggerel:

Stolen Sweets

"At ten o'clock, when the house is still,
The maid leans out on the window-sill,
And gives her hand to the gallant bold
Who has waited an hour in the bitter cold. . . .

But maidens are coy when they want to be,
And we are all fond of mystery.
This kind of love the other beats,
For there's nothing so nice as stolen sweets."

The failure of The Carolina Insurance Company was caused by poor management —and a ruinous yellow fever epidemic in the Memphis region. Policies had been issued recklessly and excessive claims doomed the firm. Davis was untrained in business, and though he grasped the mathematical principles of actuarial tables, he had no gift for meeting the public. Ishbel Ross, *op. cit.,* p. 317; Varina Davis, *op. cit.,* Vol. 2, pp. 312–13.

McElroy, *op. cit.,* Vol. 2, pp. 631 ff, and Strode, *Jefferson Davis,* pp. 431 ff offer full accounts of the Beauvoir period, and Ishbel Ross, *op. cit.,* offers even more intimate detail, through the addition of material from correspondence of the Davis family.

The Davises left the basic accounts of the writing of *Rise and Fall,* but these fail to reveal Varina's substantial contributions to the work. The Confederate Major J. J. Hood later observed that she did nearly all of the writing and copying for the two massive volumes, and added, ". . . the world does not know what Mrs. Jefferson Davis suffered all these long, trying years at Beauvoir." Note on clipping from Jackson (Miss.) *Daily News,* June 2, 1908, State Archives, Montgomery.

The later writings of Davis are indebted to James Redpath, a young Scot who edited the *North American Review,* and came to admire Davis despite his own Abolitionist leanings. Redpath said of Davis, "I never met any public man who reverenced the Constitution as Mr. Davis reverenced it . . . if the Constitution had been lost, I think Mr. Davis could have rendered it from memory."

Major Walthall's contributions may also have been undervalued. Not only did this veteran tour the South, collecting material for Davis; he persisted until Washington officials opened to him Confederate records seized at the end of the war. The Federal government bought the papers of many of the leading Confederates, but Davis refused to part with those left to him.

Attacks on Davis in the war memoirs of Beauregard and Johnston—and the latter's charge that Davis had stolen much Confederate gold—are ably discussed in Connelly, *op. cit.,* pp. 79–80. Varina Davis, *op. cit.,* Vol. 2, offers a strongly partisan view, in pp. 854 ff. The original Johnston charges were published in the Philadelphia *Press,* 18 December, 1881.

19 "My ambition lies buried"

The dramatic story of the Compromise of 1877, and the role of the New York *Times* in this unsavory affair, are retold in Henry, *op. cit.,* pp. 571 ff.

McElroy, *op. cit.,* Vol. 2, pp. 672 ff, pictures Davis on the lecture trail and emphasizes the influence of this tour upon Southern public opinion. Carl Schurz gave an extreme view of the Davis postwar role. "[He] stimulated the brooding over the past disappointments rather than a cheerful contemplation of new opportunities. He presented the sorry spectacle of a soured man who wished everybody else to be soured, too." (McElroy, *ibid.,* p. 617.) McElroy contended that there was no evidence of such an effect from the Davis speeches.

There is, however, evidence that the rather vain Davis saw himself as the one legitimate Southern spokesman. Burton Harrison, who wrote on the capture of Davis for *Century* magazine, found his former chief displeased even by this friendly account, and hesitated to write further about his years with the Confederate President. Davis, Harrison said, was "very sensitive to criticism or to any remark by a friend which is not all praise."

20 "No infidelity to the Union"

The story of the Lee monument in Richmond is discussed, as it relates to the theme of "The Image Molders," in Connelly, *op. cit.,* pp. 27 ff; also consulted: Ulrich Troubetzkoy, "The Lee Monument," *Virginia Cavalcade,* Spring 1962, pp. 5 ff; numerous Richmond newspaper articles, particularly by R. B. Munford, Jr., Richmond *News-Leader,* May 5, 29, 1930; and Herbert T. Ezekiel, *News-Leader,* May 28, 1935.

Contemporary issues of the Richmond *Dispatch,* and "The Programme of Exercises . . . in Laying the Corner Stone . . . ," Richmond, 1887 were also useful.

The lingering influence of the reverence for Lee, exhibited so forcefully in Richmond in May 1890, was brought home to the author by President Harry Truman, who wrote to protest the "solecistic" sin of referring to the General as

"Robert Lee" in the pages of a military biography. "Our great heroes are all too few," Truman said, and he urged that they be treated with the utmost respect; this, he said, was the theme of his collections in the Truman Memorial Library in Independence, Mo.

The quotations from Bernard deVoto are from *Saturday Review,* March 6, 1937, p. 8.

EPILOGUE

The brief sketches of the chief actors in this narrative are drawn from entries in the *Dictionary of American Biography;* also, for Judah P. Benjamin, see Meade, *op. cit.;* John Breckinridge, W. C. Davis, *op. cit.;* Jo Shelby, Rolle, *op. cit.;* Edwin Stanton, Thomas and Hyman, *op. cit.:* Virginia Clay, Nuermberger, *op. cit.;* Varina Davis, Ishbel Ross, *op. cit.*

The lingering echoes of the Civil War are presented throughout Connelly, *op. cit.;* the quotation from D. S. Freeman is from *Time,* Oct. 18, 1948; further details from B. Davis, *Our Incredible Civil War,* N.Y. 1960 (republished as *The Civil War: Strange and Fascinating Facts,* N.Y. 1982).

The career of Traveler's skeleton is taken from releases of Washington and Lee University; Charles McDowell, now a Washington columnist and television commentator, served as a guide in the Lee Chapel at about age twelve, and recalled the story of presenting the miniature skeleton as that of Traveler in colthood. The Richmond *Times-Dispatch,* May 7, 1967, has a report on Traveler's post-mortem career by Web deHoff.

Lee's frustration in seeking a pardon and restoration of his civil rights are detailed in Flood, *op. cit.*

Index

Abbeville, Ga., 138, 142
Abbeville, S.C., 74, 75, 89, 90, 109, 112–14, 116–18, 121, 169, 189
Abraham, Capt. Lot, U.S.A., 184
Adams, Provost Marshal, U.S.A., 187
C.S.S. *Alabama,* 35
Alaska, 227
Alexander, Brig. Gen. E.P., C.S.A., 185–86, 268
Allegan, Mich., 142
Allen, Gov. Henry W. (La.), 195
Amelia Courthouse, Va., 88
Anderson, Col. Archer, C.S.A., 268
Anderson, Brig. Gen. Joseph, C.S.A., 22
Anderson, Maj. Robert, U.S.A., 88
Andersonville (Ga.) prison, 141, 208, 255
Andrews, Eliza, 114, 126, 128, 129, 183, 185
Andrews, Judge Garnett, 126, 183–84
Antietam, (Md.) battlefield, 192, 271
Appleton & Co., publishers, 248, 252, 253
Appomattox Courthouse, Va., 58–9, 93, 193, 228, 230, 233
Appomattox River (Va.), 17
Arizona, 227
Army of Northern Virginia, 12–13
Ashmore, Otis, 184, 187
Astor, Lady Nancy, 270
Athens, Ga., 108
Atlanta, Ga., 6, 90, 141, 152, 228, 259, 260
Atlanta (Ga.) *Constitution,* 263
Atlantic Coast Line R.R., 275
Augusta, Ga., 105, 113, 115, 152, 155–56, 238
Augusta (Ga.) *Constitutionalist,* 119
Aullville, Mo., 277
Averasboro (N.C.), battle of, 166

Bahamas, 160ff.
Baltimore, Md., 210, 219, 220, 235
Baltimore & Ohio R.R., 219
Bank of Georgia, 126
Bank of Virginia, 186*n*
Barnum, P. T., 158, 217
Barringer, Judge Victor C., 84
Bates, Lewis F., 85–6
Beauregard, Gen. P.G.T., C.S.A., 42, 65, 66–7, 71, 229, 242, 247, 271
Beauvoir Plantation (Miss.), 248–52, 254–55, 259
Bee, Pvt. Andrew, U.S.A., 143–45
Bee, Brig. Gen. Hamilton P., C.S.A., 196
Belford & Co., publishers, 280
Benjamin, Sec. of State Judah P., C.S.A., 24, 54, 60, 61, 67, 71, 80–81, 85, 92, 102, 121, 206, 237, 252
  background, 30, 47–8
  bravery of, 162
  in England, 162, 237

escape, 159–63
later life, 273–74
leaves presidential party, 125–26
personality, 30, 47, 60, 103, 106, 125
Benjamin, Natalie (Mrs. Judah P.), 48, 274
Bentonville (N.C.), battle of, 66
Bermuda, 90, 129
Bibb County, Ala., 228
Bimini, 161, 162
Bingham, John A., 277
Birmingham, Ala., 228
Blackford, Col. William, C.S.A., 38–9, 58–9
Booth, John Wilkes, 87
Boston, Mass., 177
Boston *Transcript,* 105
Bragg, Gen. Braxton, C.S.A., 95, 106–07, 110, 117, 121, 126, 129
Bratton, Dr. James, 106
Brazil, 191, 198
Breckinridge, Cabell, 56, 163, 164
Breckinridge, Clifton, 162, 163*n*
Breckinridge, Sec. of War John C., C.S.A., 19, 30, 35, 79, 83, 85–6, 91, 96, 103, 106, 107, 108, 112, 117ff., 123*n,* 124, 129, 130, 187, 238
background, 31, 69–70
escape, 159, 163–67
flees Richmond, 56–7
foresees Confederate defeat, 57
later life, 275
leads troops in action, 56
leaves presidential party, 130
named Secretary of War, C.S.A., 70
personality, 31, 69, 84, 96, 121–24
praise of, 31, 69–70, 96
as Vice-President of U.S., 69–70
Breckinridge, W.C.P., 163
Brierfield plantation (Miss.), 280
British Honduras, 191, 198
Broad River (S.C.), 106
Broad Trail, Chief, 278
Brooke, John M., 45
Broun, Col. William, C.S.A., 22
Brown, Robert (Jefferson Davis slave), 29, 137, 201, 206, 249
Bruce, George, 41
Bryant, Capt. O.E., U.S.A., 189
Buchanan, Adm. Franklin, C.S.N., 45
Bulloch, James D., 95
Burkeville, Va., 38, 52
Burr, Frank A., 254
Burt, Col. Armistead, C.S.A., 75, 90, 114
Burton, Brig. Gen. Henry S., U.S.A., 218–19
Byrd, Sen. Harry F., Jr., 285

Caldwell, Lt. J.F.J., C.S.A., 17–8
Calhoun, John C., 9, 75
Caloosahatchie River (Fla.), 161
Camden, S.C., 168
Campbell, Capt. Given, C.S.A., 78, 96–7, 107, 127, 137, 140, 142
Canada, 170, 191, 206, 207, 221, 223, 232ff., 236, 275
Canby, Maj. Gen. E.R.S., U.S.A., 136
Cardenas, Cuba, 167
Carleton, George, publisher, 217
Carlota, empress of Mexico, 197
Carlota, Mexico, 198, 276
Carolina Insurance Company, 238, 248
Carrington, Maj. Isaac, C.S.A., 22
Cary, Constance (Mrs. Burton Harrison), 22, 146, 275–76
Catawba River (S.C.), 105
Censorship, 6, 118–19
Chambersburg, Pa., 196
Chancellorsville (Va.), battle of, 271
Charleston, S.C., 47, 129, 169, 199, 228, 239
Charlotte, N.C., 14, 28–9, 53, 65, 72, 82–97, 167, 238
Chase, Chief Justice Salmon P., U.S.A., 204
Chattanooga, Tenn., 228
Chattanooga (Tenn.), battle of, 142
Chenault, The Rev. Dionysius, 122, 184, 186–87
Chesnut, Brig. Gen. James, C.S.A., 73
Chesnut, Mary Boykin (Mrs. James), 66, 73–4
Chester, S.C., 73
Chicago, Ill., 227
Chicago (Ill.) *Tribune,* 232
Chickamauga (Ga.), battle of, 80
Chief Joseph, 278
Chisman, Maj. S.R., C.S.A., 77
Chittum, C.G., 240
Clark, Gov. Edward (Tex.), 195
Clark, Brig. Gen. John B., Jr., C.S.A., 195

Clark, Capt. Micajah, C.S.A., 6, 49, 53, 73*n*, 78, 121ff., 136–37, 187–89, 204, 254
Clay, Clement Claiborne, 26–7, 49, 50–1, 57–8, 73, 108, 111–12, 152–53, 155, 173, 174, 175, 205, 246, 247
  death of, 279
  letters to his wife, 111–12, 246
  as prisoner, 211–14
  surrenders, 152–53, 212
Clay, Henry, 48, 130
Clay, James B., Jr., 130, 163, 163*n*
Clay, Virginia Tunstall (Mrs. Clement Claiborne Clay; Mrs. David Clopton—"Clay-Clopton"), 27, 152ff., 173, 175, 176, 200–01, 245–47, 260
  background, 111–12
  diary, 279
  domestic life, 111–12, 246
  helps to free husband from prison, 211–14
  later life, 279
  letters to husband, 246, 247
  memoirs *(A Belle of the 'Fifties)*, 279
  personality, 27, 175 *passim*
  vanity, 112, 246
Cleveland, Ohio, 278
Clopton, Judge David, 279
Clover, Va., 51–2
Cokesbury plantation (S.C.), 106–07, 108
Cole, Maj. James R., C.S.A., 77
Cole, Col. Robert G., C.S.A., 239
Colfax, Schuyler, 203
Collins, Fla., 164
Colorado, 227
Colt, Samuel, 180
Columbia, S.C., 238, 257
Columbus, Ga., 141, 229
Compromise of 1877, 256–58
Concord, N.C., 84
Confederate Cabinet, 24, 30–2, 44–50, 72 *passim*
  "final" sessions (in sequence),
  Danville, Va., 53–4, 57, 59–60
  Greensboro, N.C., 65–7, 70–2
  Charlotte, N.C., 92–3, 94
  Fort Mill, S.C., 103
  Abbeville, S.C., 117–18
  Washington, Ga., 126–27
Confederate currency, 6, 14, 15, 29, 46, 74–5, 266
Confederate government, 29, 44–9 *passim*
  longevity of influence, 282–85
  weaknesses of, 20–1, 50, 154–55, 247–48 *passim*
Confederate treasure, 24–5, 33–4, 53, 65, 65*n*, 73, 73*n*, 79, 104, 113, 118, 121, 122–23, 123*n*, 124, 129–30, 136–37, 141, 146
Confederate Treasury Department, 6, 24–5, 53
Confederate troops, 5, 16–18 *passim*
  lack of discipline, 34, 76–7, 122ff., 129, 131, 183–85
  units:
    11th Virginia Infantry, 269
    45th N.C. Infantry, 77
    Kershaw's Brigade, 36
    Shelby's Iron Brigade, 194–98, 276–77
Conyngham, David, 76
Cooper, Dr. George, U.S.A., 209, 221
Cooper, Adjutant General Samuel, C.S.A., 49, 80, 87, 96
Craven, Lt. Col. (Dr.) John J., U.S.A., 180–81, 200, 202, 205, 207–10, 237
  diary, 209
  dismissed from Fort Monroe, 209
  his *Prison Life of Jefferson Davis*, 217–18
Crawfordville, Ga., 154
Crazy Horse, Chief, 278
Crump, Judge W.W., 25, 52, 53, 130, 183–84
Cuba, 163 *passim*, 191, 235
Cumberland Island, Ga., 238
Curry, Capt. John, 160

Dana, Charles A., 177, 179–80, 201, 263
Danburg, Ga., 124
Danville, Va., 15, 17, 24, 52–62, 192, 233, 270
Danville (Va.) *Register*, 54
Davis, Attorney General George, C.S.A., 30, 64, 71, 80, 85, 167–69, 222
  background, 30, 48
  later life, 275
  leaves presidential party, 94

Davis, Jefferson,
amnesty granted, 237
and Andersonville prison, 208, 233, 255
appearance, 7–8, 21–2, 52, 126, 128, 215, 221, 222
assassination plots against, 234
bravery, 144, 175, 178–79
as businessman, 236, 237–38, 248
capture of, 139–48
citizenship restored, 285
and Confederate treasure, 53, 65, 79, 113, 121, 123–24, 127, 129, 136, 187–89, 253–54
conflicts with Confederate Congress, 7
criticism of, 6 *passim,* 20–1, 27, 39, 49–50, 66, 101, 107, 149–50, 154–55, 246, 253–54, 261
death of, 263
defends leadership of Confederacy, 249, 251–52, 253–55
defies U.S. conquerors, 232, 258–61, 262–63
despairs of Confederate cause, 79–80, 118
and "disguise," 137, 143–45, 150, 157–58, 200–01, 284
dissolves Confederate government, 127
as enigma, 10, 19–20, 39, 50, 258–62
execution urged, 55, 105, 157, 203, 214
in exile, 232–34
farewell to escort troops, 128
farewell to U.S. Senate, 9
funeral services, 263–64, 281
health, 7–8, 9, 20, 139, 173, 175, 181, 201–02, 205, 215, 220, 232, 255, 262
intellectual interests, 9, 208, 209
humor of, 103, 117
impoverished by war, 14, 15, 112–13, 187–88, 223, 232–34, 235–36, 238
impulsiveness, 137–38, 178–79
indicted for treason, 192, 215, 234, 235
letters to Virginia Clay, 247
letters to his wife, 72, 92–3, 131, 138, 207, 248, 257
Lincoln's death, and, 85–6, 87–8, 108–09, 150–51, 152, 174, 177, 201, 203–04, 214–15, 218, 219
as martyr, 55, 182, 223
memoirs of, 233, 248–55
military aspirations of, 8, 9–10, 13
opposes emigration of Southerners, 198
opposes national reunion, 89, 90–1, 198, 232
and peace negotiations, 26, 67, 71–2, 78, 84, 91–4, 189
personal attacks upon, 8, 13, 20, 66, 101, 243–45, 247–48, 253–54
personality, 7, 10ff., 19–20, 21–2, 27, 82, 128, 174, 221, 236
post-war financial problems, 234, 238, 248, 250–52
post-war popularity of, 241–42, 258–63
praise of, 49, 117–18, 126, 128, 174, 175, 218, 252, 254, 260, 261, 263–64
pre-war career, 8–9, 246
pride, 8, 236, 248
as prisoner, 173–82, 200, 205, 207–09, 214–21, 280
protests treatment in prison, 178–80, 202, 205, 215
prosecution by U.S., 192, 203–04, 214–15, 219–20, 221–23, 234–36
public appearances, 235, 241–42, 258–63
public attitudes toward, 7, 10, 52, 63–4, 85, 101, 126, 149–50, 151–53, 157, 182, 209–10, 218, 221, 223, 232, 233–34, 241–42, 258–63
recklessness, 137–38, 144, 179
refuses opportunities to escape, 153, 174, 177–78, 205
refusal to surrender, 13–4, 25–6, 54, 67–8, 72, 83, 103–04, 117–18, 125, 135, 258–63
relationships:
with Judah P. Benjamin, 30, 47, 53–4, 60, 67, 71, 92, 103, 125–26, 237, 252
with Virginia Clay, 27, 58, 111, 153, 175, 176, 245–47, 260, 279
with Joseph E. Johnston, 60, 65–7, 70–2, 247–48, 252, 253–54, 268
with Robert E. Lee, 8, 9, 11, 12–4, 17, 22, 24, 58, 89, 232ff., 241–42, 254–55

with Alexander Stephens, 21, 154, 156–57, 175
release from prison, 220–21
and religion, 21, 59, 87, 178, 223
"rescue" of his family, 137–38
reward for capture of, 108–09, 141, 150, 219, 219*n*
and Secession, 9, 10, 178, 191, 204, 208, 220–21, 237, 252, 253, 260, 261
as U.S. Secretary of War, 9
self-confidence, 10, 13, 50, 208
slaves and his, 26, 29–30, 137, 140ff., 206, 249
stubbornness, 8, 10, 12, 13, 14, 26–7, 50, 90, 117–18
temper, 13
urges cooperation with Federal government, 259–63
U.S. policy toward, 173–82, 200–02, 206–23, 234–37
women, and, 58, 221, 236, 243–47

Davis, Jefferson, Jr., 15, 175–76, 206, 250, 252
Davis, John (Jefferson Davis's slave), 26
Davis, Joseph, brother of Jefferson Davis, 8
Davis, Margaret ("Maggie"), daughter of Jefferson Davis, 14, 15, 250, 252, 253
Davis, Sarah Knox Taylor, first Mrs. Jefferson Davis, 68, 246
Davis, Bishop Thomas P., brother of Attorney General George Davis, C.S.A., 168
Davis, Varina Anne ("Winnie; "Piecake"), daughter of Jefferson Davis, 14, 74, 90, 114, 146, 173, 215, 220, 260, 262, 280, 282
Davis, Varina Howell, Mrs. Jefferson Davis, 7, 12, 28–9, 72–5, 114–16, 130–31, 173, 222, 223, 234, 235, 236, 255
appearance, 8, 73, 281
appraisal of husband, 10, 20, 53
background, 12
capture of, 139–48
criticism of, 8, 280, 281
escape plans, 14–5, 90, 92, 109, 115
in Europe, 236–38, 239, 249
financial problems, 14, 15, 27, 188, 188*n*, 189, 206, 233, 280
flees Richmond, 14–5
grieves over Lincoln's death, 89
helps to free husband from prison, 206–07, 214–17, 218–21
health, 220, 243, 249, 279–80
hostility toward captors, 144, 150, 151, 176, 201, 202, 215–16, 278
hysterical moods, 144, 201, 251
jealousy, 245–46, 249–51, 252
and Johnston's surrender, 115
later life, 279–82
letters to husband, 53, 74, 75, 89–90, 115, 126, 207, 220, 245–46, 249–50
memoirs *(Jefferson Davis . . . A Memoir by his Wife)*, 280
in New York, 279–82
personality, 8, 10, 12
urges husband to escape, 89, 115, 126, 144
urges husband to write his memoirs, 233

Davis, William ("Billie"), son of Jefferson Davis, 206, 250
Dennison, Postmaster General William, U.S.A., 79
desertion:
Confederate army, 5, 8, 11, 20, 54, 76, 83, 116
U.S. Army, 11

DeVoto, Bernard, 271
Dibrell, Brig. Gen. George, C.S.A., 78
Dickinson, Lt. Julian G., U.S.A., 144
Dickinson, Capt. William, C.S.A., 105
Dickison, Col. J.J., C.S.A., 164
Disraeli, Benjamin, 237
Dorsey, Mrs. Sarah Anne, 250–52
Douglas, Adele Cutts (Mrs. Stephen A.), 212–13
Douglas, Stephen A., 217
Dry Tortugas, Fla., 166
Duke, Maj. Gen. Basil, C.S.A., 96, 106, 117, 118, 121, 128, 163
Duluth, Minn., 283
Dunham, Charles A. (alias Sanford Conover), 203–04
Durham's Station (Durham), N.C., 84, 91
Dwight, Capt. Charles, C.S.A., 35–6

Eagle Pass, Tex., 195
Early, Lt. Gen. Jubal A., C.S.A., 196, 251, 265, 268
Echols, Maj. William, C.S.A., 212
Edgefield (S.C.) *Advertiser,* 119
Egypt, 191
Elliott Key, Fla., 166
Elzey, Maj. Gen. Arnold, C.S.A., 126
Emory, Capt. Fred, C.S.A., 96
Evarts, Attorney General William M., U.S.A., 222
Everhart, The Rev. George M., 87–8
Ewell, Lt. Gen. Richard S., C.S.A., 34ff., 57

Farmville, Va., 56
Fayetteville, N.C., 47
Ferguson, Brig. Gen. S.W., C.S.A., 96, 122
Ferguson, Tom (Breckinridge's slave), 163, 164, 166–67
Field, Kate, 280
Five Forks (Va.), battle of, 16
Flournoy, Brig. Gen. George, C.S.A., 196
Ford, President Gerald R., 285
Forrest, Lt. Gen. Nathan B., C.S.A., 135, 138, 152
Fort Dallas, Fla., 166
Fort Delaware, Pa., 174
Fort Lafayette, N.Y., 169
Fort Mill, S.C., 103
Fort Monroe, Va., 173–82, 200–02, 205, 207–09, 213–16, 218–19, 220–21, 278, 280
Fort Pickens, Fla., 275
Fort Sumter, S.C., 42, 88, 203
Fort Warren, Mass., 174
Franklin (Tenn.), battle of, 152
Freeman, Douglas S., 283

Gainesville, Fla., 164, 168, 188
Galveston, Tex., 229
Garnett, Dr. A.Y.P., 49, 54
Garrett, John W., 219–20
Gary, Brig. Gen. Martin W., C.S.A., 106
Gasparilla Pass, Fla., 161
Georgetown, D.C., 277
H.M.S. *Georgina,* 163
Geronimo, Chief, 278
Gettysburg (Pa.), battle of, 16, 271
Glazier, The Rev. Ezechiel, 160
Gone with the Wind (Mitchell), 283
Gordon, Maj. Gen. John B., C.S.A., 18, 268
Gorgas, Brig. Gen. Josiah, C.S.A., 22, 39, 107, 228, 255
Gorgas, Dr. William C., 39
Grady, Henry W., 260, 263
Grant, James, 27
Grant, General and President U.S., U.S.A., 6, 16, 18, 58, 67, 78–9, 93, 104, 105*n,* 120, 177, 193, 208, 212, 277
Grant, Gen. U.S., III, U.S.A., 283–84
Graves, Capt. W.P., C.S.A., 59–60
Greeley, Horace, 26, 51, 55, 206, 207, 209, 211, 213, 219, 220, 222
Green, Ben, 212
Greene, Maj. Gen. Nathanael, U.S.A., 259, 260–61
Greensboro, N.C., 3, 4, 53, 54, 60–1, 62, 63–72, 75–8, 79, 95, 169, 170, 188, 238, 276
Greenwood, S.C., 106

Halleck, Maj. Gen. Henry W., U.S.A., 104, 158, 177, 180
Halpine, Col. Charles, U.S.A., 217–18
Hampton Roads, Va., 174, 271
Hampton, Lt. Gen. Wade, C.S.A., 90–1, 229, 258, 259, 268
Hardeman, Brig. Gen. William P., C.S.A., 195–96
Harnden, Lt. Col. Henry, U.S.A., 141–42, 219*n*
Harper's Weekly, 54–5, 157
Harris, Gov. Isham G. (Tenn.), 196
Harris, Joel Chandler, 190–91
Harrison, Burton, 14–5, 22, 25, 28–9, 53, 57, 60, 65, 80–1, 86 *passim,* 114ff., 130–31, 138ff., 173–74, 221, 223
  later life, 275–76
Harrison, Mrs. Burton. See Constance Cary.
Harrison, Fairfax, 276
Harrison, Francis, 276
Hartsuff, Brig. Gen. William, U.S.A., 95
Harvie, Lewis, 24, 31
Haughton, The Rev. Thomas A., 84
Havana, Cuba, 163, 167, 235
Hawkinsville, Ga., 138

Haw, Joseph, 33
Hawthorne, Brig. Gen. Alexander T., C.S.A., 196
Hayes, J. Addison, 250
Hayes, Pres. Rutherford B., 256–57
Helen (Jefferson Davis' slave), 144–45
Hendera, John, 27, 29
Hiatt, John, 81
Hicks, Col. William (of the British army), 276
High Point, N.C., 82
Hill, Benjamin H., 152, 259
Hillis, Robert E., 240
Hilton Head, S.C., 211
Hindman, Brig. Gen. T.C., C.S.A., 196
Hiram College (Mich.), 142
Hoare, Joseph A. (alias William Campbell), 204
Hoge, The Rev. Moses, 47, 60
Hollywood Cemetery, Richmond, Va., 281
Holt, Judge Advocate General Joseph, U.S.A., 194, 204, 211, 212, 214
Hood, Lt. Gen. John B., C.S.A., 73, 152, 283
Houston, Sam, 8, 48
Houston, Tex., 283
Howell, Jefferson D., 25, 173, 174
Howell, Margaret ("Maggie"), 14, 90, 130, 140, 146, 149, 155, 215, 220, 233
Howell, Gov. Richard (N.J.), 12
Howell, Mrs. William, 201, 232, 234, 235
Hudson, Capt. Charles, U.S.A., 150
Huntsville, Ala., 212, 214, 246, 247, 279

Idaho, 227
Indian River (Fla.), 68, 142, 165
Inflation, 5, 8, 15, 74 *passim*
The International Chamber of Commerce and Mississippi Valley Society, 248
Irving, William, 22
Irwinville, Ga., 139–48, 164

Jackson, Lt. Gen. Thomas J. ("Stonewall"), C.S.A., 47, 266, 271, 285
Jackson, Mrs. Thomas J., 268
Jacksonville, Fla., 238
Jamaica, 191
Jamestown, N.C., 81
James River (Va.), 17, 35–7, 221
Japan, 191
Jefferson, President Thomas, 32
"Jim Limber" (Jefferson Davis's ward), 90, 157
Johnson, President Andrew, 79, 86, 87, 91, 105, 108–09, 141, 150, 152, 170, 191, 193, 210, 212–14, 215, 216–17, 218, 219, 236, 237, 275, 277
  later life, 278
Johnson, Reverdy, 193
Johnston, Gen. Albert S., C.S.A., 48, 146, 271
Johnston, Gen. Joseph E., C.S.A., 6, 12, 23, 60, 65, 66–7, 69, 70–2, 75, 78, 84, 91, 93–4, 242, 247–48, 252, 253–54, 268–69
Johnston, Mayor William, Charlotte, N.C., 85–6
Johnston, Col. William Preston, C.S.A., 25, 29, 48, 88, 101, 126, 136, 137, 146, 149, 173, 174, 239–40
Jones, J. William, 251–52
Jones, Jim (Jefferson Davis's slave), 131, 140, 142–43
Jones, John Beauchamp, 31
Juarez, Benito, 197
Jupiter Inlet, Fla., 165

Kansas, 227
Kansas City, Mo., 277
Kashgil, the Sudan, battle of, 276
Kean, Capt. Robert G., C.S.A., 49, 96
U.S.S. *Kearsarge*, 35
Kennaway, Sir John, 228
Kentucky (Jefferson Davis's mount), 29
Kershaw, Gen. Joseph, C.S.A., 36
Key Largo, Fla., 166
Key West, Fla., 169
Knight's Key, Fla., 161
Koones, C.M., 240
Khrushchev, Nikita, 284

Ladies' Lee Monument Assn., 265–66
La Grange, Ga., 122, 152, 169
Lake City, Fla., 168
Lane, Mrs. Thomas Hill, 168
Langhorne, Chiswell ("Buck"), 269–70
Lanier, Sidney, 182

Lawley, Francis, 21, 22, 58
Lawton, Quartermaster General A.R., C.S.A., 56, 130
Leach, James, 20
Leadbetter, Brig. Gen. Danville, C.S.A., 195
Lee, Agnes, daughter of Robert E. Lee, 39, 238, 268
Lee, Annie, daughter of Robert E. Lee, 238
Lee, Maj. Gen. Fitz, C.S.A., nephew of Robert E. Lee, 268
Lee, Maj. Gen. George W. Custis, son of Robert E. Lee, 11–2, 268
Lee, Gen. Henry ("Light Horse Harry"), father of Robert E. Lee, 238
Lee, Mary Custis (Mrs. Robert E. Lee, Sr.), 28, 39–40, 60, 240
Lee Memorial Assn., 239, 241, 242, 265
Lee Memorial Episcopal Church (Lexington, Va.), 265
Lee, Mildred, daughter of Robert E. Lee, 268
Lee monument, Richmond, Va., 265–69, 283
Lee Monument Assn., 265–66
Lee, Gen. Robert E., C.S.A., 6, 8, 39, 51, 56–9
  aggressiveness, 12–3, 240
  appearance, 10–1, 12, 58, 267
  applies for pardon, 193, 231, 285
  background, 12–3
  begs aid for troops, 11–2
  citizenship restored, 285
  as college president, 230–32, 241
  as commander-in-chief, C.S.A., 8, 10
  as Confederate folk hero, 10, 192–93, 231–32, 238–39, 241–42, 265–69, 282–83
  conflicts with Jefferson Davis, 8, 11, 12, 24, 88–9, 232, 235, 242
  congratulates Davis on release from prison, 232–33
  and criticism of Jefferson Davis, 12, 234–35
  death of, 239–40
  defends Jefferson Davis, 194
  denounced, 266
  and fall of Richmond, 15–8, 19–23, 31–2
  forecasts Confederate defeat, 11–2, 57
  funeral of, 240–41
  health, 10–1, 16, 230, 238–39
  indicted for treason, 192, 215, 234, 235
  memorials to, 239, 265–69
  military career, 12–3
  and oath of allegiance, 192–93, 231, 285
  opposes emigration from South, 192, 194
  as peacemaker, 88–9, 192–94, 230–32, 239
  personality, 12, 14, 16, 58–9, 67, 230–32, 238–39, 240
  post-war influence, 230–32, 239
  praise of, 232, 238–39, 242, 266 *passim*
  prosecuted by U.S., 193
  surrender of, 57–9, 60, 67–8, 75, 88
  tours the South, 238–39
Lee, Capt. R.E., Jr., C.S.A., son of Robert E. Lee, 59, 67–8, 268
Lee, Maj. Gen. William Henry Fitzhugh ("Rooney"), C.S.A., son of Robert E. Lee, 268
Lennoxville, Quebec, 234
Leovy, Col. Henry, C.S.A., 117, 125–26, 159
Leovy, Mrs. Henry, 117, 189
Lesley, Maj. John, C.S.A., 160
Letcher, Gov. John (Va.), 24
Lexington, N.C., 82–3
Lexington, Ky., 275
Lexington, Va., 230–32, 239
Lieber, Judge Francis, 214–15
Lincoln, President Abraham, 55–6, 59, 91, 181
  assassination, 85–8, 89, 108–09
  funeral procession, 95
  illegal war acts, 1861, 69
  last Cabinet session, 78–9
  lenient policy toward South, 18, 56, 72, 78–9, 204, 277
  in Richmond, Va., 55–6
Lincoln, Mary Todd (Mrs. Abraham), 59, 70
Little Sorrel, Stonewall Jackson's mount, 285
Liverpool, England, 129, 236
London *Daily Telegraph,* 273

London *Illustrated News,* 80, 276
London *Times,* 21, 273, 274
Long, Col. Armistead, C.S.A., 17
Longstreet, Gen. James, C.S.A., 16, 268
Louisville *Commercial,* 243–45, 247, 254
Lowell (Mass.) *Sun,* 261–62
Lubbock, Gov. Francis R. (Tex.), 19, 21, 25, 29, 64, 126, 136, 146, 149, 173, 174
  background, 48
Lynchburg, Va., 17
Lyons, James, 222

McCardell, Lt. William, C.S.A., 164
McCarthy, Carlton, 266
McCausland, Maj. Gen. John, C.S.A., 196
McCullough, Sec. Treasury Hugh, U.S.A., 219
McLeod, H.A., 160–63
McNeil, Capt. Archibald, C.S.A., 160
McRae, C.J., 206
Macon, Ga., 113, 115, 135, 141, 146 *passim,* 157, 163*n*, 212, 262
Madison, Fla., 136, 163, 164
Magruder, Maj. Gen. John B., C.S.A., 196
Mahone, Maj. Gen. William, C.S.A., 229
Majestic Hotel, New York City, 282
Mallory, Sec. of Navy Stephen R., C.S.A., 21, 30, 35, 59–60, 63–4, 71, 79–80, 91, 103, 106, 113, 121, 152, 169
  background, 30, 45
  later life, 274–75
  leaves presidential party, 122
Manassas–Bull Run (Va.), battle of, 65, 70, 271
Manatee River (Fla.), 160
Marshall, Col. Charles, C.S.A., 266
Marshall, Brig. Gen. Humphrey, C.S.A., 115–16
Marshall, Tex., 69
Maury, Commodore Matthew Fontaine, 45, 196
Maximilian, Emperor of Mexico, 104, 119–20, 195 *passim,* 276
Mayo, Mayor Joseph (Richmond, Va.), 24, 40
Memminger, Sec. Treasury Charles C., C.S.A., 45, 239, 247–48
Memphis, Tenn., 228, 237–38, 243–44 *passim*
Memphis & Charleston R.R., 243–45
Mercié, Marius Jean Antonin, 266
U.S.S. *Merrimac* see C.S.S. *Virginia(I)*
Merritt, Dr. James B., 204
Metairie Cemetery (New Orleans), 264
Mexican War, 8, 12, 107, 246
Mexico City, 197
Mexico as Confederate haven, 55, 69, 119, 191, 194–98, 276
Miami, Fla., 166
Michigan, University of, 142
Midway Island, 227
Miles, Brig. Gen. Nelson A., U.S.A., 177 *passim,* 205 *passim*
  later life, 278–79
Milledgeville, Ga., 131
Milton, Gov. John (Fla.), 43
Minnigerode, The Rev. Charles, 21–2, 223
Missionary Ridge (Tenn.), battle of, 107
Mitchell, Margaret, 283
Mobile, Ala., 88, 136
Molineux, Brig. Gen. Edward L., U.S.A., 187
U.S.S. *Monitor,* 271
Montana, 227
Montgomery, Ala., 141, 169, 259
Montreal, Canada, 232, 234
Monumental Church (Richmond, Va.), 266
Morehead, Gov. Charles S. (Ky.), 195
Morehead, Gov. John M. (N.C.), 65
Moreno, Don Francisco, 275
Morgan, James M., 28
Morse, Samuel F.B., 180
Moses, Maj. Raphael J., C.S.A., 130, 187
Moss, Mrs. J.D., 124, 187
Mount Olivet Cemetery, Washington, D.C., 284
Murfreesboro (Tenn.), battle of, 107
Murphy, Pvt. P., C.S.A., 164
Murrah, Gov. Pendleton (Tex.), 195
Myakka River (Fla.), 161
Myers, William, 85

Naples, Fla., 161
Nassau, 90, 129, 163, 168
National Archives, 284, 285
Nebraska, 227
Negro troops:
Confederate, 11, 24
Union, 11, 41
S.S. *Neptune,* 167
Nevada, 227
Newark, N.J., 180
Newberry, S.C., 75, 113
New Orleans, La., 47, 48, 159, 191, 235, 247, 252, 257, 263, 268, 281
New Smyrna, Fla., 168
New York City, 95, 213, 223, 227, 241, 250, 275
New York *Daily Mail,* 266
New York *Daily News,* 196
New York *Herald,* 177, 215, 239
New York *Post,* 42
New York *Sun,* 263
New York *Times,* 55, 105, 119, 173, 217, 256, 264
New York *Tribune,* 26, 55, 209, 219, 233–34
New York *World,* 260, 261, 263, 280
Norfolk, Va., 183, 192, 215, 229
North Carolina, war effort of, 82–3
North Dakota, 227
Northrop, Commissary General Lucius B., C.S.A., 11
Nugent, Richard, 131

Oath of allegiance to U.S., 68*n,* 191–93, 214, 285
Ocala, Fla., 168
Ocmulgee River (Ga.), 138
Oconee River (Ga.), 137
O'Conor, Charles, 207, 211, 213, 215 *passim*
Omelia, Mrs. (Jefferson Davis' housekeeper), 14, 26–7
Orr, James L., 101, 107
O'Toole, Sgt. Joseph, C.S.A., 164–67
Ould, Judge Robert, 222

Palatka, Fla., 238
Palestine, Tex., 274
Palm Beach, Fla., 165
Palmer, Brig. Gen. W.J., U.S.A., 105, 108
Parker, Capt. James H., U.S.A., 145
Parker, Capt. William H., C.S.N., 25, 31, 33–4, 52, 65, 73 *passim,* 113, 118, 121
Parsons, Brig. Gen. Monroe, C.S.A., 196
C.S.S. *Patrick Henry,* 37
Peace River (Fla.), 161
Pember, Mrs. Phoebe Y., 40
Pendleton, Brig. Gen. William N., C.S.A., 229
Pensacola, Fla., 275
Perkins, Judge John, 190, 196
Petersburg, Va., 5, 16, 27
Pettigru, James L., 75*n*
Phifer, William, 85
Philadelphia, Pa., 227
Philbrook, Chief Teller Walter, Confederate Treasury Department, 25, 53, 73, 113
Pickett, Maj. Gen. George E., C.S.A., 16
Pickett, Mrs. George E., 268
Pierce, President Franklin, 9, 176, 203, 212, 220–21
Pleasanton, Maj. Gen. Alfred, U.S.A., 195
Polk, Gen. Trusten, C.S.A., 196
Pollard, Edward, 6, 20
Porter, William Sydney ("O. Henry"), 77–8
Post-war America, 227, 237, 256–58
Post-war South, 149–50, 190–92, 193–94, 214, 227–29, 235–36, 252, 256–58
industrialization begins, 227–29
revival of regional pride, 241–42, 252, 258–62, 265–71, 281 *passim*
Potter, Henry A., 151
Preston, Brig. Gen. John S., C.S.A., 73
Preston, General William, C.S.A., 196
Price, Lt. Gen. Stirling, C.S.A., 195
Pritchard, Lt. Col. Benjamin, U.S.A., 141–42, 143, 144, 146–48, 157, 219*n*
Pulitzer family, 280, 282

Quarles, Mann S., 24–5

Raleigh, N.C., 82, 238
Rankin, Robert S., 61
Reagan, Postmaster General John H., C.S.A., 19–20, 24, 30, 44, 49, 64, 66–7, 71, 79, 91–2, 103, 112, 119ff,

136–38, 146, 149, 169, 173 *passim*
background, 30, 46
later life, 274
Reconstruction ends, 256–58
Redmoor plantation (Va.), 202–03
Reed, William B., 222
Richardson, Maj. B.W., C.S.A., 267
Richmond, Va., 88, 183–84, 192, 221–23, 234ff. 265ff.
burning of, 33, 35–6, 39–40, 52
fall of, 5–43
Richmond, Va. bank deposits, 25, 52, 65*n,* 116, 116*n,* 183–86, 186*n,* 187
Richmond, Va. Blues, 267
Richmond & Danville R.R., 24, 30–2, 44–52, 60–2
Richmond *Dispatch,* 241–42
Richmond *Examiner,* 6, 20
Richmond *Times,* 34
Richmond *Whig,* 23, 118–19
Rio Grande River (Tex.), 111, 194–97
The Rise & Fall of The Confederate Government, by Jefferson Davis, 248–53
U.S.S. *Robert E. Lee* (nuclear submarine), 283
Robertson, Dr. J.J., 126
Robertson, Mrs. J.J., 128
Roosevelt, Eleanor, 95
Roosevelt, Elliott, 95
Roosevelt, President Theodore, 95
Ruffin, Edmund, 42–3, 86–7, 202–03
Ruffin, Edmund, Jr., 203
Russell, Corp. Richard, C.S.A., 164, 165, 167
Russia, 227

St. Albans, Vt., 51
St. John, Commissary General Isaac, C.S.A., 56, 119, 130, 251
St. Johns River (Fla.), 164–65, 238
St. Luke's Episcopal Church, Salisbury, N.C., 84
St. Martin, Jules, 47, 80, 85
St. Paul's Episcopal Church, Richmond, Va., 19, 21–2
St. Peter's Episcopal Church, Charlotte, N.C., 87–8
Salisbury, N.C., 84, 238
Saluda River (S.C.), 106
Sandersville, Ga., 136
Santa Fe River (Fla.), 164
Sauls, George, 165
Savannah, Ga., 129, 152, 156, 157, 201–02, 206, 212, 238, 259ff.
Savannah River (S.C.-Ga.), 108, 122–24, 152, 156, 184, 187
Sayler's Creek (Va.), battle of, 57
Schofield, Maj. Gen. John, U.S.A., 170
Scott, Sir Walter, 270
Selma, Ala., 141, 152
Semmes, Adm. Raphael, C.S.N., 34–5, 36–8, 45, 68, 76, 95–6, 164, 169–70
as brigadier general, C.S.A., 54
Semmes, Cadet Raphael, Jr., C.S.N., 54, 169
Semple, James A., 129, 130, 187
Sewanee, Tenn., 230, 244, 247
Seward, Secretary of State William H., U.S.A., 78, 85, 108, 285
Shawneetown, Ill., 151
Shea, George, 206, 207, 211, 213, 215, 222
Shelby, Maj. Gen. Jo, C.S.A., 194–98
later life, 276–77
Shell, Augustus, 222
Shenandoah Valley, 239
Shepherd, Col. Elliott, U.S.A., 266
Shepherd, Lewis, 185
Sheridan, Maj. Gen. Philip, U.S.A., 16, 18, 38
Sherman, Gen. William T., U.S.A., 6, 18, 23, 71, 72, 75–6, 84, 91–2, 104, 177, 228
Shiloh (Tenn.), battle of, 48, 271
Shumate, Mary Anne Chenault, 186–87
Sitting Bull, Chief, 278
Slave migrations, 198–99
Slavery and peace negotiations, 71–2
Smith, Charles H. ("Bill Arp"), 229–30
Smith, Gen. Edmund Kirby, C.S.A., 26, 69, 83, 110–11, 125, 135, 163, 196
Smith, Gerrit, 218, 220, 222
Smith, Judge Joseph, 111
Smith, Gov. William ("Extra Billy") (Va.), 24
Smithsonian Institution, 180, 216
South Carolina, 72–5, 89–90, 101–18
South Dakota, 227
Southern expatriates, 190–91, 194–98
Southern Historical Society, 251–52, 265
Southside R.R., 57

Spanish-American War, 278
Spotted Eagle, Chief, 278
Springs, Col. A.B., 103
Springs, Eli, 103
Springs, Johnny, 103
Stamps, Mary, 246
Stanton, Secretary of War Edwin M., U.S.A., 78–9, 85, 91, 93, 104, 105, 150, 174, 177, 179–80, 181, 182, 194, 204, 207, 213–14, 216, 217, 219–20, 223, 236, 237, 284
  later life, 277, 278
Stanton, Mrs. Edwin M., 277
Statesville, N.C., 170
Stephens, Vice President Alexander H., C.S.A., 21, 154–55, 156, 169, 173
  later life, 273
Sterling, Ada, 279
Stevens, Sen. Thaddeus, U.S.A., 207, 213, 217
Stoneman, Maj. Gen. George, U.S.A., 60, 78, 84, 85, 104–05
C.S.S. *Stonewall,* 174
Stribling, Adm. Cornelius, U.S.N., 104
Stuart, C.E.L., 123*n*
Stuart, Maj. Gen. J.E.B., C.S.A., 38, 195, 271
Sulivane, Capt. Clement, C.S.A., 36
Sumner, Sen. Charles, U.S.A., 236
Surratt, Mrs. Mary, 203, 277
Sutherlin, Maj. W.T., C.S.A., 52
Sutherlin, Mrs. W.T., 61
Suwannee River (Fla.), 164
Swan, Judge W.G., 196

C.S.S. *Tallahassee,* 68, 164
Tallahassee, Fla., 141, 164
Tampa, Fla., 160
Taylor, Lt. Gen. Richard, C.S.A., 26, 94, 103, 108, 135–36
Taylor, Col. Walter, C.S.A., 17
Taylor, President Zachary, 29, 246
Tennessee River (Tenn.-Ala.), 228
Tenney, Judge W.T., 252
Terrell, Brig. Gen. A.W., C.S.A., 196
Texas A&M College, 248
Thompson, Jacob, 50–1, 108
Thorburn, "Colonel" Charles E., 68, 126, 136, 140, 142–43
Tilden, Samuel J., 256–57
Tilghman, Tench, 96, 105–06, 108, 128
Titlow, Capt. Jerome, U.S.A., 178–79
Tomlinson, A.R., 5–6
Toombs, Maj. Gen. Robert, C.S.A., 114–15, 130, 170
Traveler (R. E. Lee's mount), 16, 59, 230, 240, 283, 284–85
Trans-Mississippi Department, C.S.A. ("Second Confederacy"), 69, 109–11, 126, 129, 163, 195–96 *passim*
Tredegar Foundry, Richmond, Va., 22, 37
Tresca, Capt. Fred 160ff.
Trenholm, Anna (Mrs. George A.), 30, 45, 85
Trenholm, Secretary of Treasury George A., C.S.A., 14, 30, 65, 71, 85, 94–5, 103, 119, 169, 251
  background, 45–6
  later life, 275
  leaves presidential party, 103
Tucker, Dallas, 22
Tucker, John Randolph, 222
U.S.S. *Tuscarora,* 174

Underwood, Judge, John C., 222
Union sentiment in the Confederacy, 20, 64, 75*n,* 126
United Confederate Veterans, 266, 269–70
United Daughters of the Confederacy, 279
U.S. Court of Claims, 186*n*
U.S. Military Academy, 8, 9, 66, 151, 152, 230, 242
U.S. Naval Academy, 68
U.S. Patent Office, 180
U.S. Troops,
  lack of discipline, 146–47, 150–51, 185–87
  units:
    4th Michigan cavalry, 141–47, 151, 219*n*
    1st New Jersey infantry, 180
    1st Ohio cavalry, 135, 141, 219*n*
    9th Vermont cavalry, 41
    1st Wisconsin cavalry, 141–47, 219*n*

Valentine, Edward, 239, 241
Van Benthuysen, Alfred, 96
Van Benthuysen, Jefferson D., 96

Van Benthuysen, Capt. Watson, C.S.A., 96, 121, 188–89, 234
Van Buren, Pres. Martin, 48
Vance, Gov. Zebulon B. (N.C.), 21, 82–3, 170
Vanderbilt, Cornelius, 220, 222
Vaughn, Col. J.C., U.S.A., 96
Venezuela, 191
Vera Cruz, Mexico, 163
Vicksburg, Miss., 110
Vienna, S.C., 122
C.S.S. *Virginia* (I) (U.S.S. *Merrimac*), 271
C.S.S. *Virginia* (II), 35, 36–7
Virginia Military Institute, 230, 240, 250, 285
Vizetelly, Frank, 80, 83–4, 102, 128, 137
  later life, 276

Waldorf Astoria Hotel, New York City, 282
Wallace, Brig. Gen. William, C.S.A., 106
Walthall, Maj. W.T., C.S.A., 249
Washington Artillery (New Orleans), 268
Washington College, 230–31, 240, 269
Washington, D.C., 112, 157, 164, 170, 174, 175, 181, 203ff., 212–13, 214, 219–20, 231, 271, 276–77, 279, 284
Washington, Ga., 90, 109, 111, 113, 115–16, 118, 123, 126–29, 163, 170, 183ff., 189, 276
Washington & Lee University, 241, 265, 284
Watts, Gov. Thomas H. (Ala.), 108
Weed, Thurlow, 181
Weill, Abram, 28–9, 73, 85
West Virginia, 227
Wheeler, Maj. Gen. Joseph, C.S.A., 77, 155, 174, 268
Wheless, Paymaster John F., C.S.N., 25, 118
White Sulphur Springs, W. Va., 282
White, Col. William Elliott, C.S.A., 103
Whittington, Mrs. Alphonso, 64
Wigfall, Louis, 196
Wilcox, Maj. Gen. Cadmus, C.S.A., 196
Wilder, Brig. Gen. John T., U.S.A., 228
S.S. *William P. Clyde*, 157, 173–76, 200–01, 211–12
Williams, Brig. Gen. John S., C.S.A., 196
Williams, Pvt. Walter, C.S.A. ("The Last Man"), 283
Wilmington, N.C., 47, 275
Wilson, Col. James, C.S.A., 56, 164, 166, 167
Wilson, Maj. Gen. James H., U.S.A., 109, 140–41, 150ff., 219*n*
Wilson, President Woodrow, 156
Wilson, Mrs. Woodrow, 283
Wirz, Henry, 141, 208, 284
Wise, Capt. George, C.S.A., 192
Wise, Gov. Henry A. (Va.), 13, 51
Wise, Lt. John, C.S.A., 51–2, 57
Withers, Dr. Robert, 58
Wood, Capt. John Taylor, C.S.N., 29, 54, 63, 68, 76, 94, 115, 125–26, 136, 139, 140, 143, 144, 147–48, 164, 165–67
Woolson, Pvt. Alfred, U.S.A. ("The Last Yank"), 283
Wounded Knee Creek (S. Dak.), battle of, 278

Yadkin River (N.C.), 83–4
Yeoman, Lt. Joseph, U.S.A., 135, 141, 219*n*
Yorkville (York), S.C., 106
Young, Lafayette, 106
Yulee, David, 188, 204

About the Author

BURKE DAVIS, author of more than forty books, is best known for his Civil War narratives, including *To Appomattox* and, most recently, *Sherman's March*, which is also available from the Vintage Civil War Library. His numerous biographies include three of Confederate Commanders: *They Called Him Stonewall, Grey Fox: R.E. Lee,* and *Jeb Stuart, The Last Cavalier*. The father of two young novelists, Angela Davis-Gardner and Burke Davis III, Burke Davis is a native of North Carolina.